Consuming
Joyce

Consuming Joyce

100 Years of *Ulysses* in Ireland

JOHN MCCOURT

BLOOMSBURY ACADEMIC
LONDON • NEW YORK • OXFORD • NEW DELHI • SYDNEY

BLOOMSBURY ACADEMIC
Bloomsbury Publishing Plc
50 Bedford Square, London, WC1B 3DP, UK
1385 Broadway, New York, NY 10018, USA
29 Earlsfort Terrace, Dublin 2, Ireland

BLOOMSBURY, BLOOMSBURY ACADEMIC and the Diana logo are
trademarks of Bloomsbury Publishing Plc

First published in Great Britain 2022

Cover design by Rebecca Heselton
Cover image: James Joyce, Trieste, Italy, c1912 © Granger Historical
Picture Archive/ Alamy Stock Photo

A catalogue record for this book is available from the British Library.

A catalog record for this book is available from the Library of Congress.

ISBN: HB: 978-1-3502-0581-9
         PB: 978-1-3502-0582-6
        ePDF: 978-1-3502-0583-3
        eBook: 978-1-3502-0584-0

Typeset by Integra Software Services Pvt. Ltd.
Printed and bound in Great Britain

To find out more about our authors and books visit www.bloomsbury.com
and sign up for our newsletters.

For Alice

CONTENTS

ABBREVIATIONS

CB	*Catholic Bulletin*
CE	*Cork Examiner*
CH 1, 2	Robert Deming, *James Joyce: The Critical Heritage*, 2 vols. (London: Routledge & K. Paul, 1970).
EH	*Evening Herald*
EP	*Evening Press*
FW	James Joyce, *Finnegans Wake*, ed., John Bishop (London: Penguin, 1999). References appear as page number plus line number. All *Finnegans Wake* editions carry the same pagination.
II	*Irish Independent*
IM	*Irish Monthly*
IP	*Irish Press*
IS	*Irish Statesman*
IT	*The Irish Times*
JJ	Richard Ellmann, *James Joyce: New and Revised Edition* (New York: Oxford University Press, 1982).
JJQ	*James Joyce Quarterly* (University of Tulsa, 1963 –)
JSA	*Joyce Studies Annual* (University of Texas, 1990–2003, Fordham University, 2007 –)
LII, LIII	Richard Ellmann, ed., *Letters of James Joyce*, vols II and III (New York: Viking Press, 1966)
NYT	*The New York Times*
OCPW	Kevin Barry, ed., *James Joyce: Occasional, Critical, and Political Writing* (Oxford: Oxford World Classics, 2008).
SI	*The Sunday Independent*

SL   Richard Ellmann, ed., *Selected Letters of James Joyce*
            (London: Faber and Faber, 1992).

ST   *The Sunday Tribune*

U   James Joyce, *Ulysses*, ed., Hans Walter Gabler (New York:
            Vintage, 1986).

Introduction
Consuming Joyce:
100 Years of Ulysses in Ireland

James Joyce, like Leopold Bloom, was fascinated by advertising, sales and consumption, and by the ways in which the attention of consumers was won and held. This was particularly true when it came to *Ulysses*. He was fully engaged in the complex process of both its material production and its promotion. For both artistic and commercial reasons, he was understandably invested in seeing that it was bought, consumed and, to borrow a term from *Finnegans Wake*, 'receptionated' (FW 370.18) by the largest body of readers possible. His two principal earlier publications, *Dubliners* and *A Portrait of the Artist as a Young Man*, had enjoyed but scant commercial success and brought little or no financial reward: after an exhausting seven-year battle, *Dubliners* was published in 1914 just two weeks before the assassination of Archduke Franz Ferdinand, the event that triggered the outbreak of the First World War. By the end of that year, just 499 copies of *Dubliners* had been sold (120 of which Joyce had purchased and sold on to his Triestine English language students). Joyce would have been paid rights only upon achieving 500 sales over the year. In the first half of 1915, a mere twenty-six copies were sold and sales dwindled to just seven over the second six months.

Little wonder, then, that when it came to *Ulysses*, there was hardly a moment in the initial life of the book that he did not follow closely and try to manage and influence. While many press notices saw his novel in the terms he later used himself – as 'his usylessly unreadable Blue Book of Eccles' (FW 179.26–27) – Joyce and Sylvia Beach, his eternally patient and generous publisher, were careful to market it not only as a unique artefact but also as an expensive, profit-making commodity, which would initially have to win over wealthy book purchasers rather than so-called common readers. Many of these early purchasers must have hoped their initial outlay would prove a canny long-term investment. Joyce was fully cognizant of the power of reviews to generate sales and can be seen commenting, for example, in a letter to Robert McAlmon in March 1922, about the 136 orders which came about as a result of a 'notice (first to appear) from the *Observer*' (*L1*, 182). Given the limits within which Shakespeare and Company was working, quality and price would have to predominate over any hopes of mass production. Worn down by seven years of tireless work, everything was at stake for Joyce whose critical reputation, in 1922, was still very much in the making.

How his novel would be bought and consumed in Ireland would particularly preoccupy him and is the principal subject of this study. The verb 'to consume' suggests multiple meanings such as 'to do away with completely' (destroy); 'to spend wastefully' (squander); 'to use up' (finish); 'to enjoy avidly' (devour); 'to engage fully' (engross); 'to utilize as a customer'. All of these meanings are relevant to the fate in Ireland of *Ulysses* in particular and of Joyce more in general over the past 100 years. There is little doubt that many people in Dublin would have preferred if Joyce had never been heard of again following his flight to the continent in 1904 with Nora Barnacle, and many more would have had little or no sympathy with his notorious publication travails, believing (not entirely incorrectly) that he had brought many of them on himself through his uncompromising stances. On 11 September 1912, the Dublin printer John Falconer had gone so far as to burn the entire run of 1,000 copies of *Dubliners* in sheets intended for the first edition to be published by Maunsel & Co. Like many others, Falconer believed that Joyce had spent his talent poorly. When the collection was finally published, many Irish reviews endorsed this view. The *Irish Daily Independent* described *Dubliners* as an 'example of muck raking […] That sort of realism which we thought had been safely interred (amid hoots) in the French Pantheon'. Joyce had broken 'a silence which might with advantage to himself have been left intact' and his book was an unfortunate example of 'Talent wasted'.[1] While *Ulysses*, as we shall see, would be greeted with similar hostility in Ireland (as elsewhere), it also attracted a small yet conspicuous number of readers who engaged with it avidly from the start and others, who enjoyed it fully and were, we might even say, consumed by it.

This book focuses principally on *Ulysses*, which is the book that defines Joyce in the public consciousness in the same way that *La Divina Commedia* defines Dante for Italy and the world or *War and Peace*, Tolstoy. Yet when tracing the history of the reception or consumption of *Ulysses* in Ireland, it is impossible to separate that single work from Joyce's entire output or from Joyce himself. Down through the century since *Ulysses* was published, Joyce's overweening personality has encroached constantly and, at times, it has felt impossible to separate the dancer from the dance.

---

[1] A copy of this review is held in the Stuart Gilbert papers at the Harry Ransom Center, University of Texas, Box 17, folder 10.

This is the first book that attempts to provide a reasonably representative picture of the Irish reception of *Ulysses*. It follows various, often inter-connecting channels in its explorations of the book's treatment in academia, in schools, in newspapers, in theatre, in subsequent Irish creative writing and in popular Irish culture more generally. *Ulysses* and the Irish State are exact contemporaries, and as Irish society grew and developed down through the decades so did our acceptance and understanding of Joyce's novel. This book presents an initial map of how *Ulysses* was consumed and received in Ireland, one that will benefit from more detailed investigation and analysis in the future. It engages with the vast body of international Joyce criticism only in so far as it is refracted through Irish responses.

Certain things can never be known about how Joyce was and is consumed in Ireland (or elsewhere). We can only speculate on private reading experiences and the opinions that have been recorded about *Ulysses* are not in the main from 'plain' readers, but rather come from (predominantly male) academics, journalists, politicians, religious leaders and letter-writers and tend to represent sharply defined and crafted positions.

In the Ireland of the early decades of the twentieth century in particular, women had to go to great lengths to make themselves heard in most public spheres. Mary Colum, one of Joyce's foremost Irish supporters in the United States, was an exceptional example of a critical voice who managed to make herself heard at home and abroad but even she recalled how Yeats had advised her that if she wished to pursue a career in literary criticism, she should specialize and, more importantly, assume a man's name, given that 'men still regarded criticism and philosophy as their own province, and would be sure to resent a woman's pushing in'.[2]

As we shall see, the journey of *Ulysses* in Ireland was also affected both by Joyce's earlier publications and by the drip feed of costly segments of *Work in Progress* in the twenties and thirties. The initial negative reaction to *Ulysses* would not have come as any great surprise to Joyce and often seemed driven by a desire to keep the book as far away as possible from Irish readers, as if it were a primer for revolution against the increasingly dominant Church or the fragile new infant State. Side by side with this, however, came a slow, intermittent and partial understanding of the work's importance in its own right as the great Irish book of the twentieth century, the one work that most fully encompasses the complexities of the Ireland to which it gives voice. This more positive judgement came belatedly, decades after the post-colonial State and state of mind gradually grew more confident and independent. While *Ulysses* was dismissed or ignored by the majority, it was always appreciated by a very small group of intellectuals and writers even in the dark inward-looking decades of the 1930s and 1940s. By the 1950s, a more open endorsement of Joyce and *Ulysses* began

---

[2]Mary M. Colum, *Life and the Dream* (New York: Doubleday, 1947), 372.

to emerge with, for example, the celebration of Bloomsday from 1954, even
if Irish academics continued to shy away from the novel (and from most
contemporary writing), fearful of its difficulties and put off by much of its
criticism of the country and of the Church, which made it too hot to handle.
They also felt little affinity with the academic Joyce industry that was taking
shape in the United States from as early as the 1930s in Harvard. As Brian
Fox has shown, 'in the 1940s, Harvard provided the setting for pioneering
works on Joyce by Harry Levin and Joseph Prescott, with the former's
1941 *James Joyce: A Critical Introduction* being credited by Geert Lernout
with "making Joyce academically respectable"'.[3] Dirk Van Hulle has cited
Edmund Wilson's 1932 *Axel's Castle* as a key intervention leading to a 'shift
away from Paris to the United States, where the centre of the Joyce industry
has remained ever since'.[4] In the decades following the Second World War,
scholarship in the United States became, partly because of its relentless
professionalism and its relegation of Irish contexts and themes to a position
of secondary importance, something of an obstacle to a more concerted
Irish engagement with Joyce. Equally, most Irish critics looked askance at
European Structuralist and post-Structuralist approaches and it was not
really until the 1980s that a proper Irish appraisal of the novel and of Joyce
finally began to take shape. Slightly anticipating this critical appreciation,
there had been a more popular reclaiming of Joyce with several key Joyce
locations, most especially the Tower in Sandycove, becoming well-trodden
places of pilgrimage. There had also been an explosion of Joyce-related
theatre, which helped to acclimatize an ever-larger public to Joyce's works
– albeit in adapted formats.

At the turn of the new millennium, this process accelerated to such an
extent (especially with the National Library's vastly expensive purchases
of Joyce manuscripts) that at times in June each year it seemed as if Joyce
was the only game in town. This eventually provoked a backlash and
genuine Joyce scholars and enthusiasts would have to fight to retain and
reinstate the integrity of *Ulysses* in the face of an increasingly consumerist
approach to the book. The tension between both a popular and a critical
appreciation of Joyce, and a more hard-edged exploitation of his image for
commercial reasons continues to this day, after what was, for *Ulysses*, a
long and tortuous journey from oddity to commodity. That journey should
not be seen uncritically, as Mr Deasy in the 'Nestor' episode might put it, as
a progressive one. For all the recognition that *Ulysses* currently receives in
being the iconic literary symbol of brand Ireland (a great little country for
doing culture in), this comes at a price. Being culturally consecrated and given

[3]Brian Fox, '"land of breach of promise": James Joyce and America', Unpublished PhD Thesis, Royal Holloway, University of London, 2014, 154.
[4]Geert Lernout, *The French Joyce* (Ann Arbor: University of Michigan Press, 1992), 22. For Joseph Prescott, see Dirk Van Hulle, 'Genetic Joyce Criticism' in John McCourt, ed., *James Joyce in Context* (Cambridge: Cambridge University Press, 2009), 116.

iconic status often coincides with the object of veneration being stripped of meaning. This is certainly the case with *Ulysses*, whose critical and even subversive potential as a means through which to read Irish society, past and present, is often muted. Although *Ulysses* is also hugely entertaining, it is not just a song at twilight. It is not a nostalgic reeling in the year 1904 that it may sometimes seem to Dublin visitors in mid-June. For all of Ireland's changes in the hundred years since *Ulysses* was first published, it is too facile to imagine that a writer of Joyce's radical power would somehow find himself at home in the secular and profoundly materialist Ireland of today. In all probability, he would find much that would surprise him and which he would celebrate but he would also turn his scrupulous gaze on the new injustices that challenge the country and doubtless be far ahead of the crowd now (as he was then) in dismantling the received wisdoms that are so often taken blindly for truth. We do not need Joyce to come back for our critical antennae to be on the alert because now, in this centenary year, *Ulysses* remains a precious resource to help us towards a more mature and critical appraisal not only of Joyce's times but also of our own, of human nature, the nature of fiction and the possibility and limits of language and therein lies much of the enduring power of Joyce's great novel. The question posed by Elizabeth Bowen back in 1941 with regard to Joyce, 'are we ready to know ourselves?',[5] is as relevant today as it ever was. If we are, the 'cracked looking glass' that is *Ulysses* is one of the best places to start.

---

[5]Elizabeth Bowen, 'James Joyce', *The Bell* 1.6 (March 1941), 40–9. Reprinted in Eibhear Walshe, ed., *Elizabeth Bowen's Selected Irish Writings* (Cork: Cork University Press, 2011), 69–74, 69.

CHAPTER ONE

'Regrettable celebrity': Joyce in Ireland before *Ulysses*

'Ireland is all through him and in him and of him; and Dublin, its streets and its buildings and its people, he loves with the whole-hearted affection of the artist. [...] He may live out of Dublin, but he will never get away from it. [...] Ireland at present will probably not love Mr. Joyce.' [1]

When *Ulysses* was finally published in book form in 1922, James Joyce's name was already much maligned in Ireland where he enjoyed what Fr George O'Neill, one of his former Jesuit teachers of English at Clongowes Wood College, called 'regrettable celebrity'.[2] *Dubliners* (1914) and *A Portrait of the Artist as a Young Man* (1916) had seen to that. Years earlier, when leaving the country, Joyce had slammed the door behind him by publishing broadsides that took aim at many of the literary figures who had helped him and at many contemporaries who would be in a position to shape his future reputation. Stanislaus Joyce recalled that his brother's decision to go into exile in Europe was seen as just 'another of his escapades'.[3] When he left, 'he

---

[1] P. S. O'Hegarty, 'Mr. Joyce's *Ulysses*'. *The Separatist*, 2 September 1922, 4.

[2] Bruce Bradley, 'James Joyce and the Jesuits: A Sort of Homecoming', 30 November 1999. https://www.catholicireland.net/james-joyce-and-the-jesuits-a-sort-of-homecoming/. 'In the forward to a collection of his own writings, published in 1946, he wrote with what seems like wistful regret: "I have introduced to college life a very small boy destined to regrettable celebrity as the author of *Ulysses*, and put a Catholic choir-book into his little hand"' (*Witness to the Stars*).

[3] Stanislaus Joyce in W. R. Rodgers, 'Portrait of James Joyce' (transcript), Broadcast on BBC Third Programme, 13 February 1950, 27.

was written off, with unconcealed jubilation, as a failure'.[4] Stanislaus claimed that Joyce 'had spurned what he called their temporising and poltroonery, their attitude of timid, covert revolt on all issues not purely national, their fear to be the same in act and valour as they were in desire; and they, for their part, with the patient memory of many a jibe, took offence at his hectoring manner'. In reality, Joyce's move to Trieste had a permanent feel to it and Joyce effectively erected a barrier between himself and his home in the irreverently titled satirical broadside, 'The Holy Office' (1905), which he fired off shortly before his departure and eventually printed in Trieste. Calling himself 'Katharsis-Purgative', Joyce announced that he would not write under any fellow Irish writer's shadow and rejected the frame of the Irish literary Revival. In constructing his voluntary exile in Europe, he rather disingenuously ignored the well-established continental literary connections of several senior Irish contemporaries, such as Yeats, Shaw, Edward Martyn and George Moore. Disrespectfully echoing and parodying the rhymes and rhythms of Yeats' 'Address to Ireland in the Coming Times', he wrote:

> But I must not accounted be
> One of that mumming company –
> With him who hies him to appease
> His giddy dames frivolitics
> While they console him when he whinges
> With god-embroidered Celtic fringes. (*P&E*, 103)

Much of this was posturing and Joyce would engage deeply with and borrow widely from the Revival authors. But as he set out, he deliberately positioned himself apart from the architects of the Irish Literary Revival who had sought to help (and enlist) him. His exilic dissent was a necessary condition for his literary path and he would have no choice but to 'recognise myself an exile: and, prophetically, a repudiated one' (*LII* 125) and to stand, as the poem puts it, 'unfellowed, friendless and alone'.[5]

The publication of *Dubliners* and *A Portrait* burnt more bridges. Quite aside from his controversial views of Irish nationalism and Irish Catholicism, Joyce's uncompromising portraits of his fellow Irishmen and women caused resentment. Writing about Ireland from abroad was never going to be simple and many thought he was fouling the nest from which he had flown. While it is true that Joyce was not as uniformly ostracized as he might want us to believe, in the early decades following his departure, his Irish admirers, in what was an increasingly Catholic country, were few and far between and usually kept their heads down. During his last visit to Ireland, in 1912, when he was engaged in a bitter and ultimately useless row with George

[4]Stanislaus Joyce, 'Joyce's Dublin', *The Partisan Review*, vol. 19 (1952): 103–9, 104.
[5]Joyce, James, *Poems and Exiles*, ed., J. C. C. Mays (London: Penguin, 1992).

Roberts of the Maunsel publishing house that had agreed, years earlier, to publish *Dubliners*, Joyce turned to his old friend, Thomas Kettle, asking him to intervene on his behalf. But Kettle, by then a respected reviewer, warned him: 'I will slate that book.' If Kettle, whom Joyce described in 1909 as 'the best friend I have in Ireland', and with whom he had studied at University College Dublin, where both were prominent in the Literary and Historical Society, 'disapproved of the unpatriotic candour of *Dubliners*' (*JJ* 63, 329), it is hardly surprising that the more general reception of Joyce's works would be hostile.

A *Portrait* did slightly better in a review in the *Freeman's Journal*, entitled 'A Dyspeptic Portrait', which praised Joyce's prose for its 'terseness and force', adding that 'even his most casual descriptions haunt the mind by their vividness and wonderful economy of line'. Unfortunately, Joyce's pen, instead of pointing to the stars, is 'degraded into a muck-rake' and Joyce 'drags his readers after him into the slime of foul sewers'. What bothers the reviewer most is that Joyce is washing dirty Irish linen before the eyes of the English reading public with his negative portrait of Dublin, of Ireland and of Irish Catholic practice. What made this all the more alarming was that influential English critics, such as H. G. Wells, were vouching for the authenticity of Joyce's portrayal:

> Like some of the best novels in the world it is the story of an education; it is by far the most living and convincing picture that exists of an Irish Catholic upbringing. It is a mosaic of jagged fragments that does altogether render with extreme completeness the growth of a rather secretive, imaginative boy in Dublin. The technique is startling, but on the whole it succeeds.[6]

In response to (or in anticipation of) reactions like this, the *Freeman's Journal* review sought to disown Joyce, to play down his Irishness, deny the racial background of *A Portrait* and claim that it was simply 'an accident that Mr. Joyce's book should have Dublin as its background'. Stephen Dedalus might just as easily have been placed as a rebellious youth 'in an English cathedral town or an American industrial centre' and 'he would have pilloried them in just as repellent a fashion'. Therefore it was wrong of 'English critics' to hail Joyce 'as a typical Irishman, and his book as a faithful picture of Irish life. It would be just as accurate to declare that De Quincey's Opium Eater embodied the experience of the average English youth' (*CH* 1, 98–9).

At a time when the Easter Rising and its immediate aftermath were being acutely felt, it is not surprising that Joyce's critical versions of Irish life would cause annoyance at home just as they were being read as representative

---

[6]H. G. Wells, 'James Joyce', *Nation*, vol. xx, 24 February 1917, 710, 712. It was reprinted in *The New Republic*, 10 March 1917, 158–60.

and authoritative outside the country where knowledge of Ireland was very limited (and usually filtered through the British media, as Joyce pointed out in his Trieste journalism). Joyce's novel could not have landed in the country at a worse time as it struggled in the initial stages of an inevitable post-colonial insecurity that was marked by extreme sensitivity to criticism, particularly when it came from beyond the borders. Joyce paid a price for challenging the sanitized and acceptable self-image of the Irish and he knew well that he could only do so 'from the safe side of distance!' (FW 228.24–25). That said, the attitude of pre-Independence Ireland was a little more open than what was to come after the founding of the Free State, when the space for dissenting views in the public arena shrank rapidly as the symbiotic relationship between Church and State solidified.

During the First World War, Joyce did receive some support from his senior Irish literary colleagues. In a letter to the Secretary of the Royal Literary Fund, Yeats wrote in praise of Joyce's 'most beautiful gift' and described him as 'the most remarkable new talent in Ireland to-day' (CH 1, 79). Even if he thought most of the Dubliners' stories 'trivial and disagreeable', George Moore told Edward Marsh that 'The Dead' 'seemed to me perfection whilst I read it! I regretted that I was not the author of it.' Yet this one story 'does not prove that Joyce will go on writing and will end by writing something like a masterpiece' (CH 1, 80). Beyond this small literary coterie, grudging or neutral nods were made to pre-Ulysses Joyce. The Irish Book Lover acknowledged that, in Dubliners, Joyce had written 'pen portraits of great power' of the city's 'many peculiar types of men and women, good, bad and indifferent'. Yet, 'one naturally shrinks from such characters as are depicted in "An Encounter" or "Two Gallants", and finds their descriptions not quite suited virginibus puerisque' even if 'one cannot deny the existence of their prototypes'. Joyce's realism and stark language were such that 'no clean-minded person could possibly allow it to remain within reach of his wife, his sons or daughters'.[7] The same journal is more effusive in its praise of what it considers Joyce's, albeit misdirected, gifts as shown in A Portrait with its jarringly 'unsparing realism'. It concedes that he 'is a master of a brilliant descriptive style and handles dialogue as ably as any living writer' (CH 1, 102). More neutral acknowledgement came from Fr Stephen Brown SJ of Clongowes in his Ireland in Fiction. He singled out the 'brutal realism' in Joyce's treatment of 'the Dublin lower-middle class and lower classes' from a 'dark and squalid aspect'.[8]

Despite these responses, Joyce's reception was not being framed primarily in Ireland. Quite the contrary. One of the principal architects of his early reputation was Ezra Pound. He saw Joyce as a realist who 'describes the thing as it is' and one who, with A Portrait, wrote the 'best novel of my

---

[7] Unsigned review of Dubliners, Irish Book Lover, vol. VI, no. 4 (November 1914): 60–1.
[8] S. Brown, S. J., Ireland in Fiction A Guide to Irish Novels, Tales, Romances, and Folk Lore (Dublin and London: Maunsel and Company, 1916), 123.

decade'.[9] He twinned Joyce with Flaubert as the master of the *histoire morale contemporaine* but there is a contradiction when Pound claims that 'it is surprising that Mr. Joyce is Irish. [...] He writes as a contemporary of continental writers' (*CH* 1, 57). How could Joyce have 'described the thing as it is' if he did not retain the very local focus that Pound denies? Pound's is, in John Nash's words, 'a calculated insult at Irish literature' but also an assertion 'that his writing bore an "international standard"' and that Joyce was a writer 'who had successfully shed his upbringing'.[10] In fact, in his provocatively entitled piece, 'The Non-Existence of Ireland', Pound asserted that Joyce had 'fled to Trieste and into the modern world' and that '[h]e writes as a European, not as a provincial'.[11] While Pound's was a gross simplification and a heavy-handed overstatement, it did favour Joyce's international status within modernism and helped to separate him from what Pound saw as the Irish Revival's 'Celtic imagination (or "phantasy" as I think they now call it) flopping about' (*CH* 1, 67).

When Pound suggested that 'if more people had read *The Portrait* and certain stories in Mr. Joyce's *Dubliners* there might have been less recent trouble in Ireland. A clear diagnosis is never without its value',[12] his words were both condescending and prescient. He was referring to the political upheaval started by 1916 but there were many other 'troubles' present in the early decades of the twentieth century that Joyce's works would attempt to uncover. Describing his own literary technique to Arthur Power, Joyce talks about his 'intellectual attitude which dissects life instead of puffing it up with romanticism'.[13] Joyce's readers could make their own diagnoses of the issues afflicting Irish society that his works laid bare. Apart from the obvious dissection of the dangers of nationalism and isolationism, many of the concerns expressed in Joyce's works had to do with questions of justice and with the treatment of the young and vulnerable. Poverty, lack of opportunity and exploitation come under his literary lens as does the neglect and poor treatment of children and young people. Economic, political and sexual frustration and repression are recurring themes, so too religious extremism, suicide, alcoholism and abuse. Nearly all of these topics were taboo in the Ireland of the first half (at least) of the twentieth century. Silence was general and those who broke it were angrily turned on as Joyce, Lennox Robinson, Sean O'Casey, Liam O'Flaherty and many others found out to their cost.

By the time *Ulysses* was finally published, mainstream Irish commentators were but little disposed to greet it with sympathy. It was, by the legal

---

[9]Ezra Pound, *Literary Essays of Ezra Pound*, ed. T. S. Eliot (Norfolk, CT: New Directions, 1954), 420.

[10]John Nash, 'Genre, Place and Value: Joyce's Reception', in John McCourt, ed., *James Joyce in Context* (Cambridge: Cambridge University Press, 2008), 42.

[11]Ezra Pound, 'The Non-Existence of Ireland', *The New Age* XVI, 17 (25 February 1915): 452.

[12]Ezra Pound, Review of *The Egoist*, February 1917; Reprinted in Forrest Read, ed. *Pound/Joyce: The Letters of Ezra Pound to James Joyce, with Pound's Essays on* Joyce (New York: New Directions 1970), 88–91.

[13]Joyce is quoted in Arthur Power, 'Conversations with Joyce' (*CH* 1, 182).

standards of the time, seen as obscene, even by Joyce's defenders such as Mary Colum, who, in her 1922 review, dismissed the attempts by Joyce admirers 'to absolve Joyce from accusation of obscenity in the book' and asked 'Why attempt to absolve him?' before answering: 'It is obscene, bawdy, corrupt. But it is doubtful that obscenity in literature ever really corrupted anybody.'[14]

Unable or unwilling to see beyond the headlined obscenity, few Irish readers would have agreed with John Butler Yeats' assessment as expressed in a letter to the Irish-American lawyer and man of letters, John Quinn:

> Joyce is a man of genius, inspired by an intense feeling for what is actual and true, and he sees the whole world, especially in his own native city, Dublin, living luxuriously in the lap of falsehood. He would awaken these people. He is a patriot, above all an Irish patriot.[15]

Quinn feared that the country's more conventional patriots would 'claim that *Ulysses* is not a picture of Irish life and is incorrect and immoral'[16] and that those US-based Irish critics, such as Ernest Boyd and Padraic and Mary Colum, who heralded Joyce's essential Irishness, were not, for all their good intentions, actually helping Joyce's cause in Ireland or abroad. In his view, it was better to promote *Ulysses* as 'a European event' in order to deny 'the Irish patriots a chance to assail it as they had assailed *The Playboy of the Western World*'.[17]

While there is truth in Joseph Kelly's view that Pound and Eliot 'changed Joyce from an Irish writer into an avantgarde, cosmopolitan writer, shucking off his provincial husk',[18] it does not tell the whole story. The 'European' Joyce, influentially promoted by Valery Larbaud, Pound and T. S. Eliot, would prevail at the expense of an Irish Joyce for many decades. As early as 1922, Shane Leslie complained in the *Dublin Review* that 'nothing could be more ridiculous than the youthful dilettantes in Paris or London who profess knowledge and understanding of a work which is often mercifully obscure even to the Dublin-bred'.[19] Yet, a very different 'Irish' Joyce lingered in the undergrowth. The purpose of this book will be to explore its slow, often painful, but gradual emergence. First, however, it is necessary to take a step backwards and take a brief look at the publishing history of *Ulysses*.

---

[14]Mary M. Colum, 'The Confessions of James Joyce', *The Freeman* 123 (19 July 1922): 450–2. Reprinted in *The Selected Works of Mary M. Colum*, ed. Denise A. Ayo (2013), http://marycolum.com/articles/confessions-ofjames-joyce/.

[15]William M. Murphy, *Prodigal Father* (Ithaca, NY: Cornell University Press, 1978), 518.

[16]Quinn's comments are quoted in B. L. Reid, *The Man from New York: John Quinn and his Friends* (New York: Oxford University Press, 1965), 547.

[17]Ibid., 530.

[18]Joseph Kelly, *Our Joyce: From Outcast to Icon* (Austin: University of Texas Press, 1998), 9.

[19]'Domini Canis' (Shane Leslie), 'Ulysses' *Dublin Review*, September 1922, clxxi, 112–19 reprinted in *CH* 1, 200-203. p. 202.

CHAPTER TWO

Ulysses in court

The fate of *Ulysses* in Ireland was influenced by the international controversy created by the serialization of versions of its early chapters. This only intensified after it finally appeared in book form. In an Ireland wearied by the War of Independence and lurching into Civil War, most people in 1922 were probably unaware of its existence; some may have chosen to ignore it; others, without reading it, dismissed it as dangerous filth. Many would reach this conclusion based on what they found out about it not so much in Irish newspapers but in the more popular British dailies that continued to sell well in the newly independent country. Beyond Ireland, very few early readers or reviewers knew quite what to make of Joyce's unprecedented new novel as it appeared, episode by episode, in New York's *The Little Review*, which was edited by the extraordinarily brave and enterprising couple, Margaret Anderson and Jane Heap. Anderson showed remarkable vision in believing so early on that *Ulysses* 'is the most beautiful thing we'll ever have' and vowing: 'We'll print it if it's the last effort of our lives.'[1] Indeed, even a keen advocate like Ezra Pound was more representative in his contradictory response. On reading the 'Proteus' episode as prepared for the *Little Review*, he complained that although the chapter was 'magnificent in spots', it was 'mostly incomprehensible'.[2] Pound later vainly attempted to make cuts to render Joyce's text less vulnerable to public policing.

Some in Ireland felt justified in dismissing Joyce because he had already been condemned for obscenity (and obscurity) in the courts and in the court of public opinion abroad. When faced with a barrage of negative comments from *The Little Review* subscribers, an exasperated Anderson had asked

[1]Margaret Anderson, *My Thirty Years' War* (New York: Horizon Press, 1969), 174–5.
[2]Forrest Read, ed. *Pound/Joyce*, 143.

her readers: 'Do you think the public will ever be ready for such a book as *Ulysses*?'[3] If this was a question Anderson felt she had to ask in ultra-modern New York, small wonder that similar questions would be asked in Joyce's 'Hibernian Metropolis'.

The sorry saga of the trials suffered by *Ulysses* demands a brief retelling here. In October 1920, John S. Sumner, the zealous and recently installed secretary of the New York Society for the Suppression of Vice, which had been founded and run by Anthony Comstock, who was also responsible for the 1873 Comstock Act that criminalized the distribution in the United States of any 'obscene, lewd, or lascivious book, pamphlet, picture, paper, print or other publication of an indecent character',[4] issued a warrant against the proprietors of the Washington Square Bookshop. Their crime was selling the July–August issue of *The Little Review*, which, in line with its policy of 'Making No Compromise with the Public Taste', carried the controversial 'Nausicaa' episode (Jane Heap and Margaret Anderson, publisher and editor, respectively, had been publishing instalments of the book since 1918). 'There is hell in New York about "Nausikaa"' (*LIII*, 30), wrote Joyce to his Zurich-based friend, Frank Budgen. This was the start of *Ulysses*'s long and painful career in the American courts. Although previous issues of the *Review* had already run into trouble under federal postal law, now Sumner was enforcing 'a New York state law (Penal Code 1141)'.[5] John Quinn, the rich, gruff and opinionated Irish-American New York attorney and patron of the arts, who bankrolled *The Little Review*, insisted on taking the case and on representing Anderson and Heap. His legal tactics were ill chosen and proved unsuccessful, partly because he disapproved of much of Joyce's content and style: 'He conceded that *Ulysses* was an experiment carried too far and that it was disgusting and repulsive. But, he insisted, it was not lascivious. The retreat did not work. The women were fined.'[6] Anderson later complained that 'not one New York newspaper came to our defense, not one spoke out for Joyce, not one cared to be identified with the *Ulysses* scandal'.[7]

The result of the case was that both the judiciary and the public came to consider *Ulysses* as 'erotica. No reputable publisher, including Ben Huebsch (who had published *Dubliners* and *Portrait*) at Viking, would take on the unexpurgated book, and Joyce would not publish it any other way'.[8] Joyce had been ill-served by John Quinn, who believed that the case was 'unwinnable',[9] as Joseph Hassett explained:

[3]Margaret Anderson, *The Little Review Anthology* (New York: Horizon Press, 1953), 297.
[4]Quoted in Kevin Birmingham, *The Most Dangerous Book: The Battle for James Joyce's Ulysses* (London: Head of Zeus, 2014), 5.
[5]Ibid.
[6]Ibid., p. 87.
[7]Margaret Anderson, *My Thirty Years War*, 226.
[8]Joseph Kelly, *Our Joyce*, 89.
[9]Joseph M. Hassett, *The Ulysses Trials: Beauty and Truth Meet the Law* (Dublin: Lilliput Press, 1916), 4.

Anderson and Heap urged their lawyer, John Quinn, to argue that Joyce's prose could not be obscene because it was beautiful literature, and Quinn's friend John Butler Yeats outlined an argument based on the societal value of Joyce's 'terrible veracity'. Unfortunately, Quinn [...] hobbled by a mind filled with prejudice and closed to opinions that differed from his own, failed to advance these potentially winning arguments. Instead he made a series of unworthy and cynical points addressed to what he chose to call the 'ignorance' of the 'stupid judges'. After his clients were convicted he failed to seek an appellate ruling on the important legal issues presented by the criminalization of an innovative piece of writing by a master stylist. Thus *Ulysses* was silenced after the serialization of fourteen of the eighteen episodes contemplated by Joyce.[10]

Silenced in the United States, Joyce turned in desperation to the Paris-based American bookseller, Sylvia Beach, who heroically undertook to publish expensive, mostly pre-ordered small runs of *Ulysses* for Shakespeare and Company, while at the same time offering Joyce generous 90 per cent royalties. Copies, in Cyril Connolly's words, 'lay stacked like dynamite in a revolutionary cellar'[11] but *Ulysses* was not on sale in the normal sense of the word except through mail order and even then it was essentially smuggled, sometimes with decoy covers, through customs. A first English edition was prepared from the Shakespeare and Company plates for Harriet Shaw Weaver's Egoist Press and published on 12 October 1922 in a limited edition of 2000 numbered copies and 100 unnumbered copies, printed on 'handmade paper', and costing £2 2s.[12] Like Beach, Weaver offered the novel on a subscription model and, within four days of publication, the impression had sold out.[13]

The reception of *Ulysses* was further complicated in 1926 when the New York publisher, Samuel Roth, began serializing it without permission in *Two Worlds Monthly*. He used Beach's edition as his text until she protested on Joyce's behalf in a letter signed by an international group of 167 writers and published in *transition* (April 1927). The letter pointed out that the republication was being made 'without authorization by Mr. Joyce; without payment to Mr. Joyce and with alterations which seriously corrupt the text'. Joyce was essentially being swindled and his text mutilated. Joyce's plight elicited little sympathy in Ireland where the Roth case became the subject of discussion in the Irish Senate during a 1927 debate on copyright. Independent Senator, J. C. Dowdall, attempted to introduce an amendment

---

[10]Ibid., 2.

[11]Noel Riley Fitch, *Sylvia Beach and the Lost Generation: A History of Literary Paris in the Twenties and Thirties*. (New York: W. W. Norton & Company, 1985).

[12]John J. Slocum and Herbert Cahoon, *A Bibliography of James Joyce, 1882–1941* (London: Rupert Hart-Davis, 1957), 26.

[13]Lloyd Houston, '(Il)legal Deposits: Ulysses and the Copyright Libraries', *The Library*, 7th series, vol. 18, no. 2 (June 2017): 134.

to proposed Irish legislation that would oblige anyone who was 'a citizen of Saorstát Eireann', and desired 'to secure copyright within the State' to 'ensure that the work be printed within the State'. In the debate about this, the Roth piracy case was raised by Labour Party Senator, William Cummins, who could not bring himself to pronounce Joyce's name but accused him of making 'a violent onslaught upon all things Irish'.[14] He then turned his ire on Yeats for his defence of Joyce before claiming: 'We were branded [by Yeats] almost as an illiterate nation, not worth printing for.' He accused Yeats of drawing a pathetic picture of Joyce as someone who attempted and failed to publish his book in various countries without success: 'I shall not name the author. Neither did Senator Yeats name the author, and I am glad because of the delicacy and the sensitiveness.' Yeats interrupted with the words 'James Joyce' before Cummins took a swipe at the petition that was 'signed by the highbrows'. Yeats again interjected pointing out that the highbrows were '150 of the most eminent men of letters [who had] signed the protest against the mutilation and piracy of James Joyce's book in America'. Instead of debating the merits of the amendment or defending Joyce against piracy, Cummins sought to discredit Yeats by associating him with Joyce:

> I would like to ask Senator Yeats to give us the history of the book which he spoke of in such feeling terms on the last occasion. I would ask him is it true that the British Post Office authorities have really refused to send this book through their channels, that it has been actually refused in America, that the indelicacy and the outrageous character of that book were of such a nature that it would not be permitted to go through the ordinary channels of delivery in any Christian country? There are eminent men in various countries, many eminent men in literature, eminent men in science, eminent men in Christian life, and I shall leave it to this House to judge which is the greater eminence, Christian eminence or the eminence that would destroy all semblance of Christianity on the face of the earth?

Yeats pointed out that some signed because they 'sincerely admired' Joyce's book, others 'did not admire it at all, and had signed simply because of the copyright issue'. Among them were 'Gentile, the Italian Minister of Education, who has restored religious teaching to the schools in Italy', 'the great Catholic philosopher of Spain, Unamuno', and Einstein. Yeats continued: 'When I heard the Senator put up Irish opinions as against these, as certainly and definitely right, then I was inclined to believe this was an illiterate nation. These things cannot be settled as easily as that. I do not know whether Joyce's *Ulysses* is a great work of literature. I have puzzled a great deal over that question.' Joyce read the six-page account of these

---

[14]Seanad Éireann debate – Wednesday, 4 May 1927, vol.8, no. 22. The entire debate can be read at https://www.oireachtas.ie/en/debates/debate/seanad/1927-05-04/9/.

proceedings in the pages of the *Catholic Bulletin*, which routinely referred to him as an obscene and filthy writer.

Ulysses was back in court in 1928 after the customs court in Minneapolis included seven copies of it in a general seizure of titles. Subsequently, in New York City, John Sumner 'rounded up five different booksellers for distributing obscenity. At least two of them – David Moss, the husband of Frances Steloff and co-owner of Gotham Book Mart, and the ubiquitous Samuel Roth [...] – were found in possession of *Ulysses*'.[15] This led to the 'The United States of America v. One Book Called *Ulysses*' landmark case. Joyce's good fortune was that the presiding Judge, John M. Woolsey, did what so many others refused to do – he actually read *Ulysses*. In his judgement, he stated that he could nowhere find in it the 'leer of the sensualist' and ruled that it was neither pornographic nor obscene. He underlined the seriousness and sincerity of the novel, singled out the excellent use of the stream of consciousness technique and defended Joyce's need to convey his characters' thoughts fully. *Ulysses*, he concluded, was not obscene even if it was 'a rather strong draught to ask some sensitive, though normal, persons to take'. Its effect on the reader was at times 'somewhat emetic' but 'nowhere does it tend to be an aphrodisiac'. This decision effectively brought a modern classic into being. It combined legal judgement with literary criticism and changed everything for Joyce.

Its first immediate effect was that Bennett Cerf of Random House instructed his typesetters to start work on preparing the manuscript for publication. One hundred copies were published in January 1934 to obtain US copyright and this was, twelve long, often soul-destroying years after Beach's edition, the first legal publication of *Ulysses* in an English-speaking country. Random House made a habit of printing Woolsey's *Ulysses* decision as a preface to its editions of *Ulysses* until 1986 while in Britain, the Bodley Head also carried it until 1960. The first Random House edition, complete with an excerpt from a particularly negative review by James Douglas in the *Sunday Express* on the dust-jacket, sold 33,000 copies within weeks. Not long after an appeal against Woolsey's decision was dismissed, the British ban on *Ulysses* was also lifted.

Although the banning of *Ulysses* did Joyce much short-term damage, he did very little to make things easier during these trials. He refused to make any changes and relished taking on the social purists. The more they attempted to silence him the more provocative his writing became. Katherine Mullin, among others, sees Joyce 'as neither victim nor hero, but [...] as an agent provocateur' who would both feed and feed off 'prevailing debates about art, morality and sexuality'.[16] Joyce was playing a long game perhaps because he knew that he would have to bide his time if his explosive work was to win out in the long run.

---

[15] Joseph Kelly, *Our Joyce*, 90.
[16] Katherine Mullin, *James Joyce, Sexuality and Social Purity* (Cambridge: Cambridge University Press, 2003), 3.

CHAPTER THREE

'An Odyssey of the Sewer': *Ulysses* in Ireland in the 1920s

'When I am dead they will raise a monument to me.'[1]

In recent decades, an unsuspecting visitor might be inclined to believe that the Irish had always warmly embraced James Joyce and read his works with interest and respect. It was never so. Yet when Joyce complained that the 'copies of *Ulysses* which I presented to certain of my fellow countrymen and fellow countrywomen were either unacknowledged or locked up or given away or lent or stolen or sold and, it seems, in all cases unread' (*LIII*, 74), he was not telling the full story and he was failing to acknowledge the tumultuous situation in which the country found itself in 1922. On 6 January of that year, the terms of the Anglo-Irish Treaty were published. The following day, Dáil Éireann voted narrowly (64 to 57) in favour. On 10 January, Arthur Griffith was elected president of the Provisional Government, Michael Collins became Minister for Finance and Eamon de Valera led fifty-six of his supporters out of the Dáil in protest against the Treaty. This was the decisive step on the path to a devastating Civil War that began in June. Joyce followed these events and all events in Ireland closely. He had long been a supporter of Griffith and of Sinn Féin and felt that 'if a victorious country terrorises over another, it cannot reasonably take it amiss if the latter responds' though he had long since despaired of this ever happening successfully:

---

[1]Fritz Senn, *Joycean Murmoirs: Fritz Senn on James Joyce* ed. Christine O'Neill (Dublin: Lilliput Press, 2007), 54.

It is high time Ireland finished once and for all with failures. If it is truly capable of resurgence, then let it do so or else cover its head and decently descend into the grave forever. [...] But telling these Irish actors to hurry up, as our fathers before us told them not so long ago, is useless. I, for one, am certain not to see that curtain rise, as I shall have already taken the last tram home.

(*OCPW*, 126)

Joyce was shocked by the Rising but Richard Ellmann erred in claiming that he 'followed the events with pity; although he evaluated the Rising as useless, he felt also out of things' (*JJ*, 399). Not for the first time, Joyce did indeed feel 'out of things' but rather than pity he worried that the Rising would not be 'complete, full and definitive', that it would fail to deliver an Ireland that was truly free. Getting rid of the British alone would not guarantee the kind of change for which Joyce (like many of the rebels) hoped, especially if the country continued to serve 'one mistress faithfully, the Roman Catholic Church' (*OCPW*, 159). With the War of Independence and later the Civil War, hope for many turned to despair. A small number of those who felt disappointed and alienated within the new Free State turned to *Ulysses*, almost as if it were a blueprint for a different Ireland. In 1924, Joyce enthusiast, P. S. O'Hegarty, depicted the destruction caused by the Civil War in his ironically titled and polemical book, *The Victory of Sinn Fein*:

Every devilish thing we did against the British went its full circle and then boomeranged and smote us ten-fold; – The Irregulars drove patriotism and honesty and morality out of Ireland. They made people ask themselves whether Ireland was worth saving. [...] They demonstrated to us [...] that we were really an uncivilised people with savage instincts. And the shock of that plunge from the heights to the depths staggered the whole nation. The 'Island of Saints and Scholars' is burst, like Humpty Dumpty, and we do not quite know yet what we are going to get in its place.[2]

Predictably, *The Nation* was highly critical of O'Hegarty's book, claiming that it contained only 'the outpourings of a vitiated mind' and 'wantonly, and foully libels the dead who died for Ireland'.[3] Two years later, in an article entitled '"Are We All Murderers?"', published in the short-lived nationalist Cork paper, *The Tribune*, dramatist D. L. Kelleher similarly described how Ireland, 'recovering out of an urge of idealism, has acquiesced in a kind of despair. There is no real logic in the idealism; there is less in the despair.' He directly compared de Valera and Joyce as though they represented different visions for the future: 'That genuine idealist and revolutionary, De Valera,

[2]P. S. O'Hegarty, *The Victory of Sinn Fein* (Dublin: Talbot Press, 1924), 126.
[3]'Mr. P. S. O'Hegarty Slanders the Dead', *The Nation*, 18 December 1924, 5.

has the roots of the matter in him. "Ireland is yours for the taking," says he to the youth who, unthinkingly, follow him. They set out to take the astral beauty that he dreams of; they fail to find it, since, being astral, it is not of earth, earthy and realisable. De Valera is right; but he forgets the implications. He is as right as James Joyce, is, though equally indiscreet, because there is no ultimate truth in the finite life of a man.' Both are accused of being hopelessly idealistic:

> There is no truth in the logical pursuit of fact piled on fact; the only truth lies in humility combined with that loose word, grace, which is love plus revelation. Have De Valera and James Joyce that combination? Hardly! They are immortal, by reason of their humility. James Joyce, like De Valera, is perfectly right and accurate and logical. Thus the two of them are grievously wrong. They argue for a world of perfection; their last word in achievement would spell boredom and annihilation. With their ideals achieved, there would be nothing to live for upon earth.[4]

The Irish reception of *Ulysses*, which was, among other things, a manifesto for an Ireland radically different from the Free State, was profoundly affected and compromised by the historical moment of its publication. Even in those tragic times, however, there was always a small, enlightened minority that bought and read it and a handful of others who went to great lengths to review it while most Irish people, if they acknowledged it at all, did so with indifference, resentment or downright hostility.

Another assumption that might be made by an unsuspecting visitor is that *Ulysses* was officially banned in Ireland. Again, this was not so. On 26 June 1924, Yeats wrote about the status of *Ulysses* in Ireland to Ezra Pound, denying a presumed seizure of copies:

> The seizure of copies of 'Ulysses' was not made... according to the Common Law of England. Ireland has no machinery whatever for seizing copies on transit under that law, though of course they are liable to prosecution under the same law as the English. The legal position here is that all English laws apply, unless specially abrogated by our Parliament. No such prosecution has taken place hitherto and 'The Irish bookshop' sell[s] copies of the books & puts it in the Window.[5]

The Nation commented in the same year that the Irish Bookshop (owned by P. S. O'Hegarty) 'was the only place outside Paris in which that unspeakable heap of printed filth, Mr. James Joyce's *Ulysses* could be openly purchased!'[6] However, according to Gerard O'Flaherty, 'copies were [...] being smuggled

---

[4] D. L. Kelleher, '"Are We All Murderers"?', *The Tribune*, vol. 1, no. 2 (19 March 1926): 10.
[5] W. B. Yeats, *The Collected Letters of W.B. Yeats*, gen.ed., John Kelly (Oxford University Press [InteLex Electronic Edition], 2002, 4574.
[6] 'Mr. P. S. O'Hegarty Slanders the Dead', 5

into the country since 1922, and in that year there was at least one copy circulating among the republican prisoners in Kilmainham Gaol'.[7] As the Free State consolidated, it arguably became more difficult to find copies of *Ulysses*. Censorship was already very much a reality in the Ireland of the 1920s. In 1925, the Minister for Justice, Kevin O'Higgins, yielded to pressure from Catholic lobbies – Catholic bishops, 'the Vigilance Association of Ireland, the Christian Brothers, and Catholic newspapers such as the *Standard*' – to constitute the Committee of Inquiry into Evil Literature with the aim of suppression.[8] The Committee, chaired by Robert Donovan, Professor of English Literature at University College Dublin, drew on the guidance of (among others) the Reverend Richard Devane, SJ, well known at the time as the author of *Indecent Literature – Some Legal Remedies*.[9] Devane saw censorship as a means to assert Ireland's moral superiority over Britain and regularly attacked 'the filthy Sunday cross-Channel papers' while supporting 'the clean tradition of the Irish Press'.[10] Few, working in Irish newspapers, dared lift their heads to oppose the clamour for censorship (apart from A. E. and a handful of his colleagues writing for *The Irish Statesman*) because they feared incurring the wrath of the Church. The Irish newspapers also knew that they stood to gain financially if some of the more popular British papers were removed from the market. For many proponents of censorship, the banning of the British papers was more pressing than any concerns with licentious literature which was, in any case, mostly unlikely to find a substantial readership. The few who did read such books would, it was hoped, be capable of coming to mature judgement. The benighted masses could not be so trusted. 'Literature', however, was not entirely out of the firing range. Back in 1923, the influential Jesuit periodical, *Irish Monthly*, had published an article entitled 'The Evil Literature Question in Ireland' outlining the risks posed by this monster stalking the land and threatening all in its path:

> There is a literature question. It looms large over the land, and is fraught with consequences beyond all reckoning. Like some fever-laden mist a literature is coming in upon us that threatens to destroy not only every vestige of our Gaelic civilization, but even the faith and virtue of our people as well.[11]

---

[7]Gerard O'Flaherty, 'Living with *Ulysses* – under Plain Cover', *II*, *James Joyce Centenary Supplement*, 2 February 1982, 7.
[8]Anthony Keating, 'Censorship: The Cornerstone of Catholic Ireland', *Journal of Church and State*, vol. 57, no. 2 (Spring 2015): 289–309, 294.
[9]This was first published in the *Irish Ecclesiastical Record* (25 February 1925, 182–204) and subsequently as a stand-alone pamphlet.
[10]R. S. Devane, *Indecent Literature: Some Legal Remedies* (Dublin: Browne and Nolan, 1925), 4, 13.
[11]T. A. Murphy, Rev., 'The Evil Literature Question in Ireland', *IM*, vol. 51, no. 596 (February 1923): 53–60, 53.

The author of this apocalyptic piece, the redemptorist priest, Fr T. A. Murphy, called for a return to the Irish language as the best means 'to erect the strongest of all barriers against the inroads of demoralising literature, to safeguard the faith of many an Irish home, and the purity of many an Irish heart, and therefore, to do a great work for God and country'.[12] Most, like the Christian Brothers, favoured the more direct route of strict censorship:

> Until this riddance takes place, there is no chance of building up a better or holier Ireland. At present the spiritualised Irishman is quickly passing away and all of the brute that is in him is being fed almost to the point of moral leprosy, to be followed by the tempest of fire from heaven.[13]

As the 1929 Censorship of Publications bill passed through the houses of the Oireachtas, pressure was maintained and the brave few who spoke out in opposition did so at their peril. *The Catholic Bulletin*[14] branded those who begged to differ or wished to temper the severity of the legislation as 'those low creatures, vulgarians, wastrels, materialists, mere Irish scum'.[15] Padraic Colum warned that the Censorship bill would 'have the effect of identifying Catholicism with the worst kind of obscurantism. Catholics will grow up in this country with the notion that the culture to which they are heirs is not able to deal with modern ideas. Ireland should be importing ideas, not seeking to restrict them'.[16] The *Catholic Bulletin* in turn attacked Colum simply by associating him with Joyce: 'the perpetrator of the colossal muck-heap called *Ulysses*' who, it announced, 'has found a bell-man in New York for one of his latest performances'[17] (this was a reference to Colum writing the preface to *Anna Livia Plurabelle* in 1928). Colum's piece was published in the *Irish Statesman* and this was indicative of the central role this publication played in persuading politicians to curb what were increasingly draconian measures. The 'politically well informed' and 'intellectually rigorous attacks on the bill' by crusading editor, George Russell, were 'the best critiques of censorship policy in the period'.[18] The bill's passage into law was not simple and there were those within the government who had

[12]Ibid.
[13]Quoted in Anthony Keating, 'Censorship', 297.
[14]The *Catholic Bulletin* was founded in 1911 by J. J. O'Kelly (1872–1957). Its first issue set the tone with an article by the Rev. Patrick Forde's entitled 'Catholic Literature'. Its first sentence was 'Why do bad and dangerous publications find a wide circulation in Ireland?' (*The Catholic Book Bulletin*, 1.1, January 1911, p. 3.) The *Catholic Bulletin* worked 'to promote wholesome literature for the family and to support vigilance committees in their opposition to undesirable publications'. It had a circulation of over 10,000 by 1914. Ibid., vii: 605.
[15]CB, March 1927, 233.
[16]Quoted in 'On the Utterance of Mr. Padraic Colum', CB, vol. XIX, no. 1 (January 1929), 9.
[17]Ibid.
[18]Peter Martin, *Censorship in the Two Irelands 1922–1939* (Dublin: Irish Academic Press, 2006), 83.

their reservations. External Affairs Minister, Desmond Fitzgerald, came under pressure from literary friends, such as Francis Hackett and Ezra Pound, who wrote with characteristic directness: 'What the HELL does this mean... Can't you keep condoms and classics in separate parts of your law books?!!!'[19] Fianna Fáil, anxious to redeem and ingratiate itself with the Church, mounted no serious opposition, with P. J. Ruttledge declaring in the Dáil: 'We cannot see [...] how in any way whatever, literature or art can suffer in the slightest degree from the passing of this bill.'[20] Even those in government who had reservations about the bill were inclined to agree with Agriculture Minister Patrick Hogan's claim: 'Thomas or Pat Murphy, who lives anywhere between Donegal and Cork, is not likely to read either Balzac or Aristophanes even in translation.' In the words of Deputy Eamonn Cooney of Fianna Fáil, 'it is the wealthy classes and not the masses that are reading these books'.[21]

Once the bill had been passed, the five-man State Censorship of Publications Board was appointed under the chairmanship of Canon Patrick Boylan, professor of Eastern languages at UCD. The structure of the first board constituted 'a precedent for all that followed until the late 1950s: it comprised a member of the CTSI [the Catholic Truth Society of Ireland] and/or the Knights of Columbanus, another leading member of the Catholic Action group (as chairman, often a cleric), together with three other Catholics [...] and a token Protestant, represented by a Trinity College academic'.[22] There was initial anxiety among the board members to find material to ban – the onus was on the public to make complaints – and they were disappointed at how few materialized. As a result the board lobbied successfully to be given a small sum to buy books but ultimately decided that the best way to proceed was to 'join the *Times* book club' and borrow the titles they thought suspicious, so as to ban them and then return them.[23] In 1926, in a submission to the Committee, the Irish Vigilance Association objected to the sale in Dublin of books by Joyce, along with works by D. H. Lawrence and Warwick Deeping but of Joyce's works, only *Stephen Hero*, published posthumously in 1944, was officially banned. This ban was lifted after an appeal in 1951 – a year in which the Censorship Board prohibited 539 of the 717 books it examined.[24] These numbers show that Ireland became more censorious as

---

[19]Ezra Pound to Fitzgerald, 16 August 1928 in Fitzgerald Papers, University College Dublin archives, P80/1207 (10–12).
[20]Dáil Debates, vol. XXXVIII, 27 February 1929, 615.
[21]Dáil Debates, vol. XXXVI, 24 October 1928, 829.
[22]Donal Ó Drisceoil, 'Censorship and the Irish Writer' in Clare Hutton and Patrick Walsh, eds., *The Oxford History of the Irish Book*, vol. V (Oxford: Oxford University Press, 2011), 285–303.
[23]Peter Martin, *Censorship in the Two Irelands*, 91.
[24]*IT*, 7 March 1953, 5.

the century progressed and a Catholic moral ethos increasingly dominated. Joyce's nephew, Ken Monaghan, left a useful first-hand account of the status of *Ulysses*:

> It is ironic to learn that *Ulysses* was never banned in Ireland under this Act but was prohibited from being brought into the country under some section of the Customs and Excise Acts. Copies of the book were confiscated at points of entry, and, of course, were never on sale openly in shops in Dublin until the middle to late 1960s. In an Irish solution to an Irish question and in much the same way, as Mr Deasy explains to Stephen Dedalus in *Ulysses*, that the Jews were never persecuted in Ireland because they were never let in, so the Irish people were saved from being contaminated by this terrible book. Enterprising enthusiasts (and there were some) smuggled copies into the country disguised under the dust covers of more innocent volumes such as Mrs. Beeton's *Cook Book*.[25]

That *Ulysses* was bought at all in the tumultuous early 1920s was a notable result. Eason's, the country's major book wholesaler, did not handle titles by Joyce as evidenced from this letter from J. C. M. Eason to A. E.: 'As to James Joyce, I need not tell you that we have not got his *Ulysses*, nor have we got any other works of his.'[26] Joyce rightly fretted that the new regime in Ireland would further complicate getting copies of *Ulysses* into the country. In a letter of 11 February 1922, he enquired if Joseph Hone had been sent a copy and suggested that 'all Irish notices ought to be sent out as with a new Irish postmaster general and a vigilance committee in clerical hands you never know from one day to the next what may occur'.[27]

Details of Irish purchases can be traced among the first 1,000 copies dispatched from Paris by Sylvia Beach. Irish buyers represented approximately 10 per cent. In 1921, Beach told Joyce that 'John M. McCormack, Noroton, Connecticut'[28] was among the early subscribers. This was none other than the renowned Irish tenor. As it turned out, Joyce gifted McCormack a signed copy during one of their meetings in Paris in 1922.[29] Meanwhile, individual buyers and several Irish bookshops ordered a significant number of copies. Of the first 100 Dutch 350-franc copies,

---

[25]Ken Monaghan, 'Dublin in the Time of Joyce', *JSA*, vol. 12 (Summer 2001): 65–73.

[26]Quoted in Donal Ó Drisceoil, 'Censorship and the Irish Writer', 289.

[27]Letter from Joyce to Sylvia Beach, 11 February 1922 in Julieann Veronica Ulin, 'Philatelic *Ulysses*', *JSA* (2018): 51–85, 51.

[28]Letter of 28 June 1921 from Sylvia Beach to Joyce consulted at the Hans E. Jahnke collection at the Zurich James Joyce Foundation.

[29]John Scary, 'James Joyce and John McCormack', *Revue belge de philologie et d'histoire*, tome 52, fasc. 3, 1974: 523–36, 531.

numbers 19 and 45 went to Peter Golden;[30] no. 37 to Fred Hanna; nos. 42
and 88 to Hodges Figgis; no. 49 to Combridge & Co. on Grafton Street;
and no. 51 to the Irish bookshop. Of the Vergé d'Arche 250-franc copies,
nos. 108 and 118 went to the Irish Bookshop. In 1955, Michael MacWhite,
the Irish diplomat who had served in Paris in the early 1920s, sold copy
no. 143, which he had presumably bought directly from Sylvia Beach.[31]
Of the Vergé à Barbes 150-Franc copies, nos. 260, 261, 262, 267, 268,
285 and 286 were sent to the Irish Bookshop, which both sold and lent
copies (no. 268 was Bulmer Hobson's copy; no. 281 went to Joseph Hone;
nos. 308 and 309 were sent, on Joyce's instruction, to Stanislaus Joyce
and Constantine Curran, respectively; while no. 313 was ordered by the
Leitrim-born journalist, M. J. MacManus, who would poke fun at the
novel in his *So This Is Dublin!*).[32] No. 376 was bought by Arthur Power;
no. 378 by L. A. (Laurence) Waldron (1858–1923), an influential former
nationalist Irish MP, businessman and stockbroker, who was also a keen
bibliophile; no. 393 was sent to Hodges Figgis; 456 went to Ernest Boyd;
516, 517 and 518 were sent to Combridge & Co.; 538 and 539 went to
Mullan & Son in Belfast; 580 and 586 to Hodges Figgis; and 591 and
596 to the Irish Bookshop. After the first 600, Sylvia Beach's records are
more sketchy, but we can see that no. 609 was bought by John J. Nolan, a
physicist who later served as president of the Royal Irish Academy; other
copies went to Lennox Robinson (751) and W. B. Yeats (939); two press
copies went to Padraic (623) and Mary M. Colum; uncovered numbers
were sent to Joyce's father, to his aunt, Josephine Murray, and to Michael
Healy. According to Stanislaus Joyce, Aunt Josephine 'kept the copy of
Ulysses, which my brother had sent her, under lock and key as if it were the
book of the Antichrist, [...] she burnt all the letters he had written her over

[30]Peter Golden was a second cousin of Terence MacSwiney (the Sinn Féin Lord Mayor of Cork,
arrested by the British government on charges of sedition and imprisoned in Brixton Prison
where he died in October 1920 after seventy-four days on hunger strike. Joyce believed he was
a distant relative and followed his case closely). Golden was a native of Macroom where he
was born in 1877. He emigrated to the United States in 1901 and worked there as an actor and
poet. A prominent journalist and activist in Irish-American circles, he supported Eamon De
Valera in the Treaty split and travelled to Ireland in August 1922 in a vain attempt to reconcile
the sides in the Civil War. His copies were returned to Ireland in 2010 and 2013. See Catherine
Ketch, 'Rare and Valuable Copy of *Ulysses* Donated to Library', *The Corkman*, 28 January
2010.
[31]'Ulysses for 27 gns', *IP*, 10 November 1955, 7.
[32]M. J. MacManus in *So This is Dublin!* (1927) describes a trip by Joyce to Dublin 'in search
of local colour' for his 'Irish Odyssey'. Joyce, we are told, 'spent considerable time visiting the
Corporation Sewage Farm, the Wicklow manure factory, and the sloblands at Fairview. Before
returning to Paris he stated that he had derived keen satisfaction from is visit to his native city'.
Joyce later used the title of McManus' book in *Finnegans Wake* – 'So This Is Dyoublong?' See
Terence Killeen, in 'Ireland Must be Important…', *JSA*, 2003, 24–5.

many years, and [...] as she lay dying, it seemed to prey on her mind, for she kept saying "The book... the book".'[33] Copy no. 819 went to Dublin publisher, Thomas Kiersey; 930 to a Mr. Murphy c/o Grosvenor Hotel on Harcourt Street in Dublin; 940 to Hodges Figgis; 923 to the National Library of Ireland. Copy 895 was bought by David or Davy Byrne, he of the 'tuckstitched shirtsleeves' who ran the 'moral pub' at 21 Duke Street, Dublin. Byrne, whom Joyce described as 'a tiresome bore' sold it on in the early 1930s to the controversial book dealer Jacob Schwartz.[34] This copy was seized under Section 42 of the Customs Consolidation Act 1876 and never made it to its new owner. It is still held today at the Postal Museum in London.[35] Sylvia Beach's records show that Norah Hoult, A. J. Leventhal and the London-based Irishman, Aeneas O'Neill, also purchased editions. *Ulysses* was also bought by several Irish libraries including Dublin's Pearse Street (no. 262). Trinity College Dublin received a legal deposit copy, which it placed on an open shelf but, as Lloyd Houston commented, 'as the immaculate condition of Trinity's copy (the pages of which remain unopened) indicates, though legal deposit could gain *Ulysses* entry into the copyright libraries, it could not guarantee the novel a willing readership'.[36] Further copies would have been ordered by Irish readers from British bookshops.

All that said, copies of *Ulysses* were hard to find and expensive to purchase. In a 1926 letter from London to Gabriel Fallon, Sean O'Casey wrote excitedly: 'Oh, be God, I ferreted out a copy of Ullysses [*sic*] at last!'[37] The same year, Hanna Sheehy Skeffington 'returned from a suffrage conference in Paris with a copy of *Ulysses*, which Joyce himself had given her as a present'. She lent it to her feminist, Republican friend, Rosamund Jacob, who 'found a lot of interesting, weird and funny stuff in it, but so much plain disgustfullness [...] that I could not read it at meals'.[38] But read it she did. *Evening Herald* journalist, John Finnegan, recalled discovering Herbert Gorman's biography at the Thomas Street Public Library and then reading *Dubliners* and *A Portrait* at the National Library around 1925. But he could not find *Ulysses*: 'The then editor of the *Herald*, Michael J. J. Brunicardi, a man of wide learning, possessed a copy of the novel, but no persuasion on my part could induce him to lend it, deeming me too young

---

[33]Stanislaus Joyce, 'Joyce's Dublin', *Partisan Review*, vol. 19, no. 1 (January–February 1952): 103–9, 107.

[34]Joyce's comment to Herbert Gorman is cited in Willard Potts, 'Joyce's Notes on the Gorman Biography', *ICarbS*, vol. IV, no.2 (Spring–Summer 1981): 83–100, 91.

[35]Full details are available here: https://www.postalmuseum.org/blog/controversial-ulysses/

[36]Lloyd Houston, '(Il)legal Deposits', 143.

[37]Letter of 12 April 1926 in David Krause, ed., *The Letters of Sean O'Casey 1910–1941*, vol. 1 (New York: Macmillan, 1975), 190.

[38]Geraldine Meaney, 'Rosamond Jacob and the Hidden Histories of Irish Writing', *New Hibernia Review/Iris Éireannach Nua*, vol. 15, no. 4 (Geimhreadh/Winter 2011): 70–4, 73.

to be exposed to such a disturbing book.'[39] He eventually purchased a copy in 1930 (the eleventh edition) and smuggled it into the country.

With a reasonable number of copies of *Ulysses* in circulation, there was more of a response than Joyce chose to admit. There was mixed reaction with many critics taking their cue from their British counterparts, such as H. G. Wells, who described it as 'insurrectionary' (*JJ*, 608). In the October 1922 issue of *Quarterly Review*, Eton and Cambridge educated Catholic convert and Irish critic, Sir Shane Leslie (1885–1971), compared *Ulysses* to a 'Clerkenwell explosion in the well-guarded, well-built classical prison of English literature', aligning Joyce's novel with the Fenian tradition of Irish violence in England (*CH* 1, 210). The Clerkenwell bombing was the largest terrorist attack to be carried out in nineteenth-century Britain; it killed a dozen people and injured over 100 innocent bystanders but failed in its intent to free a Fenian prisoner. The inappropriateness of linking Joyce's novel with this terrorist atrocity could not be clearer, and the bad faith in Leslie's assessment is all too apparent – as was his fear of the emerging Irish State, which he felt Joyce's novel partly represented. Leslie, always keen to ingratiate himself with Irish Catholicism, also claimed that *Ulysses* was an 'assault upon Divine Decency as well as on human intelligence [...] literary Bolshevism [...] experimental, anti-conventional, anti-Christian, chaotic, totally unmoral [...]'.[40] Before writing this, Leslie corresponded with Oliver St John Gogarty, who claimed that Joyce gathered his material 'from the walls of our public lavatories' and encouraged him to attack Joyce's work 'as literature, hack literature' so as to 'Stop him'.[41] Even if Joyce attempted to pass off Leslie's review as 'the best thing he could have done for the book to give it prestige in England. The fact that it is adverse, in my opinion will not count' (*LI*, 192), he also dictated a letter that responded, blow by blow, to the attack, which had contained:

> a string of reflections on the incriminating bibliographical features of Joyce's novel, noting that it had been 'printed at Dijon' (implying that no English printer was prepared to accept the legal risks of setting the novel) and 'published in Paris at an excessive price' (reflecting its publisher's desire to evade British obscenity legislation and deter a general readership) in a format 'whose resemblance in size and colour to the London Telephone Book must make it a danger to the unsuspecting'.[42]

[39] John Finnegan, 'Why the Editor Wouldn't Let Me Read *Ulysses*', *EH*, 2 February 1982, 6.
[40] Shane Leslie, '*Ulysses*', *Quarterly Review*, 238, October 1922. For a discussion of these two reviews, see John Nash, '"In the Heart of the Hibernian Metropolis"? Joyce's Reception in Ireland, 1900–1940' in Richard Brown, ed., *A Companion to James Joyce* (London: Blackwell, 2008), 108–22.
[41] Gogarty, 'My Dear Gogarty', 42.
[42] Lloyd Houston, '(Il)legal Deposits', 141.

Leslie expressed doubt as to whether 'the British Museum possesses a copy, as the book apparently could not be printed in England, and no copy could fall by law to the great national collection'. A furious Joyce dictated a reply to Leslie in Sylvia Beach's name 'stating for his information that copies had been presented to Trinity and the National Library and acknowledged with thanks'. He also emphasized 'that the British Museum ordered and paid for a copy'.[43] Leslie had done damage: as Lloyd Houston points out, his review 'prompted the Home Office to open its first file on *Ulysses* (H. O. 186.428/1) in November 1922' and it 'continued to shape official opinion on the novel in Britain well into the 1930s'.[44] Joseph M. Hone also saw danger in what he considered Joyce's political 'struggle for freedom' (*CH* 1, 297). Years later, Joyce's friend, Arthur Power, claimed that 'there was much of the Fenian about him' and called him 'a literary conspirator, who was determined to destroy the oppressive and respectable cultural structures under which we had been reared'.[45] Few of Joyce's other friends would remember him in this light, and yet, in recent years, this political aspect of his output and his own alignment with Sinn Féin have re-emerged more clearly.

The dominant response to *Ulysses* in Ireland, however, was to attack it on anti-Catholic grounds. Yet, while Joyce had major issues with the Irish Catholic Church, which he saw as ignorant, insular and bullying, his writings were steeped in Church history, philosophy and theology, which he knew far better than the vast majority of Irish Catholic clerics who denounced him. Although, as the notoriously anti-clerical Stanislaus attested, 'the earliest and most lasting influence on Jim's life was Italian – the Roman Catholic Church',[46] *Ulysses* caused disgust and outrage in an Ireland dominated by a puritanical and repressive Church that feared anything that might threaten or question its growing dominance. Even at the Dublin Radical Club, a left-wing forum for intellectual debate about art and literature set up by Liam O'Flaherty and Cecil Salkeld in 1925, Joyce's novel was the subject of debate on the basis of its supposed anti-Catholic bias when M. J. MacManus gave a lecture in January 1926 on 'The Cult of the Abnormal in Literature'. In her diary, Rosamund Jacob reported that the lecture 'was awful tosh, everything abnormal was vile, morbid, filthy, etc etc – no words were disgusting enough for *Ulysses* & its intention (to destroy man's belief in the soul) [...] you'd think it was the *Catholic Bulletin* talking'.[47] What caused offence was the

---

[43]Ibid., 141–2.
[44]Ibid., 142, footnote 54.
[45]Arthur Power, *Conversations with James Joyce* (London: Millington Publishers, 1974), 69.
[46]Stanislaus Joyce, Letter of 17 March 1929 to Stuart Gilbert. The original letter is kept in the Stuart Gilbert Collection at the Harry Ransom Center, University of Texas at Austin (hereafter HRC), Box 17, folder 9.
[47]Rosamund Jacob, 'Diaries', 16 January 1926, NLI ms 32582 quoted in Nicholas Allen, 'Reading Revolutions, 1922–39' in Clare Hutton and Patrick Walsh, eds., *The Oxford History of the Irish Book Volume V The Irish Book in English 1891–2000* (Oxford: Oxford University Press, 2019), 104.

veracity of Joyce's portrayals. This was attested to in Mary M. Colum's review, published in *The Freeman* in July 1922. Colum, who had studied at University College Dublin at the same time as Joyce, describes the book as 'the Confessions of James Joyce, a most sincere and cunningly-wrought autobiographical book; it is as if he had said, "Here I am; here is what country and race have bred me, what religion and life and literature have done to me"'.[48] Some Irish readers would have identified with elements of that portrait even if they lived their personal struggles at home rather than in exile. For Colum, *Ulysses* was far more than a personal account; it was a profound, provocative, political intervention into Irish public life:

> *Ulysses* is one of the most racial [...] and one of the most Catholic books ever written; this in spite of the fact that one would not be surprised to hear some official of the Irish Government or of the Church had ordered it to be publicly burned. It hardly seems possible that it can really be understood by anybody not brought up in the half-secret tradition of the heroism, tragedy, folly and anger of Irish nationalism, or unfamiliar with the philosophy, history and rubrics of the Roman Catholic Church; or by one who does not know Dublin and certain conspicuous Dubliners.

'Where', she asked, 'has the aesthetic and intellectual fascination of the Roman Catholic Church ever found subtler fascination?' (*CH* 1, 232–3). She backed up this view in a 1927 review in the *New York Herald Tribune*, where she claimed, anticipating a whole school of Irish Joyce criticism in mid-century, that '*Ulysses* cannot be entirely comprehensible to anybody not Irish because of the subtly national, local, and linguistic allusions and references' (*CH* 1, 373). Her husband, Padraic, in his preface to *Anna Livia Plurabelle* (1928) described Joyce as 'the most daring of innovators', yet one who had decided 'to be as local as a hedge-poet' (*CH* 1, 389). The Colums' interpretation of Joyce's Irishness and his Catholicism was consistently positive and it was not appreciated in Irish America, where Joyce was seen to be giving the country a bad name. On 5 March 1927, the influential New York-based, Irish-American newspaper, *The Advocate*, reprinted the editorial page of the *Roscommon Herald*. It lambasted 'the new school of writers in Dublin whose abominable writings have made Ireland a foul smell in the nostril of other countries' and attacked what it called 'a degenerate named James Joyce' for having 'issued a book entitled "Ulysses," which in its vileness could only be compared to a reeking cesspool'.[49] *The Advocate* also reported that '"at a recent meeting of an Irish literary group in New York City," a speaker who had once written a preface to the *Collegians*

[48]Mary M. Colum, 'The Confessions of James Joyce', npg.
[49]Stephen G. Butler, *Irish Writers in the Irish American Press, 1882–1964* (Amherst and Boston: University of Massachusetts Press, 2018), 134.

nevertheless "lauded Joyce and belittled [Gerald] Griffen [*sic*]"'. The article was referring to Padraic Colum.

A letter from Shane Leslie to Monsignor Michael O'Riordan, rector of the Irish College in Rome, was equally unforgiving and gave voice to the dismay and horror Joyce's new book was occasioning among educated Irish Catholics. He reported that he had been reading Pearse's political writings and:

> the appalling product of James Joyce – of Clongowes, a terribly blasphemous sexually perverted account of himself and friends during 24 hours in Dublin. He takes 720 pages to describe them and calls the whole *Ulysses*. I have come to the conclusion the man is diabolically possessed but alas what a waste of Irish humour and insight and fierce power of writing! The sad thing is that the French Press and some English intellectuals have hailed *Ulysses* as Ireland's return into European literature. Having Irish letters deeply at heart I have never felt more grieved – to see so splendid and horrible a book to which no scribe could add 'do chum gloria De agus honora na hEireann'.[50]

Leslie was here rehearsing the famous attack on the 'diabolically possessed' Joyce that he would soon publish, writing as 'Domini Canis' for the *Dublin Review*. In it, he denounces *Ulysses* as 'a fearful travesty on persons, happenings and intimate life of the most morbid and sickening description, we say not only for the *Dublin Review* but for Dublin *écrasez l'infâme!*' (*CH* 1, 200–1). As Geert Lernout has commented, 'Leslie makes it clear that he sees the book as an anti-Catholic attack by turning Voltaire's famous anti-clerical statement against the author of *Ulysses*. In his attack, he pulls out all the stops: the novel is "the screed of one possessed"'.[51] He hopes that Catholic Irishmen will repudiate 'the failure of this frustrated Titan' and 'the flood of his own vomits':

> We speak advisedly when we say that though no formal condemnation has been pronounced, the Inquisition can only require its destruction or, at least, its removal from Catholic houses. [...] Having tasted and rejected the devilish drench, we most earnestly hope that this book be not only placed on the *Index Expurgatorius*, but that its reading and communication be made a reserved case.
>
> (*CH* 1, 201)

Some critics, such as historian, writer and biographer, Stephen Gwynn (1864–1950), one-time Irish Parliamentary Party MP and a Protestant

---

[50]Letter from Shane Leslie to Monsignor Michael O'Riordan, 15 May 1922. The letter is kept in the archives of the Pontificio Collegio Irlandese, Rome.

[51]Quoted in Geert Lernout, 'Religion' in John McCourt, ed., *James Joyce in Context*, 333.

advocate of Home Rule, drew positive attention to the Catholic elements in Joyce's works. He described Joyce in his article 'Modern Irish Literature', which was published on 15 March 1923 in the *Manchester Guardian* as 'the first notable force' from the Catholic population to appear in modern Irish literature (*CH* 1, 300). He was well qualified to make such a claim: his wife had converted to Catholicism and their four children were brought up as Catholics, the eldest, Aubrey, becoming a Jesuit priest:

> Mr. Joyce's Stephen Dedalus is the Catholic by nature and tradition, who must revolt under the stress of an intellectual compulsion, to whom truth – the thing which he sees as true – speaks inexorably. Yet what he would shake off clings to his flesh like the poisoned shirt of Hercules. He wallows, it burns the more, but revolt persists. He can touch, taste and handle every abomination; only one thing is impossible, to profess a faith that he rejects.
>
> (*CH* 1, 300)

Joyce approvingly noted this review although he doubted its originality, telling Harriet Shaw Weaver grudgingly: 'I shall send my formal thanks to Mr Gwynn who after sixteen years of literary criticism has discovered my existence. One half of his article is taken almost verbally from the text of *Ulysses*, the other half consists of phrases which I myself set in circulation. They now come back to me' (*LIII*, 74). In the January 1923 issue of the *London Mercury*, Joseph Hone described Joyce as 'the first man of literary genius, expressing himself in perfect freedom, that Catholic Ireland has produced in modern times. [...] Certainly no Irish Protestant writer was likely to have expressed the secular Irish emotions of politics and religion with Mr. Joyce's passionate force and understanding and his entire lack of sentimentality' (*CH* 1, 299). Hone argued that Stephen Dedalus and his peers represented:

> a type of young Irishman of the towns – mostly originating from the semi-anglicised farming or shopkeeping class of the east and centre – a type which has been created largely by the modern legislation which provides Catholic democracy in Ireland with opportunities for an inexpensive university education. This young Irishman is now a dominating figure in the public life of Ireland; he was less important in Mr. Joyce's day, but had already exhibited a certain amount of liveliness.

These young Irishmen represented the future: 'Mr. Joyce's novels and stories are much more important than Synge's plays and stories, for the later writer describes, intimately and realistically, a growing Ireland, not, as Synge did, an Ireland that is passing away' (*CH* 1, 298).

With notices such as these, it was no surprise that alarm bells were ringing in the ears of the moral arbiters of conservative Irish Catholicism, who could only have felt threatened by Joyce's rebellious attitudes towards faith and fatherland. The new editor of the *Catholic Bulletin*, the Clongowes-educated Jesuit, Fr Timothy Corcoran, railed against the very fact that *Ulysses*, Joyce's 'vast, shapeless, and hideous heap of the most utterly depraved and beastly filth', was on sale in the Irish Bookshop and was being bought, read and circulated:

> The writer, who lays his scene in Dublin, and the book itself are not to be named here. Even in Paris it was not found easy to procure for the work a publisher: for Paris and her government are at last waking up to the evils of such publications. [...] The publication of this repulsive mass of brutal immorality was somehow achieved, and the book – banned in America and even in London—is displayed for sale in Ireland. The sale will not be great. The coterie of dabblers in such vile puddles is of an economic turn of mind: the usual method is to have one copy bought, and to have this one passed round the circle of those interested.[52]

Joyce, however, precisely because his works were difficult and expensive, was not seen as the biggest threat. Although his novels carried 'a taint of indecency' and were 'afflicted with a shameful mania', they were, as the *Irish Monthly* put it, 'but little read by sane folk'.[53] Joyce drew Harriet Shaw Weaver's attention to a cartoon in the comic Dublin paper, *Dublin Opinion*, which essentially described reading *Ulysses* as hard labour or torture: 'The first caricature of *Ulysses* I saw appeared in a comic Dublin paper "Dublin Opinion." A convict has called a warder. The warder says "We let you off hard labour and gave Joyce's *Ulysses* to read. What do you want now?" The convict (handing back a large volume): "More oakum!"' (*L1*, 208).

Ten years later, Charles Duff would write of the centrality of Joyce's 'Roman Catholicism' and argue that:

> Like many Roman Catholics who have discarded their religion, Joyce seldom misses an opportunity for blasphemous ridicule, and, as he is exceptionally resourceful in the use of language and deeply learned in Church matters, his considered blasphemies are apt to horrify any plain reader who has the least respect for Latin Christianity. The good Roman Catholic who reads him requires disinfection afterwards, if the Joycean darts are not to leave septic lacerations. This explains the rough manner in which Joyce's works are handled by some critics who are conscientious Roman Catholics; it also explains why they are regarded as abominations by the Irish Free State Government.[54]

---

[52]*CB*, 13.3 (March 1923): 131–2.
[53]Eoin Ua Mathghamhna, 'Obscenity in Modern Irish Literature'. *IM*, vol. 52, no. 617 (November 1924): 569–73, 569.
[54]Charles Duff (1932), *James Joyce and the Plain Reader* (New York: Haskell House, 1971), 24–5.

The final sentence is a damning, if unintended, verdict on the dominance of the Catholic Church within the newly founded Irish State, whose government is effectively reduced to an afterthought in Duff's analysis. It is not primarily Joyce's critique of Irish nationalism in the era of Cosgrave and de Valera but his alleged anti-Catholicism that causes most discomfort. The leadership of the new State, both in W. T. Cosgrave's pro-Treaty Cumann na nGaedheal government, which ruled from 1923 to 1931, and in de Valera's Fianna Fáil government, which took over in 1932 and held power until 1948, forged an identity based on Irish Catholicism and on a glorious Celtic past (both of which were unrelentingly questioned and dismantled in *Ulysses*). Elements within the Church pushed an image of the Irish people whose Catholic faith was under siege, with the *Irish Monthly* warning: 'Modern forces are not for but against the Church's mission. Today the enemy is invisible and omnipresent. The Irish Catholic is like a soldier who has turned aside the sword but is attacked by a poisonous gas.'[55] Joyce was, of course, the author of an inflammatory satirical broadside entitled 'Gas from a Burner', which he wrote in 1912 as he left Dublin for the last time having learnt that the sheets of *Dubliners* had been destroyed by the printer, John Falconer, who had feared being seen as unpatriotic. Joyce had the broadside distributed by his brother Charles in Dublin. It was a deeply personal parting shot. His more considered response to the Ireland that did not have space for his works was *Ulysses*, which contained material that would be seen to be even more noxious and as a result could only be rejected. No censorship would be needed to keep Joyce's book out of the hands (and minds) of the people because there was a consensus that anything that was seen to challenge traditional Catholic values should be repressed, if necessary, by law. As Seán O'Faoláin argued, the 1920s was a period when 'the Catholic church was felt, feared and courted on all sides as the dominant power'.[56]

If Irish Catholics reacted with singular virulence to *Ulysses*, it was also because the book portrayed the institution and their faith so unapologetically. Their annoyance was all the more pronounced when the Catholic nature of the book was pointed out by non-Catholic sources or English reviewers, such as Cecil Maitland, in his 'Mr Joyce and the Catholic Tradition', published in *New Witness* in 1922. Maitland saw Joyce's Catholic education as the source of his 'Weltanschauung'. What he thought was the failure of *Ulysses* arose 'from the fact that to a Catholic who no longer believes that he has an immortal soul, fashioned in the image of God, a human being becomes merely a specially cunning animal'. This was not Joyce's fault, 'but that of the Catholic system, which has not had the strength to hold him to

[55]*IM*, vol. 53, no. 626 (August 1925): 350.
[56]O'Faoláin is quoted in J. H. Whyte, *Church and State in Modern Ireland, 1923–79* (Dublin: Gill and MacMillan, 1980), 35.

its transcendentalism, and from whose errors he has not been able to set himself free' (*CH* 1, 273). Dubliner and former Director of the National Library of Ireland, William Kirkpatrick Magee (1868–1961), the son of a Presbyterian minister who appears under his own name in 'Scylla and Charybdis', wrote under the pseudonym of John Eglinton in *The Dial*. He claimed in May 1929 that Joyce was the first to give voice to Irish Catholic experience and through a distinctly Irish means of expression: 'The mind of Catholic Ireland triumphs over the Anglicism of the English language [...] perhaps for the first time in an Irish writer, there is no faintest trace of Protestantism, that is, of the English spirit.' We are obliged to admit that in Joyce literature has reached for the first time in Ireland a complete emancipation from Anglo-Saxon ideals (*CH* 2, 459). This was the polite version of future Trinity Provost, John Pentland Mahaffey's take that 'James Joyce is a living argument in defence of my contention that it was a mistake to establish a separate university for the aborigines of this island – for the corner boys who spit into the Liffey'.[57]

Joyce was perfectly placed to become the voice of the emerging bourgeois Catholic nation that Magee and Mahaffey found so disturbing. He had been educated by the Jesuits, side by side with young men who were being trained to assume leadership roles in the new country. Unlike his peers, he desired a very different Ireland and sought, from afar, to make a contribution towards the achievement of what he called 'the spiritual liberation of my country' (*SL*, 88), a liberation from the repressive Catholicism dominating the hearts and minds of his fellow countrymen even after they had broken free from British rule. Thus his works would, among other things, interrogate and undermine the Irish bourgeois mainstays – the family, the Irish language, the Catholic Church – upon which the new nation state was being built. Joyce despaired at the mounting dominance of the Church in a Free State Ireland where its power was no longer checked by a British counterweight: 'Now I hear that since the Free State came in there is less freedom. The Church has made inroads everywhere, so that we are in fact becoming a bourgeois nation, with the Church supplying the aristocracy [...] and I do not see much hope for us intellectually.'[58]

The beauty of it for the Catholic Church was that it could largely ignore Joyce in the knowledge that mainstream British and Irish media could be relied on to wholeheartedly condemn *Ulysses*. The negative reviews from both sides of the Irish Sea are perhaps the ones that are best known today partly because Joyce drew on them when assembling material to publicize the novel. Dublin's Unionist *Sunday Express* carried a review by James Douglas, which described *Ulysses* as:

---

[57]Gerald Griffin, *The Wild Geese; Pen Portraits of Famous Irish Exiles* (London: Jarrolds, 1938), 24.
[58]Arthur Power, *Conversations*, 1974, 65.

the most infamously obscene book in ancient or modern literature. The obscenity of Rabelais is innocent compared with its leprous and scabrous horrors. All the secret sewers of vice are canalised in its flood of unimaginable thoughts, images and pornographic words. And its unclean lunacies are larded with appalling and revolting blasphemies directed against the Christian religion and against the name of Christ.[59]

In the British *Sunday Chronicle*, an outraged Alfred Noyes found Joyce's novel the 'foulest book that has ever found its way into print'[60] while 'Aramis' in *The Sporting Times* denounced Joyce as a 'perverted lunatic who has made a specialty of the literature of the latrine. [...] Ulysses is not only sordidly pornographic, but it is intensely dull' (*CH* 1, 192, 194). More surprisingly, George Bernard Shaw refused to subscribe to the Egoist edition of *Ulysses* telling Harriet Shaw Weaver that the novel was 'a revolting record of a disgusting phase of civilisation; but it is a truthful one'. *Ulysses* was 'hideously real' (*LIII*, 50):

> James Joyce in his *Ulysses* has described, with a fidelity so ruthless that the book is hardly bearable, the life that Dublin offers her young men, or if you prefer it the other way, the life its young men offer to Dublin [...] a certain futile derision and belittlement that confuses the noble and serious with the base and ludicrous seems peculiar to Dublin.[61]

In 1924, Trinity College Dublin's Professor of English, W. F. Trench, took to the columns of AE's *The Irish Statesman* to express his exasperation at how 'the Dublin aesthete', Yeats, was promoting Joyce, a writer who 'rakes hell, and the sewers, for dirt to throw at the fair face of life, and for poison to make beauty shrivel and die' and who was far from the 'genius' that Yeats was making him out to be.[62] This was seized on gleefully by the *Catholic Bulletin* and it was later quoted in a front-page attack entitled 'Satan, Smut & Co.' printed in the *Irish Independent*. Among other things, Trench, who was 'one of the few Protestant defenders'[63] of the Censorship of Publications Bill, was probably irritated by Yeats' defence of Joyce at the opening meeting of the Dublin University Philosophical Society in November 1923. In response to the assertion by the President of the Society, W. Beare, that

[59]James Douglas, 'Review of Joyce's *Ulysses*', *Sunday Express*, quoted in Donagh MacDonagh, 'The Reputation of James Joyce: From Notoriety to Fame', in *University Review*, vol. 3, no. 2 (Summer 1963): 16.
[60]Alfred Noyes, reviewing *Ulysses*; quoted in Patricia Hutchins, *James Joyce's World*, Methuen 1957, 176, n.1.
[61]Bernard Shaw, Preface to *Immaturity* (London: Constable and Company, 1931), xxxiii.
[62]W. F. Trench 'Dr Yeats and Mr. Joyce', *IS*, 30 August 1924, 790.
[63]Peter Martin, *Censorship in the Two Irelands*, 81.

future historians would perhaps decide that Joyce was 'the most original and influential' writer of the day:

> Yeats described Joyce as being 'as voluminous as Johnson's dictionary and as foul as Rabelais' before stating that 'he was the only Irishman who had the intensity of the great novelist. [...] The miracle was possibly there: that was all he felt he had a right to say, and, perhaps, the intensity was there for the same reason as the intensity of Tolstoi and Balzac'.

Yeats' ambivalence towards Joyce was generational. His wondering if 'Joyce was merely the first drop of a shower'[64] suggests not only his awareness of Valery Larbaud's influential opinion on *Ulysses*, but also his own struggle to keep up with the times both in Ireland and in the new world of Modernism. When announcing the winners on behalf of Aonach Tailteann Literary Committee at the Royal Irish Academy, a year earlier, Yeats explained that they could not consider the work of Padraic Colum, Joyce or George Moore, because 'they have not been resident in Ireland' before adding: 'We feel, however, that it is our duty to say that Mr. James Joyce's book, though as obscene as Rabelais, and therefore forbidden by law in England and the United States, is more indubitably a work of genius that any prose written by an Irishman since the death of Synge.'[65] While this not entirely positive affirmation was met by applause among the polite Royal Irish Academy audience, it would have gone down like a lead balloon with most readers outside of this elite circle.

Other arbiters of taste struggled to offer a decisive stance on *Ulysses* or on Joyce. A piece in the *Irish Times* in 1923 comments on the difficulty of knowing how to receive, let alone read, Joyce's novel. Descriptions of it as 'unique' or 'European' are dismissed as being of little value:

> The correct mind, however, found that *Ulysses* was more than a large mouthful; it was a large stomachful. It was almost as if somebody was speaking in a language hitherto unheard, even unthought. [...] the language of *Ulysses* is not a trifle free – it is freedom itself. It is questionable whether any word forbidden in polite society is not to be found somewhere in its pages.[66]

The columnist struggles to reconcile how Joyce, the author of the 'delicate love lyrics' of *Chamber Music*, could have produced 'the stern harshness' of his current fiction. While acknowledging that the novel is possessed of 'sheer

---

[64]'The Modern Novel. An Irish Author Discussed. Mr. Yeats Admires Good Breeding', *IT*, 9 November 1923, 11.
[65]'Irish Writers. Scholarship, Fiction and Poetry. Tailteann Awards', *IT*, 11 August 1924, 7.
[66]Bruyere (probably R. M. Smyllie), 'Some Irish Artists – VI: Mr. James Joyce', *IT*, 5 May 1923, 9

force', Joyce has 'carried introspection to as far a limit as we can understand'; yet, his candour is a strength: 'He leaves out absolutely nothing: he presents the complete chain of thought and reasoning. If that were his only merit, he would still be able to claim the attention of the world as a master; for to be able to write exactly what one feels is among the most difficult of accomplishments.'

Some Irish critics took their cue from the acclaimed French critic, Valery Larbaud, who gave *Ulysses* a ringing endorsement at the famous gathering that took place at La Maison des Amis des Livres in Paris in December 1921 (with Joyce lurking behind a screen backstage). He had primed Larbaud during regular correspondence in the months leading up to the talk during which he had sent him episode proofs and a schema. When Larbaud expanded his lecture for publication in the *Nouvelle Revue Française*, Joyce was again hovering. Arguing for a 'French Joyce', Larbaud claimed that *Ulysses* was indebted to the naturalist and symbolist movements, to Flaubert and Maupassant, Lautreamont and Rimbaud. As to the Ireland to which Joyce and *Ulysses* belonged, it was, for Larbaud, European: 'He is what we call a pure "Milesian": Irish and old-fashioned Catholic; from the Ireland that has affinities with Spain, France and Italy, but for whom England is a foreign country which nothing, not even the commonality of language, can bring closer.'[67] Although this would be contested by many, especially in Ireland, it was a line that was endorsed by the Irish critic, A. J. (Con) Leventhal, who would later take Beckett's place as lecturer in French at Trinity College, Dublin. Leventhal sought to place Joyce in a cosmopolitan, European tradition in a review originally to be published in the *Dublin Magazine*, edited by Seumas O'Sullivan (*nom de plume* of James Sullivan Starkey). The mere mention of Joyce's name was enough to frighten off the printers, as Leventhal recalled:

> I had got as far as correcting the galley sheets when word came that the printers in Dollards would down tools if they were required to help in the publication of the article. At that time, the very name of James Joyce set the righteous aflame with anger, provoking an odour of sanctimoniousness that seeped into the printing presses of Ireland. [...] My disappointment was so great that together with F. R. Higgins, I started a little magazine *The Klaxon* which did not last beyond the first number and in which was printed a truncated version (to save cost) of my assessment of *Ulysses*.

Klaxon's one issue was edited by Leventhal under the pseudonym Lawrence K. Emery. The editorial announced the intention of connecting

[67]Larbaud 1922, 387. 'Il est ce qu'on appelle un pur "Milésien": Irlandais et catholique de vieille souche; de cette Irlande qui se sent quelques affinités avec l'Espagne, la France et l'Italie, mais pour qui l'Angleterre est un pays êtranger dont rien, pas même la communaute de langue, ne la rapproche.'

Irish culture with the more innovative European scene. Leventhal (writing under the Emery pseudonym) provided a helpful summary of *Ulysses* and insisted that the artist did not have to be homegrown, asserting the relevance of the many significant but exiled Irish writers (often referred to slightingly as 'emigrés'): 'It is not necessary for an artist to develop on his native soil to produce his best work.'[68] Seeing Joyce as both a 'product of his age' and 'a little ahead of it', Leventhal places him within an artistic revolution while linking him with contemporary psychology, claiming: 'He can open up a thought as a surgeon does a body.'[69] He examines the 'relationship of Joyce to modernism' and connects him with Picasso, an 'early follower of tradition breaking into new modes and expressing life from a new angle with a changed vision'.[70] He sees 'in the Dorothy Richardsons and May Sinclairs [...] the influence of the Joyce literary style' but somewhat undermines this view by asserting that '*Ulysses is* essentially a book for the male. It is impossible for a woman to stomach the egregious grossness'. Leventhal makes a nod to Valery Larbaud's approving review of Joyce and concludes that no 'discerning mind' can 'deny genius to Mr. Joyce [...]. His work will persist in spite of the efforts to suppress it'.[71]

Another supportive stance was taken by Dubliner Ernest Boyd (1887–1916), who, after a career in the British consular service, moved to New York and worked as a full-time and respected critic, writing, among other works, the highly influential, canon-making *Ireland's Literary Renaissance* (1917 and 1920), as well as *Contemporary Drama of Ireland* (1917). He offered a strikingly positive account of Joyce and was at pains to underline his belonging to Ireland in an effort to rebuff Larbaud's insistence on Joyce's formation in and debt to the continent. An abridged version of what Boyd saw as Larbaud's dismissive and ill-informed approach to Joyce's Irishness was translated and published by T. S. Eliot in the opening number of *The Criterion*. Boyd particularly objected to the claim that 'with the work of James Joyce and in particular with this *Ulysses* which is soon going to appear in Paris, Ireland is making a sensational re-entrance into high European literature' (*CR*1, 255)[72] and felt impelled to respond. Ironically, in so doing, he amplified interest in Larbaud's article among the English-speaking public on both sides of the Atlantic. His first reply, 'The Expressionism of James Joyce', published in the *New York Herald Tribune* on 28 May 1922 began a lengthy spat that would carry on until 1925, presumably to the delight

---

[68]A. J. Leventhal, 'The *Ulysses* of Mr. James Joyce', *Klaxon* (Winter 1923–24): 14–20, 14. The full text can also be consulted here. http://www.ricorso.net/rx/library/criticism/major/Joyce_JA/Leventhal_AJ.htm
[69]Ibid., 15.
[70]Ibid., 17.
[71]Ibid., 18–19.
[72]Valery Larbaud, 'The "Ulysses" of James Joyce', *The Criterion*, vol. 1, no. 1 (October 1922): 94–103.

of Joyce, who dispensed advice to both as to how each should reply to the other. Boyd misquoted Larbaud's 'rash' claim in *La Nouvelle Revue Française* as: 'Ireland makes a sensational re-entry into European literature'. Having stigmatized what he describes as Larbaud's attempt to 'cut him off from the stream of which he is a tributary' [the Irish Literary Revival], Boyd claimed that the 'logical outcome of this doctrinaire zeal of the coterie is to leave this profoundly Irish genius in the possession of a prematurely cosmopolitan reputation, the unkind fate which has always overtaken writers isolated from the conditions of which they are a part, and presented to the world without any perspective'. In Boyd's view, 'no Irish writer is more Irish than Joyce; none shows more unmistakably the imprint of his race and traditions. The syllogism seems to be: J. M. Synge and James Stephens and W. B. Yeats are Irish, therefore James Joyce is not. Whereas the simple truth is that *A Portrait of the Artist as a Young Man* is to the Irish novel what *The Wanderings of Oisin* was to Irish poetry and *The Playboy of the Western World* to Irish drama, the unique and significant work which lifts the genre out of the commonplace into the national literature' (*CH* 1, 302).[73]

Boyd's gripe was not that Larbaud exalted Joyce but that he ignored or dismissed so much other Irish writing. To claim, as Larbaud had done, that *Ulysses* had a 'European significance' where the works of Synge and Stephens did not, was 'to confess complete ignorance of its genesis, and to invest its content with a mysterious import which the actuality of references would seem to deny'.[74] Boyd was insistent on the centrality of Dublin for Joyce's writing: 'European interest in the work must of necessity be largely technical, for the matter is as local as the form is universal.'[75] In a later review of Herbert Gorman's biography, he reiterated this view. He warmly praises Gorman (a Greenwich village acquaintance of his) for his 'compact little book' that offers 'a guide' to which readers will 'gratefully turn' for its 'unpretentious sobriety of treatment', which is 'an antidote from the hocus-pocus' of 'the obscurantist illuminati' who tried:

> to isolate Joyce, to present him as a 'European' figure entirely unrelated to his own past, to his own country and its literature. To this end it was triumphantly announced in Paris that with Joyce 'Ireland makes a sensational re-entry into European literature,' a statement upon which a fitting comment was to come a year later when the Nobel Prize for Literature was awarded to William Butler Yeats.

Secondly, 'the coterie' needlessly 'embellish the already obscure and elusive' *Ulysses* until it begins 'to assume the portentousness of a cabalistic scripture'.

---

[73]This was also published in Ernest Boyd, *Ireland's Literary Renaissance* [rev. edn.] 1923: 402–12.
[74]Ibid., 412.
[75]Ibid., 411.

Worse, local 'Dublin characters, familiar to everyone living there at the time, were invested with a symbolic significance as being strange, fantastic creations of the author's brain'. In Boyd's view, Gorman's strength was that he saw Joyce not only as the isolated author of *Ulysses* but as 'an Irishman expressing a phase of Ireland as Synge or Yeats, and that his work must be considered as a continuous whole'.[76]

Such claims for the 'Irish' Joyce were not, for several decades, going to convince critics on the continent or later in North America, nor would they gain the upper hand in what passed for critical debate in Ireland. One very early exception to this was Simone Téry whose *L'Île des bardes* (1920) gave Joyce a starring role, praising his ability 'to combine literary innovation with the representation of social and political realities'.[77] Téry was a prominent French journalist based in Ireland in the early 1920s, who covered political and cultural issues for the left-leaning daily newspaper *L'Oeuvre*. Her book was warmly reviewed by Joyce's friend, C. P. Curran, in *The Irish Statesman*[78] and a second review appeared in the *Sligo Champion*:

> Mlle Terry [*sic*] finds this doleful Rabelais an Irishman in the marrow of his bones, believing that within the next hundred years James Joyce will have his statue in Dublin in the company of other literary giants. In a conversation, however, Joyce himself is described as smiling cynically and bitterly at the suggestion that he should abandon his twenty years' exile in Paris. No one wanted him back in the city his sombre and realistic genius has painted with such grim albeit loving touches in 'Ulysses,' although it was evident he was still 'remembering thee, O Sion'.[79]

Other Irish readers, essentially a group of dissenting Irish nationalist intellectuals and politicians belonging to the so-called 'revolutionary generation',[80] warmed to *Ulysses* precisely because they were disappointed at how little had changed despite the newly attained national freedom. They had been formed under the influence of Griffith, whose *United Irishman* had played such an important role in asserting the need for the coming generation to embrace modernity. They were disappointed by how the decade following 1916 had failed to deliver much of the transformational change they had

---

[76]Ernest Boyd, 'Order Established in the Literary Choas [*sic*] of James Joyce', *NYT*, 2 March 1924, BR7.

[77]Simone Téry, *L'Île des bardes. Notes sur la littérature irlandaise contemporaine. Yeats, Synge, Joyce, Stephens* (Paris: Flammarion, Paris, 1925).

[78]C. P. Curran, 'Literature and Life. French Critics and Irish Literature', *IS*, 15 September 1925.

[79]Unsigned review, 'Ireland's Doleful Rabelais', *Sligo Champion*, 29 August 1925, 6. The article was originally published in *T. P and Cassell's Weekly*.

[80]See, for example, Roy Foster, 'A Revolutionary Generation', in John Crowley, Donal O Drisceoil and Mike Murphy, eds., *Atlas of the Irish Revolution* (Cork: Cork University Press, 2017), 116–25.

been solemnly promised. Griffith, who played no part in the Rising but was imprisoned in its aftermath on the grounds that his movement had played a vital role in inspiring it, remained a beacon for many Irish nationalists throughout the difficult period from 1916 until his death in August 1922. Joyce's journalism and private letters align him with such figures, who not only shared Griffith's modernising impulse, but later drew on *Ulysses* in order to assert their beliefs. They included Desmond Fitzgerald, Eimar O'Duffy, Hobson, O'Hegarty and, later, Desmond Ryan. Most of them were more directly connected to the political events leading up to 1916 and its aftermath than they were to the Literary Revival that was a vital part of its prologue; all came to appreciate the lasting importance of that cultural surge. They were, for the most part, pro-Treaty and disenchanted with the partial liberation that the Rebellion had achieved. Thus, although *Ulysses* was set in 1904 and vividly reconstructs the past, they did not read the text in order to look back but so as to look forward. Feeling defeated in the short term, they were in search of an alternative vision for the country, something in line with what Joyce promised when describing *Dubliners* as a 'first step towards the spiritual liberation of my country' (*L1*, 63).

Joyce's novel provided a liberating space, albeit of the imagination, for it could be read as a hopeful foundational text that pitched itself not only against British domination in Ireland but also against the narrowly conservative Catholic Irish nationalist model that was aspired to by many pro- and anti-Treatyites alike. Joyce enthusiasts on the anti-Treaty side were thin on the ground although Ernie O'Malley, who served as assistant chief of staff and who wrote an accomplished literary account of the Civil War, *On Another Man's Wound* (1936), is an important exception.[81] Another was Michael Carolan, director of Intelligence for the anti-treaty forces. He had, through his friend Róisín Walsh, the feminist Republican, who served from 1926 as Dublin's first chief librarian, 'acquired the loan of the first edition of James Joyce's *Ulysses*' as C. S. Andrews, by his own admission, one of the 'dyed-in-the-wool Republicans' recalled.[82] Carolan showed him *Ulysses* 'with great enthusiasm, thumbing rapidly through the pages until reaching the famous Molly Bloom soliloquy, on which he dwelt with shocked surprise which I knew he did not feel-nor did I'.[83] Andrews later became quite a Joyce enthusiast.

Most prominent among the Griffith-inspired figures who appreciated Joyce was Desmond Fitzgerald, who had fought in the General Post Office and served as Minister for both Propaganda and External Affairs in the first Free State Governments. According to his friend and fellow minister, Ernest

---

[81]See Ernie O'Malley, *On Another Man's Wound* (Dublin: Sign of the Three Candles, 1936).
[82]C. S. Andrews, *Man of No Property: An Autobiography*, vol. 2 (Dublin: Mercier Press, 1982), 18, 29.
[83]Ibid., 18–19.

Blythe, Griffith was 'the greatest influence in Desmond Fitzgerald's early life'.[84] A poet and a man of great 'literary and intellectual tastes', Fitzgerald openly voiced his appreciation of Joyce and *Ulysses* at a time when it was far from common to do so (especially so within the government). He subscribed to the first edition of *Ulysses* and visited Joyce in Paris in 1922, telling him that he had proposed that the Free State government nominate Joyce for the Nobel Prize. Even though Joyce told Stanislaus of Fitzgerald's intention 'to send [his] name to Stockholm as a candidate for the Nobel prize', he nurtured few illusions that the Irish government would back the minister's solo run, commenting that Fitzgerald 'will probably lose his portfolio without obtaining the prize' (*LIII*, 61). It is not clear how many supporters Fitzgerald would have found around the cabinet table, but such a nomination would certainly have made a splash for Joyce and Ireland around the globe (although that would not, of course, have guaranteed victory for Joyce). Fitzgerald would probably have had the backing of Blythe (they worked together in cabinet to win state subvention for the Abbey Theatre) and the relatively liberal Minister for Agriculture, Patrick J. Hogan. Years later, in 1982, in a letter to Samuel Beckett, the Dublin architect and Joycean, Niall Montgomery, wrote: 'Heard yesterday, for the first time, from Pierce FitzGerald, who is brother of our Prime Minister, that JAJ's Nobel Prize was blocked by the government of the day at the instigation of Dick Mulcahy! Dick Turpitude!'[85] He was referring to Richard Mulcahy who served as commander-in-chief of the Irish Republican Army (IRA) following the death of Michael Collins and as Minister for Defence in Cosgrave's government. He was leader of Fine Gael from 1944 to 1959. As it turned out, nothing came of Fitzgerald's proposal and Yeats was awarded the prize to muted reaction in Ireland in 1923.

Fitzgerald's high opinion of Joyce[86] would not have won him too many friends on either side of the Treaty split, but it would have resonated within the small but significant group of Irish intellectuals (very often civil servants) who saw value in Joyce and in bringing *Ulysses* home to shake up an increasingly claustrophobic public arena. The novelist Eimar O'Duffy, who, like Joyce, had studied at Belvedere College, worked under Fitzgerald at the Department of External Affairs from late 1922, and was a prominent member of the minority that publicly praised Joyce's novel. His laudatory 1922 review was published in the *Irish Review of Politics, Economics, Art, and Literature*, which he edited along with Bulmer Hobson, P. S. O'Hegarty

[84]Ernest Blythe, witness statement to the Bureau of Military History. <http://www.bureauofmilitaryhistory.ie/reels/bmh/BMH.WS0939.pdf#page=137>. Further references to the statement will be cited parenthetically in the text to the website.
[85]Letter of 25 December 1982 quoted in Christine O'Neill, *Niall Montgomery Dublinman: Selected Writings* (Dublin: Ashfield Press, 2015), 51, 53.
[86]In 1929, while serving as Minister for Defence, Fitzgerald generously presented a copy of the French edition of *Ulysses* to the National Library of Ireland.

and Colm Ó Lochlainn.[87] All four were distinguished Republicans and declared pro-Treatyites for the most part opposed to the use of violence. They were hostile towards the increasingly dominant Catholic Church. Hobson, a Belfast-born Quaker (1883–1969), played a key role in the republican revival in Ulster but, despite his membership of the IRB, opposed the Rising and was kidnapped by its main organizers to stymie his efforts to abort it. He was the owner of copy no. 268 of the first edition of *Ulysses*, which he purchased from O'Hegarty, the co-proprietor with Edward MacLysaght of the Irish Bookshop. The Cork-born O'Hegarty joined the postal service in 1897 and was a member of the Gaelic League, Sinn Féin and of the IRB Supreme Council. He also wrote for Griffith's *United Irishman*. As an outspoken anti-cleric, he argued in 1909 in the pages of the *Irish Nation* that 'the Church should confine itself to such matters as come within its province, and that secular matters remain secular. And we are anticlerical, all of us, in that sense, and rightly so. It is an ancient battle, that has had to be fought in every country in the world, and we also must fight it nay, we are fighting it. And if we are to emancipate the Nation we must fight it to a finish'.[88]

O'Hegarty worked in London for the Post Office between 1902 and 1913 and was involved in the IRB there (swearing in his close friend, Michael Collins, as a member). He was one of 'a group of young civil servants living in London between 1900 and 1914 who were, collectively and individually, to become of major political significance. [...] Padraig Ó Conaire, Robert Lynd, and Bulmer Hobson were also members of the circle', and O'Hegarty 'retained lifelong friendships with Lynd and Hobson'.[89] A member of the Irish Volunteers, O'Hegarty was working in Shrewsbury during the Rising, which he thought was an error, attributing the same opinion to Griffith who, in his view, held 'that a Rising by a minority was unjustifiable'.[90] In 1918, he refused to take the Oath of Allegiance and resigned his position in the Post Office. He later held the position of secretary of the Irish Department of Post and Telegraphs. O'Hegarty was also the editor of *The Separatist*, a short-lived, pro-Treaty paper set up in 1922 by the IRB, which stood for 'the complete separation of Ireland from England'.[91] O'Hegarty was a critical but keen early admirer of *Ulysses*, which he reviewed in the penultimate issue

---

[87]Eimar O'Duffy, 'James Joyce's *Ulysses*', *Irish Review of Politics, Economics, Art, and Literature*, vol. 1, (9 December 1922): 12–13.

[88]O'Hegarty's article of 4 September 1909 in the *Irish Nation* is quoted in W. P. Ryan, *The Pope's Green Island* (Boston: Small, Maynard, 1912), 180–1.

[89]Tom Garvin, 'O'Hegarty, Patrick Sarsfield (P. S.)' in James McGuire and James Quinn, eds., *Dictionary of Irish Biography* (Cambridge: Cambridge University Press, 2014). http://dib.cambridge.org/viewReadPage.do?articleId=a6801.

[90]P. S. O'Hegarty, *The Victory of Sinn Fein*, 134.

[91]O'Hegarty is quoted in Keiron Curtis, *P. S. O'Hegarty (1879–1955): Sinn Féin Fenian* (London: Anthem Press, 2009), 9.

of *The Separatist*, noting both its 'continental' and its 'Irish' credentials. He praised Joyce for taking the English language and using it:

> As it never before was used, and used it triumphantly; he has massed it and manoeuvred it as one masses men at army manoeuvres and does it successfully. He has taken the old, decorous, staid, mould of English prose, broken it up completely and remoulded it into a thing which is Continental rather than English. He has put into *Ulysses* not a story merely, but an epoch, the comedy and tragedy of many lives, and of the people of his own generation.[92]

In quasi-religious terms, he asserts Joyce's patriotism: 'Mr Joyce loves Ireland, especially Dublin [...] not [...] in any "wrap the green flag" sense. But Ireland is all through him and in him and of him'.[93] While admitting that the book caused him 'a certain amount of nausea', he lauds Molly Bloom's monologue as 'the achievement of a master, one of the really big things in modern literature'. This is in marked contrast to Mary M. Colum, who enthusiastically praised the novel as 'an epic of Dublin', but felt Molly Bloom was the 'exhibition of the mind of a female gorilla who has been corrupted by contact with humans'.[94] O'Hegarty, who, on his death, owned four first editions of *Ulysses*, read Joyce's novel as a declaration of Irish cultural independence and stated that 'no Englishman could have written this book. [...] Dublin is all over it, its idiom, its people, its streets, and its ways, its atmosphere, and its intellectual daring'. He underlined how Joyce has given Ireland a unique literary shape and an unprecedented presence on the world-literature stage:

> Here is a big book, perhaps the biggest book that has ever been done in English in the form of fiction. [...] Dublin, its streets and its buildings and its people, he loves with the wholehearted affection of the artist. He may live out of Dublin but he will never get away from it. Ireland at present will probably not love Mr. Joyce, but he had done her honour and stands with Wilde, Moore and Synge in representing the Irish spirit.[95]

Another 'very percipient review'[96] of *Ulysses* was penned by Eimar O'Duffy, the former Irish volunteer who had been deeply involved in pre-revolutionary events and had accompanied MacNeill to his famous showdown with Pearse over the planned insurrection and was present when the countermanding order was issued. He was utterly disenchanted with the violence of 1916

---

[92]P. S. O'Hegarty, 'Mr. Joyce's *Ulysses*', *The Separatist* (2 September 1922): 4.
[93]Ibid.
[94]Mary M. Colum, 'The Confessions of James Joyce'.
[95]P. S. O'Hegarty, 'Mr. Joyce's *Ulysses*', 4.
[96]'An Irishman's Diary', *IT*, 30 June 1958, 6.

and its aftermath, and felt that the War of Independence had been more trouble than it was worth and that the revolutionary impulse to change the country had largely been unrealized. He was critical of the Catholic imprint that dominated the events of Easter 1916 and the dangerous glorification of the military over the political.[97] O'Duffy wrote a cutting critique of the Rising in his semi-fictionalized *The Wasted Island*,[98] which was lambasted. The *Catholic Bulletin* called for it to be not just banned but burnt.[99] In the *Irish Review*, O'Duffy described *Ulysses* as 'the epic of modern Ireland'[100] and uses his review to ask what love of country means at a time when the country is tearing itself apart in a civil war: 'True patriotism' is not the province of the 'gunman' or the 'political theorist' but of the 'common man': 'The tram conductor, the milkman, and the fireman, who carry on with their work while the bullets are flying round them are better patriots than the men who are firing the rifles and braver men too when everything is considered.' Joyce shows a 'love of country' that 'excels that of the common man and receives even less recognition. [...] Ireland is his Beatrice, whom he loves without hope and without return though he is a great artist, perhaps the greatest artist in prose now living'. Thus, O'Duffy believes, 'it is time for Ireland to realise that in James Joyce she has produced a great artist [...] and that in *Ulysses* Joyce has produced a very great work'. He probably never imagined how many decades would pass before his country came to this realization.

---

[97]Frances Flanagan, *Remembering the Revolution: Dissent, Culture and Nationalism in the Irish Free State* (Oxford: Oxford University. Press, 2015).

[98]O'Duffy, *The Wasted Island* (New York: Dodd, Mead, 1920).

[99]Unsigned review of *The Wasted Island* in *CB*, 10 (February 1920): 119–20.

[100]Eimar O'Duffy, 'Review of James Joyce', *Ulysses*, *Irish Review*, vol. 1, no. iv (9 December 1922): 42–3.

CHAPTER FOUR

Ulysses in Catholic Ireland in the 1930s

If the 1920s had been a difficult decade for Joyce and other writers in Ireland, things only got worse in the decade that followed. These were the years of the Great Depression, a period in which Ireland attempted to seal itself off, economically and culturally, from the wider world. The international financial slump was used to strengthen the argument for building the economy as a self-sufficient entity based less on industrial capitalism and more on rural small farming. Many aspired to making culture equally self-sufficient. The newly elected Fianna Fáil government under de Valera introduced heavily protectionist economic policies and engaged in the deleterious Anglo-Irish Trade War that would drag on until 1938, causing further impoverishment. The push to favour farming over a capitalist industrial economy had the added benefit of being consistent with Catholic social teaching and especially Pope Pius XI's 1931 encyclical, *Quadragesimo Anno*, which denounced the evils of modern capitalism.

Even if Belfast's *Irish News* was mostly on the money in its insistence that 'the young people of Ireland have no use for James Joyce' (this was a rebuttal of Humbert Wolfe's claim 'that Yeats's poetry has gone down the sluices of the Shannon water power scheme. Young Ireland prefers the writings of James Joyce, who has invented a language which might be called Disperanto, because it is universally unintelligible'),[1] Joyce stayed in the public eye. Occasionally, however, he was appreciated and his denigrators

---

[1] Anon, 'Poet's Licence', *Irish News*, 25 November 1930. The writer continues: 'I did not find anyone who was prepared to champion James Joyce as his literary favourite. The great majority of those to whom I spoke had not read him, and said so frankly. Others knew him only through reviews of his books, and the few who had read his works were not inclined to boast about the matter.'

challenged. In 1929, *Honesty* republished an interview with the great tenor, John McCormack (who had been made a Papal Knight in 1928 and became a Privy Chamberlain to the Pope in 1929), which had first been published in the *New York World*. He defended Joyce's work as 'a great tour de force' and dismissed charges that it was filth before giving the interviewer a copy of 'Tales Told of Shem and Shaun' (which Joyce had gifted to him), asking him to read it and then tell him what he thought of the new book.[2]

Benedict Kiely also recalled 'impassioned' praise for Joyce coming from an unexpected quarter, that is from a 'cultured' Irish Christian Brother 'with literary tastes' in Trigonometry class in his Ulster secondary school in the 1930s:

> He defended Joyce to a class of half-comprehending young fellows, not just because Joyce was a great writer but because he was a great Irish writer, a national possession, something to be proud of. And because it was evident from the attitude of certain parties in Britain and the USA towards the great novel, *Ulysses*, that yet another attempt was being made to do the Irish down. That the book had been published and praised in France simply went to show that the most civilised people in Europe were with us as they had been with us in the past: sails cracking in Bantry Bay, if only the luck and the weather had been with us. He could not approve, he told us, of literary criticism by Customs and Excise.[3]

But a lone swallow or even a lone Christian Brother does not a Spring make and Joyce largely remained in the nation's bad books. There were regular notices about the trial of *Ulysses* and Judge Woolsey's decision along with many short, usually baffled reviews of instalments of *Work in Progress*. New critical works on Joyce such as Louis Golding's *James Joyce* (1933) received dutiful but unenthusiastic reviews. The first of Joyce's many manuscript sales was noted as was the news that the film rights to *Ulysses* had been acquired by an American film syndicate. Journalists speculated that a 'very sensational' film version was likely and that it would be 'interesting to see what manner of Dublin they will make in Hollywood'.[4] As it turned out, Warner Brothers' interest came to nothing. Later in the decade, a similar project, this time from Paramount with Charles Laughton to play Bloom, was also mooted but again came to nothing. There were regular updates about Joyce's health, his all-too-regular eye operations and his 1931 marriage in London:

> He wore dark glasses, but looked very well, as he came out from his registry office wedding in London last week-end. The story is that he and

[2]'An Interview With John McCormack', *Honesty*, 23 November 1929, 15.
[3]Benedict Kiely, *The Waves behind Us* (London: Methuen, 1999), 5–6.
[4]'An Irishman's Diary', *IT*, 11 October 1932, 4.

his wife went through a marriage ceremony on the Continent twenty-seven years ago, but that this last ceremony in London was to give Mrs. Joyce, as his wife, full benefit of the English law.[5]

The papers also reported the death of Joyce's father, John Stanislaus, and, all told, were far more at home handling his celebrity than they were engaging with his writings. Positive or even neutral notices about *Ulysses* tended to cause a minor flurry of indignation in the letters pages, such as this, from P. M. Finigan, decrying a letter by Francis Hackett in favour of Joyce:

> Never before in my experience of your paper have I read a letter in which there was such evidence of the use of the muck rake, of malice, detraction and misrepresentation. Your correspondent's reference to his reading of James Joyce's *Ulysses*, to sterlised [*sic*] education and under-developed celibate teachers, etc; is simply revolting. I am amazing that your columns should be polluted by such vapouring from the cesspool of a diseased mind.[6]

Joyce's growing global prominence (he made the front page of *Time* magazine on 29 January 1934 to mark the publication of the first legal and authorized edition of *Ulysses* in the United States) made it increasingly difficult and anomalous to dismiss him as a self-exiled muckraker or to simply ignore him. Even if Joyce was clearly at odds with the Free State's increasingly hegemonic Catholic ethos, some shred of embarrassment began to be felt about his lack of official recognition in the country. To have ignored him entirely would have been both churlish and self-damaging. As the critic, Stephen Gwynn put it, in an address to the Associated Booksellers of Great Britain and Ireland at the Gresham Hotel: 'There was another name, which, whether they liked it or not, had European significance – that of James Joyce. Personally, he would not recommend everyone of his acquaintances to read James Joyce, but he recognised that there was great talent in his work, and it was silly to deny it.'[7]

What many at government or official level did was to name check Joyce, acknowledge his fame, but avoid saying anything of substance about his writing. The 1932 *Saorstát Eireann Irish Free State Official Handbook*, edited by Bulmer Hobson, was a good case in point. It positioned Joyce among the distinguished Irish writers of his day: 'The list of eminent Irish men and women writing fiction today is a remarkable one. Critics differ in their estimates of the genius of Mr. George Moore and Mr. James Joyce, but they are at least two writers who have had an enormous influence on

---

[5]'Ireland in London', *IT*, 11 July 1931, 6.
[6]P. M. Finigan, 'Dublin in Decay', *IT*, 24 May 1935, 4.
[7]'The Book Trade', *IT*, 14 July 1930, 5.

the English novel in our time.'[8] Ernest Blythe, now vice-president of the Executive Council, speaking in 1930 at the Booksellers' Congress in Dublin, probably went as far as he could by simply acknowledging Joyce's presence among Ireland's leading contemporary writers:

> This country has given birth to many eminent writers, some of whom, unfortunately, have shaken the dust of the city off their feet, but I believe that all of them have a great deal of affection for Dublin. James Joyce has left Dublin – I do not know whether he will come back or not – but anybody who reads his books will see that he is showing a great deal of interest in his native city.[9]

Blythe was criticized for these hesitant comments by the *Catholic Bulletin*, whose negative editorial was picked up by provincial newspapers, such as the *Waterford News and Star*, which noted: 'The Editor does not forget to call attention – as the "News" did a short time ago – to Mr. Ernest Blythe's exhibition of tenderness for that past master in pornography, Mr. James Joyce.'[10] Later in his speech, Blythe reverted to shoring up the party line on the draconian censorship regime and claimed that 'none of the books that were condemned was of any appreciable literary value, and nobody would lose by being unable to get a copy of any of them'. 'None of them', he concluded disingenuously, 'was a book likely to have a very wide circulation'.[11] Given the economic state of the country in these years, few, in any case, could have afforded to buy Joyce's books. To claim, however, that the banned books had no 'appreciable literary value' was a blatant lie at this time in which books, and especially those by Irish authors, were being banned *en masse*. By the first half of 1936, 715 books had been banned, causing *The Irish Times* to list some of the Irish 'victims', such as Clarke, Beckett, O'Faoláin, before asking: 'Are they all immoral?'[12] By the end of the decade, the Censorship Board had banned 1,193 books giving substance to *The Irish Times* opinion that 'only in the totalitarian States is the censorship more rigid than that which rattles its padlocks in Dublin'.[13] By 1943, the figure was 1,700. While it is true, as Wexler has argued, that 'censorship advertised the work of Joyce [...] far beyond the avant-garde audience',[14] there is less evidence to back his conclusion that it had the immediate knock-on

---

[8]Bulmer Hobson, *Saorstát Eireann Irish Free State official handbook* (Dublin: Talbot Press, 1932), 280.
[9]Quoted in *IT*, 12 July 1930, 7.
[10]'Some Excellent Irish Periodicals', *Waterford New and Star*, 8 August 1930, 9.
[11]Ibid.
[12]*IT*, 9 May 1936, 7.
[13]'London Letter', *IT*, 18 May 1939, 6.
[14]Joyce Piell Wexler, *Who Paid for Modernism? Art, Money, and the Fiction of Conrad, Joyce, and Lawrence* (Fayetteville: University of Arkansas Press, 1997), 91.

effect of helping to sell copies outside of a small coterie. Advertising, name recognition, fame and notoriety were all very well but equally not of much use when copies of *Ulysses* remained so difficult to obtain. A short article entitled '*Ulysses* in the "Bus"', published in 1937 in *The Irish Times*, reports seeing a 'country girl in the late twenties [...] engrossed in a big book. [...] it was James Joyce's *Ulysses*, of all things'. 'How', the journalist wondered, did the girl on the number 65 bus 'obtain possession of it?'[15] This anecdote reveals that *Ulysses*, despite no formal ban, was still contraband in Ireland and that Joyce's ongoing predicament was that his notoriety continued to dwarf his book sales. There was truth in Myles na gCopaleen's 1956 claim that 'Ireland, north as well as south, subsists in a maze, or celtic twilight, of hidden, underhand and undeclared censorships',[16] and in his dark assertion that there had been no need to ban *Ulysses* because 'any person asking for it in a bookshop would probably be lynched'.[17]

The relentless censorship policy and the asphyxiating atmosphere it created undoubtedly hurt Joyce, but it was more damaging for less acclaimed Irish writers, mostly hoping to sell their books on the home market, even if they tended to wear their bans as a badge of honour. Liam O'Flaherty was right in accusing what he called the 'soutaned bullies' of hurling 'the accusation of sexual indecency at any book that might plant the desire for civilization and freedom in the breasts of their wretched victims'.[18] Voices of moderation and inclusion were seen as contrarian and were pushed to the margins of the halting public debate in what was, increasingly, a restrictive and puritanical Catholic confessional state. As is all too clear today, active censorship was only the tip of the iceberg.

One of the few stalwart publications that had consistently given space to differing views, *The Irish Statesman*, was described by the *Catholic Bulletin* as a 'persistent carrier and sprayer of moral Disease'[19] and folded in 1930. In the words of Austin Clarke, 'a howl of primitive delight greeted its disappearance'.[20] A disillusioned A. E. moved to England two years later. W. B. Yeats was also 'profoundly alienated by the narrow, puritanical and Catholic bourgeois nationalism that abounded in the new state'.[21] The disappearance of the *Irish Statesman*, partly caused by two expensive legal cases, negatively affected Joyce, depriving him of regular exposure in the country but this was gleefully celebrated by the ever-adversarial *Catholic Bulletin*, which had used countless editorials to condemn the publication

---

[15]'"Ulysses" on the Omnibus', Irishman's Diary, *IT*, 4 March 1937, 4.

[16]Myles na Gopaleen, 'Censorship', *IT*, 9 February 1956, 8.

[17]Myles na Gopaleen, 'J-Day', *IT*, 16 June 1954, 4.

[18]Liam O'Flaherty, 'The Irish Censorship' (1932) in *The American Spectator*, cited and reprinted in J. Carlson, ed., *Banned in Ireland* (London: Routledge, 1990), 140.

[19]*CB*, October 1930, vol. XX, no. 10, 909.

[20]W. R. Rodgers, *Irish Literary Portraits* (London: BBC, 1972), 200.

[21]Frances Flanagan, *Remembering the Revolution*, 30.

and its promotion of modern Irish literature. It listed six instances of its 'spread of moral rottenness'. Between the first (a review of 'the filthy journal *To-Morrow*') and the third instance ('the publication, for W. B. Yeats, of his undelivered speech on Divorce') came, almost inevitably, the accusation of giving prominent space to Joyce who was, the *Bulletin* complained, 'styled with dreary iteration "Ireland's greatest artist"':[22]

> The persistent commendation and advocacy, in articles, reviews, editorial paragraphs, of the obscene works of James Joyce, and especially and by name, of his book called *Ulysses*. These commendations cover the entire period from August, 1924, to the collapse of the journal in Spring, 1930.[23]

The *Irish Statesman* had indeed paid a lot of attention to Joyce but much of it was mixed. Commenting on a 1927 edition of *transition*, an unsigned article complained that Joyce 'is like a terrier who burrows energetically into a hole so that at last one only sees an agitated ceaseless waving of the tip of its tail: a great literary talent wasting itself on obscurities which it will never be worth anyone's while to unravel'.[24] More often comment was cautiously positive but Joyce would not be the only writer that would lose out in the absence of what the *Bulletin* called 'The Plunkett House weekly journal' (in reference to its major backer, the Anglo-Irish agricultural reformer, Horace Plunkett), which 'has always paraded its cult of writers whose works are deeply tainted with obscenity'. The reason for this relentless attack was that the *Irish Statesman* had, under A. E.'s guidance, managed to exercise a moderating role on government. Its disappearance deprived the cultural world of its key voice in the ongoing struggle between what Nicholas Allen calls 'literary authority and political power in the early Irish Free State'.[25]

The foundation of the Irish Academy of Letters in 1932 was an attempt by Irish writers to reclaim some of that lost authority. This was also the year of the vast and triumphalist Eucharistic Congress in Dublin, which came hot on the heels of the 1929 Catholic Emancipation centenary celebrations. The title of the British Pathé film of the event captures its scale and success: 'Phoenix Park, Dublin. A million people kneel in Worship when Pontifical High Mass is celebrated, with solemn splendour & majestic ritual, at conclusion of International Eucharistic Congress.' Marking the fifteenth centenary of Saint Patrick's arrival, it was the greatest show of Catholic force that the country had ever seen. Joyce watched from afar and referred to the event in *Finnegans Wake* as the 'neuchoristic congressulations, quite

[22]*CB*, vol. XX, no. 5 May 1930, 424.
[23]*CB*, vol. XX, no. 10, October 1930, 910.
[24]'Magazines', *IS*, 10 September 1927, 21.
[25]Nicholas Allen, 'Free Statement: Censorship and the Irish Statesman' in Fran Brearton and Eamon Hughes, eds., *Last Before America – Irish and American Writing* (Belfast: Blackstaff Press, 2001), 97.

purringly excited' (*FW* 234.20–22). Closer to home, writers and artists cannot but have felt a further compression of the space available for free expression. All of which fed into the establishment, by Yeats and Shaw, of the academy. Although they wished to reward literary accomplishment, they were also concerned to bring together the country's most prominent writers to oppose literary censorship. The whole project was less about self-aggrandizement and more about the survival of writers and the defence of space for critical debate. Not surprisingly, the academy was constantly attacked by *The Catholic Bulletin*, which associated it with George Russell (the 'Mahatma') and the 'whole Bureau of Billyboys' and their 'parade of putridity'.[26] Most of the leading Irish literary figures of the day including James Stephens, Oliver St John Gogarty, F. R. Higgins, Padraic Colum, Seán O'Faoláin, Frank O'Connor, Austin Clarke, Lennox Robinson, Brinsley MacNamara and St John Ervine agreed to join but Joyce declined and became, through his absence, all the more conspicuous. Yeats' invitation had seemed genuine: 'Of course the first name that seemed essential both to Shaw and myself was your own. […] If you go out of our list it is an empty sack indeed.' Yet it did not have the desired effect on Joyce who replied somewhat primly: 'it is now thirty years since you first held out to me your helping hand' and asking him to 'please convey my thanks also to Mr. Shaw whom I have never met'. Joyce wished the academy well while arguing that he had no place in it: 'I feel quite clearly that I have no right whatsoever to nominate myself as a member of it' (*SL*, 365). This rather self-serving '*Non serviam*' allowed Joyce to steal the show as it made the news around the world with the *New York Times* headlining its piece: 'Joyce Rejects Bid of Irish Academy'.[27]

Joyce's refusal would have irritated but not surprised his fellow Irish writers who must have resented a lack of solidarity from their most famous compatriot who had spent a decade drumming up international solidarity for his own literary battles. Several of them had signed the petition on his behalf against Samuel Roth's piracy just a few years earlier. Some of these writers and many of Joyce's Irish readers were already alienated by each expensive new instalment of *Work in Progress*, which would eventually be published as *Finnegans Wake*. Seán O'Faoláin penned a series of articles complaining about the 'prohibitive price' of 'Anna Livia Plurabelle' and described *Work in Progress* as one of the most 'pathetic literary adventures I know, pathetic chiefly because of its partial success, for even the most sympathetic and imaginative will have smiled wanly several times as they read, and laughed in despair long before the end'.[28] O'Faoláin's main issue was that Joyce's use of language ignored the need

[26]*CB*, vol. XXIII, no. 9, September 1933, 694–5.
[27]*NYT*, 28 October 1932, Section BOOKS ART, 17.
[28]Seán O'Faoláin, 'Almost Music', *Hound & Horn*, II (January–March 1929): 178–80, 180.

for 'universal intelligibility'. In various articles and reviews,[29] he accused
Joyce of engaging in 'maltreatment of language', using it in an utterly
idiosyncratic 'merely ahistoric' way. In Joyce's hands, language loses its
representative power: 'It comes from nowhere, goes nowhere, is not part
of life at all. It has one reality only, the reality of the round and round of
children's scrawls in their first copybooks, many circles of nothing.'[30] From
Paris, Eugene Jolas jumped to Joyce's defence in his 'The Revolution of
Language and James Joyce' which was part of *Our Exagmination Round
His Factification for Incamination of Work in Progress* (1929), a book
of essays, as Kevin Dettmar put it, that was 'orchestrated (and titled) by
Joyce himself'.[31] Samuel Beckett's contribution, entitled 'Dante… Bruno.
Vico. Joyce', was penned just a few short months after he had arrived in
Paris and was written with Joyce almost literally reading over Beckett's
shoulder.[32] Beckett maps out Joyce's relationship with Dante, discussing
their common exile, their use of language, and the question of authority and
the role of the writer in establishing himself in language. Striving to paint
both Dante and Joyce as reaching beyond provincial concerns, he describes
Dante as he 'attacks the world's Portadownians', an attempt, this, to vilify
campanilismo (excessive attachment to one's home place or country). The
whole piece reads like a response to O'Faoláin, a justification of Joyce's use
of language, and, in Dante, it finds a historical precedent for Joyce's literary
enterprise. The fact that Joyce had to draw on and pilot a 22-year-old to
plead his cause and justify himself before the court of Irish critical opinion
speaks volumes for how precarious his reputation was in Ireland at this
point. In any case, the entire *Exagmination* was greeted coolly in Dublin
where it was seen as further evidence of Joyce being served by a subservient
and acquiescent clique.

John Eglinton's 1935 comments about Joyce as 'a mechanical inventor'
who had lost his way but was supported by 'a company of very able
henchmen' were shared by many in Dublin:

> I am all for lucidity and logic, and the writer who in his work raises a
> problem […] of what he means, appears to me to bring into annoying
> prominence his own idiosyncrasy. These new 'telescoped' words affect
> me as monstrosities, like the Siamese twins, repulsive in their congenital
> deprivation of the inborn right of words to individuality. Words should

[29]See Seán O'Faoláin, 'The Cruelty and Beauty of Words', *Virginia Quarterly*, vol. IV (April 1928): 208–25; 'Almost Music', *Hound & Horn*, II (January–March 1929): 178–80, and some shorter pieces in *The Irish Statesman*.
[30]Seán O'Faoláin, 'Style and the Limitations of Speech', *Criterion*, vol. VIII (1928): 67–87, 86.
[31]Kevin J. H. Dettmar, 'The Joyce That Beckett Built', *James Joyce Quarterly*, vol. 35/36, nos. 1–4 (Summer–Fall 1998): 605–19, 605.
[32]Ibid., 610.

exist to do the bidding of the mind, but Joyce's palace of art is an unruly house in which words are masters.[33]

Each new excerpt of *Work in Progress* seemed to alienate Joyce from his own readers and to complicate the acceptance of *Ulysses*, which was tarred retrospectively with the same charge of needless obscurity. Ernest Boyd, who had been an enthusiastic promoter of *Ulysses*, regretted the obscure turns that 'Work in Progress' was taking but also Joyce's refusal to join the academy (of which he himself was an associate member) and felt that it 'emphasized his desire to be disassociated from the intellectual life of his country'. Boyd's description of the academy being 'formed primarily as a protest and protection against the encroachments of censors and politicians upon the independence and integrity of Irish literature'[34] is instructive. The original invitation sent by Yeats and Shaw to prospective members emphasized these issues. Censorship could lead to confining 'an Irish author to the British and American market, and thereby make it impossible for him to live by distinctive Irish literature'. By wielding their influence 'collectively and unanimously', they hoped that the censors could be more successfully opposed.[35] There are many possible motives for Joyce's refusal to join. Perhaps, like the editorialist of the *Catholic Bulletin*, he worried that the academy was a relic of the Ascendancy or he feared that Yeats was using his name as a red rag to taunt more extreme Catholic opinion. Whatever his reasons, Joyce was missing the point or was not interested in it. The academy was an attempt by Irish writers to unite in opposition to politicians 'bent upon stifling all manifestations of freedom of thought' and as such it was virulently attacked especially in clerical quarters. In any case, even if Joyce was not a member, he might as well have been because he was repeatedly singled out for attack by those who opposed the academy. A typically vitriolic assault came from the Clongowes-based Jesuit, Fr Patrick Gannon, who denounced the academy as a 'mutual admiration society' in a vociferous public lecture at Dublin's 2,000-seat Theatre Royal. His lecture is typical of the clergy's approach: there is a refusal of the modern, a dismissal of the Anglo-Irish, but also of those nefarious Catholic writers who, like Brinsley MacNamara, laid bare the grim realities of life in small town Ireland. All foreign influences are to be repulsed along with those Irish writers who have found success abroad or by virtue of being abroad. Branding them 'émigrés', Fr Gannon believed that by their absence they had forfeited the right and lost the competence to write about Ireland. The academy should have included those who had 'given the best expression

[33] John Eglinton, *Irish Literary Portraits* (London: Macmillan, 1935), 155, 157–8.
[34] Ernest Boyd, 'Joyce and the New Irish Writers', 700.
[35] Invitation from W. B. Yeats and G. B. Shaw to potential members to join the Irish Academy of Letters, MS 31,015, NLI.

of literature of the mind and heart of Ireland [...] a faithful mirror of Irish life'. Instead:

it was only the life of Ireland as seen through squinting windows by the eyes of men who would seem to have dabbled disastrously in the works of that arch-charlatan, Freud. It left whole areas of our life unexplored and unexplained in order to concentrate upon the sordid, the morbid, the macabre and the unclean. [...] It was hard to see by what authority they had been invited to come over and be crowned with a wreath of shamrocks, instead of bays, as a mark of national veneration.[36]

A. E. defended the academy and Joyce in the *Irish Times*, accusing Fr Gannon of 'public bad manners' in his claim that 'the art of the majority of its members is an art devoted chiefly to the cesspool'. He took issue with Joyce being compared to Ovid, who is accused of alluring 'his readers to pleasures which may be called sinful'. That charge, A. E. insists, could not be brought against Joyce 'even in the frankest pages' of *Ulysses*. Joyce is, rather 'the profound surgeon of the soul, probing its abscesses'. Fr Gannon, he concluded, 'is not sensitive enough to be a critic of literature'.[37] A. E., who had his supporters among the more liberal clergy, such as the Jesuit, Fr Thomas Finlay, vice president of Horace Plunkett's Irish Agricultural Organisation Society, was being too generous. Fr Gannon and his followers did not seek to be critics of literature; they wished to ensure that their flocks were sheltered from all literature, native and modern, which they felt undermined their Catholic Irish worldview. The debate did not end with A. E.'s intervention. Another of Gannon's fellow Jesuits, Fr Arthur Little from St. Stanislaus College, Tullamore, entered the fray to argue that writers like Joyce should not be included in the academy because, in following a 'certain modern manner of writing on immoral subjects', they did not represent the ideals or the mentality of Ireland any more than the Anglo-Irish did. Literature should represent the ideals of the majority and not be critical or adversarial but it was at its most pernicious when penned by writers of 'genius' capable of seducing their readers into evil:

Can we rely on the new academy to crown such works only as would not be regarded as immoral by the mass of the public? No member of the new academy will approve of immoral literature as such; but many seem to include under their definition of what is moral, works that are regarded as dangerous by Irish public opinion. 'A. E.' defends James Joyce and Professor Rudmose-Brown defends Marcel Proust in the letters referred to. Now, it is the very poetical genius of these writers, by which they

---

[36]'The New Irish Academy. Dublin Priest's Criticism'. *IT*, 14 November 1932.
[37]Letter from A. E to *IT*, 15 November 1932, 7.

can communicate imaginatively the experiences they describe, that makes them peculiarly seductive to evil in our eyes.[38]

Regardless of what the Academy might deem, the Irish people could rest assured, Fr Little concluded, that the censorship board, an expression of the government and hence of the people, would see to it that no unsuitable or 'evil' material would be allowed to be sold: 'The people of Ireland have, therefore, desired to be protected against immoral books. [...] If "A. E." doubts this, let him consult the censors.'[39] A. E. replied and suggested that Fr Little's order ought 'to impose on him the Pythagorean vow of silence for seven years until he has something to say, and not merely a desire to say something'.[40]

As if the Irish clerics alone were not capable of fighting their corner, the well-known English priest and writer, Fr Owen Dudley, weighed in with a lecture at the Grand Central Cinema in Limerick. Stating that the Church 'was at war to safeguard the sanctity of the home' which was threatened by 'modern scientists, philosophers, and spiritualists', he claimed that 'seventy per cent of the films and books produced at the moment advocated sensuality, free love, and lust, and displayed them in the glamorous aspect to the public'.[41] He then asked to 'register a protest against the Irish Academy of Letters' and its members, many of whom were 'literary pagans' and 'not real Irishmen'. 'James Joycese's [sic] indecency no decent Irishman would read. It would be difficult to conceive a body of literary men less representative of Ireland's mentality, morality and spirituality.'[42]

Commentary on the Academy lingered into the following year and Joyce remained a stick with which to beat George Russell. An article in the *Waterford News and Star* about a lecture by Professor Edmund Curtis to the Trinity College Gaelic Society once again attacked A. E. for giving a lecture in which he 'lauded to the skies':

> the writings of James Joyce, singling out for special praise Mr. Joyce's *Ulysses*. James Joyce possesses some admirable qualities as a story-teller, but in the immortal *Ulysses* he displays a desire – quoting the words of Macbeth – to clean his stuffed bosom of perilous stuff and in the attempt he displays merely the skill of the pornographist. It is just as if a literary man, overcome by nausea, vomited publicly. If this is the sort of stuff that is to be recommended by the new Academy, or by any of its members, then even ' a clotted mass of ignorance and superstition' [his description

---

[38]Arthur Little, SJ, 'The New Irish Academy', letter to *IT*, 2 December 1932, 4.
[39]Ibid.
[40]A. E., Letter to the Editor, *IT*, 3 December 1932, 6.
[41]'A Scathing Denunciation', *Limerick Leader*, 28 November 1932, 3.
[42]Ibid.

of the Gaeltacht] – to employ the words of Mr. George Russell – would be infinitely preferable.[43]

Some months later, in March 1933, James Stephens, interviewed by the *Irish Times*, made a rare pitch in favour of the inclusion of Joyce and Shaw in the academy, arguing that Irish writers, living both at home and abroad, had every right to be part of it:

> You should not exclude any great Irish writer from the Academy [...] whatever your personal feelings on him may be. For instance, you should not exclude James Joyce, because Joyce put Dublin on the map as far as the world was concerned, even more than the 'Sweeps' have done. Although he may have painted Dublin red, he certainly painted it in a very lifelike way.[44]

Such a liberal view was very much the minority sentiment in a country cowed by Frs Gannon and Little. Anecdotal evidence suggests that priests were not above intervening directly and confiscating an offending copy of *Ulysses* in the unlikely event of it being noticed on one of their parishioner's bookshelves: essentially, the 'people of Ireland' were not sufficiently qualified to come to their own conclusions about what they should read; hence, the academy should be made up of safe 'national' figures drawn from and representative of the Catholic population.

Joyce's refusal to lend his name to bolster attempts to protect the increasingly marginalized Irish writers cannot have helped his own cause at home. Equally, however, had he joined his mere presence would have further muddied the waters as many continued to see him as he was presented in 1931 in a venomous article in *Catholic World* by his former University contemporary (then District Justice) Michael Lennon. Lennon, with whom Joyce had seemingly been in friendly contact (he visited Joyce in Paris the same year and, after dinner, asked for and received a signed copy of *Ulysses*), attacked Joyce's father and described Joyce's own behaviour, from a young age, as being 'cynical', the result of 'the grinding poverty of his home life (that) had soured him'.[45] Lennon plays fast and loose with the facts, making every effort to discredit 'the ill-clad, unshaven, and unkempt' Joyce and describing how, on leaving University, the writer 'found wretchedly paid employment as manager of a back-street cinema. Occasionally he did hack journalism for the Old *Freeman's Journal*, and, like O'Casey, tried to write lyric poetry'. Disparaging comments follow on the nature of his relationship with Nora,

---

[43]*Waterford News and Star*, 24 February 1933, 9.
[44]*IT*, 3 March 1933, 3.
[45]Michael J. Lennon, 'James Joyce', *Catholic World*, vol. 132 (March 1931): 641–52. The typescript of this article is kept in Box seven, folder five of the Joyce Collection at the HRC. All citations are from this version.

to whom 'he did not grant the protection of even a civil marriage' and on her situation as 'the mistress' who gave birth to 'the spurious offspring'. He further claims that Joyce spent the entire First World War in Rome, working in a bank before resigning:

> to work in the department of propaganda which the British government had established in Italy for the purpose of inflaming Italian feeling against Austria so as to pave the way for the breach of solemn treaty which the Italian government had to commit as a preliminary to entering the War upon the side of the Allies. [...] The British government appears to have been satisfied with Joyce's services for which he was well remunerated.

As a result of the Roman experience with 'food shortages and military restrictions', Joyce's nerves – 'not the nerves to take kindly to intense strain' – suffered and his mind:

> staggered and reeled amid the conflict with his alter ego, the alter ego which had once prayed so hard for grace. If many quite ordinary Irish Catholics of no particular introspective turn of mind were yielding, at this time, to a process of aberration, what a criss-cross of emotions must then have been playing upon the unhappy mind that was Joyce's!

This was the background to Joyce's writing *Ulysses*, a work destined to join the list of his other failed literary productions – 'a few trite, third-rate poems, some most ordinary short stories, and as dull a play as ever was written', and *A Portrait*, 'a wretchedly constructed affair' that displays 'patches of promising, if very gross dialogue' but is 'nothing more than a safety valve for the emotions pent up within him upon the death of his mother, and his disappointment at his failure in the University'. The 'freakish *Ulysses*' opens 'the sewers of the mind to an intelligentsia saturated with pseudo-Freudianism [...] the book is not so much pornographic as physically unclean, and it reeks with religion so introduced as to make the verb selected peculiarly apposite'. And yet, Joyce was not without talent and:

> were the mood to seize him, he might be able, some day or other, to give us fine, strong prose, in which Catholics could take pride. That is to say, he may have a future as an essayist. As a poet or novel-writer, he will always fail. [...] Yet, in this man's heart there must still be the broken light of faith. It may be that as the days darken, these lights will begin to strengthen. And for Joyce, the days are darkening as for no one else. [...] Will this growing darkness lead to a great spiritual vision. Only God can tell.

Lennon's article, though far from unique, was the most scurrilous written about Joyce by an Irish commentator. Joyce did not see it at the time (the

Colums thought it better to keep it from him) but he was deeply offended when he did read it and felt his friends had done him a disservice. The accusation of secretly joining the British propaganda service particularly incensed him, also because he was alleged to have done so '"at a time [...] when the British government was carrying on a war of its own against the nationalist forces in Ireland which culminated in the Easter Week rebellion"'. Joyce claimed there could be 'little doubt' that the article had inflamed American Irish hostility towards Ulysses[46] and damaged his reputation. In January 1932, presumably on the grounds that bad publicity was better than none, Joyce wrote to Miss Weaver, telling her that he had suggested that Eugene Jolas 'should print passages from the three recent attacks on me by Lennon, O. G. and "One who knows him"' (L1, 313) in transition. O. G. was Oliver St John Gogarty, who had never forgiven Joyce for how he was depicted as Buck Mulligan in Ulysses. Joyce probably had in mind a review written by 'A Fellow Dubliner' of Stuart Gilbert's James Joyce's Ulysses: A Study in 1931,[47] which claims to interview Gogarty. The author of the review self-identifies as a Dublin contemporary of Joyce and may have been Gogarty himself or perhaps Lennon.[48] While acknowledging that Joyce's literary pedigree 'comes of first class stock' and that he 'has written very commendable prose' in A Portrait, 'it just fails in that quality which would make prose what is called first class [...] yet some responsible English writers have been praising Mr. Joyce's work in a superlative way'. This 'has come to the aid of a cabal of spurious literary people who have been trying for the past nine years to push Ulysses on the public – and especially on the foreign public – as the greatest masterpiece of modern English literature'. Gilbert is a victim, manipulated by Joyce under whose 'supervisional collaboration' the study was written. The author wonders: 'Was Joyce pulling Stuart Gilbert's leg?' (which echoes with Gogarty's later description of Finnegans Wake as 'the most colossal leg-pull in literature since McPherson's Ossian'[49]) and claims that Gilbert's 'main thesis [...] that Joyce is the modern counterpart of Homer' is unfounded. Joyce 'is constantly pulling the long Homeric bow in order to astonish the uninitiated; and he has succeeded to some extent, especially with the Americans, where classical learning is not very widely cultivated'. At the same time, 'as a tour de force in the use of the English language Ulysses is an object for just and honest admiration, even

---

[46]Willard Potts, 'Joyce's Notes on the Gorman Biography', ICarbS, vol. IV, no. 2 (Spring–Summer 1981): 83–100, 91.

[47]Oliver St. John Gogarty, 'A Fellow Dubliner', 'The Veritable James Joyce according to Stuart Gilbert and Oliver St. John Gogarty', International Forum, no. 1 (July 1931): 13–17. Reprinted, at Joyce's request in transition, no. 21 (March 1932): 273–82 (CH 1, 556–9).

[48]John J. Slocum and Herbert Cahoon, 'A Note on Joyce Biography', The Yale University Library Gazette, vol. 28, no. 1 (July 1953): 44–50, 47, speculate that Lennon is the author.

[49]Oliver St J. Gogarty, 'Roots in Resentment James Joyce's Revenge', The Observer, 7 May, 1939.

for wonder'. But Joyce's linguistic gymnastics are in vain and whatever his '*claquers*' may claim, his streams of consciousness make up:

> a jamboree of senseless syllables here and a race of long-sounding words there, the latter having meaning in themselves but no meaning when strung together. [...] It is the stream that flows from a diseased mind – Bloom's – as you will easily recognise if you examine similar transcripts of the senseless chatter indulged in by certain types of lunatics in insane asylums. [...] *Ulysses* is not a document that stands alone. The pathological records in the archives of lunatic asylums are its companions.

Joyce, in short, 'is a joke' but his jokes have none of Swift's '*sæva indignatio*'; he 'is not a mocking Dante but a mockery of him: all Dublin is his Inferno'.

At times, it must have seemed to Joyce as he looked west from Paris to Britain, Ireland and the United States, that no one really *got Ulysses* and that those who did simply chose to disparage it. In reality, in 1930s Ireland, many critics did not know how to react with 'some insisting that Joyce is a genius of the first magnitude, and others that he is merely a madman', as Brinsley MacNamara put it. At the same time, MacNamara expressed irritation that Joyce's reputation was being made abroad, 'by critics who are without intimate knowledge of the life from which it sprang'.[50] Those best placed to judge *Ulysses* were Joyce's fellow Dubliners: 'no Dubliner can escape its authentic Dublin quality'. The problem was that few locals engaged with the text. Yet it was 'against our international standing' that 'we have not issued a considered opinion of a work which has excited all the rest of the world; but this, clearly, is a job for some Dubliner who would also be a critic, and we do not now seem able to produce an intelligence of that kind'. It would be decades before this lacuna would be filled and Ireland would begin to assess Joyce's place within its own culture. In the meantime, those wishing to find help in reading *Ulysses* would have to make do with Stuart Gilbert's guide, which elicited little enthusiasm from Irish reviewers, such as Conal O'Riordan, who complained that the author of this 'seemingly erudite and undoubtedly clever, if juvenile book seems acquainted with every subject under the sun except the actual city of Dublin, which most of his readers have regarded as the essential theme of Mr. Joyce's work'.[51]

O'Riordan was correct with regard to Gilbert's ignorance of Dublin but Dublin was not his theme. In the meantime, Joyce remained outside the scope of Irish academic interest partly because the field was led by critics such as Daniel Corkery, who was appointed as professor of English literature

---

[50]Brinsley MacNamara, 'Great Influences: Recording the Spirit of the Nation', *IT Supplement*, 21 January 1932, 99.

[51]Conal O'Riordan, 'Gaudeamus', *The New Statesman*, vol. XXXC, no. 892 (31 May 1930): 247–8.

at University College Cork in 1931 (ahead of Seán O'Faoláin, his former
student). Corkery was one of the chief arbiters of the country's literary
culture and no one was better suited to this role in de Valera's isolationist
Ireland. His books, *The Hidden Ireland* (1924) and *Synge and Anglo-Irish
Literature* (1931), cemented his central role. He was dismissive of the reliance
on foreign critics to decide what was good or bad in Irish literature:

> a normal literature while welcoming the criticism of outsiders neither
> lives nor dies by such criticism. It abides the judgement of its own people,
> and by that judgement lives and dies. If this literature then be not a
> normal literature it is not a national literature, for normal and national
> are synonymous in literary criticism.[52]

Such a view did not augur well for Joyce because without 'the criticism of
outsiders' he would have been ignored even more easily at home. Corkery
foresaw no place for the exiled writer and declared that 'a normal literature is
written within the confines of the country which names it. It is not dependent
on expatriates'[53] (he equally regarded Anglo-Irish figures like Yeats as mere
interlopers, writers of colonial literature). Corkery's criteria were nationality,
religion and the land, and, as Declan Kiberd noted, 'Corkery's three notes were
the very forces which had driven Stephen Dedalus into exile'.[54] Even if they
came at these issues from diametrically opposed positions, Corkery and Joyce
were part of the same generation and, taking the very long view, Corkery is
sometimes seen today as the first post-Colonial Irish intellectual,[55] while Joyce,
who pitilessly exposed the limits of nationalist argumentation, might be seen as
the first revisionist. Back in 1923, Joseph Hone connected them in terms of the
young Irish Catholic male protagonists of their novels: 'This young Irishman
has, however, entered literature in a few other recent books besides those of Mr.
Joyce – in the books, for example, of Mr. Daniel Corkery, a talented writer from
Cork, whose *Hounds of Bamba*, a collection of stories about the Volunteers,
has been much admired' (*CH* 2, 298). Both spoke for their generation but in
very different ways. It was common to laud Corkery at Joyce's expense. One
critic, 'Sandrach', praised Corkery's second book, *The Threshold of Quiet*, for
not being 'morbid in the sense of being unhealthy or perverted like the work of
trashy writers, such as Liam O'Flaherty or James Joyce'.[56]

---

[52]Daniel Corkery, *Synge and Anglo-Irish Literature – A Study* (Cork: Cork University Press,
1931), 3.
[53]Ibid.
[54]Declan Kiberd, 'Writers in Quarantine?: The Case for Irish Studies', in *Crane Bag*, 3, 1 (1979),
9–21 reprinted in *Crane Bag Book of Irish Studies* (Dublin: Blackwater Press 1982): 341–53,
348.
[55]See Heather Laird, 'Introduction: Daniel Corkery as Postcolonial Critic', in Laird, H. ed.,
Daniel Corkery's Cultural Criticism: Selected Writings (Cork: Cork University Press), 1–14.
[56]Sandrach, 'Voice of Gaeldom', *Sinn Féin*, 8 November 1924, 8. This was probably written by
Aodh de Blácam.

Just what to do with writers like Joyce, who had 'gone astray', was a problem that exercised the minds of Irish critics and readers alike. It was Corkery's influential belief that for writers who left the country, Ireland 'was never a patria in any sense' and that expatriation was nothing less than 'a chronic disease from Goldsmith's time [...] to our own time of Shaw, Joyce and Moore'.[57] In 1934, at a meeting of the Blackrock Literary and Debating Society, Frank Carty fretted that there were too few Irish native writers at work in Ireland and too many at work abroad. While writers in other countries wrote primarily for their own people, 'Irish writers [...] worked with one eye on England and the other on America'. Most Irish writers lived abroad and:

> continued, to find their matter in Irish life, but their choice and treatment of it were governed or were imposed on them by alien considerations. [...] With the exception of Canada, Australia, and similar British colonies, Ireland was the only country under the sun whose writers were almost completely dependent on a 'foreign market'.

Carty echoed Yeats when describing 'novels which exploit Irish life for the benefit of the stranger instead of expressing it in a normal way'.[58] The bottom line for Carty and indeed for Corkery was that expatriate Irish writers were not truly Irish because their points of view had been tainted by 'alien considerations'.

If there were too few writers in Ireland there were even fewer critics and fewer again among them who were willing to take up Joyce's cause. Two who might have stepped into the fray were Frank O'Connor and Seán O'Faoláin. Ironically, both had studied with Corkery and through him as students had sneaked their first peek at Joyce's forbidden book: 'The young O'Faoláin had been Corkery's protégé, the "best friend" who was allowed to look at a copy of *Ulysses*, which Corkery kept in a locked drawer.'[59] Despite their enthusiasm for Joyce's early works and for the first half of *Ulysses*, both O'Connor and O'Faoláin were increasingly alienated by *Work in Progress* which, in Seán O'Faoláin's words, had 'taken a good idea to the extremity of foolishness' and was 'not sane enough to be literature itself' (*CH* 2, 397). This view retrospectively coloured their readings of *Ulysses* and was shared by many, among them Ezra Pound, Harriet Shaw Weaver and Stanislaus Joyce who told Stuart Gilbert that Joyce was engaged in a 'hopeless enterprise. [...] What he produces now reads like a round of drunken words dressed in each other's clothes.'[60]

---

[57]Daniel Corkery, *Synge and Anglo-Irish Literature*, 5.
[58]*IT*, 3 December 1934, 8.
[59]Bryan Fanning, 'Hidden Ireland, Silent Irelands: Seán O'Faoláin and Frank O'Connor versus Daniel Corkery', *Studies – An Irish Quarterly Review*, vol. 95, no. 379 (Autumn 2006): 251–9, 252.
[60]Letter of 19 December 1928 from Stanislaus Joyce to Stuart Gilbert. The original letter is kept in box 17, folder 9 of the Stuart Gilbert Collection at the HRC.

O'Connor initially seemed less dismissive, arguing in the *Irish Statesman* in 1930, 'that Joyce's calculated obfuscation made him a writer to be studied rather than read'.[61] Joyce had 'two obsessions, language and form', and O'Connor marvelled at how, in *Ulysses*, 'language became putty in his hands; he made it do things one had thought it impossible for language to do; at one moment it suggested the movement of waters, at another the stale air of a bawdyhouse; it was passionate, sentimental, maudlin, etiolated, violent, obscene and exquisite by turns'. While he appreciated the 'show' that was *Ulysses*, he had less sympathy for the 'Joyce of the third period'.[62]

O'Connor returned to Joyce in 1937 when he prepared a lecture on Lawrence and Joyce for broadcast on the Dublin Radio Station in the 'Great Writers of Today' series. His broadcast was cancelled at the last minute by the station which claimed that the script had not been submitted 'five days before the time for broadcasting [...] that Lawrence being dead and *Ulysses*, the book of Joyce's principally treated in the talk, being scarcely a work of to-day, the talk was not the most suitable for a "Writers of Today" series [...], and was "not suitable for general dissemination"'.[63] *The Irish Times* published O'Connor's full talk. He opened by saying that he had been 'supposed to speak to you about the great fiction writers of today' but 'there aren't any' although both Joyce and D. H. Lawrence had considerable reputations. *Dubliners* is 'the last word in cold reason; anything less mystic it would be hard to imagine' but also a 'genuine piece of exploration', an important urban text – 'the first portrayal in literature of everyday life in Irish cities'. *A Portrait* is 'an imaginative autobiography' of the 'young man who in *Dubliners* had walked the streets of Dublin with a coldly scientific eye, was revealed as a nervous tortured soul, crucified by his own human weaknesses, and by the ugliness of life about him'. Joyce is a product of the atmosphere of despair created by the fall of Parnell. His despair 'is the despair of Ireland' and it has only produced 'a violent overweening individualism', a 'desire to break forever with the tribe'. O'Connor's ambivalence grows with *Ulysses*, an 'amazing conception and an amazing book', which 'began as a short story for *Dubliners* and ended as the biggest thing in modern literature'. He reads it as a blending of Joyce's 'cold scientific spirit' of 'the refined and sensitive Dedalus' with 'the coarse, sensual, mediocre Bloom'. The death of Stephen's mother is central to the main theme of 'memory haunted'. O'Connor goes on to praise 'the perfect sense of form, the gorgeous humour' but asks 'whether

---

[61]John Nash, '"A Constant Labour": Work in Progress and the Specialization of Reading', in John Nash, ed., *Joyce's Audiences*, *European Joyce Studies*, 14 (Amsterdam and New York: Rodopi, 2002), 128.

[62]Frank O'Connor, 'Joyce – The Third Period', *Irish Statesman* (12 April 1930): 114–16 (*CH* 2, 515–16).

[63]Frank O'Connor, 'A Broadcast That Was Cancelled', *IT*, 12 July 1937, 13. The following year, on the day of his birthday, Joyce was featured in an Irish radio broadcast featuring Herbert Gorman, C. P. Curran, singer Michael O'Higgins and J. J. Hogan.

the marriage of *Dubliners* and *A Portrait of the Artist*, in Joyce's mind, was a real marriage at all'. He concludes by asking:

> Isn't Bloom, like so many of the characters in Dubliners, a piece of raw objectivity, unwarmed by the author's personality; isn't Stephen Dedalus a Narcissus, a human soul which has never been penetrated by the real world, and brought to laugh at itself and adjust its impossiblism by outside standards? I do not know; I only feel now that sometimes I want to kick the too-human Bloom into a semblance of human dignity, and box the ears of Stephen Dedalus and make him think of others' tragedy beside his own.

The poisonous sting in the tail is peremptory: Lawrence and Joyce 'are our two greatest; and they seemed to me to have failed'.

Just as O'Faoláin and O'Connor took exception to Joyce's focus on language, 'Dublin Boyd' (Ernest Boyd), in an article entitled 'Modern Transitional Literature' in *The New Statesman*, complained about contemporary 'experimental literature' and made Joyce one of his principal targets.[64] He laments Joyce's loss of 'intellectual control' and 'a tendency towards the complete breaking up and promiscuous reconstruction of language'.[65] Boyd returned to Joyce four years later in an essay entitled 'Joyce and the New Irish Writers' following the publication of the full *Ulysses* in the United States.[66] He again reclaims *Ulysses* as 'quintessentially Irish' and a 'local study of Dublin life' but partially reverses on his early keenness for the novel, which has 'evoked somewhat extravagant enthusiasm and highly exaggerated claims for its importance.'[67] He again counters Larbaud's claiming Joyce for Europe and reiterates the view that 'the "European" interest of the work must of necessity be limited to its form, for its content is so local and intrinsically insignificant that few who are unfamiliar with the city of Dublin thirty years ago can possibly grasp its allusions and enter into its spirit'.[68] Boyd claims, with some justification, that 'Irish criticism [...] is more impressed by its simple realism, photographic in detail and documentation', while admitting the power of 'Joyce's bewildering juxtaposition of the real and the imaginary, the commonplace and the fantastic'. He maintains that Joyce 'is the first, and perhaps the last, Irish Expressionist' and suggests that if Joyce has taken anything from the French, it is at best a mixed inheritance: 'the defects and qualities of the French Naturalists of the Zola school [...]

---

[64]Dublin Boyd, 'Modern Transitional Literature', *The New Statesman*, 16 August 1930, 593.
[65]Ibid.
[66]Ernest Boyd, 'Joyce and the New Irish Writers', *Current History* (New York) March 1, 1934: 39.6, 699–704.
[67]Ibid., 699.
[68]Ibid.

mocking Rabelasian ribaldry'.[69] Boyd concludes by claiming that Joyce's impact on contemporary writers was visible only in England and the United States: 'In Ireland his influence has been nil.'[70] O'Faoláin agreed when claiming, in 1941, that the overly individualistic Joyce had missed his chance to become the exemplar for Irish novelists to follow: 'Joyce did something glorious in *A Portrait of the Artist as a Young Man*, and if he had only been a little less subjective and preoccupied he might have given Irish prose a model as Gogol gave one to Russia with "The Cloak."'[71]

Although Austin Clarke disapproved of the 'coteries' that were 'formed to explain the enigmatic work of Joyce', he disagreed about Joyce's impact in Ireland. In his view, Joyce's 'revolutionary art is an influence working, for good or bad, in the minds, of younger writers'. Even if there have been 'silly imitations', he gives voice to the excitement among young writers in encountering Joyce: 'To dip into *Ulysses* is to step from the safe pavement into the very dizziness of mental traffic.'[72]

The publication of *Finnegans Wake* in 1939 did little to facilitate the success of *Ulysses* in Ireland (or elsewhere). Its timing could not have been worse. It appeared just months before Germany attacked Poland and Britain and France went to war. Dáil Éireann declared a state of emergency on 2 September, giving the government sweeping new powers including internment, and renewed censorship. There was little space for a considered appraisal of Joyce's difficult new novel. The reviewer in the *Irish Independent* made no pretence of having been remotely able to make sense of it in a review entitled 'WHASIDABOWT?' which concluded: 'At first I thought it was early Anglo-Saxon in simplified spelling. I could not understand what this weird thing was all about from beginning to end.'[73] An unsigned review calling Joyce's new work 'endlessly exciting in its impenetrability' appeared in *The Irish Times*. Although *Finnegans Wake*:

> is described as a novel, and, although in their essence all the stories of the world may be here, there is no single story that one can grasp. It may be a novel to end novels; for, if there is shape at all, its is the shape of a superb annihilation – as of some gigantic thing let loose to destroy what we had come to regard as a not unnecessary part of civilisation. One feels its power, the kind of gleaming genius behind it, but no communication of anything is achieved, perhaps simply because it is just not intended.[74]

[69]Ibid., 700.
[70]Ibid.
[71]Seán O'Faoláin, 'Ah, Wisha! The Irish Novel', *The Virginia Quarterly Review*, vol. 17, no. 2 (Spring 1941): 265–74, 267.
[72]Austin Clarke, 'James Joyce', *Everyman*, 15 May 1930, 486.
[73]T. L. 'WHASIDABOWT? Mr. Joyce's Puzzle', *II*, 9 May 1939, 4.
[74]*IT*, 3 June 1939, 7.

What the reviewer enjoys in what he terms 'one of the great milestones of literature', a book in which 'a new language may have been born', are what he calls the 'moments of beauty, the measured sounds of lyrical prose which beat upon the ear, but which do not come into the understanding, and always an airy gesture beyond the words which make it'. Yet the reader must deal with both delight and frustration as he follows:

> lingering lovely passages like flickers of gold. By following the small light they give there may be real illumination a little further on. But the light fails, and he is left to wander round and round in the maze. [...] it is a game which only Mr. Joyce can play, for he alone knows the rules, if there are any. He will take a word and twist and turn it, and chase it up and down through every language he knows.

Joyce gratefully wrote to thank *The Irish Times*, as that paper's editor, R. M. Smyllie, noted in his 'Irishman's Diary' (which he signed 'Nichevo'):

> Brinsley MacNamara reviewed it [*Finnegans Wake*] for the *Irish Times*, and I still have somewhere a letter from Joyce himself congratulating the paper on the excellence of his review. Praise from Joyce was high praise indeed. I wonder how many of his other reviewers can boast that they were congratulated by this remarkable, if wayward, genius.[75]

More commonly, however, *Finnegans Wake*, and the various instalments of it that appeared over a decade, became sticks with which to beat Joyce and retrospectively re-read *Ulysses*, mainly in a negative key.

Despite this, *Ulysses* continued to impact individual readers. Desmond Ryan, former Sinn Féin revolutionary turned journalist, author and historian, turned to Joyce as he tried to make sense of the Rising and the decade that had followed it. Having long been held 'spellbound' by Pearse, whose aide he had been at the GPO, and having looked admiringly to Collins as an 'awesome Spectra',[76] Ryan now looked to Joyce and was, by 1934, openly critical of Pearse's 'Napoleonic complex' and his 'fanatical glorification of war for its own sake'.[77] As he distanced himself from his former revolutionary colleagues, Ryan came to believe that *Ulysses* 'alone would explain the Irish revolution, for it reveals Dublin as none other than an Irishman could reveal her, an Irishman who at heart loves Dublin, and writes with all the indignation of love, the very pulse of this remorseless and

[75]*IT*, 24 May 1947, 7.

[76]R. F. Foster, *Vivid Faces: The Revolutionary Generation in Ireland, 1890–1923*, 326; Desmond Ryan, *Michael Collins* (Dublin: Anvil Press, 1932), 29–30.

[77]See Ryan, *Remembering Sion: A Chronicle of Storm and Quiet* (Dublin: Arthur Barker, 1934), 124.

brutal protest'.[78] In a lecture entitled 'Remembering Sion', given in 1934 to the Irish Literary Society in London (and published in 1968), Ryan spoke fulsomely of how Joyce had taught him to acquire freedom and revealed just how important *Ulysses* had been in influencing and sustaining a minority of often despairing dissenters within the Free State. *Ulysses* had provided a unique model through which to think and write about Ireland and the Irish, at home and in the diaspora. Therefore, Ryan 'took several leaves from the book of Mr James Joyce':

> Joyce sums up all the nostalgia of the Irish exile and suggests the whole movement of life and thought and history henceforth that any reader must find in the words: 'Remembering Sion.' [...] In his characteristic style, Joyce has given a sketch of the Irish political exile, too long to quote but what has been quoted is moving and adequate enough. And in his new use of the Psalmist's phrase recalls how Ireland lives in our memories away from Ireland.[79]

Not surprisingly, Ryan's book received mixed reviews, with the *Evening Herald* finding his interest in Joyce odd, and noting that his 'lavish praise of that writer makes painful reading'. It sorrowfully quoted Ryan's claim that 'every Irishman who knows Catholicism outside Ireland knows that Joyce is right in his onslaught on the Jansenist vices that warp and twist it too often there. There is the noble temper of Renan in Stephen Dedalus's refusal to kneel even at a deathbed'.[80] Notably, the only contemporary Irish politician that Ryan shows Joyce referencing is Arthur Griffith, signalled in *Ulysses* by Bloom as a 'coming man' (*U* 18.386). There is a sense of circularity in this, and there is good reason to believe that Joyce and *Ulysses* were not entirely lost to the clutches of cosmopolitan European modernism even in the 1930s. Although dismissed by many, *Ulysses* maintained a foothold in Irish debate even in the 1930s and acquired some importance among the idealistic though disillusioned Revolutionary generation. Although relegated to the margins, Joyce and *Ulysses* were not written out of the Irish story and had a continued relevance for those ill at ease in the conservative Ireland of the 1930s, for the disenchanted members of the 1916 generation, many of whom had been raised in the shadow of Griffith, adjudged by his political adversary, Erskine Childers, to have been 'the greatest intellectual force stimulating the tremendous national revival which took place in Easter week'.[81] Taken together, the legacies of Griffith and Joyce were vital

---

[78]Ibid., 43.

[79]Ryan, 'Still Remembering Sion', *University Review*, vol. 5 (Summer 1968): 245, 248.

[80]'Desmond Ryan's Provocative New Book *Remembering Sion*', *EH*, 1 June 1934, 6.

[81]Erskine Childers, *Poblacht na hEireann* (14 August 1922), quoted in Gerard Shannon, 'The Sinn Féin Rebellion? Arthur Griffith's Easter Week 1916', *The Irish Story* (5 April 2015). http://www.theirishstory.com/2015/04/05/the-sinn-fein-rebellion-arthur-griffiths-easter-week-1916/#.V76z1Y9OLcs.

elements for these intellectuals as they attempted to come to terms with the new Ireland. If Pearse was initially a beacon for many, in the decades that followed, Joyce, and the diametrically different vision he represented, came to take his place at least among a significant few.

Joyce also appealed to the newer generation of intellectuals that had grown up in the Free State and whose careers were taking shape in the 1930s, a time when his novels, and especially *Ulysses*, were circulating, albeit surreptitiously, in the universities. Vivien Mercier recalled reading Joyce while at Trinity in the late 1930s:

> A number of us shared in the cult and smuggled in our copies of *Ulysses* from Paris through two customs barriers. I suppose we were mostly Modern language students, though I remember some Classical men too. The Trinity drinking place was then still Davy Byrne's [...] There we used to meet barflies of the type of Lenehan in *Ulysses*.[82]

Things were more complicated in University College Dublin. In 1936, the Jesuit scholastic, Roland Burke-Savage, the Hutchinson Stewart scholar in English literature (1934), invited T. S. Eliot to participate in the inaugural meeting of the English Literary Society, of which he was auditor. Eliot accepted and stayed with the President of UCD, Dr Denis J. Coffey (1865–1945). On 23 January, Savage gave a talk entitled 'Literature at the Irish Crossroads'.[83] His respondents were Eliot and Daniel Corkery. The entire event was broadcast live on 'Athlone' (the future Radio Éireann).[84] Burke-Savage argued that there was 'a legitimate place for an Irish literature in the English tongue, expressing all the mentality, the environment, and outlook of modern Ireland' but that 'no serious attempt had been made to build up a literature that made its appeal directly to the people and their traditions'.[85] He said that he 'wanted to protest against the most common tendency of modern Anglo-Irish literature. A dash of pornography, he supposed helped to stimulate the sale of what was otherwise unattractive, but surely that was a prostitution of true literature, even if it was done in the name of the freedom of the arts'. He pointed to 'the lack of a sound philosophical position' as the cause of 'the growing weakness of Anglo-Irish literature':

> The reason why Anglo-Irish literature developed in this direction was largely because it had been the preserve of a non-Catholic clique, writing

---

[82]Vivien Mercier, 'Dublin under the Joyces', in Seon Givens, ed., *James Joyce: Two Decades of Criticism* (New York: The Vanguard Press, 1963), 295–6.
[83]A full copy of Burke-Savage's nine-page typescript, 'Literature at the Irish Crossroads,' as well as a programme of the inaugural meeting of the English Literary Society on 23 January 1936, is at the Houghton Library: bMS Am 1691 (29).
[84]*IP*, 22 January 1936, 11.
[85]Roland Burke-Savage, 'Anglo-Irish Writings', *IP*, 24 January 1936, 7.

for a non-native, foreign public. [...] Any literature which claimed to be Irish should aim at appealing to the religious consciousness which permeated the life of their people. It was in the reasoned acceptance of the Catholic tradition that the true future of Anglo-Irish literature lay. There were two possible directions for the future. Either literature could adopt, as a working hypothesis, Anglo or definitely English ideals, public order and discipline at all costs, but let the individual soul do what it would. Or else they could develop a truly Irish and Catholic ideal, which aimed at the discipline of both the individual and the public.

In response, Daniel Corkery argued that the country's literature should be written in Irish while J. J. Hogan, UCD's professor of English literature, disagreed with Burke-Savage, pointing out that 'Shakespeare's plays were readily appreciated by the Irish people, and many of them had no reference to either religion or nationality'. He quoted Cardinal Newman's statement that 'literature was the expression of the natural man, and could not be merely Catholic'. Eliot's response is given just one short paragraph in the newspaper report. In fact, his response was seven pages long. He considered 'not what Irish Literature has to do for Ireland, but what it has to do for Europe and for civilisation in general, taking into account its position in relation to the Catholic Faith on the one hand, and to England (through the English language) on the other'. Furthermore, he would assert that 'no one literature is self-subsistent'.[86] He also defended Yeats as 'the greatest living master of verse in the English language' and insisted that he had certainly 'done something for his own country'. Eliot, who had worried in advance that 'they will fling chairs about when I mention James Joyce',[87] affirmed that he:

> considered that James Joyce was the most Irish and in a sense the most Catholic writer in English of his generation. He hoped that the future of Irish literature would be perfectly Catholic. If the Catholic Faith was the true one might they not be permitted to aspire towards a literature which was English and Catholic as well as one which was Irish and Catholic.[88]

In fact he went further than the *Irish Press* suggests calling Joyce a 'great and lamentable [*sic*] isolated figure' and he argued that 'whatever he [Joyce] thinks of his education, and whatever its particular effect upon his temperament, his work is certainly an unconscious tribute to the kind of

---

[86]T. S. Eliot, *The Letters of T. S. Eliot*, vol. 8, 1936–1938, eds., Valerie and John Haffenden (London: Faber and Faber, 2019), 35–6.
[87]Letter from T. S. Eliot to Mary Hutchinson, 19 January 1936, in T. S. Eliot, *The Letters of T. S. Eliot* Volume 8, 36.
[88]'Anglo-Irish Writings', *IP*, 24 January 1936, 7.

education he received – an education without which, I believe, he would not have achieved such eminence. The mind exhibited in the work remains profoundly Catholic and religious'.[89]

The poet Denis Devlin mentioned this event in a letter to Thomas MacGreevy, pointing out that Eliot had been the first to dare to talk about Joyce 'in that place' [UCD].[90] Eliot himself remembered:

> I did speak of Joyce, and of course in his praise. [...] So far as I can remember, the great part of the audience remained in silence, but there was a considerable demonstration of applause from a group of young people at the back of the room, who were evidently well pleased that the name of Joyce should be mentioned, and his work openly preferred on such an occasion.[91]

The novelist James Hanley, whose early novels were heavily influenced by Joyce, wrote to Eliot to say that he had listened 'on the wireless':

> Need I say how thrilled I was when you spoke of James Joyce as you did, especially after Father Savage's speech. Though I am myself Irish, having a Cork mother & Dublin father I would not care to live in that country ever again; and though I owe something to Catholicism for stimulating my imagination, I am all against the clerical conception of literary ethics. It was so splendid to hear Joyce championed in his own country and by one not Irish.[92]

In Paris, Samuel Beckett was less impressed by Eliot's casting of Joyce as a Catholic writer:

> TSE has been all over the place, speaking at National to a motion affirmed by Rev. Burke-Savage, S. J., who savaged what he didn't burke, & then alone next day on Relation of Literatures, tralalala. Shem 'an unconscious tribute to a Catholic education acquired at a time when few people were educated at all.' The old fall back on pedagogics.[93]

---

[89]T. S. Eliot, 'A Reply to Roland Burke-Savage's 'Literature at the Irish Crossroads', University College, Dublin, 23 January 1936, in T. S. Eliot et al., *The Complete Prose of T. S. Eliot: The Critical Edition: Tradition and Orthodoxy, 1934–1939* (Baltimore: Johns Hopkins University Press, 2017), 293–9, 295.
[90]Letter from Denis Devlin to Thomas McGreevy, 15 March 1936. TCD 8112/9.
[91]Letter from T. S. Eliot to Patricia Hutchins, 23 November 1953, in T. S. Eliot, *The Letters of T. S. Eliot*, vol. 8, 36.
[92]Letter from Hanley to Eliot, 31 January 1936 in quoted in Ibid., 36.
[93]Letter of 29 January 1936 to McGreevy, Martha dow Fehsenfeld and Lois More Overbeck, *The Letters of Samuel Beckett Volume 1: 1929–40* (Cambridge: Cambridge University Press, 2009), 304–5.

It is very probable that among the group of applauding young people were figures such as Devlin, Charles Donnelly, Donagh MacDonagh, Brian Coffey, Niall Sheridan, Liam Redmond and Brian O'Nolan, all of whom were named by Peter Costello as being part of a 'Joyce cult' at UCD.[94] They may also have included Cyril Cusack, Niall Montgomery and O'Nolan's brother Ciarán. All of these young men looked to Joyce as an exemplar as they questioned the Catholic-Nationalist status quo. Later, they would also be to the fore in public attempts to celebrate Joyce in Ireland. The most obvious and immediate expression of their collective if critical homage was the satirical student periodical *Comhthrom Féinne* (Fair Play) which, edited by O'Nolan, often took aim at the more mainstream *National Student* and against the religious ethos of the University. Joyce was seen to stand in opposition to the provincialism and closure that was so often the target of this publication and he showed that it was possible for an Irish writer to belong within European late modernism and at the same time to be a vital voice in his own country, especially as the dismantler of national myths. Joyce was also seen as a counterweight to Yeats, who, with Synge, was among the butts of the humorous pieces in the magazine.[95] *Comhthrom Féinne* was followed by another *avant-garde* magazine called *Blather*, which again was founded by O'Nolan, along with his brother, and Niall Sheridan, and ran through 1934–5, trading mainly in caustic parodies of contemporary Ireland. This was at a time when not just pieties but Catholic social and moral teachings were being deferentially translated into law and especially into de Valera's 1937 Bunreacht na hÉireann, which was drafted by a small group of civil servants under de Valera's control and under the influence of key Catholic clerics, most especially the then Fr John Charles McQuaid. It enshrined the Catholic Church's 'special position' in the country.

Although their preferred literary targets were the sacred cows of the Revival and the political situation of the day, Joyce's highly individualistic approach to writing also came in for scrutiny. The two short-lived publications reveal an attempt to propose an alternative to Joyce's creative self-reliance. If Joyce staked everything on his own individual, egoistical imagination, they attempted to focus on the collective. Sheridan's memoir makes it clear that he considered himself part of a group and invokes O'Nolan's proclamation that 'the principles of the Industrial Revolution must be applied to literature. The time had come when books should be made, not written – and a "made" book had a better chance of becoming a bestseller'.[96] Thus Sheridan, O'Nolan, MacDonagh and Devlin planned to

---

[94]Peter Costello, 'James Joyce and the Remaking of Modern Ireland', *Studies*, vol. 93, no. 370 (Summer 2004): 127.

[95]For a discussion of these two publications, see Joseph Brooker, 'A Balloon Filled with Verbal Gas: Blather and the Irish Ready-Made School', *Precursors and Aftermaths*, vol. 2, no. 1 (2003): 74–98.

[96]Niall Sheridan, 'Brian, Flann and Myles', in Rudiger Imhof, ed., *Alive Alive O! Flann O'Brien's at Swim-two-birds* (Dublin: Wolfhound Press, 1985), 72–81.

collectively write 'the Great Irish Novel' to be called *Children of Destiny*.[97] As writers they would stay in Ireland and attempt to follow a very different model to Joyce's heroic individualism. They sought, as Anthony Cronin wrote, to dismantle the challenge of Joyce that 'would be defused by making him a mere logomachic wordsmith, a great but demented genius who finally went mad in his ivory tower. Admittedly he was a great low-life humorist as well, but he was one whose insensate dedication to something called art would finally unhinge him'.[98] The 'Great Irish Novel' to rival *Ulysses* never got written but, writing as Myles na gCopaleen in 1950, O'Nolan colourfully revisited this moment in a Cruiskeen Lawn column:

> How many of us think back, I wonder, to that far day when a handful of us, then young, ardent, met in a certain hotel to found the celebrated Irish-American syndicate to write under the name of 'James Joyce'? We had Aodh de Blacam, Niall Sheridan, myself, the Bird, Sam Beckett, Kenneth Reddin, Father Prout, Liam Gogan, Tim O'Neill, Con Curran, Beirt Fhear, Proust, Oliver Gogarty, Tom McGreevy, Joe Pike, Freud, Jimmy Joyce, poor O'Leary Curtis and myself – I appear twice because I was in the Chair, with a casting vote. Our motto was silence, exile and cunningham.[99]

By 1950, the motto had become 'Clamour, Inpatriation and Ignorance'. In the meantime, Sheridan had played a role in knocking O'Nolan's *At Swim-Two-Birds* into shape for publication in 1939 and he took an inscribed copy of it to Joyce in Paris: 'To James Joyce from the author,/ Brian O'Nolan with plenty of/What's on page 305'. What was underlined on that page was the phrase 'diffidence of the author'.[100] The literary careers of the other protagonists ended in greater compromise or disappointment. Donnelly was killed in 1937 in the Spanish Civil War, Denis Devlin enjoyed a moderately successful career as a modernist poet and a more successful one as a diplomat; Coffey, the most Catholic of the group, published several volumes of poetry; Sheridan, 'a young man of many talents', who, according to the Irishman's diary in the *Irish Times*, 'probably knows more about James Joyce than nine out of ten of the young Americans who are writing books of the subject' and 'could even give John Garvin a run for his money

[97]See Joseph Brooker, 'A Balloon Filled with Verbal Gas: Blather and the Irish Ready-made School', *Precursors and Aftermaths, Literature in English, 1914–1945*, vol. 2, no. 1 (2004): 74–98, 86.

[98]Anthony Cronin, *No Laughing Matter. The Life and Times of Flann O'Brien* (London: Grafton Books, 1989), 52.

[99]*IT*, 7 July 1950, 4.

[100]Ibid., 93. See Niall Sheridan, 'A Memory of Joyce', *RTÉ Guide*, 29 January 1982, 15 which describes his first visit to Joyce (during his Paris honeymoon) and Joyce's face 'cauterised in a crucible of long thought and suffering'.

on *Finnegans Wake*',[101] took a day job at the Irish Tourist board and wrote poetry, short stories, radio and television scripts as well as a play for the Abbey entitled *Seven Men and a Dog* (1958). He also planned but never got around to writing a biography of Joyce and later gave Richard Ellmann the material he had collected.

For this emerging generation of writers, the relevance and power of Joyce's output as an already-existing critique of all they wished to challenge in Ireland was both exhilarating and disabling. More often than not, he would show little interest in their writing. While many of them travelled to Paris hoping to get a foothold in the cosmopolitan world of the city, they found that Joyce was more interested in looking backwards to Dublin. In the words of Donagh MacDonagh, 'Joyce in his self-exile never left Dublin. He read the Dublin newspapers, listened constantly to Radio Éireann and would question his visitors closely – after they had presented the ritual gift of Hafner's sausages – as to the changed or changing topography of the city'.[102] Austin Clarke, who did break through the initial barrier of resistance but was never part of the inner circle, remembered: 'We went into the same cheap little cafe, which was usually empty at that hour, and sat there in a strange silence. What could I say to him? What could anyone say to him? I felt like a small boy in the presence of a kind but very dejected schoolmaster.'[103] Clarke recalled giving him his first book and 'when I met him again, in great expectancy, he told me he couldn't read it because it was much too long'.[104] With the exception of Flann O'Brien, the Irish writers that held Joyce's interest, such as Beckett or McGreevy, were already in Paris and he probably felt that much of what was being produced in Ireland was old hat. As Nino Franck remembered, 'the point that he was always interested in was had they broken new ground'.[105] Few, it seems, passed this test and at times it seemed that Joyce was more interested in nursing grievances with his Irish interlocutors about how little had been done for him at home than he was in supporting the next generation who came in homage. That was how it came across to Niall Sheridan:

> As we were talking he pointed at a rug on the floor. It was a woven affair with some sort of pattern in the middle of it, and he asked me could I recognise the pattern. So I didn't and he said, 'That's the Liffey from its source to its mouth, given to me by an American admirer,' And then added, 'Much more than any of my countrymen have ever done for me.'[106]

---

[101]*IT*, 24 September 1949, 8.
[102]Donagh MacDonagh, 'In the Steps of Leopold Bloom', *IT*, 16 June 1954, 6.
[103]W. R. Rodgers, ed., 'Portrait of James Joyce', 4
[104]Ibid., 9.
[105]Ibid., 10.
[106]Ibid., 7.

CHAPTER FIVE

Post-mortem: Remembering Joyce in the war years

In the 1940s, with Europe engulfed in war, neutral Ireland was more isolated than ever as it lived through the 'Emergency'. In a time of widespread material hardship, the country chose to assert its neutrality against Allied pressure to support the fight against Fascism. When Ireland refused to acquiesce to Churchill's demand that it join the war effort, he retaliated by introducing a supplies blockade that devastated Irish agriculture. There was widespread food rationing and fuel shortages. Once the war was over, Ireland remained isolated and found itself in a kind of international limbo, punished for its neutral stance. As in the past, for many people emigration was the only path out of poverty.

The decade began traumatically for Joyce as for everyone in a Europe devastated by war. The Joyces spent Christmas 1939 temporarily sheltering at St Gérand-le-Puy near Vichy and returned there in the spring of 1940 when Paris fell. A flicker of positivity came in the autumn when Padraic Colum, Eugene Jolas and Thornton Wilder wrote a public letter describing *Ulysses* and *Finnegans Wake* as 'the most influential novels of the epoch' and recommending that Joyce be awarded the Nobel Prize.[1] An *Irish Times* editorial warmly endorsed the proposal and praised Joyce's contribution to literature as 'great beyond question'. He had succeeded in bringing 'a new range of human experience into literature' and in creating 'a new technique for the novel'. The editorialist 'hoped ardently that a 1940 Prize for Literature' would be awarded 'in these barren days of European culture' and that the winner would be an Irishman: 'If the Noble Prize for Literature should be awarded to James Joyce, his honour will be shared alike by all his

---

[1]*IT*, 14 October 1940, 4.

countrymen'.[2] Unfortunately, the Prize was not awarded at all in 1940 or in the years that immediately followed.

Towards the end of 1940, Joyce and his family (except Lucia, who was confined in the Clinique des Charmettes in Pornichet à Mer near La Baule on the west coast of France) obtained visas to travel to Zurich, where they arrived just in time to enjoy what was to be their last Christmas together. Joyce fell ill soon afterwards and passed away on 13 January 1941 following an operation for a duodenal ulcer. His death was greeted with mixed reactions in an Ireland in which, as one American observer put it in a 1947 review of Harry Levin's *Portable James Joyce*, 'dour de Valera puritanism seemed to exert on the turbulent Irish temperament the unnatural sort of gloom that Stephen Dedalus knew so well in *A Portrait of the Artist*'.[3]

The mainstream newspapers gave Joyce's death prominent coverage but seemed at a loss as to whether the country had lost a Rasputin-like figure, an oddball, an anti-Christ, a writer of genius or a combination of all these. The *Irish Independent* lamented the loss of the 'Irish-born writer' and praised *Dubliners* and *A Portrait* as 'notable contributions to English literature' that 'showed great imagination, a fine use of words, an extraordinary sensitiveness to the social, political, and religious life of the Dublin of that day'. *Ulysses* and *Finnegans Wake* were described, less enthusiastically, as the 'chief works of the Continental period'. The writer argued that 'in all his writings it seems as if he were never easy about his attitude to the Church, as if his quarrel with it preyed on his mind continually' and noted that he was always 'very fond of talking about his native city'.[4]

The Belfast Telegraph reported Joyce's death rather oddly with the headline: 'The Irish Author Who Could Write Only When Dressed in White'. It claimed that Joyce 'wore a long white frock coat, white trousers, and white hat' and that 'his pointed beard hid a scar caused by a dog when he was a child, and that on this account he had a horror of dogs, although he was fond of cats'.[5] Describing Joyce as 'the author whom everybody talks about and nobody reads', the *Belfast News Letter* explained that 'his most discussed novel, *Ulysses*, was banned, and his later work [...] was unintelligible to many people'. He is described as 'living precariously' as 'a kind of wandering scholar', who 'opened a cinema in Dublin' that was 'an immediate failure'. *Dubliners* 'was an artistic success' but 'the frankness of his next book, *A Portrait of the Artist as a Young Man*, made life in Dublin difficult'.[6] In 1942, the Young Ulster Society, which had been founded by Thomas Carnduff to 'encourage a new interest in all forms of art in Ulster'

[2]'The Nobel Prize', *IT*, 16 October 1940, 4.
[3]Richard Watts Jr, 'An Irish Dante's Pilgrimage', *NYT*, 2 March 1947. https://movies2.nytimes.com/books/00/01/09/specials/joyce-portable.html.
[4]'Death of James Joyce', *II*, 13 January 1941, 6.
[5]*Belfast Telegraph*, 13 January 1941, 4.
[6]'Joyce's Career', *Belfast NewsLetter*, 14 January 1941, 4.

and was 'the only significant forum for cultural discussion in Belfast well into the 1950s',[7] held a talk on Joyce. Entitled 'The Last of the Goliards', it was given by the Rev. Canon R. S. Breene who claimed that:

for good or ill, Joyce had profoundly affected the whole trend of English literature. He traced in detail Joyce's literary progress from his production at the age of nine of a pamphlet on Parnell to *Dubliners* and 'curiosities' *Ulysses* and *Finnegan's* [sic] *Wake*, which had earned him a unique reputation.[8]

Back in Dublin the de Valera-controlled *Irish Press* announced Joyce's passing in a short, error-ridden article, which reports that Joyce 'left Dublin around 1916', after the publication of *Dubliners* ('a collection of stories about the capital's personalities') and *A Portrait*, the two books by Joyce that 'have a permanent place in great literature'.[9] He is praised for working '14 hours a day without rest' while his habit of 'laboriously re-writing' is signalled as is his use of 'a big red pencil, and writing letters so large that a few words filled each page'. Of the later works, *Ulysses* is reported to have been published 'in 1924' to 'bitter controversy'. The *Irish Press* also published a more sympathetic interview with three of Joyce's devout sisters, Eileen, Florence and Eva, 'as they sat together in a top [floor] flat in Mountjoy Square', dealing with the deaths of James and of his younger brother Charles, who had died three days earlier, and worrying about 'Stanislaus, who was living in Trieste until the outbreak of war and of whom they have heard no news since' (he was being held at an internment camp near Florence).[10] All three were defensive about their brother with Eva claiming that Joyce 'always expressed his love of Dublin and of the Dublin people, and often that he would love to live here again. [...] However some people may criticize what he wrote, he was our eldest brother and our idol, and to us, at least, his writings had the stamp of genius'. Despite having had very little contact with him for decades, she insisted that he 'had the kindest disposition, hated show and publicity, and spent all his spare time with his family, enjoying trips with them in the French countryside'. Eileen underlined his Catholic credentials: 'They say he was anti-Catholic, but he never missed a service during all the Holy Weeks he spent with me in Trieste.'

An *Irish Times* editorial heralded Joyce's importance with conviction:

Joyce probably was the most important English prose-writer of the present century. His place in the history of English prose will be greater

---

[7] John Gray, ed., *Thomas Carnduff Life and Writings* (Belfast: Lagan Press, 1994), 42.
[8] 'Young Ulster Society', *Belfast News Letter*, 30 September 1942, 2.
[9] 'Death of James Joyce', *IP*, 14 January 1941, 6.
[10] 'Sisters of James Joyce Mourn for Two Brothers', *IP*, 14 January 1941, 6.

than that of Yeats in the history of English poetry; for Joyce had an influence on world literature that Yeats never had, and his influence was the result of a single book.[11]

This was probably written by the editor, R. M. ('Bertie') Smyllie, himself. He would have enjoyed taking a cut at Yeats, who had supposedly alluded to him in the phrase, 'a drunken journalist', in his poem 'Why Should Not Old Men Be Mad?' Smyllie would have relished promoting the cosmopolitan Joyce at a time of cultural closure but he also underlined that 'Joyce was an Irishman of the Irish. He also might be described as the complete Dubliner. [...] He hardly ever wrote a line that was not steeped in the atmosphere of his native city'. Joyce's contribution to world literature would be judged by *Ulysses*, 'a work of consummate genius', that 'has been condemned as a crude essay in pornography, unworthy of an Irish writer, the product of a diseased mind, and fit to be read – if, indeed, it could be read at all – only by persons as depraved as the author himself'. 'The fact is', the editorial continues, 'that *Ulysses* has had a bigger influence on contemporary literature than any other single work in modern times'.[12] In so emphatically identifying Joyce as quintessentially Irish, *The Irish Times* was, in Terence Brown's words, 'nailing its colours definitively to the mast of a cultural pluralism and hybridity that stood opposed to the dominant Irish Ireland consensus of the day'.[13]

The death was also marked on the same day by Myles na gCopaleen in Irish in his 'Cruiskeen Lawn' column (which he had begun writing regularly in October 1940). He lamented the death of 'Séamus Seoige' and praised the authenticity of his depiction of 'the tribe', which far surpassed that of any analogous efforts written in Irish:

The death of the great Irish writer James Joyce is a cause of sorrow and regret to us. His death leaves a great void in the world of arts. In his own way he displayed to the wider world the literary genius most native of the tribe of people who inhabit this country. His work could not have been created by anyone except an Irish person and on this basis the writings he has left us are more Gaelic than many of those we have from people who never understood a word of English. With the passage of time this writer's fame will grow and in this country respect for him will increase as the generality of people come to understand what literature is.

Not until there is a comparable author writing in Irish will the mother tongue be out of danger. In the meantime we will have that comely finely-ground work 'Séadna' and 'Niamh,' 'An Béal Beo,' 'An Mháthair,'

[11]'James Joyce', *IT*, 14 January 1941, 4.
[12]Ibid.
[13]Terence Brown, *The Irish Times: 150 Years of Influence* (London: Bloomsbury, 2015), 146–7.

as well as a lot of other rubbish that is as false and as ungaelic as it is contemptible.[14]

Joyce's close Paris friend, the art critic, Arthur Power, penned a warm tribute, describing him as 'a gentle and affectionate man who loved his friends, and, in turn, was loved by them'.[15] His 'international fame [...] never swerved him to forget the simple and real things of life – his family and his personal friends'. Power focused on the ordinariness of Joyce's daily routine, his abhorrence of 'loose or bawdy talk' in an attempt to 'normalize' a figure seen as being anything but normal. He noted that 'Dublin always formed the chief topic of the conversation', thus underlining his constant attachment to the country he had physically abandoned. Power praised Joyce by honouring his integrity while at the same time distancing himself from the content of the writings:

> But what always worried me was how a man of his refined and delicate sensibility could have written the things he did write in *Ulysses*. But I never got an answer from him. In one of my worst moods I hinted to him that he had done it to gain notoriety; but I had barely uttered it when I withdrew it all, convinced, as I was, from a thousand observations of his absolute integrity. He wrote what he did because he believed it should be written. And he spent years in obscurity and poverty because he would not change so much as a line of it.[16]

Power's conclusion is a moving tribute to Joyce:

> A man's kindness is even more important than his greatness; and in my loneliness in Paris he was my constant friend – the man whom all the world was anxious to meet. [...] Everywhere he went he carried Ireland and Dublin with him, in his mind and heart. He is gone, and Dublin remains, will remain: and yet the majority of the world only knows Dublin through the medium of his personality, the personality of James Joyce. Such is the function of the artist.[17]

Less than two months later, Power was more critical, accusing Joyce of 'stuntism [...] the curse of modern art', of allowing 'his emotion to twist and contort his style' and of belittling 'life by making it appear always sordid

---

[14]The translation is by Seán Mag Leannáin. I am grateful to him for bringing this to my attention. The works referred to by Myles were: *Séadna* and *Niamh* by Father Peadar Ua Laoghaire (1904), *An Béal Beo* by Tomas Ó Máille (1936), *An Mháthair*, the collection of short stories, by Patrick Pearse.
[15]Arthur Power, 'Memoir of the Man', *IT*, 14 January 1941, 6.
[16]Ibid.
[17]Ibid.

and mean'.[18] This view was challenged by another of Joyce's Irish friends in Paris, Thomas McGreevy, who countered that Joyce 'gave to the sordid and mean things a real meaning and importance'. Elsewhere, McGreevy saw Joyce's death as removing a figure that was the last of his kind and as marking 'the end of nineteenth-century individualism in literature. He was its last great genius, like Yeats in one thing only in that he had worked out an attitude of mind which seemed to him to be valid, and he consecrated his whole life, both in his art and in his way of living, to maintaining it'.[19]

Power and McGreevy were taking part in a public debate about Irish art that was derailed into a discussion about Joyce following an assertion by Dublin architect and man of the theatre, Joseph Holloway, that it was 'a great pity that James Joyce left his native country and went away for sixteen years, only to write childish nonsense and a foreign language'. This assertion sparked lively responses in the letters pages from the sculptor and painter, Lilla Vanston, and from E. V. Briscoe, who hoped that this would not be 'his native country's epitaph on Mr. James Joyce'. Taking issue with the 'vultures', Briscoe challenges the claim that 'the world could not yet assess the value of Joyce's work' by pointing out that Joyce 'has been acclaimed through the world by men of genius as one of the great figures of our time'. He appeals for those who have never read Joyce to 'stop hurling fatuous abuse at the man, and, still worse, at those who do understand and admire him. ("Bogus intellectuals, irresponsible youths, *poseurs*, etc.")'.[20] This provoked a flurry of facetious responses, including one by Ashbourne Porter who defined himself as a 'literary *poseur* by profession' and recounted trying to steer a conversation 'round to an argument about the meaning of the word "Gulmansibthonffaeddioude," which occurs with such regular monotony in modern works of genius'. He concludes by pretending to offer a compliment: 'To-day I am glad to see in the *Irish Times* that there actually exists in Dublin a man who not only "understands and admires James Joyce," but has even read him.'[21] A reply came from Oscar Love, a probable pseudonym for Brian O'Nolan. He suggests that critics should attend a school, 'such as that described in *Alice in Wonderland*', where pupils 'were taught "Drawling, Stretching and Fainting in Coils"' and could learn phrases such as 'The Truminous Bandersnatch'. Love thus connects Joyce's use of language with Lewis Carroll's *Alice's Adventures in Wonderland* and his poem 'Jabberwocky'. He concludes by referencing Swift and Gulliver's 'Land of Houyhnhmns' where 'Gulliver learnt, from a bay mare, the meaning of "Yahoo" and "Hbuun-Hbuun"' and by bemoaning the fact 'that art critics possess little horse sense'.[22]

---

[18]'Joyce, the Artist and Writer', *IT*, 6 March 1941, 6.
[19]See Hugh J. Dawson, 'Thomas MacGreevy and James Joyce', *JJQ*, vol. 25 (Spring 1988): 307.
[20]E. V. Briscoe, *IT*, 7 March 1941, 3.
[21]Ashbourne H. Porter, *IT*, 8 March, 4.
[22]Oscar Love, *IT*, 10 March 1941, 3.

Some provincial newspapers reported Joyce's death. The *Connacht Tribune* published a short though positive piece but failed to mention any of his books, noting only that his 'writings provoke world-wide discussion' and stressing the local angle: 'In 1904 he married Nora, daughter of the late Mr. And Mrs. Thomas Barnacle, Bowling Green, Galway. A sister, Mrs Mai [*sic*] Monaghan, and a sister-in-law, Mrs Kathleen Griffin, reside in Galway.'[23] The *Tuam Herald* referred to the author as 'the "stormy petrel" of twentieth century literature, by reason of the controversy centred in his writings' and claimed that his 'death has removed from this earth another of those Irish geniuses – a man whose name is almost assured of literary immortality'.[24] The *Meath Chronicle* was of a very different view and mocked the suggestion that a memorial should be built (a proposal made in the letters page of *The Irish Times*) offering its support for 'the man who, in Thursday's issue, suggested as an appropriate memorial a public convenience on the Ticknock road'.[25]

At the other end of the spectrum, Micheál Mac Liammóir led the small chorus of cultural voices that openly and genuinely mourned the passing of 'another great son' of Ireland:

> Perhaps the most significant and exciting figure now writing in English. No Irish writer has created such a store of worship and of hatred, no Irish writer has scourged us with such remorseless whips. It was Joyce more than Yeats, more than Wilde, more than Shaw, who rode his Irish horse with such a savage war cry into the literary courts of Europe and forced the critics to say: 'Ireland is at the door, and we have got to let her in!' Joyce was a genius. It would be well that his own people should salute him before they are forced to their feet by the rest of Europe.[26]

The Irish government did little to embrace Joyce even on his death. When Frank Cremins, Ireland's permanent delegate to the League of Nations in Berne, informed the Department of External Affairs in Dublin, where Éamon de Valera was minister (he was also, simultaneously, Taoiseach), of Joyce's passing, de Valera swiftly decided against sanctioning any official diplomatic presence at the funeral which took place on 15 January 1941 at the Fluntern cemetery. This left the coast clear for Lord Derwent, the British Minister to Berne, to own the scene. In a well-judged speech that was both respectful and witty, he captured a sense of both the Irish and the cosmopolitan Joyce:

---

[23]'Irish Writer Dies in Switzerland', *Connacht Tribune*, 18 January 1941, 6.

[24]'James Joyce', *Tuam Herald*, 25 January 1941, 2.

[25]'Appropriate', *Meath Chronicle*, 23 August 1941, 3. This may have been an attempt to connect Joyce to Honor Bright (who is mentioned in *Finnegans Wake*), a prostitute who was murdered in 1925 in the Dublin mountains at the Ticknock crossroads in 1925.

[26]MacLiammóir's comments are quoted in J. J. Finnegan, 'Joyce is Dead', *EH*, 13 January 1971, 7.

I confess I am not familiar with the attitude that Irishmen as a whole have adopted towards Joyce's work; but in any case Joyce belongs to Europe, both by his continual choice of residence there, and by the detached and strange grandeur of his work – for are not Stephen Dedalus and Ulysses-Bloom type figures which, while bathed in an Irish atmosphere, stand out against a much larger horizon. [...] I consider it eminently suitable that this cosmopolitan gathering should be assembled here to-day to bid a last farewell to a man who, wherever domiciled (as an Italian paper has pointed out), seems to have had no creative thought in his mind that was not intimately connected with the Ireland of his birth.[27]

Derwent also underlined the importance of Ireland's writers in the ongoing relationship between Britain and Ireland:

And now all that's over. George Moore is gone; Yeats is gone; and now Joyce. But of one thing I am sure – whatever be the rights and wrongs of the relations between England and Ireland, I know Ireland will continue to take the finest and most ironical of revenges on us; she will go on giving us great men of letters.[28]

When Derwent was delivering his eulogy, de Valera's officials in the Department of External Affairs were fretting about whether or not Joyce had died a Catholic. The Department Secretary, Joe Walshe, who feared that German victory was close but refused to intervene on behalf of Joyce's Jewish friend and long-time helper, Paul Léon (who was later killed by the Nazis), wrote to the Irish Embassy in Berne: 'Please wire details about Joyce's death. If possible find out if he died a Catholic? Express sympathy with Mrs. Joyce and explain inability to attend funeral.' From Berne, Cremins replied in some detail about Joyce's illness but denied any knowledge of his religious state.[29]

Some Irish diplomats were privately more than happy to meet and help Joyce. One among them was Sean Lester, who, during his time as secretary of the League of Nations, attempted to help him to obtain a visa for Lucia to travel from Nazi-occupied France. They met as Joyce passed through Geneva in December 1940. Lester had reviewed *A Portrait* many years earlier in the *Freeman's Journal*. They had dinner and a long chat as Lester remembered in his diary: 'Joyce told me that he had only spent 10 days in Ireland during the last 30 years – some day I hope I shall get the story of his departure from him.' In response to Lester's asking 'Why do you not go home?' Joyce

[27]Derwent's speech was quoted in an article about Joyce and Zurich published in *IT*, 4 February 1949, 7.
[28]W. R. Rodgers, 'Joyce's Funeral', *IT*, 20 June 1964, 11.
[29]Cian Ó hÉigertaigh, 'Léon's Last Letters', *IT*, 4 April 1992, 33.

answered: 'I am attached to it daily and nightly like an umbilical cord.'[30] A month later Joyce was dead. Lester 'tried to attend the funeral but was unable to get away from Geneva. His suggestion that Frank Cremins, Chargé at the Irish Legation at Berne, attend was not taken up: "F. won't, says he can't leave. Too busy coding and decoding telegrams"'.[31] The more likely explanation is that the government denied him permission to attend mostly to avoid incurring any clerical displeasure. Even in death, Church organs, such as The *Irish Rosary* (published by the Dominicans), found little good to say about Joyce whose passing was marked in an editorial that opened: 'We never found occasion to write about James Joyce when he was alive and we feel no inclination to write about him now that he is dead.' But write about him, it did, and at length, describing Joyce's evil influence, the boundless admiration he enjoyed in the press, his bartering of an 'intellectual pearl of great price for the husks of intellectual sin', his having 'fouled the nest which was his native city', through his blasphemy and obscenity, and his failure to be 'reconciled to Christ' on his deathbed. The editorial defends those who were unjustly charged of 'provincial vandalism' for 'arraigning a literary genius for his unchastity and unchristianity'.[32]

Thus, had the Joyces been looking for an Irish or indeed any priest to officiate they would have struggled to find one if Mary Colum's experience in New York was anything to go by. She remembered that 'when Joyce died and some of his friends in New York wanted to have the customary Mass said for him, every priest approached, even the Jesuits whose pupil he was and for whom he preserved a great respect, refused on the grounds of Joyce's alienation from the Church'. The chaplain of Columbia University, Fr George Ford, finally did have 'the customary prayers said' but Colum indignantly contrasted this treatment with 'people far less Catholic than James Joyce like Paderewski and George Cohan [who] were given all the rites, and in the Cathedral'. Colum's explanation for this was that '[he] had done the unforgivable thing in English-speaking Catholicism: written freely of sex'.[33] It would have been at least as difficult to have a mass said in Ireland.

In 1937, Joyce had reported to his friend C. P. Curran that Herbert Gorman, who had travelled to Ireland to gather material for his biography, 'said he had a great time in Eire but at Clongowes it seems the password was "O breathe not his name"' (*SL* 386). This policy still held good. Neither the *Clongownian* nor the *Belvederian* – the annuals of the two Jesuit schools that had given him an education for which he had always expressed gratitude – published a word in memory of their famous alumnus. Back

[30]Gerard Keown, 'Sean Lester: Journalist, Revolutionary, Diplomat, Statesman', *Irish Studies in International Affairs*, vol. 23 (2012): 143–54, 150–1.
[31]Ibid.
[32]This editorial is quoted in a commemorative piece written to mark the thirtieth anniversary of Joyce's death. J. J. Finnegan, 'Joyce Is Dead', *EH*, 13 January 1971, 7.
[33]Mary M. Colum, *Life and the Dream* (New York: Doubleday, 1947), 381.

in 1926, in an article by the young Eoin O. Mathamhna (Eoin 'the Pope' O'Mahony) surveying Clongowes writers, Joyce was openly excluded with the words: 'The work of Mr James Joyce cannot come within our purview', before the author lamented that 'it is now twenty-five years since William P. Kelly penned a story dealing with the college life of half a century ago. Since then no work of fiction of respectable dimensions has been brought out'.[34] The *Belvederian* did publish an obituary of Joyce's brother Charles, who was not, as the obituarist noted (presumably sticking his neck out as far as possible), 'so talented as his elder brother'. Charles 'was always proud of getting a first prize in Christian Doctrine, and used his knowledge with telling effect in later life at many a Catholic Evidence Guild meeting in Hyde Park London'.[35] Not to give Joyce an obituary was extraordinary, according to Bruce Bradley S. J., former headmaster of both Belvedere and Clongowes: 'They always printed obituaries of their past pupils, whether they had achieved glory or otherwise.'[36] Sixteen years later, Fr J. C. Kelly, SJ, 'broke with the unspoken tradition of several generations by contributing a long and appreciative review of Joyce's recently published *Letters* in the 1957 edition of *The Belvederian*.'[37] He also reviewed J. Mitchell Morse's *The Sympathetic Alien: James Joyce and Catholicism*, a work that had studied Joyce as one of a cohort of brave Catholic thinkers who have stood for the individual as against the authorities. In Fr Kelly's view:

> James Joyce was not primarily interested in Catholicism. His interest was in constructing works of art out of his raw material. He himself was part of that raw material, which was Dublin and Dubliners: a city and a people predominantly Catholic. Critics who care little or nothing for religion are somewhat disconcerted by the quantity of Catholic references Joyce put into his work. It all seems morbid and unnecessary. But Joyce wrote as he did because he refused [...] to blink the fact that Dublin's consciousness – even in its most ribald, irreverent and rebellious moods – is soaked in Catholicism.[38]

If Joyce's former schools baulked at his very name, University College Dublin was less hesitant in laying a claim. The influential Literary and

---

[34]Eoin O. Mathamhna, 'Clongowes and Its Neighbourhood in Literature', *IM*, vol. 54, no. 631 (January 1926): 690–7, 696. According to Peter Costello, Ellmann's account of the history of Rev. Charles O'Connell, a grand-uncle of Joyce, was 'hopelessly confused. The priest he identified was in fact a Cornelius O'Connell, born in Co. Cork and no relation of these O'Connells [viz., the family of Ellen]. [...] By relying on information from the notorious Eoin O'Mahony and an anonymous source, he was led astray, perhaps deliberately.' (see Peter Costello, *James Joyce. The Years of Growth, 1882–1915* (London: Roberts Rinehart, 1992), 40.
[35]*The Belvederian*, 1941, quoted by Bruce Bradley, 'James Joyce – Old Clongownian', n.p.g.
[36]Quoted by Katie Donovan, 'Joyce and the Cardinal', *IT*, 31 July 1990, 6.
[37]Bruce Bradley, S. J. *James Joyce's Schooldays*, foreword by Richard Ellmann (Dublin: Gill and Macmillan, 1982), 2.
[38]Fr John C. Kelly, S. J., 'Joyce and Catholicism. The Dublin Consciousness', *IT*, 20 August 1959, 7.

Historical Society announced that its business would be suspended for a day as a mark of respect following the death 'of a former member of the Society, James Joyce [...] the best-known figure that has come from University College, Dublin' whose 'writings have carried the name and the reputation of the University into every part of the world'.[39]

Some belated pushback against Catholic condemnation of Joyce came from Patrick Kavanagh in a review of Thomas Merton's *Elected Silence*, which also reflected Kavanagh's own outsider status and his tortured Catholicism:

> For Irish readers the most remarkable fact about Merton's conversion will be the large share the Irish Jesuits had in it – not the writings of Fathers Devane or Gannon, or the enthusiastic work of Father Browne's Central Library, but the Jesuit boy, James Joyce. How pleased the Irish Carmelite priest must have been when he was able to introduce Merton to the head of the Trappist monastery: 'Father, here is the man who was converted to the Faith by reading James Joyce.' This will not seem strange to perceptive readers; for Joyce's work is steeped in the blood of tortured Catholicism. Joyce was also one of the best interpreters of Thomism there has been.[40]

Elsewhere Kavanagh underlines Joyce's 'spiritual honesty' when reviewing *The Capuchin Annual* (1942), which contained an article by Fr Michael OFM, who strongly recommended Canon Sheehan's output as infinitely superior to 'the threefold squalor of Joyce's underworld that carried him back to classic Dedalus and dead *Ulysses*'. In Fr Michael's words:

> If we need wings, we of the new Ireland, let us not flap the wings of the carrion crow of Joyce crying 'Ireland belongs to me,' to savage her and her religion, to drag them, with a sneer, through the pits of hell, but let us take the wings of Sheehan the priest, the uncloistered monk, and let Ireland in her word be the priest of the world, the monk of the west, to carry the unutterable mysteries of grace, and the whole graciousness of nature to what we will hope will be a new and better world.[41]

In an article ostensibly written to praise Sheehan, most of Fr Michael's energy goes instead into denigrating Joyce. The difference between Sheehan and Joyce 'is the whole hierarchical world of difference between reverence and blasphemy, between the priest and the pervert, between the Saviour and

---

[39]'Memories of James Joyce', *IT*, 20 January 1941, 3.
[40]Patrick Kavanagh, 'Review of Thomas Merton, *Elected Silence*', *IT*, 10 September 1949, 6.
[41]Father Michael O. F. M. Cap., 'Twilight and Dawn', *The Capuchin Annual*, 1942, 263–87, 287.

His adversary'.[42] Joyce is guilty of overreaching, of riding 'out the revolt till his medium burst in the midst like the frog who would be the cow in the fable'. The only positive message that can be taken from Joyce's excessive manipulation of English is that it may cause the Irish to readopt their native tongue: 'But the imp in the Irishman will add: the devil's cure to the King's English. Joyce in one sense has a message of hope for resurgent Gaelic. English is worn out, try your own so untried medium, and don't be bothering us with your meretricious art.' Joyce is dismissed as flashy and empty as the author asks: 'What is the use of style if we have nothing to put it on – just another suit of clothes without a man inside.'[43]

Kavanagh takes issue with how the 'Irish writer is described as a man who portrays his people as scoundrels and everything evil for the purpose of making money in the English and American markets':

> One doesn't need to be an admirer of the last two books of James Joyce to realise that it was his artistic (spiritual) honesty that brought him to poverty and a grave in a foreign land. 'Woe to the man with projecting unfathomables in his being,' wrote Amiel. Joyce said he would fight the world with 'silence, exile and cunning.' If he had been really cunning he would have stayed at home and written for the *Saturday Evening Post*.[44]

Kavanagh concludes by claiming that 'intellectually, the Catholic Church in Ireland is in a weak position, and not because the intellects are unavailable, but because there is no sense of the critical appraisement to select the clear, shining diamond from the dross of sentimentality, pretence and unthinking piety'.

Elizabeth Bowen published perhaps the most convincing Irish tribute to Joyce in March 1941 in *The Bell*, founded just a year earlier by Seán Ó Faoláin to fill the space vacated a decade earlier by the *Irish Statesman*.[45] Long an affectionate admirer of *Dubliners*, which she called 'the best book of stories ever written',[46] and which clearly influenced her own writing, Bowen noted the 'uneasy politeness caused by his death', which was 'felt by few in his own land as a personal tragedy. He died, as he lived the later part of his life, outside Ireland. Those of us who met him, met him in Paris, where he was almost an object of pilgrimage'. C. P. Curran would

---

[42]Ibid., 272.

[43]Ibid., 271–2.

[44]Patrick Kavanagh, 'The Irish Catholic Front: *The Capuchin Annual* for 1942', IT, 10 January 1942, 5.

[45]Elizabeth Bowen, 'James Joyce', *The Bell*, vol. 1, no. 6 (March 1941): 40–9. Reprinted in Eibhear Walshe, ed., *Elizabeth Bowen's Selected Irish Writings* (Cork: Cork University Press, 2011), 69–74.

[46]Elizabeth Bowen, 'Portrait of a Woman Reading', *Chicago Tribune, Book World*, 10 November 1968, 10.

later recall that 'to be a Dubliner of his generation was the passport to his house in Paris, or wherever he lived, in his later years' and visitors were quite frequent.[47] Bowen, perhaps because of her own complicated sense of belonging in Ireland, was sensitive about his exile and lack of connection: 'It is surroundings that tie us closely to people, that are the earth of friendship. And that physical, associative tie with his countrymen Joyce broke when he went to live abroad.'[48] It broke perhaps for his fellow countrymen, many of whom looked on the mere fact of expatriation as a black mark, but for Joyce the tie remained.

A few years later, the then exiled Irish essayist, Hubert Butler, who, like Joyce, had spent time in Trieste, wrote perceptively about Joyce and exile:

> As a young man Joyce had a clearly conceived ideal – he believed that Ireland could realise itself by becoming more European and the choice must have presented itself to him frequently of being a European in Ireland or an Irishman in Europe. The second alternative was chosen only when it was clear that it was the least impossible of the two.[49]

But the choice came at a high price and Butler indirectly alluded to this when he later published his translation from the Greek of C. P. Cavafy's 'The City', which he dedicated to the 'memory of James Joyce and Trieste'. In Butler's translation, the 'You' of the poem refers to Joyce (but also to himself):

> You said: 'I'll seek some other land, far off, with sails unfurled.
> I'll find a worthier town than this and some serener clime.
> For here ambition foiled is like a crime,
> the quickening impulse of the heart is dead,
> and sluggish thoughts entomb the past like lead.'[50]

The mere fact of leaving does not necessarily gift the exile with freedom; rather, he will find 'Your city will go with you'. If Butler underlined the burden of Joyce's belonging, Bowen appealed for a moving away both from the Irish habit of casting him as a notorious exiled rebel and from what she called 'worship' from abroad, a foreign veneration that was resented and complicated his acceptance at home. Ireland needed to find a way to embrace Joyce on its own terms:

---

[47]W. R. Rodgers, ed., 'Portrait of James Joyce', 7.

[48]Elizabeth Bowen, 'James Joyce', 69.

[49]Hubert Butler, Undated 9-page manuscript entitled 'James Joyce in Trieste', 3–4. Crampton family papers, Bennettsbridge, Co. Kilkenny [papers in possession of the Crampton family]. Cited in Robert Benjamin Tobin, 'The Minority Voice: Hubert Butler, Southern Protestantism and Intellectual Dissent in Ireland, 1930–72', PhD Thesis, Merton College, Oxford, 2004, 67.

[50]Hubert Butler, 'The City', *IT*, 10 April 1948, 4.

Europe and America have acclaimed Joyce. But it is in our power, as
his people, to know him as other countries do not. His death [...] need
not estrange him from us, but rather bring him back. We have given to
Europe, and lost with Europe, her greatest writer of prose. The shy thin
man with the thick spectacles belonged to us, and was of us, wherever
he went. He has not asked us for a grave—we have too many graves
already. It is not with his death that we need concern ourselves, but with
the life (our life) that, still living, he saved for us, and immortalised, line
by line.

Bowen called on her readers to 'strip from Joyce the exaggerations of foolish
intellectual worship' from abroad and to 'take him back to ourselves as a
writer out of the Irish people, who received much from our tradition'. Joyce
was 'before all an Irishman [...] Ireland had entered him: it was the grit
in his oyster shell' and asked if it was 'not Joyce's fundamental Irishness
that has defeated, and in some cases, antagonized, the critics forced into
pronouncements by his death? The English can never know us – and are we
ready to know ourselves?'[51]

Bowen was correct in pointing out that praise from abroad had made it
more difficult for Joyce to be accepted at home. Shortly after his death, she
insisted that 'the contradictions of Joyce's nature ought not to perplex his
own country's people: we have them all in ourselves'. She criticized what
she saw as the English refusal of anything that was not 'plain speech and
properly drilled thought'. English reaction to Joyce's work as to his death
was cold, as John Nash commented: 'Joyce's obituary in *The Times* (London,
14 January 1941) was so grudging that it seems a wonder they bothered to
give his death notice at all.' It 'spurred T. S. Eliot to declare that Joyce was 'the
greatest man of letters of my generation' and *Ulysses* 'the most considerable
work of imagination in English in our time'.[52] Bowen rightly complained
of France's 'tragically silent' reaction to Joyce. French Joyce reception had
largely begun and ended with Valery Larbaud. Bowen bemoans that 'the
slow mails hold up, for us, what America has to say' but her basic point was
that Ireland needed to work out what it wanted to say about Joyce – 'the
reviewers' nightmare' – rather than await 'awkwardly, signs from abroad'.[53]
Her view pointed to an Irish post-colonial insecurity in which we seemed to
give more weight to how we appeared to the outside world than to how we
appeared to ourselves. This was an expanded national version of wondering
what the neighbours might think rather than to looking internally to the
substance of the problem.

---

[51]Elizabeth Bowen, 'James Joyce', 69.
[52]John Nash, 'Genre, Place and Value: Joyce's Reception, 1904–1941' in John McCourt, ed.,
Joyce in Context (Cambridge: Cambridge University Press, 2009), 41.
[53]Elizabeth Bowen, 'James Joyce', 72.

Later, Bowen returned to write about the centrality of Ireland in Joyce's consciousness and his attachment to Dublin, when warmly reviewing Patricia Hutchins' *James Joyce's World*. She described how he managed 'to alter the world's conception of prose literature' having exiled himself from his native city, 'yet without cease, re-living Dublin obsessively, he made it both source and scene of his art. The Irish capital exists, therefore, for thousands who have never in actuality known it'.[54] Bowen also reviewed Herbert Gorman's *James Joyce: A Definitive Biography* (1941), noting how the work celebrates Joyce as a 'European writer' and as 'a detached man' who lived for his writing: 'He sustained with a simplicity that was disconcerting and that appeared cryptic the prominence into which he had been thrust. He had desired no more – and no less – than the consummation every writer desires: the consummation of his books finding their mark.'[55] Bowen defines his detachment as 'a continuous heroic act of the spirit. Nothing was spared him: extreme poverty, repugnant work for a living, frustrations, humiliations, physical pain, a sense of exile were by him felt to the full – but they were surmounted'. She also deals sensitively with his leaving the Catholic Church: 'He was reared and educated in a religion from which a deep nature does not without crisis secede, and from which a lonely nature dreads to detach itself.' Despite all the privations and difficulties, 'never was there a less pitiable man. [...] Joyce's equanimity triumphed, through everything: it was a combination of an unmoved belief in his art with a Jesuit-instilled rule of self-discipline'.

Elsewhere, Gorman's biography – and Joyce himself – got shorter shrift. The *Belfast Newsletter* described Joyce as 'one of the most unfortunate writers the world has known' because of the 'agony and disappointment of his publishing history'. Gorman wins praise, however, for writing 'a realistic biography, free from false sentiment'. The Unionist newspaper noted Joyce's views on the revival of the Irish language with satisfaction: 'He was unrelenting in his aversion to this movement. [...] He feared, too, that a national immersion in Gaelic would cut Ireland still further off than she was from the great central current of European culture. Many in the North of Ireland, and perhaps in the South too, will say "Amen" to that.'[56] The *Irish Independent* published a trenchant review of Gorman's biography, which claimed: 'James Joyce has been little more than a name to most people in this country. That is, perhaps, as well. For he did little of which his countrymen could be proud.' Gorman's version of Joyce's life is seen as having unwittingly furnished a cautionary tale about the fate of one who leaves the flock in 'the picture it paints of the pathetic struggle of Joyce, bereft of any spiritual

---

[54]Elizabeth Bowen, Review of Patricia Hutchins, *James Joyce's World*, *The Tatler and Bystander*, 8 May 1957, 2.
[55]Elizabeth Bowen, 'Portrait of the Artist', a review of *James Joyce: A Definitive Biography* by Herbert Gorman. *Spectator*, 14 March 1941.
[56]Unsigned review, *Belfast Newsletter*, 8 March 1941, 6.

anchorage and contending manfully against his terrible ailment as he tried to make ends meet'. Joyce's 'chief claim to notoriety rests upon the authorship of one book which is, perhaps, the most foul and blasphemous in the English language'. Gorman is condemned for writing 'in the true tradition of the Joyce school' and for adopting 'the sneering tone towards Ireland and its "priest-ridden and priest-directed civilisation"'. His 'dreary book [...] is not one fit for general circulation in Ireland'.[57]

Gorman, rather than Joyce, was panned in *The Dublin Magazine* by the recently appointed District Justice (and playwright) Donagh MacDonagh, who believed that writing a biography of Joyce was an unforgiving task since it had already been done so well by the author himself. Gorman's book, however, 'is written with the most amazing lack of emotion or poetic perception. The person called Joyce with whom Mr. Gorman's book deals might have been anything, engineer, wine-merchant, baker; [...] there is no hint as to why the man who lived that life should have written *Ulysses*'.[58] Gorman does no better at the hands of Francis MacManus in the *Irish Press*. He grudgingly accepts Joyce's 'genius' only if:

> genius is the capacity for taking infinite pains [...] if genius is the ability to be possessed of one master-idea. [...] For his master-idea was this: that he, James Joyce, was a chosen one, the chosen one of modern literature. How arrogant he was has become a legend. How faithful he was to the master-idea, is part of Mr. Gorman's story.[59]

Once again Joyce's refusal of his religion is central: 'That master-idea itself conspired with other things to pervert the genius. Artistic perfection became his final beatitude. The artist in him devoured the man and the Catholic, and he became his own *lex eterna*.'[60] MacManus' ambivalence seeps through every sentence. He describes Joyce's 'prodigious memory' only to claim, in the next breath, that he was imaginatively imprisoned in Irish memory and failed to absorb what the continent had to offer:

> His writing became shut off against all his Continental experience, as if he had never left Dublin at all. Therein is a problem that the biographer does not tackle. But in hero-worship, there are no problems.

The *Irish Times* also attacked Gorman's 'negative and anæmic' portrayal of Joyce as 'a remote, colourless creature moving unobtrusively, sometimes

[57]N. N. 'A Biography of James Joyce', *II*, 29 April 1941, 2.
[58]Donagh MacDonagh, *Dublin Magazine*, vol. XCI, no. 4 (October–December 1941): 71.
[59]F. MacM. 'Portrait of an Irish Writer', *IP*, 15 April 1941.
[60]Ibid.

almost invisibly behind his vast undertaking'.[61] Gorman is guilty of adopting 'an adulatory and uncritical approach' and of a woeful lack of knowledge of the 'Irish Joyce': 'The reader is not given even a clue as to how such as the work of Yeats, or large-scale events like the 1916 rising, or the foundation of the Free State, reacted on the cunning exile.' While much of this criticism was valid, many of the lacunae would take decades to be adequately filled and these Irish critics were being unreasonable in their attacks especially in the light of the thin Irish contribution to scholarship in this area at the time. Essentially, they were choosing to shoot the messenger given that Joyce himself was now out of range.

If public praise of Joyce in Ireland was perhaps easier, if only slightly more forthcoming, after his death, so too was criticism from those who had known him and were now less reluctant to express their feelings. Just three days after Joyce died, R. M. Smyllie gave a lecture in which, somewhat tongue-in-cheek, he compared Joyce negatively with the Irish poet F. R. Higgins: 'Joyce, of course, was a world figure. Higgins was not – probably only because he died so young – but from a purely Irish point of view, the poetry of Higgins would be read, loved and recited in the cottages of the West of Ireland long after the scandals of "Ulysses" had been forgotten.'[62] Smyllie was not entirely off the mark with regard to the reception of *Ulysses* in Ireland in the decades that followed and the real object of his comment was not Joyce but the Irish cultural provincialism that was incapable of finding a space for a figure of Joyce's stature and complexity. Just a week later, Ewart Milne (1903–87) published a rather derivative (it borrows from Shakespeare, Yeats and Joyce himself), uneven but well-meant poem in memory of Joyce. Entitled 'Chamber Music', it compared the writer's 'greatness' with 'our evasion' and 'sickness' in failing to honour him and treat his works with the seriousness they merited. This took its place in the *Irish Times* among a series of memorials designed to humanize Joyce and show his worth to the nation. In 'Worth Half-a-dozen Legations', Kenneth Reddin stressed Joyce's independence and his attachment to Ireland before recalling an anecdote about how the artist, Patrick Tuohy, had advised him to turn up to Joyce's with 'a box of Olhausen's black puddings'. Joyce:

> stood aloof from other writers, having set them a new fashion in prose. He remained completely islanded in his own consciousness, or rather in that of the Dublin of thirty years ago.... One night dining in a restaurant – I think it was the Trianon – he took Tuohy and myself on (as the phrase is) in an effort of photographic memory. After twenty years' absence he challenged us, who had just left Dublin, to name the shops from Amiens Street Station to the Pillar. First one side, and then down the other. Mostly

---

[61]*IT*, 22 March 1941, 5.
[62]*IT*, 16 January 1941, 6.

he was three or four shops in front of us. When Tuohy and I left a gap, he filled it. When we named a new proprietor, he named, and regretted the passing of, the old.[63]

Joyce's worth to Ireland in its attempts to build an image abroad was frequently alluded to even in the 1940s. Even before his death, at a lecture on the early years of the modern Irish literary movement, chaired by Stephen Gwynn and delivered in the Country Shop by Maud Gonne MacBride, Patrick McCartan openly praised Joyce. McCartan, who had served as Sinn Féin's representative in the United States from 1919 until 1921, was an influential figure who won 20 per cent of the vote in the 1945 Irish presidential election.

He derided attempts to distinguish between Anglo-Irish literature and Irish literature by figures such as Daniel Corkery and members of the Gaelic League: 'These people decried partition, but were attempting to create a partition of the intellect in Ireland. Such men as Yeats, George Russell, James Joyce and G. B. Shaw had done more to make the name of Ireland respected in the American universities than all the Irish politicians – he would even say than the martyrs of Easter Week.'[64]

More praise for Joyce came in a letter to *The Irish Times* signed by a certain 'Ulysses' who recounted having travelled to Europe and 'met civilians in Italy, Austria, Switzerland and Yugo-Slavia' where he 'found among them an almost total ignorance of the names that loom so large in this country, even that of W. B. Yeats'. On mentioning Joyce's name, however, 'there was very often an immediate and enthusiastic response'. He went on to ask: 'Is it not time for Irishmen to join the rest of Europe in acclaiming the genius of this great Irish writer? Is Yeats to be the only figure on the upper slopes of our national Parnassus?'[65] A letter from Miceal Costello to the same paper in August 1941 appealed for a proper Joyce memorial:

> As Leopold Bloom might soliloquise:
> ... dead six months now. Genius I believe. Dublin centre of his universe. I haven't heard. People always making up memorials to somebody. Still afraid of him. Prophet never accepted. Pity.
> Or, to put it bluntly –
> Isn't it about time for a memorial to the incomparable James Joyce?[66]

These calls for a proper appreciation of Joyce represented a minority view. At the same time as Joyce supporters emerged, others, such as Frank O'Connor,

---

[63]Kenneth Reddin, 'Worth Half-a-dozen Legations', *IT*, 14 January 1941, 6.
[64]'"Irish Language Will Not Survive" Defence of Anglo-Irish', *IT*, 13 December 1940, 6.
[65]'Yeats and Joyce', Letter signed by 'Ulysses' to *IT*, 30 August 1946.
[66]Letter from Miceal Costello, *IT*, 9 August 1941, 3. Costello was listed among the attendees at the Bloomsday celebrations at the Tower in Sandycove in 1962.

offered more severe public judgement following his passing. In his 'James Joyce: A Post-mortem' in *The Bell*, O'Connor opens rather ungraciously with the words: 'I think I almost said "Thank God" when Joyce died'[67] and his intent appears to have been more to bury than to praise. He sought to qualify A. E.'s very early assertion that Joyce did not have genius: 'Because genius is something native, and everything Joyce created was created by sheer force of will.' He denied that Joyce had any originality: 'Joyce's writing has all the virtues of a disciple of Flaubert; it is exact, appropriate and detached.'[68] But he also has his weaknesses: 'To be absolutely faithful to what one sees and hears and not to speculate on what may lie behind it, for fear of indulging in one's own emotionalism, is a creed that produces obvious limitations.' At times – and the example he gives is 'Grace' – Joyce's conversations cease 'to give the impression of conversation at all [...] it is conversation without spontaneity, without lyric or dramatic impulse [...] it is not dialogue but mimicry'.[69] Joyce is too 'withdrawn' from his work, 'what he gives us for style is a clever imitation of another man's work, and what passes for conversation is little better than parody'.[70] *Ulysses* suffers from being 'made arbitrarily to fit into the framework of *The Odyssey*' and its organization is 'too arbitrary, pedantic and abstract':

> Almost every serious critic of Joyce has felt and said the same things about *Ulysses*: that it is the greatest book of our time, and at the same time that it isn't a great book at all; that it is on the scale of the Divine Comedy but that personally one prefers a few pages of George Moore. It is hard to define the sense of discomfort. For myself – and I am a hero-worshipper – the discomfort comes from a strong sense of artistic failure.[71]

Almost two decades later, O'Connor recorded a lecture on Joyce for Folkways records. Thomas Lask in the *New York Times* seemed genuinely shocked at its negativity. His review article opened: 'The vendetta that Frank O'Connor is carrying on with the shade of James Joyce has now spread to another front.' O'Connor is accused of reading Joyce's output 'as a progress to obscurity' and his basic point seems to have been that Joyce 'managed to hoodwink all those who have devoted themselves to his books'. Lask concludes: 'James Joyce by Frank O'Connor does nothing for either man.'[72] O'Connor's vehement dismissal of Joyce can only be explained in terms of his own artistic agenda and his desire to emerge from Joyce's shadow but

---

[67]Frank O'Connor, 'James Joyce: A Post-Mortem', *The Bell*, vol. 5, no. 5 (February 1943): 363.
[68]Ibid., 364.
[69]Ibid., 365.
[70]Ibid., 366.
[71]Ibid., 369–70.
[72]Thomas Lask, 'James Joyce Criticized by O'Connor', *New York Times*, 26 April 1959, X15.

both he and Seán O'Faoláin felt somewhat stymied because Joyce brought
the narrative forms that were their bread and butter to a culmination point
only to then undermine them in his later fiction.

That there was a negative consensus towards Joyce was confirmed by the
American critic, S. L. Goldberg, author of *The Classical Temper*, who claimed
that most Irish critics saw '*Ulysses* as an elaborate joke'. As an exception,
Goldberg singled out *Three Great Irishmen* (1953) by Arland Ussher
(1899–1980), which contained 'a lively essay on Joyce [...] of a somewhat
different calibre'.[73] The original articles that made up what Ussher himself
later called his 'somewhat wild and undocumented book'[74] were published
in *The Dublin Magazine* almost ten years earlier in 1945. A philosopher, art
critic and Gaelic scholar, Ussher offers thoughtful comments on Joyce and
on 'the Joyce-cult' while at the same time capturing well the critical moment
in which he is writing:

> James Joyce presents the paradox of an experimenter in form whose
> material is as local and ancestral as Glasnevin Cemetery. Thirty years
> ago, to praise James Joyce was an act of some daring; today it needs an
> almost equal daring to criticize him. For my part, I seem compelled to
> commit both of these solecisms.

In his preface, he states his belief that one cannot 'fully comprehend either
Joyce's achievement or his limitations without having some acquaintance
with the Irish character, and even with that character as reflected in
Gaelic literature'. Joyce 'is the first Irishman of genius (as distinct from
the descendants of the Planters) who has attained to complete expression
in English prose. [...] Joyce was an Irish literary technician who found it
expedient to work abroad'.[75] Joyce should be read as 'a great humorous
writer' but 'Catholic Ireland, by and large, has not yet heard of her
greatest son – or heard of him only as a squalid expatriate, who wrote
some blackguardly books in Paris, calling for immediate suppression by the
authorities'.[76] He counters the 'ingenious school which believes that Joyce
dedicated his industrious life to the – doubtless delightful – task of hoaxing
the public'[77] but thinks too much stress has been placed on the Homeric
parallels in *Ulysses*, arguing that its chief qualities 'are the un-Homeric ones

[73]S. L. Goldberg, *The Classical Temper: A Study of James Joyce's 'Ulysses'* (London: Chatto & Windus, 1961), 21, 316.
[74]Quoted in Willis E. McNelly, 'Twenty Years in Search of a Footnote', *JJQ*, vol. 9, no. 4 (Summer 1972): 452–60, 454.
[75]Arland Ussher, *Three Great Irishmen, Shaw, Yeats, Joyce* (New York: The Devin-Adair Company, 1953), 9–10.
[76]Ibid., 119.
[77]Ibid., 10.

of urbanism and urbanity. *Ulysses* is the great book of the town – the modern epic of Everyman: the better title for it would have been Bloomsday'.[78] His early description of Joyce as 'a dissident disciple of the Master [Yeats]'[79] was pioneering:

> Joyce, in the eighteen episodes of *Ulysses*, found a handy framework for diurnal and nocturnal experience, as Yeats in the twenty-eight moon-Phases (which have also their analogue in the twenty-eight schoolmisses of *Finnegans Wake*) found a natural setting for human types, for both the two Celts – obsessed, like John Scotus, with circles – had caught a Vesuvian spark from the proto-Hegelian Neapolitan, Vico.

Joyce is 'Ireland's first great native writer – her Dante or her Chaucer', expressing not only his own age but also 'those buried ages' and achieving a 'great collective Yeatsian "dreaming back"'.[80]

In a very different tone, Myles na gCopaleen's thrice-weekly 'Cruiskeen Lawn' column offered ongoing reflection on Joyce and his work and alternated between hostility and praise. O'Nolan enjoyed nothing more than having a go at American Joyceans – so much so that he occasionally fell into error in doing so. It was almost as if Joyce critics, by definition, were all American or should have been. Even Trinity graduate Vivian Mercier gets tarred with this brush in a review of a book about Joyce 'to be published soon in America':

> Joyce, it seems, had a hand in the Koran. Ah yes. He also did the Aeneid, the Bhagavat-Ghita, most of Dante's stuff, King Lear, all the quartets of Beethoven as well as a few things of Seumas's. (There's not a word, however, about him founding the Mount Street Club, the Hammond Lane Foundry and the old Theatre Royal! Or about doing the frescoes in my study in Santry!) The book is published as far as I can make out by two Americans Mr. Seon Givens and Mr. Vivien Mercier and it's called *JAMES JOYCE: Two Decades of Criticism.*[81]

Myles' frequent references to Joyce would have had the effect of familiarizing readers with his work and of taking him down from his pedestal. By now it was possible for a conservative figure, like Abbey Director, Ernest Blythe, to defend Joyce's work in an address to the Literary and Historical Society at University College Dublin:

[78]Ibid., 120.
[79]Ibid., 126.
[80]Ibid., 121, 127.
[81]Myles na gCopaleen, 'Cruiskeen Lawn', *IT*, 18 August 1948, 4.

Replying to a speaker who had described Joyce's *Ulysses* as pornographic, Mr. Blythe described the work as an extremely acute and penetrating psychological analysis. 'I do not see any reason why it should be banned or stopped. It is not pornographic.'[82]

However, it remained difficult to buy or borrow *Ulysses*. John Jordan described how he went into the National Library in Dublin in 1946, aged sixteen, and asked to read *Ulysses* but the librarian refused his request. He managed to borrow the book the following year from Lady Longford 'who lived around the corner'. He subsequently read it during his final year of school along with his friends, Donal O'Farrell and the future painter, Patrick Swift. In his own words, the 'imaginative engulfment of *Ulysses* had been well and truly initiated'.[83]

Some good news for Joyce's long-term reputation in Ireland came in 1947 with the announcement that Paul Léon had gifted an important collection of Joyce materials to the National Library of Ireland through Count O'Kelly de Gallagh, former Irish minister in Paris. Noting that the 'author of *Ulysses* and *The Portrait of the Artist* bestrides contemporary letters like a colossus', *The Irish Times* grandly expressed the 'hope that the years will see the development of a "Joyce collection" in order to refute the charge that Ireland often fails to acknowledge her most brilliant children. Cosmic imaginations deserve, at least, the tribute of a display-case in the National Museum'.[84] Although it would take more than half a century to be realized, this important gift was the start of the National Library's major Joyce collection.

If the 1940s opened in Ireland with the elevation of John Charles McQuaid to the position of Archbishop of Dublin, the decade drew to a close with a change of government, which saw John A. Costello becoming Taoiseach. When the national coalition came to power in February 1948, the new Taoiseach sent a telegram to Pope Pius XII expressing the wish 'to repose at the feet of Your Holiness the assurance of our filial loyalty and our devotion to your August Person, as well as our firm resolve to be guided in all our work by the teaching of Christ, and to strive for the attainment of social order in Ireland based on Christian principles'. Even if the government had changed, the Catholic emphasis was as intense as ever, and in such a scenario it was clear that Joyce and *Ulysses* would continue to find space only in the literary margins of society.

Proof of this was evident in the decision not to participate at the James Joyce Exhibition held in Paris in 1949 at La Hune gallery on the Boulevard

---

[82]'Abbey Director Explains Why Gaelic Plays Fail', *IT*, 30 October 1944, 1.

[83]John Jordan, 'Joyce without Fears: A Personal Journey', in Hugh McFadden, ed., *Crystal Clear: The Selected Prose of John Jordan* (Dublin: Lilliput Press, 2006), 43.

[84]'Treasure Trove', *IT*, 23 August 1947, 7.

Saint-Germain. This was an exhibition and an auction of the books, manuscripts and furniture from Joyce's Paris flat, together with part of Sylvia Beach's archive. It was organized principally by Maria Jolas to raise money for Nora. It presented the Irish government with a unique opportunity to acquire significant Joyce materials for the National Library (which were instead bought by the University of Buffalo) or at least to offer moral support but it chose to do neither. Madame Jolas wrote to *The Irish Times* expressing her surprise at reading that '"Mr. Sean MacBride, Minister for External Affairs, is a great admirer of *Ulysses*". […] For, however great an admirer of *Ulysses* Mr. MacBride may be, there would appear to be an unwritten law which forbids official expression of his admiration'. She recounted how an invitation asking him to 'do us the very great honour of inaugurating it, or in any case grant us his distinguished patronage,' had elicited, 'a fortnight later, the brief statement from a private secretary that the Minister "regretted very much that he would be unable to open the exhibition to James Joyce"'.[85] A similar letter to the Irish ambassador in Paris received no reply. This left the path open for the British Minister Plenipotentiary in Paris to step in as patron. Arthur Power later blamed 'the Catholic Church's intellectual domination and preponderating influence' for the refusal of the Minister to support the exhibition.[86]

Madame Jolas criticized 'official Irish reticence towards this illustrious son' and recalled how a letter from John J. Slocum, president of the James Joyce Society in New York 'to the President of Eire on the subject of a possible transfer of Joyce's remains to Irish soil', had received no reply. Jolas wondered how long Joyce would have to remain in exile and closed by quoting the positive assessment of him by the *Osservatore Romano*,[87] which had left Joyce, in the words of his friend, Nino Franck, 'full of joy'.[88] Slocum, an American diplomat and scholar, met Nora and formed the view that 'Mrs Joyce will never be happy until his body is brought back to Ireland. She is a devout Catholic and feels that his body should rest in the land of his fathers'. While this interpretation does not correspond with other views of Nora's position with regard to Joyce or Catholicism, it spurred Slocum to seek the repatriation of Joyce's remains (following the return of Yeats' body in September 1948). In his letter to President Sean T. O'Kelly in 1948, he took the repatriation of Yeats' remains as a precedent and asked:

> if it is unreasonable to think that James Joyce might be so honoured someday, and that in so honouring him, his country would be honouring

---

[85]Maria Jolas, 'Letter to the Editor', *IT*, 22 November 1949, 5.

[86]*IT*, 11 January 1950, 5.

[87]'Letteratura Irlandese contemporanea', *L'Osservatore Romano*, 20 October 1937, 3. The article was written by E. R. (Monsignor Ennio Francia). This had already been quoted by Jolas' husband, Eugene, in an article entitled 'Homage to the Mythmaker', *transition*, 1938, 169–75.

[88]W. R. Rodgers, 'Portrait of James Joyce', 12.

itself. [...] If you were to express to me even a belief that such a return of his body to Ireland was possible, I think that I could start his friends in Zurich, in Paris, in London, in New York and even in Dublin, working on it wholeheartedly.

Slocum pointed out that 'the Church was the fount of his inspiration, the mould in which his genius was formed' and, referring to *L'Osservatore Romano*'s positive article, argued that 'there is sufficient evidence that the Church itself recognises his contribution to the tradition of Catholic letters'. Anthony Jordan continues the story:

> Slocum's letter to O'Kelly was dealt with by Valentin Iremonger, private secretary to Seán MacBride, de Valera's successor as minister for external affairs. He spent several months challenging Slocum's reading of *L'Osservatore Romano*. He got the Irish ambassador to Italy, Michael MacWhite, to locate the article and interview its author. He wrote to Patrick Lynch, private secretary to Taoiseach John A Costello, that the article could hardly be construed as 'evidence that the Church itself recognises Joyce's contribution to the tradition of Catholic letters'. Slocum never got a reply to his letter, and a note made at the Department of the Taoiseach on July 15th, 1949, recorded that no action was to be taken.[89]

Even if Irish officialdom continued to ignore Joyce, the second half of the 1940s did see the scattered beginnings of a local Joyce industry, albeit a cottage industry that engaged with his works part-time and sometimes under cover. They were, in Stanislaus Joyce's description 'lone wolves', sometimes with connections to the continent.[90] Perhaps the most significant figure to emerge was John Garvin, a prominent civil servant who, using the pseudonym 'Andrew Cass', announced himself on the scene in a long article entitled 'Sprakin Sea Djoytsch'.[91] This was, for the most part, a useful introduction to *Finnegans Wake*, the work of 'a revolutionary artist' and is the start of Garvin's work of identifying Joyce's Irish sources (Anglo-Irish literature, from 'Irish history or current Irish life'). He insists that an understanding of Joyce's 'vicious circles' is needed in order to grasp 'the mechanism behind the lay-out of his book', and talks of 'a succession of waves in the line of time [...] the nature and form of Joyce's own thought exemplify the disintegration which characterises a civilisation in the trough of one of these waves'. He situates the *Wake* just before the

---

[89]Anthony J. Jordan, 'Remembering James Joyce, 77 Years to the Day after His Death', *IT*, 13 January 2018. https://www.irishtimes.com/culture/books/remembering-james-joyce-77-years-to-the-day-after-his-death-1.3347837.

[90]Stanislaus Joyce, 'Joyce's Dublin', 107.

[91]Andrew Cass, 'Sprakin Sea Djoytsch', *IT*, 26 April 1947, 7.

'Hitlerian deluge' and sees the novel as 'the Wake of the West', written by a Joyce who is 'the last word on our history and literature'. After him there will only be 'the deluge'. Joyce's novel is 'an apposite commentary on the world which stopped in 1939', one in which 'the historic emotions of the exhausted continent are recollected in sleeping senility'. Garvin points to the self-reflexivity of *Finnegans Wake*, to how the text itself helps to orient the reader who should possess 'an aptitude for simultaneous absorption of multiple references comparable to the countinghouse clerk's ability to add a column of several digits in one tot'. At the same time, he believes that the text 'can also be absorbed, like music, without precise knowledge of the underlying themes'. Garvin also takes aim at Joyce for having produced '626 pages of what looked like gibberish', for having 'done nothing [...] to keep the public in touch with him' and for expecting 'the world in general, and Ireland in particular, to acclaim his achievement'. He sees Joyce as an 'expatriate and apostate' and argues that 'his forsaken country and his lost creed remained the ineluctable basis of all Joyce's cosmic symbolism. The pilgrim of eternity expounds universality with a Dublin accent'. Betraying a hostile attitude towards Joyce as a representative of the Irish diaspora, Garvin describes *Finnegans Wake* as 'the smile-and-tear fantasy of an Irish emigrant' bearing 'a good deal of the stage-Irish unreality which most émigrés develop'. Joyce's 'self-portraits [...] give the impression of an intellectual Paddy droning his inexplicable ranns by the waters of babylong, supping somewhat stronger waters to cheer him in his exile... nursing various personal ills and grievances, but ever with an eagle eye on Skibbereen'. Joyce's failure was that he 'remained imprisoned in the Chamber of Horrors which he had created for himself in his youth [...] Instead of the cosmopolitan which he hoped to become "out in Europe," he remained merely an Irish Exile' and *Finnegans Wake* became more than anything else, 'his nostalgic dream' of his lost home. Joyce's Irishness is criticized as a sign of his failure to fully get away and immerse himself in Europe: 'Joyce failed to secure cosmopolitan emancipation from what he regarded as the nationalistic shackles of his youth.' As a result, 'the ghost of Ireland dogged him wherever he went', 'his preoccupation with things Irish was [...] nurtured and exaggerated to the point of fantastic unreality by his exile'. The later Joyce 'regretted the hasty decision of his youth' to become a 'farsoonerite' but his arrogance and intellectual isolation prohibited him from 'effecting a reconciliation, but it is obvious that he would have welcomed an invitation from his compatriots, that his ears, eyes of his darkness, harkened for the strains of "Come Back to Erin."' Joyce's failure to return to dwell among the Irish was due to his 'satanic pride' and to 'mere embarrassment, the "shame" that places a psychological barrier between "brothers"'. The close of *Finnegans Wake* is read as a straightforward depiction of Joyce's unbreakable exile. It is Joyce himself who is 'sighing wearily in the accents of Anna Livia': 'Lonely in my loneliness. For all their faults. I am passing out. O bitter ending! I'll slip away before they're up. They'll never see. Nor know. Nor miss me' (*FW* 627, 34–6).

What is surprising about this conclusion is its failure to take into consideration what might have greeted Joyce had he actually decided to return home. It is hard to imagine as disruptive a figure as Joyce being given a heroic or a harmonious welcome. If a declared Joyce fan like Garvin could still, in 1947, refer to his 'satanic pride', what might Joyce have expected from the less enlightened? Similar negativity was stigmatized by L. A. G. Strong when, in 1949, he was 'invited to lecture to the Royal Dublin Society' and proposed to speak on Joyce, only to be 'informed in tones of dignified reproach that such a subject would not be acceptable to the members'.[92] When Kees Van Hook described Joyce in 1949 as 'the greatest writer that ever came out of Ireland [...] the most universal mind since Dante' and claimed that Joyce exercised 'a world influence on letters, second to none in our time',[93] this provoked a backlash in the letters pages of the *Irish Times* in which Joyce was accused of what was, by now, a familiar litany of 'sins': 'wilful obscurity, deliberate filth, continual blasphemy, pretension and affectation, senseless tampering with the English language, inaccuracy in unfolding Dublin life, and finally, plain dullness and perhaps madness itself'.[94] Calls were made for a 'movement to "debunk" Joyce and all his works'.[95] One correspondent, 'D. R.', bearing a rather large chip on his shoulder, admitted to having 'little Latin and less Greek' and wrote that he had 'heard most of the highbrow arguments' from 'the favoured few [...] who know better' and 'have swooned in ecstasy when "Eureka" through the smoke they detect a classical allusion [...] For the rest of us – the great illiterate mob – how can we expect to understand and appreciate this delicate work of art? Better leave it alone'.[96] The letter concluded in capitals: 'JOYCE WAS A LUNATIC' followed by the qualification, 'But, then, I am an ignoramus'. Another letter writer, A. Wilhelmina Wilson, suggested that 'the Civic Guards be instructed to seize as many copies of these noxious books as possible and burn them in some public space'. 'The Third Reich', she continued, 'dealt with unsuitable literature in this way with excellent results'. Not all respondents got the sarcasm. In any case, there would have been no need for mass burnings of *Ulysses* because copies continued to be thin on the ground if the testimony of one 'Young Irishman' in another letter was representative. He described calling at the County Library in Dundalk. On asking for a copy, he was told that none of Joyce's books were kept in the library 'as the head librarian did

---

[92]L. A. G. Strong, *The Sacred River: An Approach to James Joyce* (London: Theodore Brun, 1949), 13.

[93]Kees Van Hoek, 'Letter to the Editor', *IT*, 2 December 1949, 5.

[94]Douglas U. Wilson, 'Letter to the Editor', *IT*, 29 November 1949, 5. Wilson's letter forcefully counters these charges.

[95]T. C. P., 'Letter to the Editor', *IT*, 25 November 1949, 5.

[96]*IT*, 1 December 1949, 5.

not think they were suitable'.[97] He wondered if this was the case elsewhere in the country and anecdotal evidence would suggest that it was. Another letter writer worried that his daughter had 'overheard a young man in a library in Dublin asking if they had Joyce's *Ulysses* in stock'.[98] The answer was not given but was presumably negative and drew a brief comment in Latin 'O sancta simplicitas'. Eventually Oscar Love, aka Brian O'Nolan, weighed in:

> It is unfortunate that there should be so many expecting from modern writers more elegance and purity than the great public can digest in this age of bustle. How many queues there are at cinemas to view scenes of grossness, brutality and falsehood! How many are there outside city churches waiting to dwell on portrayals of present-day life and the shocking evils which are continually horrifying us?[99]

He signed off by suggesting that 'the present bitter critics of James Joyce' read *Chamber Music*. The lines he quotes draw attention to hypocrisy and denial, twin pillars of so many elements of Irish society at the time:

> Be not sad because all men
> Prefer a lying clamour before you.
> Proudly answer to their tears
> As they deny, deny.

[97]*IT*, 7 December 1949, 5.
[98]*IT*, 16 December 1949, 5
[99]*IT*, 8 December 1949, 7.

CHAPTER SIX

The fiftieth anniversary of Bloomsday: Inventing a tradition

Familiar problems persisted in the 1950s in the new Republic of Ireland (which had replaced Eire or the Free State in 1949). It was a decade of stagnation in which the still mostly rural economy struggled to provide adequate employment, and incomes rose far more slowly than in other European countries. For many, the only route to a steady job was across the sea to Britain. With approximately half a million people emigrating, Ireland (with East Germany) was the only country in Europe to see its population decline. The Catholic Church's dominance continued and was instrumental in the collapse of the Inter-Party government following Dr Noel Browne's resignation as Minister for Health. This was after his controversial Mother-and-Child scheme lost both Cabinet and party support following the Catholic hierarchy's condemnation of it as contrary to moral law. Browne had proposed to introduce free maternity care for mothers and free healthcare for children but the Church felt that this was in direct opposition to the rights of the family. *The Irish Times* published the correspondence on the issue between Browne and the Irish bishops and concluded in an editorial: 'The most serious revelation, however, is that the Roman Catholic Church would seem to be the effective government of this country.' The Church's considerable victory was enabled by opposition to Browne's proposal within what Joseph Walshe, Ireland's first ambassador to the Holy See and former secretary general of the Department of Foreign affairs, proudly called 'the most Catholic Government in the whole world'[1] and by the hostility of the

---

[1] Quoted in Dermot Keogh, *Ireland and the Vatican: The Politics and Diplomacy of Church-State Relations, 1922–1960* (Cork: Cork University Press, 1995), 241.

Irish Medical Association. However, as the following decades came to show, it turned out to be pyrrhic. In the short term, the subsequent 1951 general election saw Fianna Fáil scrape back into power and de Valera, partly because of his close friendship with McQuaid, would continue to be better able at avoiding conflict with the hierarchy than his predecessor, the equally devout John A. Costello.

The censorship regime, meanwhile, continued unabated. In a single year – 1951 – the Censorship of Publications Board banned 539 of the 717 books that it examined. The value of Irish literature as a force for a small young country attempting to make an impact in the wider world was lost on successive governments partly because the writers were at odds with the dominant Catholic ethos. Outspoken criticism of the Church was not tolerated and Joyce still came in for attack from religious quarters. In 1953, the *Redemptorist Record* published an unrelentingly negative article about 'the tragedy of James Joyce' entitled 'Dark Angel'. Joyce, according to H. A. McHugh CSSR, 'had chosen, like Lucifer, "to err, to fall, to triumph." Beauty would be his god'. Even as a young boy, Joyce 'had to be unusual even in evil'. He was a writer endlessly looking backwards: 'The burden of his writing is memories.' Having left Dublin 'for the next thirty-seven years his literary work went on. In sum it is not great. In quality it is unequal and already badly dated'. Joyce never lived up to his own high aspirations and 'it was his torment that he never got beyond being a bad Catholic'. He is compared to John of the Cross who 'in the winepress of Christ [...] was crushed into immortal radiance'. Joyce, 'the tall slight boy', who hoped '"to live, to err, to fall, to triumph,"' was 'crushed into proud and challenging evil. He would be a dark angel. There is no explaining him unless as the mystic who failed'. Joyce might have been another St John; instead, he chose to live 'within himself' and found 'like Lucifer, an emptiness of God. Over his pages the pain of loss rages in wild blasphemy, in frenzied obscenity and a chaos of speech. A human soul aware of its thirst for the Infinite expresses in prose a long-drawn sob of anguish that may become everlasting'.[2]

In the light of such views, it is not surprising that Stanislaus Joyce's 1950 review of Patricia Hutchins' *James Joyce's Dublin* for *Irish Writing* ran into trouble. On receiving Stannie's draft, the editor, David Marcus, wrote to tell him that 'greatly to our regret', they felt they could not publish it without omitting the following sentence:

> Through the spy-hole of the confessional, it (the Catholic Church) comes – like the totalitarian systems, which, in fact are modelled on it, and like them in the name of an inhuman ideology – between parents and children, between lover and sweetheart, between man and wife, between friend

[2]H. A. McHugh, CSSR, DCL, 'Dark Angel The Tragedy of James Joyce', *The Redemptorist Record*, (July–August 1953): 98–100.

and friend, with this only difference that totalitarian systems, being new, deem it wiser to exert their influence on the young.[3]

Marcus was rightly worried about a backlash if he published such an open attack on the Church: 'Our fear is publishing such an expression would be that it would alienate such a large section of our readers as to cause a complete fall in circulation and so, perhaps, terminate our existence.' Stanislaus refused to omit the reference to the Church and published the review in the *Partisan Review*, including, in a footnote, his correspondence with Marcus.

Yet, for all the bleakness, the 1950s was also decade of renewed creativity, much of which took aim at the institutionalized pieties of the Irish State. Many creative talents emerged or consolidated their reputations, often looking to Joyce for inspiration, although his legacy was never simple or straightforward and was often felt more as a burden than as an enabling force. The material Joyce heritage in the country grew, not through State intervention but through the generosity of his former friends and supporters. Foremost among them was Harriet Shaw Weaver. She initially intended to donate the manuscript of *Finnegans Wake* to the National Library of Ireland but was strongly discouraged from doing so by Nora, who resented the Irish government's earlier refusal to repatriate Joyce's remains. Irish Minister for External Affairs, Sean MacBride, attempted to hit all the right notes in a letter to Nora on 12 July 1950:

> I should like you to know that I personally and I am sure my colleagues in the Irish Government, as well as the Library itself, are deeply sensitive of how desirable it is from the nation's point of view that the manuscript of this great work should be deposited in your husband's native city. We are proud that James Joyce, one of the greatest Europeans of his time, was also a son of Ireland and we feel that the presence in the Library of the manuscript of [what] may be his greatest work would be a fitting commemoration of that fact.[4]

Nora was unmoved and Miss Weaver felt she had to follow her wishes and donated the *Finnegans Wake* manuscript to the British Museum. She compensated by gifting the manuscript of *A Portrait of the Artist as a Young Man* to the National Library along with other material that the Joyce family was not aware of including Lucia Joyce's *A Chaucer ABC*. Richard Hayes, director of the library, wrote to her on 27 June 1951 expressing gratitude for 'the wonderful support you gave for so many years to Mr Joyce's work

[3]Stanislaus Joyce, 'Joyce's Dublin', 103.
[4]Anthony Jordan, 'Remembering James Joyce, 77 Years to the Day after His Death', *IT*, 13 January 2018, 148.

and Ireland is under a very great debt to you for all that. The Joyce family seems determined that we shall have as little as possible; why I do not know. You must do what you think is best. I wonder what Joyce himself would have wished'.[5] The material was handed over in July 1951 in a ceremony at the Irish Embassy in London hosted by Ambassador F. H. (Freddy) Boland, who had known Joyce from his time in the Paris legation. Miss Weaver was accompanied by the Irish Joyce scholar, Patricia Hutchins. Clearly Boland's diplomatic skills were considerable as Miss Weaver agreed to further donate a Joyce portrait by Wyndham Lewis to the National Gallery of Ireland and to gift the very first copy of *Ulysses* (with the inscription: 'To Harriet Weaver in token of gratitude – James Joyce – Paris 12 February 1922') to the National Library on Saint Patrick's Day, 1952. It was a considerable coup and currently is today the prize exhibit at MoLI, the Museum of Literature Ireland at Newman House.

While enlightened public servants, like Boland and Richard Hayes, were fully aware of Joyce's importance, public representatives lagged behind. Occasionally, an elected representative, such as W. B. Stanford, Regius Professor of Greek at Trinity College Dublin and long-serving member of the Irish Senate, would make Joyce's case in public debate. But Stanford wasn't just any public representative. He was already publishing internationally on Joyce's use of Homer's *Odyssey*[6] and was, in a way, the country's first academic Joyce scholar (even if Joyce was only one string on his considerable intellectual bow). During a reading of a 1949 Local Government Bill, Stanford called on the government and on his fellow senators to think of the value of Ireland's great writers, such as Swift and Thomas Moore, who 'did more to win friends for Ireland's nationhood than any manufacturer or any farmer':

The resources of modern Ireland are far better known in Egypt or Peru for the writings of W. B. Yeats and James Joyce than for our stock exchange or our turf development schemes. That, I think, is an incontrovertible fact. Take the Shannon scheme of which we all think so highly [...] It is a pigmy scheme amongst the hydro-electrical schemes of Europe. But Jonathan Swift is no pigmy in any literature. James Joyce and W. B. Yeats are giants in the literature of the world. There is a difference. Canada will always produce better wheat than we can produce. Denmark will always produce as good butter and eggs. But what Canadian or Danish name, with the possible exception of Hans Andersen, can compare with the great literary and artistic names we can mention. There is none.[7]

---

[5]Cited in Anthony Jordan, 'The English Woman Who Bankrolled James Joyce', *IT*, 29 November 2019.   https://www.irishtimes.com/culture/books/the-english-woman-who-bankrolled-james-joyce-1.4098075.
[6]See, for example, W. B. Stanford, 'Ulyssean Qualities in Joyce's Leopold Bloom', *Comparative Literature*, vol. 5, no. 2 (Spring, 1953): 125–36.
[7]https://www.oireachtas.ie/en/debates/debate/seanad/1950-07-20/7/.

Stanford's speech was reported verbatim by Myles na gCopaleen in his *Irish Times* column on 31 July.[8] Although this message would gradually sink in over the next few decades, all too often the names of Joyce and Yeats were exploited by officialdom without any adequate investment being made in an infrastructure capable of honouring and remembering them. Work in that direction would be done, for several decades to come, by their fellow writers and enthusiasts rather than by the institutions of the State.

One among them was Belfast broadcaster and poet, W. R. (Bertie) Rodgers, who wrote and made a very substantial two-part radio documentary on Joyce in the 1950s for the BBC's Third Programme as one of his well-regarded Irish Literary Portraits programme. He spliced together a rich range of interviews with Stanislaus Joyce, and with his sisters, Eva and Eileen. Important friends and supporters, including C. P. Curran, Frank Budgen, Harriet Weaver, Sylvia Beach, Adrienne Monnier, Carola Giedion, Nino Franck, Madame Léon, Madame Jolas, Arthur Power, Niall Sheridan, along with other less supportive voices, such as those of Oliver St John Gogarty and Frank O'Connor, fleshed out Joyce's life and literary achievements. Although it was followed with interest in Ireland, Patrick Kavanagh took vituperative exception to this broadcast and attacked Rodgers in what Bruce Stewart has termed his 'spiteful poem'[9] 'Who killed James Joyce?' which, aping 'Who Killed Cock Robin?', took aim not solely at Bertie Rodgers but at the academic Joyce industry. Years later Brendan Kennelly applauded this 'successful demolition of all those pompous, solemn academics whose idea of happiness is the discovery of some trivial allusion in *Ulysses* or *Finnegans Wake*'.[10] The poem suggests that 'mighty Ulysses' was slain and that the weapon used 'was a Harvard thesis'.[11] But Rodgers' 'broadcast Symposium' also played its part:

> Who carried the coffin out?
> Six Dublin codgers
> Led into Langham Place
> Who said the burial prayers? –
> Please do not hurt me –
> Joyce was no Protestant,
> Surely not Bertie?[12]

The implication was that Joyce was being superficially commemorated and not read with appropriate critical seriousness but Kavanagh's closing

---

[8]*IT*, 31 July 1950, 4.
[9]Bruce Stewart, 'Another Bash in the Tunnel: James Joyce and the Envoy', *Studies: An Irish Quarterly Review*, vol. 93, no. 370 (Summer 2004): 133–45, 139.
[10]Brendan Kennelly, 'Patrick Kavanagh' in *Ariel* (July 1970): 7–28, 20.
[11]Patrick Kavanagh, 'Who Killed James Joyce?' (1951) in John Ryan, ed., *A Bash in the Tunnel* (Brighton: Clifton Books, 1970) 51.
[12]Ibid.

sectarian jibe was not one of his finer moments. He appears to have
nurtured a particular animosity towards Rodgers, whom he described in
an unpublished article destined for *Kavanagh's Weekly*, as 'a remarkable
bucklepper [...] a word-weaver, a phrase-maker the equal of any Radio
Éireann writers'.[13]

Kavanagh's poem was part of the most concerted early Dublin response to
Joyce, the 1951 special issue of John Ryan's Irish literary periodical, *Envoy*,
which commemorated the tenth anniversary of Joyce's death with a series of
reflections on the writer by Irish literary figures. Ryan had founded *Envoy* just
two years earlier with Valentine Iremonger, a poet and then private secretary
to External Affairs Minister Seán McBride, so as to address the absence of a
'monthly magazine wholly devoted to literature and the arts', as they put it
in their opening editorial. The cast of contributors was drawn mostly from
the anti-conformist, bohemian crew that hung out with Ryan, mainly in
McDaid's in Harry Street. Collectively they sought to make *Envoy* into a
critical forum for Irish and international writing while transferring the spirit
of their McDaid's conversations into print. The Joyce issue of *Envoy* was, in
Terence Brown's words, the 'first Irish periodical to attempt a full-scale critical
response to Joyce's work since the *Irish Statesman* ceased publication'.[14] An
expanded version, entitled *A Bash in the Tunnel*, was published in 1970.[15]
The original volume's mostly grudging tone was set by Brian O'Nolan's
'carelessly written'[16] title piece, 'A Bash in the Tunnel' (published under the
semi-pseudonym of Brian Nolan), which shows that his resentment at Joyce's
self-absorption, his exile, and at the astonishing self-belief that allowed him to
put his artistic mission at the centre of his entire life. In a mixture of defensive
posturing, faint praise and open disparagement, he also manages to celebrate
Joyce's humour and his linguistic playfulness, writing of 'the utterly ignored
fact that Joyce was among the most comic writers who have ever lived. Every
time I get influenza I read about the Citizen and his Dog; penicillin has nothing
on them'.[17] His description of how humour as 'the handmaid of sorrow and
fear, creeps out endlessly in all Joyce's work' and of how Joyce with 'laughs
[...] palliates the sense of doom that is the heritage of the Irish Catholic'[18] is a
description that perhaps better fits his own work. He concludes:

[13]The Peter and Patrick Kavanagh Archive, University College Dublin, Box Kav B I Vii.
[14]Brown, Terence. *Ireland: A Social and Cultural History, 1922 to the Present* (Ithaca and
London: Cornell University Press, 1985).
[15]John Ryan, Introduction to *A Bash in the Tunnel* (Brighton: Clifton Books, 1970). The new
contributions were by Patrick Boyle, Francis Harvey, Monk Gibbon, Aidan Higgins, John
Jordan, Benedict Kiely, J. B. Lyons, John Montague, Edna O'Brien, Eoin O'Mahony, Ulick
O'Connor, Bernard Share and there were reprints of earlier material by Samuel Beckett,
Thomas McGreevy, Stanislaus Joyce, Arthur Power and J. F. Byrne.
[16]Thomas Hogan, 'Joyce's Countrymen', *IT*, 21 April 1951, 6
[17]Myles na Gopaleen, 'J-Day', *IT*, 16 June, 1954.
[18]Brian Nolan, 'A Bash in the Tunnel' in John Ryan, ed. *A Bash in the Tunnel*, 20.

Perhaps the true fascination of Joyce lies in his secretiveness, his ambiguity (his polyguity, perhaps?), his leg-pulling, his dishonesties, his technical skill, his attraction for Americans. His works are a garden in which some of us may play. All that we can claim to know is merely a small bit of that garden. But at the end, Joyce will still be in his tunnel, unabashed.[19]

Monk Gibbon was far less positive and claimed that 'Joyce excites in some of us a fundamental antipathy, like that of a man who cannot stop telling us about the dog-dirt on his boots' and at times it seems hard to understand why this collective group even bothered.[20] In his diary contribution to the same volume, Kavanagh praises *Ulysses* as his 'second favourite bedside book', as 'a very funny book' but also 'a very wearying book'. His biographer confirms: 'It had been his book at breakfast for several years, propped on the table against his typewriter like an altar missal on a lectern, and he had read and reread the same comic chapters like a priest reading his breviary.'[21] Kavanagh claimed that 'the most outstanding quality in Joyce is his Catholicism or rather his anti-Protestantism. [...] His reason made him a bad Catholic, but whatever the defects of Catholicism, he saw that Protestantism was a compendium of all those defects'.[22] Kavanagh also contested Joyce's self-image as a martyr to the cause of art, writing that there 'was nothing in Joyce's life of noble self-sacrifice', rather he was a 'very clever cynical man', and, in 'the more violent parts of *Ulysses*', 'an unmannerly child enjoying destruction. Hate and pride'.[23] John Garvin was hardly any more positive. Writing about *Ulysses*, he claimed that 'its interminable trimmings and its stuffed Odysseus promoted from a short story to balance the pretentious epic of Telemachus, enabled Joyce to get off his chest a great deal of juvenile resentments and self-pity'. The lack of punctuation in 'Penelope' is 'a mere trick designed to hide the fact that a great deal of the alleged run-on thinking is in fact nothing more than a characteristic piece of pungent Joyce prose'.[24]

Denis Johnston's contribution, 'Short View of the Progress of Joyceanity', is a belated defence of 'Oliver St. John Gogarty's notorious tirades against Joyce in 1939 and 1941'.[25] Having poured scorn on the intensity of American Joyce scholarship, on a 'mass of misinformation provided by people like his brother Stanislaus, and by a biographer [Gorman] who do not wish to tell

[19]Ibid.
[20]Monk Gibbon, 'The Unraised Hat', in John Ryan, ed., *A Bash in the Tunnel*, 212.
[21]Antoinette Quinn, *Patrick Kavanagh: A Biography* (Dublin: Gill and Macmillan, 2001), 455.
[22]Patrick Kavanagh, 'Who Killed James Joyce?' 49.
[23]Ibid., 50–1.
[24]John Garvin, 'Childe Horrid's Pilgrimace', *Envoy* (April 1951), 22–3.
[25]Bruce Stewart, 'Another Bash in the Tunnel: James Joyce and the Envoy', 134.

us the whole story for reasons of good taste',[26] Johnston claims that Gogarty landed a blow for common sense by deriding the academic fixation with Joyce. He recalled the 'catastrophic' reaction to Gogarty's words: it was as if 'he had deliberately belched at mass'. By 1950, Gogarty was still calling America 'the chief infirmary for Joyceans'[27] and lamenting in *The Times Herald* (Dallas): 'This is a moment in the history of art where cross-word puzzles, detective stories and distortions take the place of literature and beauty. And when we consider that America is the original home of smoke signals, the popularity of Joyce here can be explained.' Gogarty continued to nurture old grudges describing himself as the 'writer of this little notice [...] once called "an accessory before the act"' of Joyce's *Ulysses*. The United States may be called with more justice 'an accessory after the act'. Gogarty questions 'the sanity' and 'the literacy of the Joyce enthusiast' and confesses to feeling 'anger' at the 'presumption' of those who 'set themselves up as Joyce guides [...] although they have never been to Dublin'. The 'Joyce fetish' is a reflection on 'the educational system of the present day that permits such a stampede from the touchstones and the standards of literature' and bemoans the pre-eminence of 'the bizarre instead of the beautiful, of disruption instead of construction, the scaffolding instead of the mansion. To the kindergarten with them all'.

The authors of the *Envoy* articles were, in the words of Thomas Hogan, a pseudonym used by the Irish diplomat, Thomas (Tommy) Woods, in the *Irish Times*: 'irritably repelled by the solemn and reverential approach of the latter-day American scholiast who rummages incessantly among the Joyce rubble, coming up now and then with a particularly mangled piece of old hat.'[28] For all the volume's gripes and limits, Hogan noted its significance on the basis 'that it gathers together a collection of serious Irish writing about Joyce, something that has hitherto been lacking (except, of course, as Mr. Montgomery mentions, in the essays of Mr. Beckett and Mr. McGreevy)'. In another *Irish Times* opinion piece, writing as 'Thersites', Woods took issue with articles by J. B. Priestley and Cyril Connolly in the *Sunday Times*. One of Priestley's criticisms of Joyce was that 'he did not influence directly scores of younger novelists'. Thersites can only think of Christopher Isherwood and Flann O'Brien. His counter-argument is

whatever Joyce's influence has been, it has not been manifested in the form of imitations of his work. [...] one could say very much the same thing about Proust [...] But just as there are no new *Finnegans Wakes*, so there have been no new *A la Recherche du Temps perdu*. [...] Joyce's value

[26]Denis Johnston, Progress of Joyceanity', *Envoy* (April 1951), 14.
[27]Oliver St John Gogarty, 'They Think They Know Joyce', *Saturday Review of Literature*, xxxiii (18 March 1950), 8–9, 36–7, reprinted in *CH* 1, 765.
[28]Thomas Hogan, 'Joyce's Countrymen', *IT*, 21 April 1951, 6.

is negative - like that of a scientist who carries out a series of experiments on a new drug which shows that it is of absolutely no value at all. Joyce has proved to be blind alleys what we rather thought would, in fact, be blind alleys. We are grateful to him for the proof, however. But his value is also positive.

He also disagrees with Priestley's final verdict that Joyce is not 'a master novelist at all' but 'a great eccentric comic poet in prose'. Priestley exemplifies the limit of

> an attitude towards literature which makes people wonder what is wrong with Joyce that he does not fit in with their creeds and categories instead of wondering what is wrong with their creeds and categories that Joyce does not fit in with them. 'Rules' obviously have a very different sense in literature from what they have in other branches of human life. A man who does not obey the rules in football or cricket is just a bad footballer or cricketer. But a man who disobeys the rules in literature may very well be a major writer, like James Joyce.[29]

One, who had few doubts about Joyce's status, was R. Shelton Scholefield or better the 'decent Dublinman called Sam Suttle',[30] who published a letter in the *Irish Times* in April 1951 proposing the foundation of a James Joyce society in Dublin (a Joyce society was already established in New York and had a membership approaching 350 by 1954[31]). Scholefield drew attention to 'the ridiculous position in which we stand vis-à-vis the world by our persistent ignoring of this great Dublin-born artist. After all we *are* in the tourist market, and these misguided foreigners think quite a lot of Joyce'. He suggested the 'raising of a subscription, limited to 2/6 a head so as to make it popular, and to Irish citizens, so that the wrong may be righted "within the family" to place a plaque on 2, Brighton square' and proposed the formation of a Dublin Joyce Society with a view to gathering Joyce materials and to redeeming 'the slight on Joyce's memory'.[32] Séamus Kelly backed up this appeal in his Quidnunc column where he reported having received 'a most heartening response [...] from Clonakilty in Co. Cork to Castleblayney in Co. Monaghan'.[33] He served on the original council with Suttle, Niall Montgomery, 'the blushing violet who writes authoritatively about Joyce over the nom-de-plume of Andrew Cass', C. P. Curran, Lennox Robinson, 'the hydra (or malta) headed monster who calls himself Myles na

---

[29]Thersites, 'Private View', *IT*, 8 January 1955, 6.
[30]'An Irishman's Diary', *IT*, 16 June 1962, 10.
[31]'An Irishman's Diary', *IT*, 25 February 1954, 5.
[32]Joyce's actual birthplace was 41 Brighton Square, *IT*, 4 April 1951, 7.
[33]'An Irishman's Diary', *IT*, 23 June 1954, 5.

Gopaleen, Flann O'Brien or Brian O Nualláin', and 'a transient called Ernie Anderson [...] who was included because he was one of the few Americans who had ever come to Dublin without claiming that he knew Joyce well in his Paris days'.[34]

Within months, plans were afoot to hold Dublin's first Bloomsday celebration which was described in *The Irish Times* as the 'Oddest "pilgrimage"' the city had ever seen (it was undoubtedly one of the booziest): 'In a vintage cab Joyce devotees and one distant relative of the writer visited all the places mentioned in the book to mark the 50th anniversary of "*Ulysses* day." The rest of Dublin took no notice.'[35] The event was led by Anthony Cronin, John Ryan, Brian O'Nolan, Patrick Kavanagh, Con Leventhal and Tom Joyce (the author's cousin). Kavanagh immortalized the happening in poetry:

I made the pilgrimage
In the Bloomsday swelter
From the Martello Tower
To the cabby's shelter.[36]

Ten years later, he recalled being 'one of the faithful band who went "out" on the fiftieth anniversary of Bloomsday' and he noted that the expedition 'got scant courtesy from many people', some of whom would later become involved in Bloomsday. On their way back from the Martello tower, the group stopped at various public houses and some 'well known publicists appeared on the scene to have a good laugh at us. Will we get pensions for our day's outing?'[37] Anthony Cronin later recalled that the pilgrimage had been Brian O'Nolan's idea.

It would be wrong to say that in 1954 Joyce was a neglected figure in Ireland. He was, in many quarters, seriously disapproved of, *hated* might not be too strong a word to describe the attitude. Not only the Church and the devout disapproved of him. Politicians feared to make any reference to a notorious blasphemer [...] Even the literary establishment disapproved.[38]

Cronin underlines the significance of the celebration as 'an assertion of his importance to us as well as a rebellion against dullness, hypocrisy and ignorance'.

---

[34]'An Irishman's Diary', *IT*, 16 June 1962, 10.

[35]*IT*, 26 June 1954, 9.

[36]Quoted in Vivien Igoe, 'Bloomsday of Yesteryear', *IT*, 15 June 1979, 10.

[37]Patrick Kavanagh, untitled article, *RTÉ Guide*, 26 June 1964. https://www.rte.ie/archives/2014/0616/624179-patrick-kavanagh-on-irelands-first-bloomsday-1954/

[38]Anthony Cronin, 'The First Bloomsday', *The Blackrock Society* (2004): 66–7, 66.

All those who took part knew the book more or less by heart. Even Kavanagh, who, in accordance with his general policy of running down any Irish writer, young or old, living or dead, who was the object of any praise, here or elsewhere, sometimes expressed reservations, would frequently and for the most part gleefully quote it. And Myles, though fed up with being described by those who knew no better as a 'Joycean' writer and therefore occasionally impelled to snarl at the mention of the name, fully understood the greatness of the master and his achievement. And as for my younger self, 1 believed – and, incidentally, still believe – that Joyce was not only the greatest European novelist of the twentieth century, but one of the greatest writers who ever lived, worthy to be mentioned with Shakespeare, Tolstoy and Homer.

The editorial in *The Irish Times* to mark 'the golden jubilee of Bloomsday' was far less convinced:

Only time will prove whether or not *Ulysses* is one of the world's great novels. [...] He [Joyce] has received from Ireland less than the official honour to which he is entitled. However, there are signs that this state of affairs is changing, and that as time passes, more domestic recognition may come his way. When the hundredth anniversary of Bloomsday comes around, Leopold Bloom either may be forgotten, or may stand in stony effigy as high as Nelson stands today.[39]

The year 1954 saw *Ulysses* being drawn on for commercial reasons when the dry cleaning company, Prescotts, ran an advertisement featuring a specially commissioned portrait of Joyce by the noted Irish artist, Seán O'Sullivan, and a tortuously explicative text, which read:

Prescotts... Bloomsday... Dubliners... To-day is the fiftieth anniversary of Bloomsday. 16 June 1904, was the day which James Joyce immortalised in *Ulysses*, in which the central character is Leopold Bloom... And when I sent her for Molly's Paisley shawl to Prescott's... Trams: a car of Prescott's dyeworks... Even then Prescotts had given decades of dependable cleaning to Dubliners.

In truth, as early as 1940, Davy Byrne's had been headlining its newspaper advertisements with a capitalized version of Bloom's description from *Ulysses*: '"DAVY BYRNE'S MORAL PUB" – James Joyce in "Ulysses"'.[40] A puff piece, published the following year to mark the bar's passing into new hands, noted that it had 'always been a good pull-up for intellectuals',

---

[39]*IT*, 16 June 1954.
[40]*IT*, 23 March 1940, 9.

such as William Orpen, Liam O'Flaherty, Donn Byrne, Nora Hoult, Maurice Walsh and, of course, Joyce who 'was lost in his harsh dreams of Dubliniana and his idealism of a new language'.[41] Davy Byrne's was cast as the birthplace of various literary characters such as the 'psychopathic Mrs. Bloom' who is linked with Liam O'Flaherty's 'gentleman of the emotions, Mr. Gilhooley'. It would not be long before many more Irish companies with far less substantial connections began to follow suit.

Radio Éireann was slow to celebrate the fiftieth anniversary of Bloomsday and was outperformed by the BBC, as the *Irish Press* pointed out: 'Put end-to-end the B.B.C. Third Programme offerings on *Ulysses* that evening totalled three hours fifteen minutes – as against a neat, semi-factual, semi-whimsical talk from RE by H. L. Morrow.'[42] In the *Irish Times*, G. A. Olden reported on a BBC radio talk by Stanislaus Joyce on the backgrounds to *Dubliners* but lamented the fact that rumours that the BBC Third Programme was going to dramatize *Ulysses* had turned out to be false:

> We also heard, rightly or wrongly, that Cyril Cusack had been engaged to play Dædalus, and that 'pressure groups' – blessed phrase! – in Radio Éireann were opposed to the loan of Irish players to take part in the undertaking. Like many another brave but tricky project, the dramatising of 'Ulysses' seems to have been shelved *sine die*.[43]

Olden suggested that Radio Éireann might seize the challenge even though 'it would not be decorous or advisable to dramatise the whole book [...] But much could be made of the funeral, the discussion on "Hamlet" in the library, and Mr. Bloom's pilgrimage from the Freeman's Journal to Davy Byrne's'. This would give Radio Éireann the opportunity 'to prove that they had heard of Joyce, and that they realised that he was a remarkable literary artist with some subtlety of analysis'. Olden concluded that Joyce was 'still regarded in official circles as an unorthodox crank who went abroad to write the dirty books that nobody in Ireland would print, and a good job, too' before suggesting that a censored version of *Ulysses* could be prepared that would be suitable for general public consumption:

> We owe it to Joyce's memory. [...] it could be done without the transmission of a single sentence to which the most benighted county council could take exception. So let it not be inferred that I am advocating Filth for the Unformed Minds: after all '*Ulysses* must be a discouraging document for those in search of a furtive leer.

[41]'A Famous Dublin "Pub"', *IT*, 11 October 1941, 5.
[42]*IP*, 21 June 1954, 4.
[43]G. A. Olden, 'R. E. Should Tackle Joyce's "Ulysses"', *IT*, 25 February 1954, 4.

As it turned out, the BBC Third Programme did transmit a number of broadcasts, including talks by William Empson on 'The Theme of *Ulysses*' and by Seán O'Faoláin on 'Music in *Ulysses*'. Two episodes from the novel, 'Paddy Dignam's Funeral' and 'At the Newspaper Office', arranged by poet and award-winning broadcaster Peter Duval Smith and featuring Cyril Cusack and Jack MacGowran, were also broadcast. An edge was added to this production by Duval Smith's being engaged in a lengthy affair with Empson's wife, Hetta, adding irony to Empson's claim in his parallel talk that *Ulysses* contained a 'secret subtext' in which the author was praising the idea of 'a consenting triangle between his leading characters, Stephen Dedalus and Leopold and Molly Bloom'.[44]

The broadcast of 'Paddy Dignam's Funeral' had an unexpected epilogue. Reuben J. Dodd Junior heard it by chance and wrote a letter of complaint to the BBC claiming 'that the programme was open to the interpretation that he was a moneylender, and that he had tried to commit suicide, a criminal action in Ireland in 1904 as well as in 1954'.[45] The BBC replied that 'the person in the episode [...] to whom Joyce gave a name similar to your own, was described as a moneylender, and we do not feel therefore, that anyone could reasonably identify this person with yourself'.[46] Annoyed at this rebuff, Dodd sued in the Dublin High Court in a case that competed for media attention with Patrick Kavanagh's traumatic libel suit. Dodd's case was heard by Mr Justice George D. Murnaghan, whose uncle, James Murnaghan, had been a judge of the Supreme Court until 1953, and long before that, a friend of Joyce at University College Dublin. Dodd, a former schoolmate of Joyce, claimed that the writer 'had a personal dislike for me because of what he alleged my father did to his father. And so, when he wrote his book, *Ulysses*, in or about the year 1904, he made some disparaging references, including moneylending transactions, to a Mr. Reuben J. Dodd'.[47] As Dodd explained in his affidavit, Joyce's father had taken a loan from his father but 'tried to get out of his obligations towards my father' who 'refused to return the title deeds until there had been full compliance with the transaction'. The passage complained of was, in Dodd's view, 'a malicious and deliberate libel upon me and its dissemination by the B.B.C. exposes me to personal humiliation and injury. The whole incident described was a malicious falsehood, and in particular that I attempted to commit suicide'.[48] Having

[44]See Vanessa Thorpe, 'Empson and His Several Types of Infidelity', *The Observer*, 29 October 2006, 20.
[45]Patrick Callan, '"One and Eightpence Too Much" – Suing James Joyce through the Agency of the BBC, 1954 to 1955'. Typescript of lecture given at the Trieste Joyce School, June 2019.
[46]'Dublin Lawyer tells B.B.C. – "*Ulysses* Broadcast A Libel On Me"', *IP*, 7 July 1954, 1.
[47]*Evening Echo*, 8 October 1954, 1.
[48]'Action over *Ulysses* Broadcast', *EH*, 8 October 1954, 8.

asked 'Does anyone listen to that programme?'[49] Justice Murnaghan gave
liberty to Mr E. M. Wood, SC (assisted by Ulick O'Connor) to issue
a summons, on behalf of Dodd, against the BBC seeking damages for
alleged defamation. The plot thickened when Joyce's inveterate nemesis,
Oliver St John Gogarty, joined Dodd's legal team in the spring of 1955
and demanded that the BBC provide 'the scripts because it was still a
moot point whether broadcast material [...] was to be regarded as libel
or slander. Expert opinion in England was that if such material was read
from scripts it was libel, but that if it was spoken (scripts not being used)
it was slander'. Mr W. O'B. Fitzgerald, SC, for the BBC submitted that
'Mr. Dodd was not entitled to discovery, the application being, he said,
in the nature of a "fishing" application'. When Justice Murnaghan denied
access to the scripts,[50] Dodd appealed to the Supreme Court where the
chief justice, in agreement with the other members of the court, said that
'an order for discovery should have been made'. The BBC rather bizarrely
'denied that there had been a prepared script'[51] but this was patently
untrue. This had been prepared by Duval Smith, who duly deleted the
offending reference to Dodd for subsequent broadcasts on 19 June and
19 November 1954, and this helps explain why Dodd took his case not
against the Joyce estate but against the BBC. The Joyce estate was, in fact,
exempt from liability.

> John Lane, as the publishers of *Ulysses* in England, had signed a contract
> outlining 'very precisely the excerpts to be used', but 'no express
> warranty' had been included in the contract form. The publishers had
> received permission from the 'administrators of the Estate of the late
> James Joyce'.[52] The ensuing case hinged on Duval Smith's unauthorised
> insertion of the Dodd surname into the radio script. The legal action
> vindicated Joyce's insistence, as stated in 1932, that 'My text is to be
> published as I wrote it, unabridged and unaltered.' Duval Smith readily
> acknowledged to the BBC legal team that he had made 'various small
> alterations (here as elsewhere) in Joyce's text when I prepared the script,'
> all for the 'sake of clarity simply'. He insisted that the 'only one that
> affects the present case is the explicit description' of RJD as a 'bloody

---

[49]Ibid. Although the BBC claimed that its broadcasts were not intended for listeners in the
Republic of Ireland, they did have an audience there. As Patrick Callan has noted, an RÉ listener
survey carried out for the week before Bloomsday showed that 4 per cent of the radio audience
sample in Ireland listened to the Third Programme, 'despite the fact that it is sometimes difficult
to receive "The Third" satisfactorily in this country'. This was reported in Sean Hughes, 'Radio
Review', *II*, 19 June 1954, 6.
[50]'Solicitor's Application Refused', *EH*, 26 May 1955, 9.
[51]'Solicitor's Action against B.B.C.', *II*, 24 June 1955, 2.
[52]Walford [Crocker's] to Assistant Solicitor [BBC], 13 [?] October 1954, BBC Dodd file (quoted
in Callan, 6).

money-lender', and that this designation had been 'expressed strongly in the original text'.[53]

The BBC legal team gathered in September 1955 and included two Irish senior counsels, three Irish solicitors and two English lawyers. The Irish members of the team warned that if the case went to a jury it would find for Dodd. They further warned that a jury might be biased against such a high-profile British institution and would be hostile 'owing to the unpopularity of Joyce in Dublin amongst all but the intellectual élite'. As Patrick Callan has noted, 'they drew attention to "certain passages" from *Ulysses* that were of an "unsavoury, not to say immoral, nature which might be regarded as disgusting to an Irish jury". The Irish lawyers believed that a jury might then be inclined to award damages "far beyond what he had clearly suffered as a result of the broadcast"'.[54]

The libel suit was settled out of court 'for a sum of damages and a sum for costs satisfactory to Mr. Dodd' and the BBC expressed 'its regret for any pain or injury the broadcast had caused him'.[55] Ulick O'Connor later said that the settlement was 'a considerable sum in those days. Reuben was delighted at this substantial financial contribution to his later years'.[56] He received £650 including legal costs. Dodd died two years later. His short obituary notice was dominated by his connection with Joyce and carried mention of his lawsuit which had done much to amplify the alleged libel against him.[57]

In 1954, a new wave of American interest was heralded by the arrival in Dublin of the then Yeats biographer, Richard Ellmann. In letters to the Irish papers, he announced that he was writing a Joyce biography and asked 'if any of your readers who were associated with him would communicate with me at the address below'[58] (he was staying in Killiney). A week later this was picked up in an article entitled 'Sin and Games' which reported that Ellmann was 'writing a life of James Joyce (according to my ledgers, he is the 238th American to attempt this grim task)'.[59] This period was the apex of hostility among Dublin's intellectual community towards Joyce's American academic supporters. There was impatience with the predominance of American

---

[53]Patrick Callan, '"One and Eightpence Too Much"', 6.
[54]Ibid., 10. Callan here quotes a memo dated 28 December 1955 from L. P. R. Roche, the BBC's assistant solicitor who was in charge of the Dodd case. The memo is kept in the BBC Dodd file.
[55]'Solicitor's Libel Suit Settled', *II*, 29 November 1955, 8.
[56]Ulick O'Connor, 'Real Life Ulysses Character Who Caused a Literary Stir.' *SI*, 12 February 2012, 16. https://www.independent.ie/opinion/analysis/ulick-oconnor-real-life-ulysses-character-who-caused-a-literary-stir-26820766.html
[57]'Mr. Reuben J. Dodd', *II*, 5 October 1957, 7.
[58]'Richard Ellmann, Letter', *IP*, 17 June 1953, 6; *IT*, 26 June 1953, 7.
[59]'Sin and Games', *IT*, 7 July 1953, 4.

New Criticism, which emphasized close reading and saw literary works as self-contained, almost sealed off from the world. Irish critics believed that reading Joyce without proper knowledge of the Irish contexts that had informed his works was pointless and that tenured Americans critics were not paying sufficient attention to these elements. As a result, they could not see the wood from the trees.

An example of this hostility was Brian O'Nolan's production of what many believe is a fake interview with John Stanislaus Joyce that found its way to Paris and into the well-intentioned hands of Madame Jolas, who published it verbatim in the 1949 *Joyce Yearbook*.[60] It was prefaced as having been 'given to an unidentified journalist who called on Mr. Joyce père at the request of his son in Paris'[61] and was later mined by a host of respected Joyce critics including Robert Scholes, Richard M. Kain, Richard Ellmann and Hugh Kenner. In 1950, John Kelleher gave a copy of the *Yearbook* to Niall Montgomery, who took a glance and burst out laughing before hurrying Kelleher off to show it to O'Nolan who 'seemed as surprised as Niall was by its (the interview's) apparition in print, but took its publication as another proof of foreign and scholarly fatuity'.[62] Although there is no absolute proof that the interview was written by O'Nolan, it may well be a Mylesian hoax. When asked if he knew anything about the quality of the water in the Liffey, John Stanislaus Joyce answers: 'Not a damn bit because I never drank it without whiskey in it.' Joyce's 'father' also claims 'I was considered a celebrated bowler [...] I was made a lot of and was taken around by the boys on their shoulders; and my God the quantity of whiskey that I drank that night!', all of which seems perfectly in line with a character prone to exaggeration and melodrama. So much so that, as Terence Killeen has suggested, it was actually John Stanislaus himself who gave the interview and enjoyed every moment of playing up his own part with his interlocutors. Killeen further reports that 'Ellmann asked O'Brien's friend, Niall Sheridan, about the issue' and he, 'rather amazingly, confirmed [...] that he and O'Brien had indeed called on Joyce senior in late 1930 or early 1931. He added, however, that neither wrote down anything about it and that the published interview did not reflect what transpired on their visit'. Killeen also notes that Herbert Gorman drew on material in the interview that 'was indeed among Joyce's papers at the time, since there was nowhere else that Gorman could have obtained it. Moreover, all the details in it do fit the known facts of John Stanislaus's life. So, improbable as it

---

[60]'Interview with John Stanislas [*sic*] Joyce (1849–1931)', *A James Joyce Yearbook*, ed. Maria Jolas (Paris: Transition Press, 1949), 159–69. John V. Kelleher's review of Hugh Kenner's *Dublin's Joyce* in the *Virginia Quarterly Review*, 33 (Winter 1957): 132–5, reveals that it was penned by O'Nolan.

[61]See Margaret Heckard, 'The Literary Reverberations of a Fake Interview with John Stanislaus Joyce', *JJQ*, vol. 13, no. 4 (Summer 1976): 468–71.

[62]Ibid., 468–9.

may initially seem, it does look as if the interview is genuine and that it was probably commissioned by Joyce'.[63]

Even if the interview is authentic (and if it is, John Stanislaus is in full performance mode), Dublin Joyceans would have been only too happy to imagine that Myles na gCopaleen had pulled the wool over the eyes of Joyce's foreign followers. He took unrelenting aim at American Joyce scholars. On one occasion, he wrote that he did not 'wish to provoke still another world war by invading America's monopoly of comment on the value of Joyce's work' before discussing the Joyce 'stooges, mainly American'.[64] This was the period in which 'Joyce's position in contemporary criticism' was, as Kain put it, 'in the process of consolidation. The period of extravagant claims and badly printed manifestoes has given way to the stage of enlightened explication of individual works'.[65] Unwilling or unable to join in or perhaps believing the explications to be less enlightened than the Americans would have wished, the Irish response was to make fun of the Americans engaged in this work, at the 'shower of gawms who erupt from the prairie universities to do a "thesis" on James Joyce',[66] those 'poor demented punkawns' who were responsible for 'a veritable deluge of thremendious illiteracy foaming' over 'Joyce's pedantry, aridity and tourdeforcity'. These were soft targets for Myles's mocking pen.[67]

Similarly, when writers from closer to home waxed overly lyrical about Joyce, they too came in for censure. A case in point was L. A. G. Strong's *The Sacred River*, a celebratory study that casts Joyce in heroic terms and sees *Ulysses* as 'a great Catholic novel'.[68] Strong praises Joyce for doing what the Church failed to do:

> He would go down into hell, in the steps of Odysseus, Dante, and Swift. From its depths, accepting life's deepest pain, he would raise a triumphant cry, as Shakespeare did in Lear and Hamlet and Macbeth [...] He would make a ladder joining hell to heaven, after Blake, and with Blake link religion with the feminine principle in life. Inspired by the Romantics, he would open wide the gate between conscious and unconscious, shadow and light. Side by side with the prophets of his own time, he would make friends with the shadow, look on the great archetypes, face his own darkness, and redeem it.[69]

---

[63]Terence Killeen, 'An Alleged hoax an Irishman's Diary: Mystery of Flann O'Brien "interview" with Joyce's Father', 16 April 2013, 15.

[64]Myles Na Gopaleen, 'J-Day', *IT*, 16 June 1954.

[65]Richard M. Kain, *Fabulous Voyager: James Joyce's Ulysses* (New York: The Viking Press, 1959), 303.

[66]Myles na Gopaleen, *IT*, 3 January 1959, 9.

[67]Myles na Gopaleen, 'JJ & US', *IT*, 6 June 1957, 8.

[68]L. A. G. Strong, *The Sacred River*, 79.

[69]Ibid., 161.

All of which was too much for Myles who complained that Strong should have known better and been less gullible than 'the alien commentators'.[70] Of similar mind was the often acerbic Donagh MacDonagh, who bemoaned the continuing influx of books about Joyce's writing, saying: 'The bottom of the Joyce barrel has long been in sight and it is unlikely that in the future any but the expert will find much to interest him.'[71] His most succinct and effective put-down to American Joyce criticism came in a verse preface to his consequently irrelevant review of S. L. Goldberg's *The Classical Temper: A Study of James Joyce's Ulysses*. It began: 'Books about books about books are a bore/Now Mr. Goldberg has written one more/ [...] Nothing is said that was not said before –/ Books about books about books are a bore.'[72] At the same time, he occasionally did recognize what he considered serious scholarship and gave a warm review to Slocum and Cahoon's Joyce bibliography.[73] Often, however, instead of properly reviewing the volumes that came his way, he slipped into unsubstantiated speculation, on one occasion writing about Joyce's supposed penchant for 'going either to the top of a high building or to a deep cellar where he would not be heard and howling, long vulpine howls, which seemed to relieve for the moment the tension and the strain under which he lived'.[74]

It is no surprise to learn that in the course of his research in Dublin in the 1950s, Ellmann sometimes found himself being stonewalled. One case in point was that of Reuben J. Dodd, who was introduced to Ellmann by a somewhat cautious Ulick O'Connor. He was worried that the elderly 'Dodd might have felt apprehensive in the presence of an academic author like Ellmann who had written a biography of Yeats and had a world reputation'. Nothing could have been further from the case. From his hospital bed in James' Street, Dodd listened patiently to Ellmann as he outlined his credentials as a biographer. O'Connor did little to conceal his delight at Dodd's behaviour:

> At the end of a somewhat lengthy presentation, Reuben looked at Ellmann with unblinking eyes and just said, 'How's your father.' This is an old Dublin trick if you wanted to upset someone. Poor Ellmann looked blankly and said, 'But you don't know my father.' Reuben said nothing. Game, set and match.[75]

---

[70]Myles na gCopaleen, 'Joyce Re-approached' (Review of L. A. Strong, *The Sacred River*), *Irish Writing*, X, 1, January 1950.

[71]Donagh MacDonagh, 'The Bottom of the Barrel', *IP*, 15 June 1957, 4.

[72]Donagh MacDonagh *IT*, 19 August 1961, 6.

[73]John J. Slocum and Herbert Cahoon, *A Bibliography of James Joyce* (London: Rupert Hart-Davis, 1953). Donagh MacDonagh, 'A Two Guinea Tour of the Joyce Country', *IP*, 2 January 1954, 4.

[74]Donagh MacDonagh, 'The Bottom of the Barrel', 4.

[75]Ulick O'Connor. https://www.independent.ie/opinion/analysis/ulick-oconnor-reallife-ulysses-character-who-caused-a-literary-stir-26820766.html.

Travellers to Dublin keen on visiting Joyce sites were often greeted with incredulity. The *Irish Independent* reported the arrival of 'Frank Rahill, of Wisconsin, a newspaperman, now doing "promotion" for the "Milwaukee Sentinel"' Rahill, it was reported, was part of the Joyce cult, which was big 'in Canada and the United States. There is a Joyce Society, there is a monthly bulletin, and there is even a map of Dublin issued in which all the places mentioned in *Ulysses* are located'. Frank's aim, the reporter noted, was 'to visit in eighteen hours all the places that Joyce, Daedulus and Bloom did in the book in the same time'.[76] If he was seeking local help in this enterprise then he would have his work cut out for him. In 1952, Quidnunc described how a Dublin tour guide defended his own refusal to deal with 'Joyceana' on his tours. 'In the voice of a spinster lady refusing a pint of porter', the guide claimed that 'this man Joyce was disapproved of by all right-thinking people, and that he was not, therefore, a suitable subject of interest for decent tourists'. Things were not much better in 1957 when another American visitor, Mr E. Echikson, 'a true aficionado of the master's', had to go off 'solo, lamenting that there was nobody in Bloomsborough-Dublin to take a pilgrim round the Dedalian shrines'.[77] The columnist regretted that some quick-thinking Dubliner had missed the chance to make a few bob. Two years later, leading architect, Michael Scott, talked about the 'very great interest indeed in Joyce not only among visitors but among a lot of Dubliners as well'[78] and pushed for Bórd Fáilte to 'signpost Joyce's Dublin' along with that of O'Casey, Yeats and Shaw. He looked to the example of London where 'there are plaques honouring people of far less importance than James Joyce'. The tourist board was reported to have 'considered from time to time the possibility of publishing a booklet on Joyce giving directions and information on the places mentioned in his works' but had taken no action. With good reason, then, in 1959, a little over a month after Seán Lemass was installed as Taoiseach, in a Dáil debate on the tourist traffic bill, the progressive young Fianna Fáil T. D., Donogh O'Malley, complained that

> the Tourist Board, in their wisdom, never seem to pay the slightest attention to a tremendous potential which we have in Ireland, and particularly in Dublin, as a tourist attraction. I refer to the efforts of the people who visit this country, and Dublin in particular, to trace some of the characters and locations referred to by James Joyce in his various writings. [...] Five out of six Americans [...] will ply you with questions about various aspects of Joyce's work and the various places mentioned by him in his books. It is a serious reflection on the Tourist Board that up to now they have not

---

[76]'Leader Page Parade', *II*, 14 June 1950, 6
[77]'An Irishman's Diary', *IT*, 25 June 1957, 6.
[78]'Signposting the Dublin of James Joyce', *IT*, 11 August 1959, 5.

thought it worth their while even to put up plaques or produce a proper handbook or guide to these places.'

He noted the growing number of students taking Joyce as the subject of their theses (citing Myles na gCopaleen's column as a source for this information!) and expressed, as 'a matter of tremendous national importance', that some public money might be spent to produce a handbook to publicize Joyce, but also Seán Ó Casey ('there is not even a plaque on his house') and George Bernard Shaw. He called on the Tourist Board to step in and on the minister to 'use his good offices in the matter'.[79] The response from Minister Jack Lynch was non-committal:

> Deputy O'Malley was on a plane rather higher than I expected, up with Lady Gregory and James Joyce, but I can assure him that while the singing of the praises of these writers and the perpetuation of their memories would not be germane to this Bill, I believe that An Bórd Fáilte do not overlook the tourist value of the association of these famous literary people with this country.

In 1958, Sean J. White struck a rare note in favour of American Joyce scholarship, noting that a 'great number of books on Joyce have appeared from America and some of them are not very good, but all our laughing does not evaporate the fact that not one Irishman with the resounding exception of his brother, Stanislaus (family shouldn't count) has published a worthwhile book, biography, critical or exegetical, about James Joyce or his work'.[80] What appeared in Ireland were a number of books, hybrid mixes of memoir, biography, and critique, by friends and former friends of Joyce. Among them, Eugene Sheehy's *May it Please the Court* (1951), J. F. Byrne's *Silent Years: An Autobiography with Memoirs of James Joyce and Our Ireland* (1953) (Byrne had been the model for Joyce's character, Cranly), *Our Friend James Joyce* by Mary and Padraic Colum (1958), and, a decade later, C. P. Curran's *James Joyce Remembered*. In the *Irish Press*, White praised the Colums for being 'so delicate in their sympathy and so unpushing in their personal claims that their book excels all the others of its kind for agreeableness and is second only to Stanislaus's, inevitably, for atmosphere and authentic recollection'.[81]

For many years, Stanislaus had effectively been the most influential Irish Joycean (and Joyce). He played a key role as mediator between his brother and his critics but at times felt that he had something of an exclusive hold

---

[79] Dáil Éireann debate, 9 July 1959, vol. 176 no. 7. https://www.oireachtas.ie/en/debates/debate/dail/1959-07-09/4/

[80] Sean J. White, 'A Frenchman and Joyce', *IP*, 9 August 1958, 5.

[81] Sean J. White, 'Joyce, the Jesuits and the Colums', *IP*, 14 February 1959, 4.

on Joyce and his reception. As he told Herb Cahoon, 'you must remember that I was my brother's first disciple'.[82] Stanislaus saved an extraordinary collection of letters and materials and hoped to write his own version of his brother's life: 'My aim in writing is to present my brother's character and outlook as I knew and understood them in about thirty years of life together.'[83] He died in 1955 having written just the Dublin chapters of what became *My Brother's Keeper*.[84] Stanislaus' project would have been marred by his abiding desire to protect and defend his brother (this, despite his own feeling of having been abandoned and even betrayed by him); by drawing on his own reactions to people known to both of them in place of Joyce's own; by his lack of sympathy for Joyce's later writings and lifestyle. Despite these considerable provisos, what we do possess of his commentaries remains valuable and Stanislaus has often been the subject of rather unjust criticism. His *Dublin Diaries*,[85] although doctored in his own favour, provides an insightful, intimate sense of life in the Joyce family in Dublin while *My Brother's Keeper* is also a uniquely valuable, if somewhat sanitized, close-up portrait. It was coolly received in Ireland, where Stanislaus was remembered with even less affection than his older brother, as 'a revealing and revolting document'.[86] Yet Stanislaus had every right to consider himself the keeper of the flame. After all, he and Joyce 'grew up together side by side, they filled one home, not with glee, but with the revolt of the young and vigorous against encroaching squalor, penury and the slow declension of a father who led his family a Danse Micawber'.[87] Later, he had kept Joyce afloat for a decade in Trieste. In the words of MacDonagh, 'James distilled his bile in many a foreign furnished room and etched his Dublin on a perdurable plate; Stanislaus, turned puritan-atheist, lost love of country, family and faith. He died as needlessly as James, leaving this bitter dossier unfinished'.

One of the most repeated charges against Ellmann's biography is that it is tinged with 'Stannic acid',[88] that it depends too much on Joyce's brother's vision of things and allows Stanislaus' point of view to function as a filter. Stanislaus' collection formed one of Ellmann's most important sources but Joyce's brother should not be held responsible for the biography's shortcomings, nor inculpated for being a 'ghostly' and 'distorting' presence

---

[82]Letter of 6 March 1950 to Herb Cahoon. A Copy of the Letter Is Kept in the REC, Box 6.

[83]Quoted from a letter from Stanislaus to Ellworth Mason reported by Mason to Ellmann in a letter dated 11 December 1958 and kept in the REC, Box 156.

[84]Stanislaus Joyce, *My Brother's Keeper* ed., Richard Ellmann with a preface by T. S. Eliot (New York: Viking, 1958).

[85]George H. Healey, *The Complete Dublin Diary of Stanislaus Joyce* (Ithaca: Cornell University Press, 1962).

[86]Donagh MacDonagh, 'James Joyce and His Brother', *IT*, 31 May 1958, 6.

[87]Ibid.

[88]Bernard McGinley, *Joyce's Lives. Uses and Abuses of the Biografiend* (London: University of North London Press, 1996), 20.

in the first half of the book.[89] In short, his influence on Ellmann has been overestimated. From the outset, Ellmann was cautious about asking Stanislaus questions and worried that his chief source 'would resent my milking him too much'.[90] In addition, he sometimes dismissed what now read like sound, unbiased versions of events as recounted to him by Stanislaus, preferring instead to rely on Joyce's livelier fictional renderings.

John Garvin, writing as Andrew Cass, although prone himself to taking jabs at American Joyceans, conceded in 1959 that anyone looking for a critical guide to Joyce would have to look to the United States:

> Some of us here have tended to deride the work of trans-Atlantic glossators as jejune or derivative, a waste of Skelton keys broken in Yale locks. But American research at its best is no laughing matter. It is well organised and well financed and can add to the corpus of exegesis when conducted by men like Kenner, Kain and Magalaner, who possess the zeal and ability to get the facts and interpret them sanely.[91]

For the moment, Garvin and Niall Montgomery were, in the words of John Jordan in 1969, 'the acknowledged Irish Joycean mandarins'.[92] Montgomery entered the academic fray with his 'Joyeux Quicum Ulysse' (published in *Envoy* in 1951) and 'The Pervigilium Phoencis', which was published by the *New Mexico Quarterly* in 1953.[93] Christine O'Neill notes that 'Montgomery was disappointed that subsequent Joyce criticism did not refer to his article, and when *A James Joyce Miscellany* appeared in 1959 he was aggrieved by Henry Morton Robinson's essay, entitled "Hardest Crux Ever", which he felt recycled his ideas without acknowledgement'.[94] In 'A Context for Mr. Joyce's Work', Montgomery stressed the role of Ireland in Joyce's concern with both form and symbol.[95]

Another often forgotten Irish Joyce studies pioneer is Patricia Hutchins. A native of Bantry, her first book, *James Joyce's Dublin* (1950), received mixed reviews. The *Irish Press* largely dismissed it as 'primarily a picture book' and complained that 'it carries hero-worship to absurd lengths. Nothing connected with Joyce seems too trivial to be pounced upon by Miss

---

[89]Ibid., 21.

[90]Letter of 30 August 1953 from Richard Ellmann to Oxford University Press. REC, Series I, Box 179.

[91]Andrew Cass, 'Twenty Years A-Flowing', *IT*, 5 February 1959, 5.

[92]John Jordan, 'Joyce without Fears: A Personal Journey', 37.

[93]Niall Montgomery, 'Joyeux Quicum Ulysse', *Envoy* 5 (1951): 31–43; 'The Pervigilium Phoenicis', *New Mexico Quarterly* XXIII (1953): 437–72.

[94]Christine O'Neill, 'Niall Montgomery', 7.

[95]Niall Montgomery, 'A Context for Mr. Joyce's Work' in Maurice Harmon ed., *The Celtic Master: Contribution to the First James Joyce Symposium Held in Dublin 1967* (Dublin: Dolmen Press, 1969): 9–15.

Hutchins'.[96] The problem for the reviewer was not so much Hutchins but Joyce himself; indeed, the review opens regretfully with the words 'One may dislike James Joyce, one cannot ignore him.' Hutchins' volume was welcomed in a review entitled 'The Joyce Industry' by Radio Éireann's Director of Features, Francis MacManus, who praised the 'colourful, thoughtful and often eloquent text written by a Joycean devotee'.[97] Unlike many, 'instead of talking about the notion [of an attractive book about Joyce and Dublin] Miss Patricia Hutchins has acted on it [...] with tact and taste' even if her work probably will not satisfy 'those G. I's of Joycean scholarship, the foot-slogging Americans in search of D.Ph's':

> The initial trouble with a book of this kind is to prevent it from becoming a mere illustrated guide-book since Joyce's references to Dublin and its suburbs are multitudinous. He is one of those rare cases in literature of writers becoming their cities. Dante, too, became Florence, venomously and affectionately and pathetically, but he was unfortunate in not being followed soon after his death by a Miss Hutchins, eager to record pictorially and in words old streets, old houses, old haunts.

Encouraged by L. A. Strong, Hutchins published *James Joyce's World* in 1957. It portrayed Joyce's many backgrounds in Ireland, England and Europe following Joyce, as Donagh MacDonagh put it 'on his bitter pilgrimage through Europe'.[98] This was warmly reviewed by Micheál Mac Liammóir, who described Joyce as 'the most spectacular figure in modern Irish literature whether one thinks of writers Catholic or Protestant, or of Gaelic or Anglo-Irish tradition, and probably for the historian the most exasperating, for his work was himself'.[99] Ultimately, however, Hutchins has 'failed – to pluck out the heart of a mystery. For indeed there is no personal mystery left for the plucking; all that was vital has been poured into the work of Mr Joyce himself'. As part of her research, the pioneering Hutchins, who had already played a central role in gathering material for the first volume of Joyce letters (which would carry only Stuart Gilbert's name as editor), carried out important interviews with figures such as Carl Jung, Ezra Pound and Stanislaus Joyce. She reviewed an extended re-edition of Gilbert's book on *Ulysses* in *Irish Writing* in 1952, praising the 'great deal of unobtrusive learning' that lay behind it.[100] She followed this up with an accomplished article on the importance of Joyce's letters as a source for understanding the

---

[96]M., 'In Joyce's Footsteps', *IP*, 26 September 1950, 6.
[97]Francis MacManus, 'Review of James Joyce's Dublin, by Patricia Hutchins', *Irish writing*, no. 14, March, 1951, 61.
[98]Donagh MacDonagh, 'The Bottom of the Barrel', *IP*, 15 June 1957, 4.
[99]Micheal MacLiammoir, 'Joyce's Work Was Himself', *Truth*, 3 May 1957, 503.
[100]Patricia Hutchins, 'Review of James Joyce's *Ulysses*' by Stuart Gilbert', *Irish Writing*, no. 18. (March 1952): 55–6, 56.

fiction and Joyce's motivations.[101] As Peter Costello pointed out, 'late in life she resented, if such a lady of old fashioned manners could be said to resent anything, the rising control of American academics over a field in which she had been an early and ill-rewarded worker'.[102]

Her correspondence with Gilbert also offers a revealing insight into the attitude of Joyce's family to the writer. Joyce's younger sister, May Monaghan, was the 'most helpful to me over my own work' and had 'a more detached and perhaps more balanced view than others of the family'. May's son, Ken Monaghan, essentially agreed with this assessment, pointing out that 'Eva and Florrie, particularly Florrie, had taken very badly to the attention which their brother brought them. Florrie became introverted and paranoid, and blamed all the family's misfortunes on her brother. When she went out in the street she felt that people were pointing at her'. He also recalled Florrie warning him never to tell people that he was related to Joyce and that she and her sister Eva 'were terrified people would know they were sisters of James Joyce'. His mother, on the other hand, 'was very proud of her eldest brother and we were always aware that he was there. She always warned that we shouldn't advertise the fact of our relationship too much but that we should also never deny it'. Monaghan's father was more typical and referred to Joyce as 'that anti-Christ' while, in Monaghan's memory, the 'vast majority and the opinion in general was that he was a sort of disgrace to the country'.[103] The family of Joyce's younger brother, Charles, felt similarly. When Hutchins tracked them down, she was shocked to find out that Charles' son 'had recently burnt all – letters, first editions of *Ulysses*, *Finnegans Wake* and other books' somewhat to the regret of his wife. Despite having to fend for four children, he felt it was unscrupulous to make 'money out of irreligious writings!' Following his mother's death in January 1948, he made up his mind, as he told Hutchins, 'to destroy them all – to cut off my part of the family altogether from his work. I didn't care for Joyce or his writings'. He claimed that although his parents had been friendly with Joyce in the later years in England, his mother had also said that she would destroy the letters and declared himself 'quite satisfied in my mind about what I have done'.[104] One of his own sons, Robert, who later joined forces with Ken Monaghan and Senator David Norris and became one of the driving forces of the Joyce Centre on North Great George's Street, only discovered his Joyce connection in 1982.

Occasionally Irish Joyceans had good reason to feel aggrieved about American dominance. William Brockman has reported how in 1957, on the grounds that it would damage his forthcoming volume of the *Critical*

[101]Patricia Hutchins, 'James Joyce's Correspondence,' *Encounter*, VII (August 1956): 49–54.
[102]Peter Costello, 'Review of *Joyce and the Joyceans* by Morton P. Levitt', *Studies: An Irish Quarterly Review*, vol. 91, no. 363: 308–11, 309.
[103]'"Awful Man" Cast a Dark Shadow', *II*, 17 June 1998, 3.
[104]Letter of 8 August 1948 from Patricia Hutchins to Stuart Gilbert. The letter is kept in the Stuart Gilbert Collection at the Harry Ransom Center, University of Texas.

Writings, Richard Ellmann blocked a publication by UCD academic Eileen MacCarvill to be entitled *James Joyce: A Documentary*.[105] This would have included essays, reviews, poems and stories by Joyce, and would have been a unique Irish contribution to Joyce publishing. While Ellmann's role may have been somewhat less important than Brockman suggests and while MacCarvill never intended to include 'poems and stories', it is still a mystery as to why it was never published. More than anything else, Ellmann and Mason probably elbowed her out by getting there first – offering Viking Press their *Critical Writings* in September 1956.[106] Ellmann was notoriously territorial when it came to Joyce materials and, when helping broker the purchases of Joyce collections, which were being competitively stockpiled by American Universities, great and small, it was not beyond him to request the buyer have a clause inserted that guaranteed him sole access for periods of one to three years.[107]

It is worth taking a look at the relevant correspondence that survives. MacCarvill sent Slocum page proofs and described her own project in her 'Note on the Author':

She has made a study of Joyce in his student years setting him into the pattern of the literary, cultural and historical Ireland of his time which is the background of all his writing. For this purpose she had access to the records of the Department of Education of University College Dublin and of the Royal University of Ireland. Her introductory essay is therefore an objective and factual statement of Joyce's activities as an undergraduate and his academic achievements complementary to his own subjective picture in *Stephen Hero*.[108]

Slocum wrote to Herbert Cahoon on her behalf, suggesting 'that a University press interested in a prestige publication might well grab this'.[109] Cahoon, however, immediately wrote to Ellmann to warn him of the danger that

---

[105]William S. Brockman, Learning to Be James Joyce's Contemporary? Richard Ellmann's Discovery and Transformation of Joyce's Letters and Manuscripts', *Journal of Modern Literature*, vol. 22, no. 2 (Winter 1998/1999), Special Issue: Joyce and the Joyceans; 253–63.

[106]In a letter of 26 September 1956, Mason wrote to Huebsch at Viking Press, announcing their plan to 'bring into a single volume a large number of out-of-the way writings of James Joyce. This book, for which we suggest the title <u>The Critical Writings of James Joyce</u>, we should like to offer to you for publication.' Quoted in Amanda Sigler, 'Joyce's Ellmann: The Beginnings of James Joyce', *JSA*, (2010): 3–70, 49.

[107]When the University of Kansas was considering buying the Stanislaus Joyce collection, Ellmann advised his friend Weiss if he 'could stipulate that the material not be available to anyone but me for a year'. Cited in Amanda Sigler, 'Joyce's Ellmann', 51.

[108]Appendix entitled 'A Note on the Author', attached to her letter of 29 November 1957 to John J. Slocum. I consulted this material at the Beinecke Library, Yale. See also Eileen MacCarvill, *The Collection of Joyce Exam Papers and University Calendars*, Unpublished Manuscript, Zurich James Joyce Foundation.

[109]Letter of 3 December 1957 from Slocum to Cahoon kept at the Beinecke Library, Yale.

this 'publication would very seriously conflict with a volume that Ellsorth [*sic*] and you are preparing for Viking.'[110] That same day, Cahoon wrote to MacCarvill, praising her book but also alerting her to the fact that Ellmann and Ellsworth Mason 'have in active preparation a book to be called the *Uncollected Writings* of James Joyce [...] which would include, with extensive annotations, all of the essays, reviews and other writings which you have in your book. [...] The Ellmann-Mason publishing arrangement is with the Viking Press'.[111] He asked her if her agreement with the Joyce Estate envisaged an American publication and suggested she should talk with Viking. Ellmann, meanwhile, wrote to Marshall Best at Viking asking 'Is there anything that can be done to prevent our being anticipated by this book?'[112] Best was less than optimistic: 'Our only hope is that the Estate can oblige or persuade her to hold back from America entirely and to delay publication in Ireland as long as possible.'[113] Ellmann then wrote asking Joyce's literary executor, Harriet Shaw Weaver, for help to block the publication. As it turned out, Ellmann and Mason did not publish their volume until 1959, which suggests that their project was far less advanced than Cahoon had earlier believed. MacCarvill replied cautiously to Cahoon, telling him that she had hoped to publish 'a limited edition for distribution to libraries throughout the world'. In other words, she had in mind a narrowly academic publication which would not in any way have detracted from Ellmann's enterprise. She also recounted how John Dulanty, former Irish ambassador in London and 'a great admirer' of Joyce (*LIII*, 223) (he attended his London wedding), had applied in 1954 to the Joyce Estate for permission for her 'to publish 35 book reviews from the *Dublin Daily Express* and for certain Italian articles'.[114] This application reached the Estate along with another by Joseph Prescott of Wayne State University. It was agreed that Prescott would publish the Italian material and MacCarvill the book reviews and the Joyce Estate granted permission to this effect. MacCarvill paid rights, but then Stanislaus Joyce intervened to claim his right on 'all of these articles' and MacCarvill was forced to revise her plans once again. Although Stanislaus died soon afterwards, MacCarvill had been stymied. Ellsworth Mason published an edition in 1955 under his and Stanislaus' name entitled *The Early Joyce: The Book Reviews, 1902–1903*.[115]

---

[110]Letter from Herbert Cahoon to Richard Ellmann, 7 December 1957. Richard Ellmann Collection, University of Tulsa. Series I, Box 6.

[111]Letter of 7 December 1957 from Herbert Cahoon to Eileen MacCarvill.

[112]Richard Ellmann to Marshall A. Best, 11 December 1957. Richard Ellmann Collection. Series I, Box 6.

[113]Marshall A. Best to Richard Ellmann, 10 January 1958. Richard Ellmann Collection. Series I, Box 52.

[114]Letter of 16 December 1957 from Eileen MacCarvill to Herbert Cahoon.

[115]Stanislaus Joyce and Ellsworth Mason (eds), *The Early Joyce: The Book Reviews, 1902–1903* (Colorado Springs: The Mamalujo Press, 1955).

Soon afterwards, the Joyce Estate asked MacCarvill, through Valentine Iremonger, at the time first secretary of the Irish Embassy in London, if she was still interested in the rights of the Italian articles. She was. She was told by Mr Munro of Munro, Pennefather and Co., representing the Joyce Estate, that 'the rights you have got are not exclusive to you and that applies in practically every case'. Given that Ellmann and Mason were to publish *The Uncollected Works*, MacCarvill offered to make many exclusions for her work which was to be published by Messrs. Clonmore & Reynolds of Kildare Street even if she was also keen to find an American publisher. A month later, in January 1958, she received bad news from Miss Weaver, who wrote on behalf of the Estate with regard to the clash between her book and that of Ellmann and Mason. Weaver told her that when she agreed rights with the latter (on behalf of the Estate) she had not realized 'that rights for publication in America had been accorded to you, now the prospective publishers' on hearing that your book is out 'are disturbed lest it should affect adversely the sales of their forthcoming book. [...] I hope their fears are groundless'.[116] MacCarvill believed they were and took legal advice to make sure she had permission to proceed with her publication. Finally, she told Cahoon that Padraic Colum had written an introduction to her intended book and wrote to Indiana Press to see if they would be interested in publishing it. In February, she wrote again to Cahoon requesting that he return her manuscript. He did so expressing regret that his efforts to find a university press willing to publish it had come to nought and his pleasure at the news that Colum would write the introduction. The correspondence stops here but what is evident is that the Ellmann–Mason axis was successful in blocking MacCarvill's efforts. In doing so, they sent a proprietorial warning shot that certainly did little to encourage other Irish Joyce scholars entering the field.

MacCarvill, who was introduced as a speaker at the first international symposium in Dublin in 1967 as 'a rarity – a genuine, well-mannered, disinterested Dublin Joycean',[117] did publish a booklet in French in May 1958 entitled *Les Années de formation de James Joyce a Dublin*.[118] Just thirty pages long, it includes useful (and for the time, original) descriptions of Joyce in Belvedere and at University College Dublin and discussions of his L&H Mangan lecture. It emphasizes Joyce's Irishness and his debt to Dublin: 'son point de départ et son aboutissement étaient sa ville natale,

---

[116]Letter of 11 January 1958 from Eileen MacCarvill to Herbert Cahoon.
[117]Austin Briggs, 'The First International James Joyce Symposium: A Personal Account', *JSA*, vol. 13 (Summer, 2002): 5–31, 18.
[118]Eileen MacCarvill, *Les Années de formation de James Joyce a Dublin* (Paris: Éditions Minard/ Lettres Modernes, Archives des lettres modernes, no. 12, 1958). MacCarvill also regularly reviewed books on Joyce. See, for example, reviews of Eugene Sheehy's *May It Please the Court* (IT, 24 November 1951, 4) and of Padraic and Mary Colum's *Our Friend James Joyce* (IT, 14 February 1959, 6).

Dublin'.[119] An extended English-language version of this work was 'still in proof with the Dolmen Press when she died. Ellmann's action seems to have effectively snuffed out her tentative career as a Joyce scholar'.[120]

Thus, in the 1950s, Irish Joyceans, not to mention Irish female Joyceans, remained but a marginal presence in published Joyce criticism and scholarship. Many felt aggrieved that generously funded Americans were hogging the field and were establishing the rules for scholarly Joyce combat and effectively deciding on his status, which was now higher than ever. As Harry Levin asked in a preface to his *Critical Introduction*: 'Has there ever been so short a transition between ostracism and canonization?'[121] But Joyce was far from canonized in Ireland where critics, such as Donagh MacDonagh, continued to harp on about the importance of his Irishness and of contextualizing his work within the Dublin of his youth, claiming that Joyce might as well have spent his life living in Cabra: 'Joyce in his self-exile never left Dublin. He read the Dublin newspapers, listened constantly to Radio Éireann and would question his visitors closely – after they had presented the ritual gift of Hafner's sausages – as to the changed or changing topography of the city.'[122] His entanglement with Ireland and every aspect of Irish life became mythologized. In 1954, Denis Gwynn, professor of Modern Irish History at University College Cork, recalled being introduced to Joyce by Ezra Pound in Paris in 1921 and commented:

> When Joyce left Dublin for Austria, almost without resources as a young man, he determined to keep in daily touch with Ireland while he worked at the vast novel he had in view. He could not afford to buy all the Irish daily papers ever day; but he arranged to have at least one every morning. For years in that strange exiled life, he read every line of these daily newspapers, including the advertisements, and the births, deaths and marriages, and all such announcements. As a result of such intensive study, he had a far more minute knowledge of what was happening in Ireland from week to week than any ordinary person would have at home.[123]

Thus, writers like Myles Na gCopaleen felt justified in claiming that 'nobody but a Dubliner could appraise its [*Ulysses'*] subtlety'.[124] As late as 1970, prominent Dublin Joycean, Gerard O'Flaherty, made the same point saying

---

[119]Ibid., 30.
[120]Peter Costello, Review of *Joyce and the Joyceans*, 309.
[121]Harry Levin, *James Joyce: A Critical Introduction*, 2nd Edition (London: Faber & Faber, 1960), 14.
[122]Donagh MacDonagh, 'In the Steps of Leopold Bloom', *IT*, 16 June 1954, 6.
[123]Denis Gwynn, 'The Cult of James Joyce', *CE*, 22 June 1954, 4.
[124]Myles na gCopaleen, *IT*, 6 June 1957.

'he could not see how a non-Catholic or a non-Dubliner could possibly appreciate Joyce's *Ulysses* fully'.[125]

Many of their American counterparts were close readers who privileged the autonomy of Joyce's texts and sought to universalize themes that were, for the Irish, local. There was a clash between Joyce's Irish followers, sometimes former friends trying to grab a minor space in the growing Joyce spotlight, through personal reminiscence or local knowledge, and the growing American brigade jostling for position in the race to produce the Joyce book that would launch or consolidate a university career. Some, like Irish critic, Vivien Mercier, stood somewhere in-between and played to both galleries. He described attending a gathering of the New York James Joyce Society, presided over by Padraic Colum, and meeting an American Joyce bibliographer whom he advised, rather justifiably, 'not to waste time and money sending his book to Ireland for review, because it would infallibly be butchered to make an Irish Saturday'.[126] One such filleting was carried out, in his inimitable way, by Brendan Behan, in the *Irish Press*:

> An American, upon being introduced and being told I was from Dublin, asked me if I had known James Joyce. I regretted that I did not have that honour, but told him that my mother had cooked a meal for W. B. Yeats in Madame Mac Bride's house in Stephen's Green and that the poet turned up his nose to the parsnips. 'He did not like parsnips?' said the American reaching for a note-book. 'You're sure this is factual?' 'It is to be hoped,' I replied, 'that you are not calling my mother a liar?' 'No, no, of course not. But she might have been mistaken. Maybe it was carrots,' he added, hastily. 'You must think I'm a right thick to have a mother that cannot tell a carrot from a parsnip.' 'No, certainly not, I'm sure you wouldn't. I mean I'm sure she could. But this is very important.' He wrote in the book: 'Parsnips, attitude of Yeats to.' 'And you say he didn't like Stephen's Green, either. Now, what sort of vegetable are they?'[127]

Occasionally the twain did meet. Padraic Colum, in particular, was a point of connection between the Irish and the Americans while Niall Montgomery was known to be generous in helping foreign critics and translators of *Ulysses*. Although admitting 'a considerable quantity of shale in the Joycean academic machine', short-story writer and critic, John Jordan, saw 'on the native side', 'a burden of resentment that good American dollars, especially, should be lavished on a local who started off little better than many another middle class Irish boy, an education by the Jesuits and a B.A. from University College, Dublin as his equipment'. The Irish veered between 'extravagant

---

[125]*IT*, 12 August 1970, 5.
[126]Vivien Mercier, Joyce in Gotham, *IT*, 11 March 1953, 6.
[127]Brendan Behan, 'The Poet Yeats Disliked Parsnips', *IP*, 1 November 1958, 11.

praise and snide depreciation of those of their fellows who have been successful by international standards. And a fair share of the depreciation goes to the intellectual and the artist'.[128]

In the 1950s, there were increasing calls, particularly at university level, for a more accepting attitude to Joyce and his writings. In 1955, the barrister and man-of-letters, Eoin O'Mahony, gave a lecture to the National University Women graduates' Association in Newman House, praising Joyce for putting UCD on the map along with Cardinal Newman before suggesting 'that an effort should be made to have a Mass said for Joyce's soul'. His fellow speaker, Lorna Reynolds, then a lecturer in English literature at University College Dublin, insisted instead that it was time 'we behaved like grown-ups and regarded Joyce as somebody we are proud of'.[129] These years also saw leading Irish actors recording readings from Joyce's works. Cyril Cusack and Siobhan McKenna led the way: Cusack recorded extracts from *A Portrait* in 1959 (and *Chamber Music* and *Pomes Penyeach* in 1971) and then excerpts from 'Shem the Penman' and 'Anna Livia Plurabelle' with McKenna in 1961. E. G. Marshall read excerpts from 'Nausicaa' and McKenna from 'Penelope' in 1958, although this latter record was not released in Ireland because the distributors, Irish Record Factors, mistakenly believed that *Ulysses* itself was banned in the country and that their record would, as a consequence, be seized. *The Belfast Telegraph*, which rarely missed an opportunity to report on censorship in 'Eire', carried McKenna's comment that she had made the record three years earlier in New York and that 'there was nothing obscene about it'. This withholding would simply increase its 'curiosity value'.[130] This report spurred a reply from Ciaran Mac An Fhaill: 'It is high time that the silly campaign to depict "Eire" as the Censor's paradise and England as the Artist's Utopia, was called off. Miss McKenna has pricked that particular bubble very effectively.'[131]

The closing years of the 1950s saw *Ulysses* at the centre of an unseemly row at the Dublin Theatre Festival that would not be resolved until 1962. The festival, founded in 1957 by Brendan Smith, would play a crucial role in shaking up and revitalizing the often-drab Irish theatre of mid-century but its early years were beset with controversy. Its scheduled staging, firstly at the 1957 Festival and subsequently at the 1958 edition, of an adaptation of *Ulysses*, by Belfast playwright Allan McClelland, which had originally been seen at the Unity Theatre in London, fell foul, along with Sean O'Casey's *The Drums of Father Ned*, to censorship because of a row involving the Archbishop of Dublin, John Charles McQuaid. The disagreement arose

[128]John Jordan, 'Joyce without Fears', 37.
[129]*IT*, 26 October 1955, 5.
[130]'Siobhan Needled By Ban on Her Record', *Belfast Telegraph*, 9 May 1959, 1.
[131]*Belfast Telegraph*, 6 May 1959, 10.

when 'a letter was received from the Archbishop's Secretary asking if the Tostal Council had sanctioned productions of the new play by O'Casey and a dramatisation of *Ulysses*'.[132] Sources close to the Archbishop made it clear that he did not approve of the programme and would refuse permission for a Solemn Votive Mass (or an ordinary Low Mass) to take place at the beginning of the festival. This rapidly turned into a 'crusade against the two plays', which was 'internationalized when the two secretaries of the Hierarchy's standing committee, Bishop MacNeely of Raphoe and Bishop Fergus of Achonry', took the extraordinary step of sending a letter to the American bishops in which they explained to their 'Venerable Brethren' that 'in spite of strong objection and protest by His Grace the Archbishop of Dublin', An Tostal had 'decided, at a recent meeting, to proceed with this project'.[133] As a result, McQuaid 'had felt compelled' to cancel the Mass on account of Tostal's selection of O'Casey and Joyce. They asked their powerful American counterparts to apply pressure on de Valera's government to ban objectionable plays from the stage. The letter was the subject of a row when New York's Cardinal Spellman raised the issue at a lunch with Irish Minister for External Affairs, Frank Aiken, and the Ambassador to the United States, Frederick Boland. Although there was no official Church ban on the two plays, the organizing committee took fright and decided that while there was nothing offensive about the Joyce adaptation or the O'Casey play, it would be better not to go ahead with them. The main sponsor, Bórd Fáilte, had recommended cutting the two plays in order to avoid public controversy, effectively threatening to pull its sponsorship unless this was done. Bórd Fáilte's Chairman, Brendan O'Regan, made it clear that it was Joyce's work, and not O'Casey's, which was the real problem. The crux for the tourist board was that there might be a Catholic boycott from the United States and this would have been a disaster for the Irish transatlantic air service which was due to be inaugurated in April 1958. Hilton Edwards, producer of the Joyce play, criticized what he called an act of 'rigid censorship' on the part of the committee, which took this decision without reading the script:

> If there is nothing offensive in the play, why don't they allow it to go on? The answer is the timidity against public opinion. This is an admission that either public opinion has got something to go on – in which case they should kowtow to it – or it hasn't, in which case it should be put right by proving the play is not indecent.[134]

[132]'Equity President Criticises Decision', *II*, 28 April 1958, 12.
[133]Letter from William McNeeley, Rahoe and James Fergus, Achonry, Secretaries to Cardinal Mooney, Archbishop of Detroit 4/2/1958 quoted in Peter Murray, 'Belting the Irish State with US Croziers. Theatre, Tourism, UN Policy and Church-State Relations, 1957–58', *Nirsa*, no. 54, (December 2009): 1–23, 3.
[134]*IT*, 15 February 1958, 1.

In protest, Samuel Beckett pulled a scheduled production of three of his mime plays as well as a staging of *All That Fall* by the Pike Theatre Company. Eventually Bórd Fáilte pulled its sponsorship and the entire festival was cancelled.

The controversy dragged on for quite a while, especially in the letters pages, with one correspondent expressing the opinion that the attempt to produce O'Casey and Joyce was yet another example of how 'Dublin is suffering from an overdose of arty-boys and pseudo-intellectuals who are striving to appear smart'.[135] An alternative view, however, was that the Archbishop should not have been asked to approve a Mass in the first place. In an unsent letter to the *Irish Times*, O'Casey wrote:

> The Archbishop doesn't know (or doesn't care) that a work by Joyce or Beckett or even by O'Casey, performed in Dublin, is of more importance to Dublin than it is to any of those authors; that outside Dublin is a wide, wide world, and that this wide place is Joyce's oyster, Beckett's oyster, and even O'Casey's oyster, or that these voices, hushed in Dublin, will be heard in many another place.[136]

Padraic Colum entered the controversy by comparing Archbishop McQuaid's actions with those of Cardinal Logue, who had condemned Yeats' *The Countess Cathleen* and declared that Catholics should not attend it even though he had not read it: 'If his denunciation had prevailed, I doubt if there would be an Irish theatre to-day.' He pointed out that *Ulysses* had never been banned in Ireland, that Joyce's works had helped provoke Thomas Merton's conversion to Catholicism and that 'it may be that in the future a stage version of a part of *Ulysses* will be regarded as a modern mystery play dealing with the horror of a God-rejecting world'.[137]

After repeated requests, Sean O'Casey had reluctantly accepted the invitation to have his play performed as part of Tostal. He had noted that An Tostal was essentially going to celebrate the work of three exiles (himself, Joyce and Beckett) and had a cut at the provincial nature of much Irish writing at the time: 'which makes it look like the exiles are more fruitful than those who lag behind in their own townlands'.[138] His dismay was expressed in a series of exasperated letters to the *Irish Times* that take issue with Quidnunc's comments on Pasternak's being banned in Russia, which he compared to Joyce's better treatment in Ireland. 'Quidnunc [...] pointed out to the poor ignorant lads that the Irish people might possibly

---

[135]*IT*, 19 February 1958, 5.
[136]Unsent letter from O'Casey to *IT*, 17 February 1958, published in Robert Hogan, ed., *The Experiments of Sean O'Casey* (London: St Martin's Press, 1960), 133.
[137]Letter to *IT*, 21 February 1958, 7.
[138]Letter of 6 December 1957 to David H. Greene in David Krause, ed., *The Letters of Sean O'Casey*, Volume III (Washington, DC: The Catholic University of America Press), 503.

have thought Joyce slandered Ireland in his great work "Ulysses"; yet he wasn't banned!'[139] O'Casey thought Quidnunc was being disingenuous and replied: 'Not only banned, but blasted. Did any author suffer more than Joyce because of what he ventured to create? [...] Unofficial censors save the official ones a lot of work in Ireland.'[140] He recalled that in order to obtain a copy of *Ulysses*

> I had to wait till I got to England, and even then it had to be smuggled from France into my hand in 1926. When an Exhibition of Joycean MSS was on show in Paris, none (which means, Quidnunc "not one") of the Irish Government there attended. He is still, as far as may be possible, blasted by the sly sneers of Irish minor writers. It is well for us Irish that there remain in the country a few courageous souls who have honored the great man by preserving the Martello Tower as a memorial of remembrance.[141]

One of those courageous souls was Austin Clarke, who had known Joyce in Paris in the 1920s but had fallen out with him because of a sketch of Joyce that he had published in the *New Statesman* and the *Nation*, to which Joyce had taken offence. Clarke provoked the ire of (future travel writer) Dervla Murphy, who asserted that only 'morbidly curious adolescents, and intellectual poseurs' could want to read *Ulysses* and contested what she called 'the campaign to equate an anti-Joyce bias with absurd Catholic prudery'. There was no such prudish reaction: it was 'the satanic blasphemy of *Ulysses*, rather than the guttersnipe pornography, that must be most repugnant to Christian readers.[...] To Mr. Austin Clarke and his kindred spirits *Ulysses* may be an "acknowledged masterpiece," but to many others it remains an unwholesome literary freak, with an artificially inflated reputation'.[142]

Joyce's reputation continued to grow and was boosted by the appearance in the late 1950s of several significant publications including the first volume of his letters by Stuart Gilbert, which was warmly reviewed by Francis MacManus. He admired the very human portrait of Joyce that emerged: a man 'who could play at being the aloof genius' but 'loved his family with a tenderness which can wring the heart', a figure who was 'kind, devoted, hard-working [...] needy of affection and understanding, boyish with his delight in fame, and often gay in his scorn of the slings and arrows of outrageous fortune'.[143] Richard Ellmann's *James Joyce* was acclaimed

---

[139]Letter to *IT* of 19 July 1960 reprinted in David Krause, ed., *The Letters of Sean O'Casey*, Volume IV (Washington, DC: The Catholic University of America Press), 156.
[140]Letter to *IT*, 26 July 1960, reprinted in Ibid. 158.
[141]Ibid., 158–9.
[142]Dervla Murphy, *IT*, 19 May 1958, 5.
[143]Francis MacManus, 'The Letters of James Joyce', *IP*, 6 July 1957, 5.

around the world with many reviewers calling it the definitive biography. In the *Irish Press*, Seán J. White was hugely impressed and described it as 'an epic biography'[144] but not everyone in Dublin was quite so taken by it, as Brendan Behan noted:

> About Kellman's or Ellman's is it ... – Ellman's life of Joyce, I thought it a very conscientious piece of work. There are 618,000 inhabitants of the city of Dublin that – no, you have to leave out the children – there are ½ million citizens of that city who think that they could have written it better, but opening times and closing times pressing on them so hard they never got around to it.[145]

In *The Irish Times*, John Garvin stated that he would recommend it simply 'in the hope of discouraging others'. He does not like the picture of Joyce that emerges but that is not Ellmann's fault. Garvin does not like Joyce: 'The composite picture that emerges from his successive appearance down the line of time could be charitably entitled a Portrait of the Artist as a Sick Man, a man full of fears, jealousies, superstitions and grievances [...] that were self manufactured.' He departed to the continent not because 'he had been hounded by his countrymen. The hound was, in fact, his own persecution complex, and the towering height to which he aspired was the peak of melodrama from which he could flash his antlers and claim to look down on the hate of those below'.[146]

If the decade began with a commemoration in *Envoy* of Joyce ten years after his passing, it ended with the news that his death mask, created by sculptor Paul Speck, at the request of his friend, the art critic, Carola Giedion-Welcker, whom Joyce had met in Zurich in 1930, had been brought to Dublin. 'Last week', the *Irish Times* reported, 'feeling that its proper place was Joyce's birthplace, she gave it to a Dubliner who wishes to remain anonymous. [...] The owner intends to lend it to the National Library or to the National Museum but ultimately, he hopes that it will be the central exhibit of the Joyce Museum which Michael Scott proposes to set up in the Martello Tower beside the Forty-foot'.[147] It would take another few years but this significant arrival would eventually become one of the central exhibits at the Joyce Tower museum which would become a reality just a few years later.

[144]Seán J. White, 'Portrait of the Artist and the Man', *IP*, 23 January 1960, 7.
[145]Brendan Behan, 'Brendan Behan on Joyce'. A lecture delivered before the James Joyce Society at the Gotham Book Mart in New York City, 1962.
[146]Andrew Cass, 'Portrait of the Artist as a Sick man', *IT*, 6 November 1959, 7.
[147]'An Irishman's Diary', *IT*, Saturday, 25 April 1959, 6.

CHAPTER SEVEN

Taking the Tower

The 1960s and 1970s were decades of political, social and economic transformation around the world, and Ireland was no exception. Change began towards the end of the 1950s with Ireland joining the International Monetary Fund and the World Bank in 1957. The decades of closure and protectionism were coming to an end, mainly as a result of the first programme for economic expansion (1958–63), drawn up by the influential secretary of the Department of Finance, T. K. Whitaker. The election of Seán Lemass as Taoiseach in 1959 (replacing de Valera) accelerated the transformation and saw the country applying in 1963 and again in 1966 to join the European Economic Community (both applications were blocked by France) before acceding in 1973, a year often remembered for the international oil crisis.

In 1960 John F. Kennedy was elected as the first 'Irish' US president and he made an historic visit to Ireland three years later. The previous year, Pope John XXIII launched the Second Vatican Council, which brought profound change to the Catholic Church despite the protestations to the contrary from Archbishop McQuaid, who, on his return from Rome, hubristically declared: 'You may have been worried by much talk of changes to come. Allow me to reassure you. No change will worry the tranquillity of your Christian lives.'[1] In 1961, Teilifís Éireann was inaugurated and with it television became available to the majority (people living on the east coast had already been watching BBC and ITV from the early 1950s). This opened the way for greater public discussion of issues long considered taboo and, over the decades that followed, RTÉ (as the merger between the old radio station, Athlone, and Teilifís Éireann was called) would provide a national platform for unprecedented public questioning of the political, religious,

---

[1]Quoted in Dermot A. Lane, 'Vatican II: The Irish Experience', *The Furrow*, vol. 55, no. 2 (February 2004): 67–81, 67.

moral and cultural status quo. As Robert Savage has noted, 'television was a critical component in the transformation that altered Irish society throughout the 1960s and into the 1970s'.[2]

While battles for civil rights raged around the world and the 'Troubles' began in Northern Ireland, the Republic also enjoyed some significant positive change such as the introduction of free post-primary education by Minister Donogh O'Malley (1969). Two years earlier, Brian Lenihan, the Minister for Justice, introduced a new Censorship of Publications Act (1967) that limited the period of prohibition orders on books to twelve years. This allowed for the immediate sale of over 5,000 previously banned books. While these individual ministers and the government as a whole (led by Jack Lynch) won praise for these actions, as often has been the case with social change in Ireland (i.e. the divorce referendum or the gay marriage referendum in more recent times), the people were comfortably ahead of the mainstream politicians (and of much of the press).

All this gradually facilitated a growing appreciation of Joyce and *Ulysses*, which was being read by a minority, impatient for change, as a beacon of a different, more liberal Ireland. Some young Dubliners emigrating from the country felt duty-bound to get hold of a copy once they were out of Ireland. This did not, however, mean that they would actually read it. Those who stayed and bought it often did read it, carefully. Limerick campaigner for non-denominational education, Patsy Harrold, for example, read *Ulysses* after her husband had purchased it in London and returned to reread it 'at least once a year' after that. Former Labour T. D. Jan O'Sullivan remembered Harrold's 'open, curious intelligent mind; she grew up in a very restricted Ireland and her political motivation was to change that'. Joyce was a means to many like Harrold to see beyond the repressions of what was still a deeply clerical society.

Most people, however, continued to view Joyce with suspicion or simply ignored him. He was off people's radars for the simple reason that his works were not part of the secondary school curriculum. Prior to 1967, the primary poetry anthology for students aged from twelve to fifteen was 'New Intermediate Certificate Poetry', edited by Patrick J. Kennedy.[3] Padraic Colum was the only living 'Anglo-Irish' poet that featured. In 1967, the introduction of a new Intermediate level necessitated the production of a new anthology. Augustine Martin, who had joined the English department of UCD as a lecturer specializing in Anglo-Irish literature in 1964, edited the short story and co-edited the poetry volumes of the *Exploring English* series that supplanted Kennedy's work. The short-story volume included a slew of modern and contemporary Irish writers in what was the most innovative

---

[2]Robert J. Savage, *A Loss of Innocence? Television and Irish Society 1960–72* (Manchester: Manchester University Press, 2010), 383.

[3]P. J. Kennedy, ed., *New Intermediate Certificate Poetry* (Dublin: M. H. Gill & Son, 1955).

development within the new syllabus. Dermot Bolger, in his introduction to a re-edition of the anthology, wrote of 'how revolutionary' it had been:

> The choice of stories was made by a syllabus committee of the Department of Education, who were in turn influenced by an energetic Association of Teachers of English, among whom Martin himself, Veronica O'Brien, Tom O'Dea and Fr Joe Veale were prominent. But while a committee may have helped to select the stories, Martin's approach of 'exploring' the texts was equally revolutionary in terms of conventional teaching and of opening up the imaginative possibilities of language to the relatively young minds who were being exposed to adult themes and ideas.[4]

All of which was true. And yet, in an excellent list that included modern and contemporary figures, such as Brian Friel, Brendan Behan, Liam O'Flaherty, Frank O'Connor, Seán O'Faoláin, James Plunkett and Mary Lavin (and numerous other non-Irish writers, predominantly men), there was no place for the writer who was the father of them all, James Joyce. Writer, Éilís Ní Dhuibhne, recalled:

> Part of my school was in the house where Leopold and Molly Bloom lived. The nun who taught us English referred to the literary associations of the building with mild exasperation. She was impatient with the Joyce industry before it had even started. Still, she didn't discourage us from reading this troublesome man, whose works had not made it onto the school syllabus, not even into the ground-breaking *Exploring English Part One* [...] (perhaps it was just a copyright thing?).[5]

He did scrape into the less popular *Exploring English 2*, the prose anthology, edited by James J. Carey that completed the three-volume series. Carey included the version of the speech in defence of the Irish language given by John F. Taylor, at a Trinity College Historical Society debate in October 1901, that Joyce had included in the 'Aeolus' episode of *Ulysses* (and which Joyce himself had recorded in 1924).[6] The three anthologies were the standard texts until the early 1990s. Joyce remained entirely absent throughout this period from the Leaving Certificate curriculum.

If schools were still wary of Joyce, his old Alma Mater, UCD, was more willing to be associated with him as was noted in 1961 by Owen Sheehy

---

[4]*II*, 4 September 2011. https://www.independent.ie/entertainment/books/review-introduction-from-exploring-english-1-short-stories-we-did-for-our-inter-cert-edited-by-augustine-martin-26767970.html.

[5]Éilís Ní Dhuibhne, 'Joyce's Shadow'. https://www.ucd.ie/ucdonjoyce/writings-on-joyce/articles/joyces-shadow-eilis-ni-dhuibhne/index.html.

[6]James J Carey, *Exploring English 2: An Anthology of Prose for Intermediate Certificate* (Dublin: Gill and Macmillan, 1967).

Skeffington in a Seanad debate. Skeffington, who had known Joyce in Paris during his period as an assistant at the École Normale Supérieure, voiced his approval that 'one of the graduates in whom the authorities [at UCD] now take pride in their brochure was James Joyce. [...] They mention James Joyce by name. I think that is a sign and a token of the broadening of minds'.[7] In fact, as early as 1950, Michael Tierney, the UCD president, was referring to his institution as 'the college of Gerard Manley Hopkins and James Joyce'.[8] However, as Terence Killeen commented, the intellectual atmosphere at UCD 'was not conducive to an intensive engagement with his work'.[9] Fritz Senn's description of Roger McHugh, the first professor of Anglo-Irish literature, as being 'of the generation that was still sceptical about Joyce, and he never quite warmed to him', and yet was 'kind and erudite, an expert on Joyce', is illuminating.[10] Augustine Martin, one of UCD's emerging stars, was also, in early career, ambivalent, complaining in 1965 about an overly obsequious attitude to Joyce, especially among younger writers for whom he 'is now become a God'.[11]

Old arguments about Joyce's relationship with Catholicism persisted and even if they were engaged in with a little less heat and slightly more light, they were also a sign of how Ireland's academics were ignoring international scholarship and revisiting local rows. At an informal symposium on Joyce and Catholicism held at the Dublin University Laurentian Society, Geoffrey Thurley, a lecturer at Trinity, claimed 'that Joyce had ceased to be a Catholic' while John Jordan, then a lecturer at UCD, said 'that Joyce was not rejecting Catholicism but the simulacra of it which he found in Victorian Ireland. [...] Having assimilated the teachings and disciplines of his mentors more thoroughly than they had themselves, he out-jesuited the Jesuits'. Jordan insisted that Joyce never ceased to be a Catholic, 'finding evidence for this in the profound effect for good produced on others by his work'. Augustine Martin disagreed and asked 'if indeed Joyce was a Catholic alienated only by the conditions in Ireland, why did he reject the Faith completely even when he found himself so close to the purer European stream of Catholicism?'[12]

Another sampling of the contrasting views of Joyce was heard at the inaugural meeting of the 1961 UCD Literary and Historical Society, where a younger student generation pitched itself in defence of Joyce against more critical establishment figures. In his inaugural address, Dermot Bouchier-Hayes complained that the 'only place where Joyce was appreciated now

---

[7]https://www.oireachtas.ie/en/debates/debate/seanad/1961-01-10/4/.

[8]Richard M. Kain, *Fabulous Voyager*, 296.

[9]Terence Killeen, 'Ireland Must be Important... ', *JSA*, vol. 14 (Summer 2003): 20.

[10]Fritz Senn, *Joycean Murmoirs*, 37.

[11]Augustine Martin, 'Inherited Dissent: The Dilemma of the Irish Writer', *Studies: An Irish Quarterly Review*, vol. 54, no. 213 (Spring 1965): 1–20, 4.

[12]*IT*, 26 February 1966, 7.

was in the American Universities' and said 'it was fitting that 20 years after Joyce's death they should come together to honour this great man' who 'had educated the Irish by telling them what they were really like'. Professor Roger McHugh responded that he could not

> completely accept the thesis that the solution to Ireland's problems was by reading Joyce. We were not yet a completely free people, and there were many unresolved problems. Joyce's work was merely part of an intellectual heritage. The speaker had made the mistake of sympathising too much with his subject.

Poet James Liddy said the country should have a sense of 'collective guilt' for its treatment of Joyce, 'the greatest writer of our times, certainly the greatest technical writer. It was because of the great love which Joyce had for his country that his betrayal and rejection by Ireland was so shameful'. In an article published the same year in the *Kilkenny magazine*, Liddy declared that he felt disgusted and degraded at the way Joyce was treated and at how 'his memory [was] attacked and insulted after his death'. He blamed 'gombeen nationalism' and 'gombeen Catholicism for obscuring Joyce's great works'.[13] The final speaker at the L&H event, Fr Peter Connelly, professor of English at St Patrick's College, Maynooth, denied that Joyce had been driven from the country and doubted that his books could be seen to offer a reliable interpretation of modern Ireland:

> He chose to go into exile and this self-chosen flight was his favourite pose on the Continent. In his psychology there seemed to have been a need to fight and many of the famous betrayals were faked. Defence of the treatment given to his books was not necessary. Ireland was not the first to reject him. The first people to reject his books were English censors. Joyce was not here in 1916 and, therefore, he was not the interpreter of the consciousness of Ireland, certainly not the modern Ireland of the past 30 years.[14]

Fr Connolly, a forward-looking literary cleric who had spoken out against censorship in the 1950s, took a softer line in another lecture entitled 'Joyce and the Irish', which he delivered at the College of Commerce. While acknowledging that 'anti-Irish, anti-Catholic and obscene stains are certainly to be found in his works', he pointed to a 'popular fallacy' that 'consists in taking them out of their context and exaggerating their true proportions. The result is an approach to Joyce which is not proper to literature and

---

[13]James Liddy, 'Coming of Age: James Joyce and Ireland', *Kilkenny Magazine*, vol. 5 (1961): 25–9, 25.
[14]*IT*, 14 January 1961, 9.

which misses the mark. [...] Joyce is taken too seriously as a propagandist because he is not taken seriously enough as an artist'.[15]

Historian Owen Dudley Edwards took issue with how Joyce's depictions misrepresented Ireland and were being misread and amplified abroad. He contested that Joyce had been driven from the country and, in a series of articles in *The Irish Times*, complained that 'the Yanks have bought James Joyce big, and are getting their money back in degrees for dissertations which in the view of some should have won penitentiary sentences'.[16] There was little 'quality or accuracy' in American understandings of Joyce, 'he is swallowed whole', while 'the Joyce-O'Casey image of the "rejected" Irishman of letters' dominates. 'From a reading of Joyce, O'Casey and, to a lesser extent, O'Connor, the American, lacking the background which enables him to sift evidence and assess the realities, builds up a terrifying image of the clericalist, censorship dominated republic.'

Niall Montgomery was of like mind when voicing his annoyance at the many foreign Joyce scholars who uncritically accepted Joyce's version of Dublin as *the* version of the city. 'Certainly he has "immortalised" something, but it's not Dublin.' He describes how a French Joyce reader, on visiting the city for the first time, 'felt, as a reader of Joyce, that he knew the town well, the squalor, the sense of a dead city, the feeling of failure'. But the realities of 1904 Dublin were very different, as Montgomery drolly noted:

> Ireland is not a poor country and Dublin, though it lacks the Babylonian splendour of Cork, is not quite the leper-haunted shantytown the Joyce pilgrims come to see. ('What ails James?' his father is reported to have asked. 'Is the boy all in it?'). [...] Perhaps Mr. Joyce, member of a Cork family which overshot the town and landed in lower Drumcondra, never really saw Dublin. Drumcondra yes, and the suburban fields![17]

F. S. L. Lyons also argued that Joyce's was not a true reflection of the Dublin he had left behind and that historians had a duty to correct this:

> Was the Abbey Theatre, were the plays of J. M. Synge, the product of paralysis? Did Yeats's poetry proceed from paralysis? [...] Was Hugh Lane's grandiose conception of a gallery of modern art to house his collection of Impressionist pictures a sign of paralysis? [...] were the emergence of Sinn Fein, the growth of the Gaelic League, the rise of organised labour, symbols of a rebirth of paralysis? Above all, was the city which, just 10 years after Joyce's letter was written, burst into a flame of revolution, not quenched until the Union with Britain was dissolved,

[15]'Priest lectures on James Joyce', *IT*, 9 February 1961, 7.
[16]Owen Dudley Edwards, 'America's Image of Ireland (2)', *IT*, 11 January 1963, 8.
[17]Niall Montgomery, 'Dublin's Dublin', *IT*, 16 June 1962, 10.

really in the grip of an inexorable paralysis? [...] as the historian must insist, the prevailing characteristic of Dublin in the opening years of this century was tension, not paralysis.[18]

One could dismiss these comments on the ground that the cultural 'revolution' that Lyons describes involved a minority of the population, but if we take the larger perspective of the century following the Famine, the enormity and relentlessness of Ireland's change become more apparent. Joyce's early writings contributed to the sense of an Ireland paralysed by history as it may well have seemed to be in the Parnell aftermath and when he left it in 1904 but *Ulysses* also communicated a sense of change and of the possibility of change despite offering only a snapshot of Dublin on just one single day of that same year.

Although Irish academics were adept at picking holes in the theses of their American counterparts, they continued to underperform when it came to producing their own rival studies that might have set the contextual record straight. In 1970, Gerard O'Flaherty was among many to complain about the still scant Irish contribution: 'In spite of the insights given to us by such brilliant Joyceans as John Garvin, Niall Montgomery and Dr. Eileen McCarville [sic] there is as yet only one full length book on Joyce's work by an Irishman. This is a very modest addition to what has come to be known as The Joyce Industry.'[19]

Where the Irish did make a singular contribution in the 1960s was in a series of theatrical productions that succeeded in making Joyce more accessible and acceptable to a growing segment of the public. The year 1961 saw Mary Manning's adaptation *The Voice of Shem* performed at the Eblana. Manning was an Irish actress and an Abbey playwright who had also worked as a film critic at the *Irish Statesman* before moving to the United States where she was a co-founder of the Poet's Theatre in Cambridge. *The Voice of Shem* boasted an impressive cast that included Marie Kean in 'one of her finest roles as Anna Livia plurabelle', May Cluskey, Arthur O'Sullivan and Patrick Bedford.[20] David Norris later described this as 'riotously funny, and the most stimulating production I have ever attended in this city'.[21] It became the basis for Mary Ellen Bute's film version of *Finnegans Wake*, which won an award at the Cannes Film Festival in 1965. Bute was a long-time member of the New York James Joyce Society and an experimental filmmaker. This, her last film, was a genuine labour of love starring Martin J. Kelley as Finnegan, Jane Reilly as Anna Livia Plurabelle, Peter Haskel as Shem, Page Johnson as Shaun

[18]F. S. L. Lyons, 'James Joyce's Dublin', *Twentieth Century Studies* (November 1971): 7–8.
[19]Gerard O'Flaherty, 'The Joyce Industry', *IP*, 22 April 1970, 12.
[20]'Impressive lyricism of Joyce', *IP*, 12 September 1961, 5.
[21]David Norris, 'It was all my uncle's doing', *IP*, 12 January 1991, 17.

and had Harvard's first professor of Irish Studies, John V Kelleher, as the 'commentator'.[22] It was shown on RTÉ in 1973.

A huge stage success came in 1966 with Hugh Leonard's *Stephen D*, an accomplished adaptation of *A Portrait* and *Stephen Hero*. It was first produced at the Gate as part of the Dublin Theatre Festival. Originally, Hugh Leonard had conceived *Stephen D* as a one-man play for Cyril Cusack but he was 'the wrong age for the part'.[23] He then approached Norman Rodway, who told him 'you need Peter Sellers for that'.[24] Leonard subsequently rewrote *Stephen D* as a full-scale play and cast Rodway in the leading role. He rather modestly (and modesty was not his forte) declared that in his adaptation 'every word [...] can be found in Joyce's originals'.[25] The play is episodic in structure and uses a flashback framework beginning in the distant past. Stephen is initially played by two actors, one as Stephen the narrator, the other, Stephen as a child and a teenager. The play ends with some of the diary entries from *A Portrait*, the repetition of the first paragraph of the novel, and a partial quotation from Joyce's broadside 'Gas from a Burner'. Stephen's line 'I will not serve' closes the adaptation. Phyllis Ryan, who produced the play for Gemini Productions, remembered the mixture of excitement and unease in the lead-up to the first Dublin performance:

> Back in the Festival office with Brendan Smith to discuss finances, I deliberately did not dwell on the extraordinary elation charging the Gate Theatre, but there was a hint of tension in the way Brendan questioned me. Would the play cause riots, run into trouble with the authorities? Was I sure that it was not offensive to Church or State? Of course I lulled his anxieties, although I really did suspect that there would be trouble from some quarters. I did not think the Church would be overly concerned. After all, Joyce was the most famous Jesuit student ever, and the Jesuits had kindly lent us a store of old cassocks, with black cloth wings coming from the shoulders. But I realized that Brendan was worried about losing his sponsorship, and that was serious. I believed that *Stephen D* would be a real turning point in Irish theatre.[26]

She was right. It was also a turning point in Joyce's reception in Ireland even if Leonard somewhat blunted the subtleties of Joyce's complex Stephen. Ryan recalled how the premiere, held on 24 September 1962 at the Gate, went off:

---

[22]Kelleher, a highly respected Joyce scholar at Harvard, was close to Harry Levin in the 1940s when he was writing *James Joyce: A Critical Introduction* (1944).
[23]Hugh Leonard, 'Leonard: Difficult to Say No!' in Des Hickey and Gus Smith, eds., *A Paler Shade of Green* (London: Leslie Frewin, 1972), 194.
[24]Ibid., 177.
[25]Hugh Leonard, *Stephen D*. (London: Evans Brothers, 1964), 4
[26]Phyllis Ryan, 'In orbit with James Joyce', in Phyllis Ryan, ed., *The Company I Kept* (Dublin: Town House, 1996), 173.

Into the second half, Fitz's [Director, Jim Fitzgerald] wizardry was evident, permeating the script as it unfolded before a rapt gathering. Then the audible gasp, as the nature of Joyce's arguments against religious orthodoxy, delivered with icy clarity by Norman, hit home, causing at least a dozen over-sensitive Catholics to vacate their seats and make for the exit. They were hardly noticed. The audience remained riveted. When the curtain fell, there was a silence, and pandemonium broke loose with cheers and countless curtain calls. On the following day, the reviews were favourable beyond our wildest dreams, and as the week wore on, foreign critics wrote eulogies about *Stephen D* and all associated with it.

Stephen D enjoyed a sell-out run in Dublin and served as an entrée for many into the life and works of Joyce. It was also Leonard's first international success and the first Dublin Theatre Festival production to go directly to the West End where it enjoyed a record-breaking 119 performance run at St Martin's Theatre. *The Evening Press* in Dublin enthused. 'Not since the Abbey players first electrified London has there been a welcome like this.' Seamus Kelly in the *Irish Times* noted that it was 'a virtually unanimous rave.'

The fact that *Stephen D* was not produced by the Abbey reflected on the continuing conservatism of the National Theatre, which was still under the stewardship of Ernest Blythe, who refused T. P. McKenna permission to play the part of Cranly. He left the Abbey Company in order to play the role and this was the beginning of an illustrious career in London. With good reason, an editorial in the *Irish Times* would complain:

> The Abbey continues to produce plays which no longer attract a discriminating audience, excite exclamations of patronising obituary from visiting critics, and dare not open abroad because no audience outside Dublin would tolerate them. [...] The Abbey Theatre is not a national theatre. It was. To dignify it with that name now humiliates the living no less than it mocks the dead.[27]

Stephen D fuelled some controversy when a special charity performance in aid of the Irish Centre in Camden Town was attended by the Ambassador in London, Cornelius Cremin. This courtesy 'aroused some comment among those who remembered an occasion not too long ago when our then Ambassador in Paris declined to open an exhibition in honour of Joyce'.[28] A year later, Kelly remembered: 'At the pre-first night, at a show for Irish charities attended almost exclusively by expatriate Irishry, applause mingled about fifty-fifty with protests and, there were the traditional walks-out that

---

[27]'The Abbey', *IT*, 20 February 1963, 7. *Stephen D* enjoyed a revival directed by Joe Dowling at the Abbey in 1978 with Barry McGovern in the title role.
[28]Seamus Kelly, 'Joycean Actor Is Told to Go and Back a Horse', *IT*, 13 February 1963, 5.

have signalized the triumphs-to-be of some early Synge and early O'Casey.'[29] Not for the first or last time, some of the Irish expatriates present revealed themselves to be in something of a time warp. The opening act was both sniggered at and heckled by the London Irish audience, then, as the second half of the play began, Hugh Leonard heard a woman seated near him in the auditorium say: 'I suppose we're in for another session of blasphemy?' She was not representative, however, because 'the audience, though pretty obviously shocked, were also hypnotized and compelled to a stunned attention by Joyce's blazing sincerity.'[30]

Further success awaited *Stephen D* in Paris (at the Theatre Montparnasse), in Amsterdam and Zurich, and in the United States, where it enjoyed an off-Broadway production with Roy Schneider winning an Obie for his performance in 1968. Critic Michael Billington praised Leonard's 'great skill' in showing 'Joyce cutting loose from the restrictive bonds of family loyalties, patriotism and religion' and ending 'the play on a fine note of exultant defiance with the hero going into permanent exile'.[31] These were the very qualities that caused discomfort in a minority present in Irish audiences. One theatregoer took the trouble to write to *The Irish Times* announcing how she 'was sickened, disgusted and appalled at the whole theme. God – the Creator of human beings and of all things – is mocked, sneered at and jibes are thrown at the Jesuits. This adaptation of two books by James Joyce is openly blasphemous and in very bad taste'. The letter-writer, who signed him/herself 'Low-Brow', was not without a sense of humour and included a postscript that read: 'A note on the programme tells me that "This theatre is disinfected throughout with Jeyes Fluid and Cooper's Aerosol" – a thoughtful precaution taken by the management in the interests of their patrons, but, unfortunately, it does not affect the mind!'[32] *Stephen D* became 'an intruder into many an Irish home' when it was broadcast in 1964 on BBC as part of its 'Festival' series of plays and on RTÉ the following year.[33]

The year 1962 also finally saw Dublin's Eblana Theatre staging *Bloomsday*, the *Ulysses* adaptation by Belfast playwright, Allan McClelland, that had originally been seen at the Unity Theatre in London and in New York and had been scheduled for the Dublin Theatre Festival in 1957 and again in 1958 but had been controversially cancelled. Ronnie Walsh and Anna Manahan starred as Bloom and Molly, with Manahan winning warm praise for her performance that was 'nothing short of magnificent' and 'surpasses even Miss Manahan's "Rose Tattoo" triumph. For me, it puts her on the

[29]'An Irishman's Diary', *IT*, 12 February 1964.
[30]Seamus Kelly, 'Joycean Actor Is Told to Go and Back a Horse', 5.
[31]Michael Billington, 'Hugh Leonard', in James Vinson, ed., *Contemporary Dramatists* (London: St James Press, 1973), 481.
[32]Letter signed 'Low-Brow', *IT*, 4 June 1965, 11.
[33]Finbarr Slattery, 'Who Was This Fellow James Joyce Anyway?', *Kerryman*, 21 October 1967, 10.

same plane as Magnani'.[34] It returned to the larger Gate Theatre in 1964 and was prominently reported in the news with the *Sunday Independent* even carrying a story entitled 'Bloomsday kittens in search of a home', which reported that Manahan's cat had given birth to five kittens on 16 June and had been named 'after characters in "Bloomsday" – Stephen, Gerti [*sic*], Molly, Poldy and Buck'.[35] Clearly Joyce was becoming part of popular culture. A televised version with Milo O'Shea as Bloom and June Tobin as Molly was broadcast as part of the BBC's 1964 Festival season. It was hailed as 'a production in which an alpine height of accomplishment was reached'. Much of the merit went to O'Shea, without whom 'this production could have been the outstanding disaster of the BBC's list of drama presentations' had he not 'figuratively hoisted the entire dramatisation onto his shoulders and carried it for an hour and three-quarters'.[36]

At the 1963 Dublin Theatre Festival, Leonard followed up on the success of *Stephen D* with a second Joyce play entitled *Dublin One* at the Gaiety. Directed by Barry Cassin, the first act dealt with 'Counterparts', 'An Encounter' and 'Grace', while the second included 'Ivy Day' and 'Two Gallants', with 'A little Cloud' functioning as an epilogue.[37] The adaptation was 'set in the framework of an illustrated lecture' given by an actor playing 'a modernized Ignatius Gallagher', who projected slides of Dublin's streets, houses, people to introduce the stories and evoke their settings. Leonard also found space to introduce the semi-fictional character of John Joyce, Joyce's father, who played the role of Tom Kernan in 'Grace', of Mr Henchy in 'Ivy Day' and of Farrington in 'Counterparts'. Like its predecessor, *Dublin One* played a role, as Gus Smith later commented in the *Sunday Independent*, in making Joyce 'palatable': 'Up to that time Joyce tended to be regarded as remote, enigmatic and surrounded by intellectual mystique. [...] Leonard showed that Joyce wasn't actually born with two heads.'[38] It was also televised in three parts in August 1965 and featured Donal Donnelly, Martin Dempsey, David Kelly, Dermot Tuohy and May Cluskey. Leonard returned to *Dubliners* in 1975 with an adaption of 'The Dead', which was broadcast on RTÉ to great praise. The *Irish Times* reported that 'Mr Leonard caught perfectly the mood and atmosphere of the original. [...] The dinner party scene was magnificent; so, too, was the dancing of the quadrille'.[39] Ray McNally as Gabriel and Pauline Delany as Gretta were lauded for their fine acting.

Joyce finally made it into the National Theatre – the Peacock rather than the main Abbey stage – in the 1969 production of Harry Pollock's

---

[34]*IT*, 18 June 1962, 6.
[35]'Bloomsday Kittens in Search of a Home', *SI*, 12 July 1964, 1.
[36]Peter Cleary, 'B.B.C. Touch Heights with "Bloomsday"', *SI*, 14 June 1964, 27.
[37]Jos Lanters, *Missed Understandings: A Study of Stage Adaptations of the Works of James Joyce* (Amsterdam: Rodopi, 1988), 18.
[38]Gus Smith, 'Is This the Way to Honour Joyce?' *SI*, 24 January 1982, 14.
[39]Ken Gray, 'Little Light on Nuclear Power', *IT*, 10 February 1975, 8.

forgettable (and forgotten) *Night Boat from Dublin*, based on Joyce's letters. A year later, having given a rave review to Harold Pinter's *Exiles* at the Mermaid in London, the *Evening Herald*'s respected critic, John Finnegan, suggested bringing it to the Abbey. He praised Pinter for giving 'new, leaping life to a play that up to now has been looked upon as a theatrical non-event' and ventured that 'Joyce's own city deserves to experience this astonishing tribute from one writer to another'.[40] His suggestion fell on deaf ears but Dublin did get its own production of *Exiles* in 1973 when it was performed at the Peacock under Vincent Dowling's highly praised direction. Bosco Hogan played Richard Rowan in a 'marvellously good performance' while Kevin McHugh was a 'splendid, smouldering' Robert Hand.[41]

In 1971, *Ulysses in Nighttown*, written by Marjorie Barkentin under the supervision of Padraic Colum, enjoyed a successful run at the Peacock. Directed by Tomás MacAnna, it stretched the Abbey's resources, with some fifty-five roles filled by twenty actors with Joe Dowling as Bloom and Frank Grimes as Stephen Dedalus. A new production was seen in the Abbey in 1974 with Dowling again playing Bloom and Eileen Colgan as Molly. An American Broadway production of the play earned Fionnula Flanagan a Tony Award nomination for her performance as Molly alongside Zero Mostel in the role of Bloom. This led Flanagan to write her acclaimed one-women show, 'James Joyce's Women', which was directed by Burgess Meredith and which she later made into a film that was not released, due to a difficult negotiation with the Joyce Estate, until 1985.

While Joyce's works now regularly enjoyed prominent success on stage and screen, his shift to the mainstream was also evident in what became, from 1960 onwards, an annual Bloomsday celebration at the Tower in Sandycove. Bloomsday events received ample coverage in the media that often focused on the presence of celebrity cultural figures. Sylvia Beach took part in the 1960 Bloomsday at the Tower but also recorded a talk entitled 'Shakespeare and Company' 'about the fortunes of her bookshop in Paris', which was broadcast on Radio Éireann in August 1960. That same year, John Huston, who would later direct the acclaimed film of Joyce's 'The Dead', led calls for the Tower, which he had helped the architect, Michael Scott, and John Ryan purchase in 1954 for £4,700, to be turned into a Museum.[42] His involvement added glamour to the enterprise. Newspapers eagerly reported that he was in Reno filming 'Misfits' with Marilyn Monroe (this was the occasion of the famous photo of her reading *Ulysses*) and as 'doing his own bit of the Joyce

[40]J. J. Finnegan, 'Abbey Should Try for "Exiles"', *EH*, 21 November1970, 6.

[41]John Boland, 'A rich, exciting "Exiles"', *IP*, 23 February 1973, 6. The only previous production was a once-off performance on 18 January 1948 at the Gaiety, directed by Josephine Albericci, with Godfrey Quigley, Peggy Hayes, Joan Wall, Barry Keegan, Joyce Sullivan and Brian Cassidy. The *Irish Press* called it 'all tract and very little play'. 'Joyce's "Exiles" at Gaiety', *IP*, 19 January 1948, 9.

[42]Vivien Igoe, 'Early Joyceans in Dublin', *JSA*, vol. 12 (Summer 2001): 81–99, 82.

Museum propaganda work there, soliciting contributions from the several rich film people on the set for this project. For it, the organising committee require a sum of about £5,000, of which it is understood they have about £500 in hand'.[43] The dormant Joyce Tower Society was reconstituted and an impressive group of donors, including T. S. Eliot, Maria Jolas, Thornton Wilder, Frances (Fanny) Steloff, founder of the Gotham Book Mart (and one of the main movers behind the influential James Joyce Society which had been formed in New York in 1947), all chipped in. Huston contributed 'the then considerable sum of a thousand dollars to get the Museum launched'.[44] Material donations formed the body of the permanent exhibition: 'Samuel Beckett presented Joyce's famous family waistcoat; Maria Jolas gave his last cane, Sylvia Beach brought in photographs, a prospectus for *Ulysses*, and a page of notes in Joyce's hand; Cyril Cusack provided an edition of *Ulysses* illustrated by Henri Matisse.'[45]

The 1960 annual Irish Exhibition of Living Art (the annual exhibition of the Royal Hibernian Academy) featured a controversial portrait of Joyce by the young Basil Blackshaw. Donagh MacDonagh sought to purchase it for the Tower collection. He wrote to the papers announcing that he had organized a whip-round that had raised '£17 in cash from 17 admirers of the portrait and the subject' but still needed to raise a total of £78-15-0.[46] This sum was quickly gathered and one of the most significant Irish Joyce portraits since those by Patrick Tuohy and Sean O'Sullivan, both of whom had known Joyce in Paris, was secured. Others, many others, would follow by esteemed artists such as Harry Kernoff, Louis Le Brocquy and Micheal Farrell.

Padraic Colum, already installed as second President of the New York James Joyce Society, became president, Donagh MacDonagh chairman, and Sam Suttle, treasurer of the Tower Society. Together they would establish it as the most significant single location for events celebrating Joyce's place in Irish culture (even if it continued to be without heating and lighting).[47] News of the imminent opening on Bloomsday 1962 spread around the world. The honorary committee included Sylvia Beach, Samuel Beckett, Denis Johnston, T. S. Eliot and Harriet Shaw Weaver. Sean O'Casey turned down the invitation hoping that MacDonagh would forgive him 'for you know how I love and honour the name of Joyce'.[48] Sylvia Beach travelled

---

[43]'Dublin Letter', *CE*, 26 August 1960, 6.
[44]Robert Nicholson,'"Signatures of All Things I am Here to Read": The James Joyce Museum at Sandycove', *JJQ*, vol. 38, no. 3/4, Joyce and Trieste (Spring–Summer 2001): 293–8, 293.
[45]Ibid., 295.
[46]*IP*, 12 August 1960, 10.
[47]The following year the society was transformed into the James Joyce Tower Company with the following directors: Donagh MacDonagh, Christopher Gore-Grimes, Michael Scott, Niall Montgomery. Other subscribers were Seán O'Faoláin, John Ryan, Padraic Colum.
[48]Letter of 26 July 1961 from Sean O'Casey to Donagh MacDonagh. MS 37, 984 NLI.

from Paris to do the honours at the official opening in the presence of over
100 guests including Joyce's grandson, Stephen, Maria Jolas, Oliver St John
Gogarty. Louis MacNeice, W. R. Rodgers, Denis Johnston, Austin Clarke,
Seán O'Faoláin and Mary Lavin. Myles na Gopaleen singled out Miss Beach
and Madame Jolas for jocular praise:

> Those two ladies (both, incidentally, Americans) are among the toughest
> of the amazons of the literary Cumann na mBan without whom English
> literature would have by now been seriously distorted by the puritanical
> myopia of God's Englishman.[49]

Brendan Behan was also present and 'climbed the Tower like a mountain
goat' before leaving a message for Miss Beach which read: 'Throwaway is
a Good Thing for the Gold Cup. Signed. Nosey Flynn.'[50] The event received
widespread press coverage. The 'Peter Kildare' social column in the *Sunday
Press* enthused: 'At last – the giant comes back to his own'[51] while the *Sunday
Independent* carried a large photograph featuring A. J. McConnell, Provost
of Trinity College; British Ambassador, Sir Ian MacLennon; and Charles
Haughey, then Minister for Justice, all happy, finally, to be associated with
Joyce. In a sense, Joyce had finally made the journey synthesized in the title
of Donagh MacDonagh's radio documentary, 'James Joyce, from Notoriety
to Fame', which was broadcast in the same month. This probably came as
some consolation to the two Joyce sisters in attendance, May, and Eileen,
who was described as having 'looked about her and said sadly. "It is an
awful pity that all this didn't happen in his life-time"'.[52]

June 1962 brought the first substantial 'Joyce Week' offering a series of
lectures and readings featuring what was by now a familiar cast of local
Joyce supporters and academics, such as Eileen MacCarvill, James Liddy,
John Garvin, A. J. Leventhal, Niall Montgomery, but also the odd voice
from abroad, such as Richard M. Kain, and an undoubted highlight in
Cyril Cusack. In addition, the *Irish Times* published a number of special
articles to mark the occasion (and the fortieth anniversary of the publication
of *Ulysses*), including one by Padraic Fallon on Joyce as poet. He linked
Joyce back to the Celtic Twilight noting how Joyce's poems 'suggest Seumas
O'Sullivan, AE, Yeats' and contain 'an astounding number' of echoes. What
was so striking about *Chamber Music* was the extent to which it shows that
'the author of *Ulysses* was involved in the Celtic Twilight', so much so that
his early efforts are 'as second-hand as bad opera'. None of which stops
Fallon from acknowledging Joyce's greatness and seeing him in *Ulysses* as 'a

---

[49]Myles na Gopaleen, 'The Forty Fête', *IT*, 19 June 1962, 8.
[50]'An Irishman's Diary', *IT*, 4 July 1962, 4.
[51]*Sunday Press*, 17 June 1962.
[52]Tom Hennigan and Eamonn Gilligan, 'Going Places', *EH*, 18 June 1962, 9.

poet discovering himself verbally and discovering his world and uncovering it. It is purely verbal, a vast poem and no novel at all. It is Joycean form'.[53]

Not everyone was pleased by the growing prominence of Bloomsday. In 1962, Francis J. Flood, a New York resident formerly of Fairview, wrote to the *Evening Herald* to express his shock at the 'James Joyce Gimmick' pointing out that the Irish in the United States 'disown the apostate religionist and defeatist nationalist'. 'If such a museum had been mooted in the immediate days following the war of independence', he continued, 'the organised Republican soldiers would have had more to say in a very practical way'.[54] Another letter, published in 1969, from a certain Ernie Murray complained about 'the annual welter of adulation of the works of James Joyce – a lot of oul' cod' and complained about *Ulysses* as 'a vile production [...] with its page-to-page blasphemies'.[55]

Such hostility met an unexpected if indirect challenge from John F. Kennedy, shortly before his presidential visit to Ireland in 1963. An article published in May of that year described Kennedy's first post-War Irish trip in 1946 and his meeting with veteran Irish journalist, Jack Grealish, who recalled that they talked about 'things newspapermen usually talk about – stories – and the recent war, of course. And Joyce'. Kennedy 'was very interested in James Joyce and the topography of *Ulysses*. [...] the pubs, streets and landmarks of Dublin'.[56] When he addressed the joint houses of the Oireachtas a few weeks later, he evoked Ireland's diaspora and drew on *Ulysses* to make his point:

> They came to our shores in a mixture of hope and agony, and I would not underrate the difficulties of their course once they arrived in the United States. They left behind hearts, fields, and a nation yearning to be free. It is no wonder that James Joyce described the Atlantic as a bowl of bitter tears.[57]

Although this was a partial misquote (Joyce was referring to Dublin Bay in the phrase 'a bowl of bitter waters'), there was method in it and Kennedy could have been confident that few in his Irish audience would notice the slip. The mere fact that he very intentionally pronounced Joyce's name was in itself notable and would have been greeted coolly by many in the chamber. In a conversation decades later with Colm Tóibín, Arthur Schlesinger, a close friend and special assistant to Kennedy, remembered that a number of Kennedy's advisers, including Schlesinger himself,

---

[53]Padraic Fallon, 'The Light Tenor of His Ways', *IT*, 16 June 1962, 11.
[54]Francis J. Flood, Letter, *EH*, 19 June 1962.
[55]Ernie Murray, 'Poor Joyce!', Letter, *IT*, 4 July 1969, 9.
[56]Joe Kennedy, 'To two presidents he's just "Jack"', *EH*, 28 May 1963, 4.
[57]https://www.oireachtas.ie/en/debates/debate/seanad/1963-06-28/2/.

took a dim view of the censorship of books in Ireland which had continued into the 1960s and believed that the official Irish view that James Joyce was 'a dirty writer' needed to change. Thus they made sure that John F Kennedy's speech to the joint houses of the Oireachtas in Ireland contained a reference to James Joyce, which might have seemed casual to the assembled audience, but was placed in the speech deliberately as a way of suggesting that those in power in Ireland might wake up to Joyce's importance and value.[58]

Six months after the speech, in an article written the day after Kennedy's assassination, Frank O'Connor described the vital role of the American academy in recognizing the importance of Irish literature and in helping to pave the way for an Irish-American and later an Irish acceptance of the great value of the country's writers:

> The American University took the Irish literary revival and put it fair and square on every arts course, and when we mock at young Americans who come here to study Yeats and Joyce, we are mocking at the very thing that straightened the backs of men like Kennedy, so that they no longer had to go around pretending they had a great-grandmother from Antrim and were really 'Scotch-Irish'. Kennedy treated the Scotch-Irish with the same good-natured contempt with which he treated the native Irish who were afraid of James Joyce's name, and he boldly spoke of Joyce in the Dail, where previously Joyce's name had never been heard except on some debate on evil literature.[59]

In the years after Kennedy's death, there were calls to commemorate him in Ireland by renaming Westmoreland Street after him but an anonymous letter writer, using the pseudonym, 'Finnegan's Wake', asked in the pages of the *Evening Herald*, 'Why not Joyce Street?' Those seeking to name a street after Kennedy 'would do well to remember that, when the late President paid his first visit to Ireland as a Senator in 1948, he came here as a student of James Joyce, carrying a copy of *Ulysses*. If the name of this street is to be changed why not call it after the great Dubliner, Joyce?'[60] As it turned out, Westmoreland Street stayed as it was. Kennedy eventually had an Industrial Estate on the Naas Road named after him and Joyce the former Mabbot Street in Monto where he had set the Nighttown episode of *Ulysses*. At the time, this was a narrow back street in a rundown area between Talbot Street and Foley Street.

---

[58]Colm Tóibín, 'Foreword' to Richard Aldous, ed., *Great Irish Speeches* (London: Quercus, 2009), 4.
[59]Frank O'Connor, 'I Mourn the Man Who Led the Intellectuals Back into Government Says Frank O'Connor', *II*, 24 November 1963, 8.
[60]Letter from 'Finnegan's Wake', 'Why Not Joyce Street?', *EH*, 4 October 1966, 6.

The Tower was run from its opening until 1965 by the James Joyce Tower Company Ltd and Bloomsday was always a big event although the growing number of foreign visitors was not always greeted warmly. In 1963, *The Irish Times* headlined an 'Overflow Crowd on "Bloomsday"' for readings by Cyril Cusack and Patrick Bedford. More punters turned up than could be accommodated but on the plus side, 'each paid £1 admittance'.[61] The following year, the tone of complaint was similar: '"Bloomsday," said a plain Dublin man who followed yesterday's celebrations from the tower to Eccles street and then on to Brighton Square, "Bloomsday has gone to hell since the Americans took it over. Not a drink in sight"'.[62] Under the governance of the Joyce Tower Committee, Dolly (Mrs. Lennox) Robinson was the first curator. In the rather ungenerous words of Robert Nicholson, she 'was fond of a drop and did not stay long'.[63] To be fair, such a fondness would hardly have singled her out among the early Irish Joyceans. Rory Brennan recalled meeting her successor, the poet Michael Hartnett, when he was curator 'or doorkeeper as he might have put it. [...] He was reading a William Faulkner novel. He indicated the book, pronouncing "I prefer him," and then waved dismissively at the Joycean memorabilia, waistcoats and all'.[64] One positive outcome of Hartnett's time there was that he completed a draft version of his sequence, *Tao* (published in 1971). His fellow poet, Paul Durcan, later remembered Hartnett as 'the Chinese-eyed curator' who 'offered to share with me/A carafe of vodka left over/From a literary soirée of the night before./It was the day after Bloomsday./Monday, 17 June 1963'. This was from the poem, 'Ulysses', which describes the eighteen-year-old Durcan taking the 46A bus to the tower following a row with his father who refused to give him 21 shillings to buy his first copy of *Ulysses*, the Bodley Head edition. His father is shocked at this 'outrageous sum of money/Which a poorly paid judge could ill afford' for such a 'notoriously immoral book' and vows 'I'll not be party to subsidising that blackguard/Bringing works of blasphemy into this house'. However, he relents and follows his son to the tower where he buys the novel from the 'ever-courteous' curator who agrees to 'wrap the green, satanic novel' in brown paper 'which the night before had ferried bottles of vodka'. Durcan senior takes the trouble to read *Ulysses* before passing it on to his son who admits he 'found it as strange as my father/And as discordant'. The poem's *incipit* 'I am hiding from my father/On the roof of Joyce's tower' aligns Durcan with Telemachus, with Hamlet, with Stephen Dedalus, and with Joyce himself whose novel would take time to work its magic on him as, among other things, an important meditation on the father–son theme. The

[61]'Overflow Crowd on "Bloomsday"', *IT*, 18 June 1963, 6.
[62]'An Irishman's Diary', *IT*, 17 June 1964, 7.
[63]Robert Nicholson, '"Signatures of All Things"', 294.
[64]Rory Brennan, Review of *A Book of Strays*, *Books Ireland* (September 2003), 200.

poem points to his own father and to Joyce himself as an important father figure as he seeks to find his voice as a writer:

> It was not until four years later
> When a musical friend
> Gave me my first lessons
> That *Ulysses* began to sing for me
>
> And I began to sing for my father:
>
> Daddy, Daddy,
> My little man, I adore you.[65]

The habit of hiding copies of *Ulysses* in brown paper was not unusual. Hugh McFadden recalls attempting to buy it in 1962 'in Hodges Figgis (I was told that they didn't stock it). Then I tried Fred Hanna's bookshop. Same result. But Fred advised me to try a bookshop on the quays Beside the Ha'penny Bridge near Merchant's Arch, George Webb's'. He continues:

> It was possible to purchase a copy there, on request, if one seemed to have reached the age of majority, provided one made the request in a suitably quiet and grave voice. It would be retrieved from a backroom and furnished in a brown-paper bag, rather like a 'carry-out' reluctantly slipped by a 'curate' to a regular at the side-door of McDaid's afterhours, it having been ascertained first by the tetchy 'curate' that the coast was clear.[66]

This situation would appear to have changed, quite rapidly, in the mid-1960s and within a couple of years it became more readily available in most bookshops, including Easons, for purchase straight off the shelf, although some academics, visiting for the 1967 symposium, complained they still could not find copies for sale.

While Joyce was beginning to become more mainstream, some younger writers began to more openly rebel against him. Michael Hartnett, for one, wrote of the need to revitalize Irish poetry which was stuck, in his view, in a false and disabling division between two cliques, the 'Irish Catholics' and the 'Anglo-Irish'. He argued that 'a marriage must be arranged. The first step could be the breaking of the great idols Yeats and Joyce, who great while alive are deified into Molochs: the Parthenon did not inhibit the builders of the Gothic cathedrals. Then both groups could stand in the sun without the dubious benefit of heritage'.[67] Augustine Martin wrote similarly in 1965

---

[65]Paul Durcan, 'Ulysses' in *Daddy, Daddy* (Belfast: Blackstaff, 1990), 99–102.
[66]Hugh McFadden, Introduction, *Crystal Clear*, 8.
[67]Michael Hartnett, 'The Dublin Literary World', *IT*, 13 November 1968, 6.

about the predicament of the Irish writer and of 'our own modest tradition' that labours 'under the immense and crippling shadows of Joyce and Yeats'. The shadow cast by 'two such giants [...] over a social landscape as small as Ireland's' makes it 'very difficult for the fledgling writer' trying to bring 'raw material into artistic focus'. Part of the difficulty lay in the fact that neither Yeats nor Joyce was an 'orthodox, typical' writer. Neither had 'absorbed and transfigured the pieties of their country's ethos into art', neither had been part of the status quo but both had brilliantly articulated in advance the very objections to which the new generation had wanted to give voice, 'in different ways, both writers repudiated the social and religious pieties of Ireland'.[68] Both had also, in their ways, rendered those who followed in their slipstream, impossible belated, or so it must have felt.

Many senior writers, however, continued to see Joyce as enabling and deeply relevant. Kate O'Brien could not have been clearer in a 1963 lecture in which she unreservedly acknowledged Joyce's importance to her as a master in the sense of one who was a slave to his vocation:

> We know him. Perhaps we think we know him too well. It is possible that too much has been written about him too soon – but anyway his life and work are there spread out in evidence of that infatuated certainty of vocation which is the mark of the master. Like Flaubert, like Balzac, like George Eliot, like Proust, he was surrendered, without pause or aside or mercy in his thought, to what he had to do. In him the creative force carried him to the discovery of his own art of writing – he was to be alone, a revelator of new ways, new language, a new freedom of imagery and echo – and in this great audacity he succeeded – leaving the world of letters with much to brood upon, and no means at all of discarding his extraordinary contribution.[69]

Others too, of both earlier and later generations, saw Joyce as a model. For good reason, Maurice Harmon would describe Austin Clarke as a 'literalist of the imagination, more Joycean than Yeatsian by background, temperament and training, he recorded what he saw'.[70] Seán O'Faoláin, on the other hand, casting his eye over the literature produced in Ireland after 1922, fretted about 'the comparative failure of the modern Irish Novel' and pointed to the inevitable centrality of Joyce who almost singlehandedly provided a necessary 'width of personal vision': 'If one were to exclude Joyce

---

[68] Augustine Martin, 'Inherited Dissent: The Dilemma of the Irish Writer', 3–4.
[69] Kate O'Brien, 'The Art of Writing', Lecture Delivered to Graduates' Association, 2 May 1963. *Irish University Review*, vol. 48, no. 1 (2018): 145–53, 152. See also Elizabeth Foley O'Connor, 'Kate O'Brien, James Joyce, and the "Lonely Genius"', in Martha C. Carpentier, ed., *Joycean Legacies* (London: Palgrave, 2013), 11–32.
[70] Maurice Harmon, 'The Rejection of Yeats: The Case of Clarke and O'Faolain', *Studies: An Irish Quarterly Review*, vol. 82, no. 327 (Autumn 1993): 243–56, 248.

– which is like saying if one were to exclude Everest – and Liam O'Flaherty how little is left!'[71] Yeats' influence, on the other hand, had waned:

> There is no longer any question of dishing up local colour. (The Nobel Peasant is as dead as the Noble Savage. Poems about fairies and leprechauns, about misted lakes, old symbols of national longing, are over and done with.) We need to explore Irish life with an objectivity never hitherto applied to it – and in this Joyce rather than Yeats is our inspiration.[72]

A writer of the newer generation, Thomas Kinsella, also looked to Joyce because his

> stomach, unlike Yeats's, is not turned by what he sees shaping the new Ireland: the shamrock lumpen proletariat, the eloquent and mean-spirited tribe of Dan. Daniel O'Connell or de Valera or Paudeen do not deter him from his work; they are his subjects. He is the first major Irish voice to speak for Irish reality since the death of the Irish language.[73]

Kinsella identified Joyce as 'the true father'. While 'Yeats stands for the Irish tradition as broken; Joyce stands for it as continuous or healed-or healing-from its mutilation'.[74]

None of this buttered too many parsnips out in the Joyce Tower, which continued to be run on the clippings of tin and depended on the goodwill of 'a motley crew of volunteers assembled by John Ryan to fill in on the weekends'. One among them was the actor Eamon Morrissey, who would later win acclaim with his one-man show, 'Joycemen', but now enjoyed 'informing credulous visitors that James Joyce was imprisoned in the tower by the British for his activities as a freedom fighter'.[75] Despite a donation in 1963 of a thousand dollars from the Irish Institute in New York, whose president was the noted former Irish Republican Army member and leading Irish-American Sean P. Keating,[76] and other similar goodwill gestures, the Tower struggled to cover its costs. Eventually Bórd Fáilte stepped in and purchased it on behalf of the Eastern Regional Tourism Organisation. This paved the way for a reopening and relaunch in 1965 and the appointment of a more qualified curator, the twenty-year-old Vivien Veale. Later, as Vivien

---

[71]Seán O Faoláin, 'Fifty Years of Irish Writing', *Studies*, vol. 51, no. 201 (Spring 1962): 93–105, 104, 102.

[72]Ibid., 101–2.

[73]W. B. Yeats and Thomas Kinsella, *Davis, Mangan, Ferguson? Tradition and the Irish Writer* (Dublin: Dolmen Press, 1970), 65.

[74]Thomas Kinsella, 'The Irish Writer', *Eire-Ireland*, vol. 2, no. 2: 14.

[75]Robert Nicholson, '"Signatures of All Things"', 294.

[76]'For Joyce Tower fund', *IP*, 16 November 1963, 9.

Igoe, she became known as the author of *James Joyce's Dublin Houses and Nora Barnacle's Galway* (1990), a detailed account of the many Joyce homes. Veale spent a busy few years expanding the Tower's Joyce collection mostly through donations (including Joyce's guitar and cigar case from Paul Ruggiero), and under her guidance it remained open from July until October and received some 3,000 visitors over this period in 1965.[77] In an article in the *James Joyce Quarterly*, the leading Joyce journal, founded in 1963 at the University of Tulsa by Thomas F. Staley, she announced that the Tower 'aims to have the largest and best collection of Joyceana in the world. It aims to have the greatest collection of Joycean books, periodicals, records'. What continued to be absent, however, was an adequate budget and Veale had little choice but to appeal to the generosity of her mostly American readership.

According the *Irish Times*, Bloomsday had by now become 'the major literary feast-day of the twentieth century, a day which did more than somewhat to put Ireland and the city of Dublin on the literary map of the contemporary world'.[78] Joyce was also increasingly being used to sell Irish products. As early as 1961, the Ormond Hotel was advertised as being 'of "*Ulysses*" fame' and the drinks company, Cantrell and Cochrane, was promoting its beverages by quoting from Joyce's novel: 'Mr. Bloom stood at the corner, his eyes wandering over the multicoloured hoardings. Cantrell and Cochrane's Ginger Ale.' Again in 1962, Kay Peterson – one of the founders of the Shannon Duty Free – opened a women's fashion shop called the 'Anna Livia Boutique' on Dublin's Dawson Street. An article in the *Evening Press* enthused about 'Joycean titles given to every gown' and particularly appreciated the 'sweeping evening cloak made from 1,200 piece patchwork quilt over 100 years old' called 'Portrait of an Artist'.[79] The 'Dubliners Diary' in the same newspaper noted that Sylvia Beach and Louis MacNeice had been among the notorieties present for the opening. Another *Irish Times* columnist dissented from the general enthusiasm and described the new collection as 'a flagrant instance of band-wagon jumping'.[80] This new sense of the commercial potential of Joyce was an important factor in his growing acceptance in Ireland. By the 1970s, an ever-growing number of mainstream brands and businesses alluded to by Joyce were seeing the potential of the association and they were joined by others who used the Joyce name even if there was no direct link. Thus, Bloomsday or Joyce's birthday would be recorded as, for example, 'A CIGAR DAY' and readers

---

[77]Vivien Veale, 'The Martello Tower', *JJQ*, vol. 3, no. 4 (Summer 1966): 276–7. She is also the author of *A Literary Guide to Dublin* (Methuen, 1994) and, more recently, her encyclopaedic *The Real People of Joyce's Ulysses: A Biographical Guide* (Dublin: University College Dublin Press, 2016).

[78]Irishman's Diary, *IT*, 15 June 1966, 7.

[79]Women Correspondent, 'Superb Collection had great charm and Joycean idea', *EP*, 16 June 1962, 7.

[80]G. A. Olden, 'Broadcasting Your man', *IT*, 21 June 1962, 8.

would be asked to 'salute his genius with SHORT PANATELLAS by Henri
Wintermans. 1/5 each'.[81]

Precious little, however, was being done on an official level to
commemorate Joyce and too much depended on the enthusiasm and
enterprise of the willing few, although 1966 did see the beginnings of a more
commercial approach when Irish Tours and Services arranged a Bloomsday
tour 'by coach and cab, over the Ulyssean holy ground.'[82] Yet progress was
not straightforward and the Tower was as often closed as it was open, as
The Sunday Independent reported on the eve of Bloomsday 1968:

> All was shuttered at the Tower in Sandycove and nobody, not one human
> sweltering in the bright warm evening sun, gave a damn. For them, James
> Joyce was dead and buried and the anniversary of Bloomsday, just a short
> few hours away meant nothing. The same 'couldn't-care-less' attitude
> [...] was apparent in Davy Byrnes [...]. Willie O'Farrell of Sallynoggin
> summed it up: 'I'm not interested. There was some nice choice language
> in the book, but the film, from what I've heard is better.'[83]

This was a temporary lull. In 1969, plans were drawn up to buy Michael
Scott's house beside the Tower in order to establish a Joyce Centre. The
Joyce Foundation and the Tourist Board were among the interested
parties. Noel Carroll, former Olympic athlete and now assistant regional
manager of the Eastern Regional Tourism Organisation (ERTO), was
keen to develop the Tower as a tourism facility and described it as 'A
GOLDMINE in Dun Laoghaire' even if 'few of the 60,000 or odd locals
even know of its existence'. In Carroll's view, if the Tower's potential were
properly exploited, it 'could easily outstrip the Rock of Cashel or at least
equal it as a tourist attraction'. Carroll also declared himself 'convinced
that James Joyce was the greatest thing that ever happened to Dun
Laoghaire' and sought to treble 'the number of pilgrims visiting'. In 1969,
it attracted 10,000 visitors, but hopes were high that this could grow to
50,000 a year with the purchase of Scott's house for use as a space to
exhibit the materials kept in storage for lack of space. Vivien Veale stated
that she had '£500 worth of paintings of Joycean scenes under her bed'
and donations continued to arrive, among them Joyce's Trieste piano,
donated by Nelly Joyce (Stanislaus' widow) in 1970.[84] Carroll hoped to
develop a centre that would cater for both students and scholars of Joyce
as well as tourists. This would be 'the tourism of the future'. In a comment
that must have gone down like a lead balloon in the Archbishop's palace

---

[81]Advertisement published in *IT*, 2 February 1971, 18.
[82]'An Irishman's Diary', *IT*, 16 June 1966, 7.
[83]*SI*, 16 June 1968, 2.
[84]'Joyce Piano Showpiece for Museum', *IP*, 10 April 1970, 9.

in Drumcondra, Carroll claimed that 'people don't visit Rome to enjoy the Italian sun: they go there to visit the Vatican. [...] It's the same with Joyce's tower'.[85]

Among the items this expanded Tower hoped to display was George Leinwall's Joyce library – one of the largest private collections in the world, including some 1,200 Joyce items and valuable first editions and practically all the Joyce criticism up to that time. The collection, which the Maryland-based Leinwall wished to donate, was valued at $50,000.[86] He was also willing to spend several months a year at the Tower as honorary librarian to the collection. However, officialdom in Dublin, while happy to toast Joyce for a once a year photo opportunity, was not willing to make the necessary investment to guarantee that the volumes would be properly archived and secured. Because the cultural budget available in Dublin was never going to cover the £50,000 needed to buy and convert Scott's house,[87] ERTO sought 'American aid through organisations like the Gulbenkian Trust and the Kellogg Foundation'.[88] Ultimately, however, the *Irish Independent* had to report that '18 months of appeals to American foundations, the government and Bórd Fáilte Eireann for the funds necessary, have been futile'. The situation was, in the words of Noel Carroll, 'a national tragedy'.[89] The *Irish Independent* devoted an editorial to urging government action:

> It is a sad reflection on our priorities that the James Joyce museum located in the Martello Tower at Sandycove will not open this year through lack of funds to repair the deterioration and dampness inside the building. It becomes tragic when one realises that an American collector of Joyce relics has promised to present his priceless collection to the Irish Joyce Foundation if they can house it properly. We can afford to pay an annual sum of £12,000 to the Chester Beatty Library, but nothing towards providing a decent museum for the relics and mementos of our great literary son. The Department of Finance has shown a readiness to accept a role as patron of the arts in a limited way in the recent past. Here is a golden opportunity; Bórd Fáilte's funds are 'over committed'. The same goes for much other money. But would it be entirely disproportionate if the Minister for Finance were to make a grant in aid to the Joyce foundation to ensure that a proper building can be found for the collection?[90]

[85]'"Goldmine" in the Tower…', *EH*, 9 July 1970, 5.
[86]'Joyce works for Dublin', *II*, 6 October 1969, 23.
[87]'ERTO Plans a Joyce Centre', *IP*, 11 April 1970, 3.
[88]'Joyce Works Offered to Dublin', *II*, 6 October 1971, 17.
[89]'Hopes for a New James Joyce Centre', *II*, 4 May 1971, 3.
[90]'Joyce Tower', *II*, 4 May 1971, 9.

Desmond Rushe wrote despairingly in the same paper:

> the only thing that will prevent it coming here is cheeseparing lunacy
> in official quarters. The combined forces of Bórd Fáilte, Eastern Region
> and Government failed to do anything. Not a finger was lifted to secure
> for Joyce's country the greatest collection of Joyceana in existence. And
> offered to us free.[91]

By 1972, Leinwall decided that he had waited long enough and it was
announced that plans 'to house one of the world's major collections of
Joycean material in a museum at Sandycove' had been scrapped.[92] The
matter was raised in the Dail by Fine Gael's Patrick Cooney, who asked the
Minister for Transport and Power, Mr Brian Lenihan, if he was aware that
the largest private collection of Joyce material in the world had been offered
to the State, 'that due to the failure to accept the offer the collection has now
been donated to a university in the United States'. The Minister, a master of
parliamentary obfuscation, replied that

> the question had been examined by Bórd Fáilte in consultation with the
> other interests concerned and as a result the board recommended the
> giving of a guaranteed loan by me under the Tourist Traffic Acts in respect
> of 60 per cent of the moneys required to finance the project. In addition,
> the board were willing to provide interest grants in respect of the loan. In
> September, 1970, I agreed in principle to the giving of the guarantee but a
> definite proposal on these lines has not emerged. It now appears that this
> collection has been donated to a university in the United States.[93]

There the matter died without as much as a word of regret from the
government, which was struggling to deal with the Troubles and a flailing
economy and was about to be hit by the international oil crisis. In the end, it
agreed to do little more than lend a part of the sum necessary to finance the
project. The material was sold to the Southern Methodist University in Dallas
Texas where it is housed in the Bridwell library. As Vivien Veale commented,
'this was a terrible loss to Ireland and an enormous disappointment for
those of us who had fought so long and negotiated so hard'.[94]

The Tower survived this blow and reopened on Bloomsday 1972 after the
completion of renovations costing £4,000 that were privately financed by
the prominent businessman, Tom Keating. He said that inspiration to fund
the repairs had come to him while he was in Berlin where 'some Germans he
was speaking to were most enthusiastic about Joyce and bemoaned the fact

---

[91]Quoted in Vivien Igoe, 'Early Joyceans in Dublin', 98.
[92]'No Money for Joyce Museum', *II*, 10 March 1972, 6.
[93]Ceisteanna-Questions. Oral Answers. – Joyce Collection. https://www.oireachtas.ie/en/
debates/debate/dail/1972-03-08/12/
[94]Vivien Igoe, 'Early Joyceans in Dublin', 98.

that the Tower was closed due to dampness'.[95] His decision came shortly after Dun Laoghaire Borough Council had shelved plans to contribute £500 towards the costs of repairing the Tower, and both Bórd Fáilte and the Eastern Regional Tourism Organisation had failed to come up with funds.[96] At the reopening of the Tower, Mr Pat Long, the ERTO manager, said he regretted having had to close it but stressed that he had been left with no choice because it was 'damp, unhealthy and dangerous'. He also revealed a rather provincial defensive motivation when he spoke 'of the fears he had felt because of the danger that Zurich and Trieste would take away from Dublin as the focal point in Joyce's life. "But I think now, with Tom's help we have managed to save Joyce for his own native city"'.[97] The phrase 'with Tom's help' served to underline that the future of Joyce heritage in Dublin was and would continue to be largely in the hands of private donors.

In any case, the tower was now structurally secure and its summer activities continued into the next decade with regular Bloomsday celebrations. Roland McHugh served as curator from 1975 to 1977. He would soon become well known for his highly regarded *Annotations to Finnegans Wake* (1980), which Declan Kiberd described as 'perhaps the most useful volume ever published on the subject [...] a massive feat of private research and public synthesis'.[98] In 1978, after yet another period of closure to allow for more major alterations, which included the installation of 'the incredible luxury of a toilet',[99] Robert Nicholson was appointed curator of the Tower and went on to run it for the next several decades.

No such happy fate awaited number 7 Eccles Street, the legendary home of Leopold and Molly Bloom, which had fallen into disrepair. In February 1965, Anthony Burgess filmed part of what would become the 'Silence, Exile and Cunning' Monitor programme on Joyce there. *The Listener* published photographs showing the sorry state of the building.[100] The following year, a Mrs Angela M. Aspinwall, who had recently moved to Dublin, expressed dismay in a letter to the *Irish Times*. As 'a keen admirer' of Joyce's works, she was shocked to discover that 7 Eccles Street 'is now all but a ruin':

> Flanked on either side by derelict houses in as bad or worse condition, No. 7 displays to an indifferent Dublin the faded remnants of an earlier elegance. For months its windows have gaped to admit the dank air of a Northern winter, and rubbish has accumulated in its mouldering

[95]'Restoration of Joyce Tower Begins Soon', *IP*, 28 September 1971, 3.
[96]'Joyce Tower Repair Plan Is Shelved', *IP*, 21 July 1971, 3.
[97]'Joyce Tower', *EH*, 18 July 1972, 9.
[98]Roland McHugh, *Annotations to Finnegans Wake* (London: Routledge & Kegan Paul, 1980). Declan Kiberd's review was published in *Irish University Review*, vol. 11, no. 1 (Spring 1981): 103–5.
[99]Robert Nicholson, '"Signatures of All Things"', 296.
[100]*The Listener* (1965), 22 April, 610; 6 May, 661. For more on this, see Ian Gunn, 'Mr Burgess Goes to Eccles Street', *James Joyce Broadsheet* (2014), no. 97, February, 1.

basement. [...] I understand that a tour of Joyce's Dublin is now one of the city's summer attractions, but if the itinerary takes in No. 7 Eccles street the effect produced upon visitors must be highly displeasing.[101]

She suggested the establishment of a Joyce centre, an idea also proposed by the Swiss Joyce scholar, Fritz Senn, who, on being asked in the *Irish Press* what Dublin was going to do about preserving Bloom's house, proposed launching a fund to buy the property and turn it into an academy with rooms dedicated to Joyce, Swift and Wilde: 'At the moment anyone interested in Joycean Dublin is completely lost in the city unless he has made contacts beforehand.'[102] Perhaps the Dublin Joyceans were too few and too busy trying to keep the Tower Museum open but appeals to save Eccles Street went unheeded. All but the ground floor façade was torn down in the spring of 1967. The site was sold on soon afterwards to the Dominican Nuns who ran their school on the same street and hoped to expand where numbers 6–8 stood. It was eventually sold on and redeveloped as the Mater Private Hospital. This was the decade of demolition Ireland. In the words of Ian Gunn, 'all this happened within weeks of the first James Joyce Symposium in Dublin in mid-June 1967, where delegates from around the globe were bused down Eccles street to look at the dust settling on the single-storey facade. The cavalry had arrived too late'.[103]

John Ryan saved the Bloom's front door and had it mounted on a wall of the Bailey pub on Dublin's Duke Street (which he owned). Around the time of its unveiling the *Evening Herald* speculated that the 'relic' would 'probably be more frequently seen by strangers in our midst than by native sons of Anna Livia Plurabelle!'[104] Patrick Kavanagh did the honours at the unveiling in characteristically belligerent fashion and could not resist an all-too-familiar swipe at the American Joyceans who, in his opinion, had hijacked Bloomsday after its promising beginnings back in 1954:

The proper inscription on this door, or rather on the wall, should be what the dead hand wrote: Bloom is a cod. I don't like Richard Ellmann's piece telling us what so-called real person lived at no. 7 Eccles Street, for such alleged realism and research clouds the myth. And the myth is all that is real. And this door is as famous to the mythology of Dublin as 221b Baker Street is to London. It is not possible for us, loaded down as we are with the weight of American madness, to discuss Joyce's importance as a writer. They have magazines devoted to something called 'Joyce Studies' and ditto seminars. So we may as well let Joyce rip in the myth.[105]

[101]Angela M. Aspinwall, Letter, *IT*, 5 May 1966, 11.
[102]'The Man Who Thinks There Is Too Much Literary Talent in Ireland', *IP*, 29 July 1966, 10.
[103]Ian Gunn, 'No 7 Eccles Street. The Demise of Ithaca', *James Joyce Online Notes*. http://www.jjon.org/joyce-s-environs/no-7-eccles-street.
[104]'The Bloomsday Door, Bailey Restaurant', *EH*, 27 June 1967, 9.
[105]Quoted in Vivien Igoe, 'Early Joyceans in Dublin', 94.

Sometimes, foreign journalists captured best the sense that so much of Joyce's Dublin was being carelessly lost. Thus, in 1972, *The New York Times* reported melancholically:

No. 7 Eccles Street is gone now. The tower at Sandycove is closed. Nelson's Pillar, the statue on O'Connell Street, was blown up five years ago by the Irish Republican Army. And Davy Byrne's pub is now a carpeted lounge with purple pillars, South Sea landscapes and a sedate clientele of young couples, businessmen and tourists. 'The Dublin that Joyce knew—so much of it is gone,' said John Ryan, former owner of the Bailey Pub (known as the Burton in *Ulysses*).[106]

A similar gloom pervaded Anthony Kerrigan's poem 'Bloomsday 1965', which despaired at the disappearance of the Joyce landscape and a city incapable of preserving key Joyce sites or even putting up its own memorial plaques. It describes 'Eccles Street condemned' and bemoans the ruined view from the Joyce Tower: 'Seaview of seagreen ruined by Michael/Scott's snot-white bathroom-of-a-late-tony-Irish house' while Davy Byrne's pub languishes 'behind Duke Street boards', Barney Kiernan's is gutted while the Ormond Hotel is 'plasticized':

Joyce's birthplace in Brighton Square –
Seedy-genteel-plaqued by a College in New Jersey.
Rain trying hard to turn back. The city falling.[107]

The reference to Brighton Square was a reminder that the impetus (and the money) to place a plaque on Joyce's birthplace – 41 Brighton Square – came from the United States. In 1963, Professor Frederick Young of Montclair State College New Jersey visited Dublin and, disturbed that no plaque marked Joyce's birthplace, set about addressing 'this sad and intolerable situation'.[108] He and his graduate class raised funds (£170) to purchase a plaque. Eventually the 35 lb. bronze plaque arrived from Newark and read: 'Birthday place of James Joyce, poet-novelist, 1882–1941, Presented by Montclair State College, New Jersey, U.S.A., Bloomsday, 16 June 1964.' In an article in praise of the Montclair students, the *Cork Examiner* commented: 'James Joyce perhaps, has never been really understood in his own city and the only thing which keeps some people from still looking askance at his works is the regard in which they are held by people of literary merit abroad.'[109] There was a good local turnout for the unveiling

[106]Bernard Weinraub, 'The City That Joyce Knew Has Changed', *NYT*, 2 February 1972, 41.
[107]Anthony Kerrigan, 'Bloomsday 1965', *Quest* 2 (Spring): 248.
[108]Milton Honig, 'Plaque to Mark Joyce Birthplace: Montclair Students Correct "Intolerable Situation"', *NYT*, 10 May 1964, 82.
[109]*CE*, 5 June 1964, 8.

with speeches from Professor Young and Niall Montgomery who marvelled
that 'neither the Electricity Supply Board nor the Pembroke Estate, nor even
Dublin Corporation had found some reason for preventing its erection'. The
owner of the house, a Miss Hoey, put a brave face on things saying 'that
anticipation of the event was worse than the actuality. Her one thought
while the ceremonies were going on was that she hoped that John Ryan,
Roger McHugh and Niall Montgomery wouldn't jump off the chair onto her
begonias'.[110] The unveiling was also attended by a lonely looking Beatrice
Behan (Brendan had died in March) and the members of the cast of Allan
McClelland's *Bloomsday*, which was running at the Gate.

If Dublin got a Joyce plaque thanks to American intervention, Zurich
went one better and had its own Joyce statue erected. The story of the
Irish involvement in this project is symptomatic of the continuing official
hesitancy wherever Joyce was concerned. An Irish priest resident in Zurich,
Father McKay, alerted the Irish Embassy in Berne to the fact that Joyce's
remains were to be transferred to a new site in a different part of the
Fluntern cemetery in Zurich and that a statue was to be built. Embassy staff
investigated and discovered that a certain 'Herr Fritz Senn' was heading a
committee for this purpose (he wasn't). Ambassador Sean Morrissey wrote
to the secretary of the Department of Foreign Affairs revealing the quandary
in which he found himself: 'It occurs to us that if we approach Mr Senn,
thus revealing our interest in the matter, we may immediately be asked and
expected to make a handsome financial contribution to the committee's
funds.'[111] Some time later, he wrote again to Dublin announcing that Joyce's
grave had been transferred and asking advice as to what would be suitable
embassy involvement in the commemoration ceremonies that were to
be held the following Bloomsday (1966), the twenty-fifth anniversary of
Joyce's death. The ambassador wrote of the local interest in Joyce (providing
evidence of the capacity attendance at a production of Hugh Leonard's
Stephen D there) and suggested that it would be in Ireland's interest to get
involved.

> Joyce enjoys an increasing vogue in Zürich, and it is our belief that much
> valuable publicity could be gained for Ireland (as a tourist country, a land
> of cultural individuality and importance, and as a centre for language
> study) by our contributing to the ceremonies of next June.

Lest these positive arguments should fail to sway the ministry, Ambassador
Morrissey underlined the negatives: 'our absence from the scene would

---

[110]'An Irishman's Diary', *IT*, 17 June 1964, 7.
[111]Letter from Ambassador Morrissey in Berne to Secretary Coffey in Dublin, 24 November
1965, quoted in Brian Dillon, 'The "Statue Affair": Diplomatic Notes on the Reinterment of
James Joyce', *The Dublin Review*, vol. 26, no. 26 (Spring 2007): 64–77, 65.

certainly occasion adverse comment' and worse, 'if we fail to take the initiative [...] somebody else will'. The 'somebody else' was the old enemy, represented, in this instance, by the British Council:

> The British Council maintain a representative in Zurich who was responsible for arranging a lecture on Yeats in Berne on June last [...] We are not unwilling to cooperate with this man if it becomes strictly necessary, but a priori it ought not in our view to be necessary when the occasion to be catered for is a purely Irish one, although it must be admitted that Joyce held a British passport.[112]

He suggested that a sum of £250 set aside by External Affairs for a visit of Micheál Mac Liammóir that had not taken place might be used to fund the Joyce event. But Dublin was not impressed and, citing drastic budget cuts, said the grant for Cultural Relations would only barely cover already-existing 'recurrent' items. Several pleading letters from Morrissey later, the department finally agreed that 'the Embassy should be represented at the commemoration ceremonies'. Spending was to be limited to £100 and John Garvin was to be invited to Zurich to give a lecture but then a new problem arose. Ambassador Morrissey wrote once again: 'It seems likely that having been instrumental in arranging the occasion that I will be asked to attend. I personally would have no hesitation in doing so but I do not know if there are strong views about this in Dublin.'[113] Happily, there were not and Garvin's visit, funded by the Cultural Relations Committee of the Department of External Affairs and in which he was also officially 'representing University College, Dublin, at the request of its President, Dr. Jeremiah Hogan, and its Professor of English, Dr. Roger McHugh',[114] went ahead. Garvin's lecture, entitled 'Portrait of the Artist in *Finnegans Wake*', was later published in the *Irish Press*.

The enduring official ambivalence towards Joyce was shared by John Garvin, still the Irish *éminence grise* on the author. When his *Disunited Kingdom* was published in 1977, Anthony Cronin commented aptly that 'the most remarkable thing' about his book was 'the hostility it exhibits towards its subject'.

> He illustrates his criticism with reminiscences and anecdotes which he has evidently been at pains for a very long time to collect and not one of them is intended to do other than degrade Joyce in the reader's eyes. [...] Nowhere does he show any clear realisation of what Joyce's stature as an artist was. [...] Dr Garvin is at positive pains to show that Joyce was not

---

[112]Ibid., 67.
[113]Ibid., 72.
[114]*IP*, 10 June 1966, 10.

only a misguided writer who merely indulged his own 'association mania' but in some ways a very unpleasant one as well.[115]

In his book and in his many lectures and articles about Joyce, Garvin repeatedly described Joyce in negative terms calling him, in 1962, 'a lonely, sick man wondering how he would be received if he was found on the shores of his native land' and an 'eavesdropper' obsessed with 'every little event that occurred back home'.[116] Later he employed terms and descriptions such as 'devious', 'porn addict', 'an intellectual corner-boy', 'talented but sick' that clashed with his declaration 'I worship Joyce this side of idolatory'.[117] Garvin believed that Joyce was neurotic and used 'his art as a raft'. He also voiced objections to Joyce's writing style, questioning his 'ill-mannered interruptions of his characters in the novel, noting that this was one aspect of his work of which he did not really approve'.[118] In 1962, he referred to 'monstrous Molly' calling her 'a phony'.[119] Niall Montgomery seems to have felt a similar discomfort around her and suggested that Joyce ('our friend from Ballybough') was one of a generation that 'knew nothing about women [...] All he could do was put in a very fat man called Molly Bloom'.[120]

Garvin's contradictory attitude towards Joyce was shared by his generation; 'a man of Victorian taste and temperament', Garvin was nevertheless fascinated, like his friends in 'literature-minded groups, particularly in the Smyllie club – a sort of Johnsonian coffee-house', by the ghost of Joyce, which 'was an inescapable quarry for debate and disorder'.[121] His attempt to come to terms with Joyce was life-long. Long before it was popular or profitable to do so, he cast light on the Irish elements in *Ulysses*, claiming that the basic theme, the main 'characters', and the historical and literary motifs of *Finnegans Wake* were all predominantly Irish, and that Shaun is 'given the accent and various other personal attributes of the quondam Irish Prime Minister, Mr. Éamon De Valera'.[122]

With or without Garvin, Irish attitudes to Joyce were evolving and 1967 was an important year. Indeed, Joseph Kelly has claimed that 'Ireland's reclamation' of Joyce began at the First International Symposium held in Dublin that year with Padraic Colum's speech on behalf of the Irish Academy of Letters.[123] American Joycean, Austin Briggs, remembered it vividly:

---

[115] Anthony Cronin, 'Life-long Devotion', *IT*, 12 March 1977, 8.

[116] 'James Joyce Portrayed as a Lonely Eavesdropper', *IT*, 22 June 1962, 6.

[117] 'Lecture Examines Joyce's Religion', *IT*, 8 December 1975, 15.

[118] 'John Garvin Talks in Maynooth on Joyce', *IT*, 17 June 1969, 10.

[119] 'Judgments on Joyce and Proust', *IT*, 23 June 1962, 4.

[120] Comment made on 'Bloom Sunday', a documentary presented and produced by Seán Mac Réamoinn and first broadcast on RTÉ Radio 1, 20 June 1971.

[121] D. F. (Donal Foley), 'Dr John Garvin an Appreciation', *IT*, 5 April 1986, 19.

[122] John Garvin, *James Joyce's Disunited Kingdom and the Irish Dimension* (Dublin: Gill and Macmillan, 1976), 38.

[123] Joseph Kelly, *Our Joyce*, 210.

Mr. Justice MacDonagh introduces Padraic Colum, who reads poem on Joyce he has written: 'The enterprise that you in secrecy had framed... we did not know the searching eyes beneath the peak of cap beheld the seventh city of Christendom reformed... we did not know... .' Hearty applause, though difficult to hear ode over faulty public address system. An aged figure, Colum is Yeatsian— 'beautiful lofty things.' Suppose that in Ireland even Colum has enemies, but it's hard to see how.[124]

Although Colum's speech signalled a significant contribution to a reconciliation between Joyce and Ireland, the Tower opening in 1962 arguably had a more lasting effect, especially for the non-academic world. Brian O'Nolan's 1962 suggestion (written as Flann O'Brien) that Joyce's body be repatriated was another key signal: 'Perhaps a member of the Joyce family would express an opinion on my proposal. A great many people would be happy to contribute to the cost of the new funeral.'[125] Ten days later, writing as George Knowall in the *Nationalist and Leinster Times*, O'Nolan cast Joyce in surprisingly straightforward and heroic terms before asking: 'Would it not be an idea to disinter the remains and rebury him at his own beloved city?' He concluded by quoting T. S. Eliot's claim 'that Joyce was the greatest master of the English language since Milton. Let us leave it at that'.[126]

Five years later, in a glowing review of Chester Anderson's *James Joyce and His World*, 'PJG', the diplomat, Paul John Geoffrey Keating (1924– 80), then stationed as counsellor at the Irish Embassy in London and later secretary general of the Department of Foreign Affairs, made an analogous proposal, which also suggests frustration in diplomatic circles at the continuing ostracization of Joyce by successive governments:

Are we to be forever content with a hollow Martello, a ruined No.7 Eccles St., a score of crumbling addresses from Cabra to Clontarf, from Bray to Fontenoy St., as Dublin's ragged reminders of all this? [...] When Joyce died in Switzerland in 1941 there was little we or our fellow-neutrals could do amid the throes of world war. But when, years later, the Municipality of Zurich decided that the bones of Joyce deserved a more fitting resting place and duly re-interred them, the opportunity was there for Dublin to lay claim to its literary immortaliser. Could we not then have saved him from continuing to moulder as a tourist attraction in a foreign clay? To read a tribute of the magnitude of Professor Anderson's is to be forced to ask oneself: Isn't it time we brought Ulysses home?[127]

[124]Austin Briggs, 'The First International James Joyce Symposium', 14.
[125]Flann O'Brien, Letter to *IT*, 20 June 1962, 7.
[126]George Knowall, 'From Clongowes to Martello Tower', *Nationalist & Leinster Times*, 30 June 1962, 12.
[127]P. J. G. 'Time to Bring Joyce Home', *SI*, 10 December 1967, 19.

While this request gained no traction, the international Joyce scholars
went ahead with what were to become bi-annual symposia, which returned
regularly to Dublin over the decades that followed. The key academic
organizers of the first symposium were Fritz Senn, Tom Staley of the
University of Tulsa, which was, under his guidance, building a substantial
Joyce collection, and Bernard Benstock of the University of Miami, already
an important centre of Joyce studies. As David Norris remembered, 'it is
greatly to the credit of this small group that they kept Joyce's reputation
alive when he was being so traduced in his homeland'.[128] A huge amount
of work was carried out by the local Irish team that was led by Gerard
O'Flaherty and included Vivien Veale at a time when the Irish universities
were not terribly keen to be involved. An impressive group of local patrons
were assembled including Seán O'Faoláin (the honorary chairman), Seamus
Kelly of the *Irish Times*, novelists Benedict Kiely and Mervyn Wall, Arland
Ussher, Niall Montgomery and Michael Scott, Roger McHugh, and A. J.
(Con) Leventhal. Giorgio Joyce and Frank Budgen were guests of honour.
Irish academic interest was thin, although UCD's McHugh, Maurice Harmon
and Eileen MacCarvill did take part and Harmon edited the quaintly entitled
and rather thin volume, *The Celtic Master: Contributions to the First James
Joyce Symposium in Dublin*.[129] In his one-page preface, Harmon, sounding
a little like Thomas Kinsella, casts Joyce as 'the originator of the Irish prose
tradition' and 'central to modern Irish life because, accepting the here and
the now, he immersed himself in the filthy modern tide that Yeats had turned
away from'.[130] Niall Montgomery considered the various contexts within
which to place and consider Joyce's writings arguing that he did not fit in a
European tradition, nor could he be framed 'as a British writer' or as part of
Anglo-Irish literature, nor as a Catholic writer even if he clearly contributed
to 'the literature of Catholicism'. Instead, 'for a man of my generation and
my class, there is truth in considering Joyce in [...] the context of Ireland.
[...] Joyce's work illuminates that context and the context it'.[131] *Ulysses*
is central to Ireland's effort to achieve 'a partial form of liberation' but
also a 'great universal work' that 'derives much of its greatness from its
perception of the character, the mores, the speech rhythms of the people of
the early twentieth century in Dublin. *Ulysses* is illuminated by Ireland and
the corollary is magnificently true'.[132] Joyce 'made the Irish Literary Revival

---

[128]David Norris, *A Kick against the Pricks: The Autobiography* (Dublin: Transworld Ireland,
2012), 182.
[129]Maurice Harmon, ed., *The Celtic Master: Essays by Donagh MacDonagh, Niall Montgomery,
Norman Silverstein, Margaret C. Solomon, Stanley Sultan* [First James Joyce Symposium in
Dublin, 1967] (Dublin: Dolmen Press, 1969).
[130]Maurice Harmon, 'Introduction', *The Celtic Master*, npg.
[131]Niall Montgomery, 'A Context for Mr. Joyce's Work', *The Celtic Master*, 9–10.
[132]Ibid., 11.

look like a lot of old rope. His was the exposition, the true expression of the life of the Irish in the early twentieth century'.[133]

Irish speakers at the symposium included Donagh MacDonagh, who spoke about 'The Lass of Aughrim' as background to 'The Dead' (and upset the local organizers by publishing his piece in advance in *Hibernia*), Eileen Veale, Gerard O'Flaherty, J. B. Lyons and Brendan Duddy (a Jesuit priest). They were among the seventy-five gathered at UCD in Earlsfort Terrace and the following day at the Gresham Hotel. In the *Irish Times*, 'Quidnunc' was dismissive of the 'Joyce posers (or symposers)', who 'were at it again hot and heavy on Thursday night'[134] and there was bemusement that Joyce was attracting so many misguided tourists: 'But an Englishman or an American cannot possibly understand it, no more than they could make sense of a family joke. The bould Jamsie Joyce was writing for Irishmen and for nobody else. I wish the Americans would learn that simple fact. They would be happier if they did.' Joyce would be 'vastly annoyed if he had the gift of clairvoyance to foresee that his books would take on the veneration which is accorded to the Talmud. Joyce is now a money-spinner for Dublin hoteliers and if he revolves in his Zurich grave I shall not be very much surprised'.[135]

With good evidence, Fritz Senn recalled: 'We, the non-Irish importers of the first symposium, had felt not only a lack of support but almost hostility, certainly the sarcastic disdain from the press.'[136] Phillip Herring concurred about the 'somewhat less than enthusiastic' reception given to the symposiasts: 'Ireland cannot really embrace him (or us) because she does not feel comfortable with him (or us). [...] there lingers the nagging suspicion that he smirks at Ireland from beyond the grave. [...] latent hostility made us feel that we were clowns paying homage to a jester'.[137]

Despite the hostility, the family of Joyce readers and academics was destined to grow. In 1969 under the headline '*Ulysses* for All', the *Cork Examiner* celebrated that at long last, 'though inevitably, we have in English a paperback edition of Joyce's *Ulysses*. And, at the incredibly low price of 10 shillings, an altogether excellent piece of work which will, I hope, extend at least its Irish readership, particularly among those who have been criticising it on moral grounds from hearsay'.[138] From the other end of the island, The *Belfast Telegraph* welcomed the publication as 'the first paperback edition published in the Commonwealth [...] a real event [...] that should widen the circle of Joyce admirers'.[139] The paperback *Ulysses*

[133]Ibid., 10–11.
[134]'An Irishman's Diary', *IT*, 16 June 1967.
[135]'Dublin Letter', *The Sligo Champion*, 30 July 1965, 4.
[136]Fritz Senn, *Joycean Murmoirs*, 53.
[137]Quoted in Joseph Brooker, *Joyce's Critics: Transitions in Reading and Culture* (Madison: University of Wisconsin Press, 2004), 206.
[138]'*Ulysses* for All – A Paperback Edition', *CE*, 24 April 1969, 21.
[139]*Belfast Telegraph*, 14 June 1969, 6.

was published on 22 April to coincide with Sir Allen Lane's fiftieth year in publishing and to mark his retirement as managing director of Penguin. He had long been a champion of Joyce's works and it was fitting that he was behind this fourth major incarnation of Joyce's novel in the United Kingdom following the three Bodley Head editions of 1936, 1937 and 1960, all of which had been expensive hardbacks. This new edition clearly had the university market in mind.

One small knock-on effect to all this was that Penguin, in response to a request from Fritz Senn, agreed to sponsor the 1969 Dublin symposium by advertising its new edition in the programme.[140] This time round, the symposiasts gathered at Trinity College, a sign, this, of the increasingly scholarly imprint of these gatherings, although there were fewer academic contiguous events including an exhibition of works by artists from London, Paris, New York, Trieste, Copenhagen, Belgium and Dublin. The guest of honour was Frank Budgen.[141] On 15 June 1969, Seán Mac Réamoinn presented an hour-long radio documentary entitled 'Bloomseve', which discussed the second symposium attended by what he referred to as 'the Joycemen': 'The Joyceans have descended on Dublin [...] and rightly so. For with apologies to Zurich, Paris, Cork, and any other place you might care to think of, Joyce is essentially a Dubliner' and yet, Mac Réamoinn commented: 'We have still among us, though in decreasing numbers, that Joyce as a man who wrote dirty blasphemous books shouldn't be the subject of a symposium at all in this fair city. Perhaps it was to reassure these that the first speaker in the first general session was an American Jesuit with an Irish name, Fr Robert Boyle.'[142] He is quoted as claiming that the Jesuits in Joyce's books were 'monstrous caricatures' and making the case for Joyce's 'respect and really for his love for the priestly work'. UCD's Roger McHugh's contribution was to criticize Joyce and the symposium. *Dubliners*, he said, 'was monotonous in its evocation of paralysis' and the quality of the symposium papers was 'very uneven. [...] Many foreign scholars particularly Americans can't get here unless they are subsidised by their universities so that they have to be reading a paper before they will get a grant'. The implication was that they had more money than sense: 'We are in the process of having some 37 papers by 37 different people and 35 participants speaking in panel discussions all in 6 days. The number of papers should be cut down drastically.' He had little idea of what would be coming down the line over the next decades.

---

[140]Fritz Senn to Penguin Books, n.d., Editorial File, *Ulysses*, Penguin Archive, University of Bristol Library, quoted in Alistair McCleery, 'The 1969 Edition of *Ulysses*: The Making of a Penguin Classic', *JJQ*, vol. 46, no. 1 (Fall 2008): 55–73, 73.

[141]'A Week full of Joyce', *IP*, 5 June 1969.

[142]'Bloomseve' (1969), [Documentary presented by Seán Mac Réamoinn], RTÉ Radio 1, 20 June 1969.

The belief that Joyce was being hijacked by American academia was also voiced in an earlier documentary, entitled 'Zurich Unveils a Monument to James Joyce', presented by Donagh MacDonagh and broadcast on 17 June 1966 on Radio Éireann. It included an excerpt from a speech given by Mary Manning at a 1962 Joyce birthday party at New York, entitled 'Myth carriage of Joycetice':

> The academic miasma which warps and whoops round the great man is thickening year by year it is almost impossible to beat your way to the real Joyce, the enjoyable Joyce. [...] *Finnegans Wake* – the biggest boon to scholarship since Moses struck the rock. Criticism in this field is no longer criticism it is vivisection. Only you wouldn't do it to a dog. Granted the master encouraged these doings by the wilful obscurantism of *Finnegans*, granted everything and you have a grant. Still I feel like throwing up when they start analysing everything to death. Personally, I think it's time the gentle reader was allowed to walk through Joyce footnote loose and fancy free.

MacDonagh did little to conceal his reserve about American Joyce scholars but also saw Joyce himself as 'the author of his own misfortune. [...] If sunny Jim Joyce of Dublin has become the Yams Yoyce of international scholarship he has only himself to blame or to thank'. Anthony Cronin engaged rather more profoundly with *Ulysses* and with international Joyce scholarship (mainly through his regular reviewing of books about Joyce in the *Times Literary Supplement* from the late 1950s on). He trenchantly declared:

> Criticism has performed no service for Joyce by the suggestion that we must unravel the book before we can understand it; and that patience, skill and drudgery in unravelment are the primary qualities commonly found in those most remarkable for receptivity and generosity of response to art or anything else. The suggestion that they are essential is part of the academic claim to indispensability – let alone usefulness – which has followed in our time as a result of the vesting of academic interests in literature.[143]

In his article, 'The Advent of Bloom', Cronin argued against attempting to figure out what *Ulysses* is about, against reducing it to 'mere, paraphrasable opinions about history or religion or our place in the cosmos: an ideology which could be discovered and exclaimed over like that of any other fashionable sage. Every recorded statement we have exhibits Joyce's

---

[143]Anthony Cronin, *A Question of Modernity: Essays on Writing with Special Reference to James Joyce and Samuel Beckett* (London: Secker & Warburg 1966), 95.

total contempt for abstract ideas, his cheerful and not at all hag-ridden scepticism about religion, his indifference to the profundities of the new psychology'.[144] He described how *Ulysses* broke new ground for the novel in eschewing plot and a contrived 'chain of causation', which is a 'falsification of life'. 'Conversation, anecdote, thought, desultory impression, image and happening are freed at last from their long subordination to plot.'[145] What *Ulysses* achieves is a 'liberation of ordinary living from the shackles of plot', thus allowing for 'an enormous extension of the range of life included'. In his 1966 book, *A Question of Modernity*, Cronin, anticipating Declan Kiberd, praises *Ulysses* for its 'redemption of our common and ordinary humanity [...] as well as the poetic intensity of its statement on the conditions of ordinary living'.[146] He also intuited the importance of the Trieste input into *Ulysses*, writing of 'Bloom's middle position between Dublin and Trieste, between the father and his associates in Ireland and the artist in the Austro-Hungarian empire – where, incidentally, old Virag, Bloom's father, was born'.[147]

With the initial symposia in 1967 and 1969, the shape of future academic Joyce gatherings was set. The symposium returned in 1973 to UCD where speakers included Conor Cruise O'Brien (then Minister for Posts and Telegraphs), Máire Mhac an tSaoi, Benedict Kiely, Seamus Heaney and Seán Mac Réamoinn while Carola Giedion-Welcker and Maria Jolas were special guests. Among the various events was a screening of Maurice O'Kelly's *Three Weeks in a Tower*, a dramatized account of the brief period in which Joyce (Chris Curran), Gogarty (Pat Daly) and Samuel Chenevix Trench (John O'Neill) lived in the Martello Tower in Sandycove. Once again, the media coverage was grudging with the *Sunday Independent* writing of 'Joyce junketings to last a week'.[148] Undeterred, after gathering in Paris in 1975, the Joyceans returned once more in 1977 for a symposium hosted by David Norris at Trinity College. Maria Jolas took part along with playwright Denis Johnston and David Norris, in the unveiling in St. Stephen's Green of a park bench to the memory of Joyce and of his father, John Stanislaus. The artist, Gerald Davis, turned up dressed as Leopold Bloom. He was to become a fixed presence as Bloom at Joyce events over the next two decades. An acclaimed artist, gallery owner, jazz music producer (creator of the Livia label) and a prominent member of the city's Jewish community, he also mounted a successful solo exhibition of paintings inspired by *Ulysses* and *Finnegans Wake* at this time. The St Stephen's Green bench came after the 1974 unveiling of a plaque in UCD's Newman House by commemorating

---

[144]Anthony Cronin. 'The Advent of Bloom' in William M. Chace, ed., *Joyce. A Collection of Critical Essay* (New York: Prentice Hall, 1974), 84.
[145]Ibid., 85–6.
[146]Anthony Cronin, *A Question of Modernity*, 96.
[147]Anthony Cronin, 'The Advent of Bloom', 95.
[148]*SI*, 3 June 1973, 7.

Hopkins, Newman and Joyce, each of whom, as Professor T. E. Nevin, dean of the Faculty of Science, declared, 'paid the penalty for being far in advance of the times in which they lived'.[149]

Although much of the impetus came from abroad, the bi-annual symposia were embraced by Dublin Joyceans, who were flanked by Bórd Fáilte and the Eastern Regional Tourism Organisation. Thus was born a cooperation between foreign academia, local Irish scholarship and tourism. Dublin, for the Joyceans, became a mecca. As a leading American Joycean, Morris Beja, would write: to be in Dublin on Bloomsday 'is always, for a lover of *Ulysses*, like being in Jerusalem on Easter Sunday. But in 1967 it was a Jerusalem in which relatively few people aside from the pilgrims from afar seemed to care very much about its Messiah'.[150] For all the local scoffing, the reality was that the international academic Joyce industry, much like the Irish Studies industry, was taking shape. The inaugural conference of the International Association for Irish Studies (Iasil) was held in 1969 at Trinity College Dublin. Among the many papers, there was only one on Joyce by Donald Torchiana of Northwestern University, a sign, this, that Joyce remained outside the remit of mainstream Irish literary studies. In the late 1960s and early 1970s, an annual Joyce summer school was organized in Dublin by Noel O'Cleirigh of the Language Centre of Ireland along with Dr Grattan Freyer, and later at the Institute of Irish Studies (with Richard Hindley as director). Leading Irish academics and cultural figures gave lectures along with a sprinkling of speakers from abroad. In 1970, there was also a Joyce segment at the Yeats School featuring Richard Kain, Clive Hart, Leland Lyons and Bernard Benstock as tutors, making this one of the liveliest Joycean summers in Ireland.

There were also intermittent signs of a slightly more generous attitude to scholarship from abroad. One work that was warmly greeted was Robert Deming's *James Joyce: The Critical Heritage*, which the *Cork Examiner* described as 'the best study concerning Joyce since Ellmann'.[151] Noting that it was 'edited in a truly magnificent fashion', the *Evening Herald* claimed that the 'genius of James Joyce was recognised when it first showed signs of blooming', pointing to early positive comments made about the author by George Russell.[152] Gerard O'Flaherty demurred and found that the Irish contributions in the volume made for depressing reading. He also claimed that Joyce was a 'writers' writer for there is virtually no one writing in English today who has not been influenced by his techniques'. Regretting that Joyce 'has never been read widely in Ireland' O'Flaherty lamented that the Irish failed to heed Elizabeth Bowen's call that Joyce be regarded as a

---

[149]'U. C. D. unveils plaque to Newman, Hopkins and Joyce', *IT*, 29 March 1974, 8.
[150]Morris Beja, 'Synjoysium: An Informal History of the International James Joyce Symposia', *JJQ*, vol. 22, no. 2 (Winter 1985): 113–29, 114.
[151]R.O'D, 'Joyce, the Man and His Work', *CE*, 2 April 1970, 6.
[152]'Russell's "Young Genius" Shocked the World', *EH*, 26 May 1970, 7.

'writer out of the Irish people', one who 'belonged to us, and was of us, wherever he went'.[153]

In 1973, Irish neurologist and occasional biographer, J. B. Lyons, published *James Joyce and Medicine*. It looked at Joyce's ill-fated plans to study medicine in Dublin and subsequently in Paris and examined his difficult relationship with Gogarty. The Dublin backgrounds to the 'Oxen of the Sun' episode and its setting in the Holles Street maternity hospital were usefully sketched and Joyce's many medical conditions were examined. The book was better received in Ireland than across the Atlantic (where Lyons was criticized for not distinguishing adequately between Joyce's real life and his fiction). In the *Irish Press*, Derek Stanford praised Lyons for his 'clarity and absence of pedantry which might well afford a shining model to those myriad Americans, these manufacturers whose murk our publishers impose upon us'.[154] Another notable publication was Edward Quinn's *James Joyce's Dublin* in 1974. Quinn was an Irish photographer best known for his friendship with and photographs of Picasso. In addition to his wonderful Dublin photographs taken in the early 1960s, his book featured quotations from Joyce's works and an introductory note by Samuel Beckett.[155]

Gerard O'Flaherty's review of Ellmann's *Selected Letters* a couple of years later was not so much another example of an Irish reviewer taking righteous issue with an American scholar but with Joyce himself. O'Flaherty's view of Joyce seems wholly negative: he is 'a rather pathetic whining young man, getting money and demanding encouragement from his dying mother. [...] he created nothing himself, his books are transmutations of his own life, and his characters are based on his family and his friends'. He also expresses dismay that Ellmann included letters from Joyce to Nora that are 'indecent and obscene [...] and should have been edited rather being included in toto'.[156]

The late 1960s brought a smattering of short TV documentaries on RTÉ, including Norma Cohen's *Joyce's Dublin* (1967), directed by Mike O'Connor and narrated by Micheál Mac Liammóir, with Joyce's works read by Ulick O'Connor, which portrays the Dublin in which Joyce lived and worked before his departure for Europe in 1904. Andy O'Mahony's *City of James Joyce* (1968), and Kieran Hickey's beautifully evocative meditation on Joyce's Dublin, *Faithful Departed* (1968), was narrated by the great Beckett actor, Jack MacGowran. Based on the William Lawrence and Son photographic collection, the film (which was shown at Dublin's Savoy Cinema in 1968) was selected as the Irish entry to the sixth Paris Biennale in 1969 and won awards at the Locarno International Film Festival (1968),

---

[153]Gerard O'Flaherty, 'Critics' Joyce', *IP*, 4 April 1970, 12.
[154]Derek Stanford, 'Joyce Autopsy', *IP*, 15 August 1973, 10.
[155]Edward Quinn, *James Joyce's Dublin* (London: Secker & Warburg, 1974).
[156]Gerard O'Flaherty, 'Grocer's Lists', *IP*, 15 May 1976, 7.

the fifth Council of Europe Film Week (1968) and the Melbourne Film Festival (1969).[157]

It was regularly broadcast on RTÉ, which gave it a special showing in 1972 to mark the fiftieth anniversary of the publication of *Ulysses*. This landmark date was also the occasion for a small exhibition of Joyce materials at the National Library. The previous year, Tom Gallagher's moving portrait of the artist at two stages in his life – as a 26-year-old in Trieste and as an older man about to depart Paris for Zurich, *Mr Joyce is Leaving Paris* – was directed by Louis Lentin for RTÉ. It was also performed in London and at the Eblana before transferring to the Gate for a successful run.

All this helped to familiarize the country with Joyce and his writings, although some disapproved. In 1966, Deputy Sean Moore of Fianna Fail told the Dáil: 'it is deplorable in times when we are trying to improve our youth that we have this obsession with James Joyce on Telifís Éireann and this use of Anglo-Saxon words. Parents have to correct their children when they use such words.' Moore, who served as Lord Mayor of Dublin in 1963–4, later complained about 'male long-haired people' and suggested they 'should have a label put on them when they appear on Telefís Éireann so that we can identify their sex'.[158] Doubtless, he would have been dismayed to hear that filming of Joseph Strick's *Ulysses* began in Dublin in 1966. The film featured Milo O'Shea as Bloom, Barbara Jefford as Molly, Maurice Roeves as Stephen and T. P. McKenna as Buck Mulligan.

Strick was not the first director to wish to make a film of Joyce's novel. After more than ten years of negotiations with the Joyce Estate, American screenwriter and producer, Jerry Wald, secured the rights when in 1960 'Fox agreed to pay $10,000 for an option on "Ulysses", giving Mr Wald the right to have someone write a movie script. If the movie was made then another $65,000 would have to be paid to the Joyce estate. [...] By 1961 a script had been written by Allen McClelland and "Ulysses" was officially in Hollywood'.[159] Wald toured Dublin locations in 1961 with a view to shooting the film the following year. The *Cork Examiner* reported that 'Mr. Peter Sellars [sic] was to have played Leopold Bloom [...] and had been practising an Irish accent in readiness for the picture'.[160] The entire plan was scuppered by Wald's untimely death, although Strick claimed that Wald had already given up on making the film: 'He said to me: "Joe, I just don't have the time to think about it now. I'm too busy with "Peyton Place."'[161]

---

[157]A book version was published in 1982 and again in 2004 as Kieran Hickey, *Faithful Departed: The Dublin of James Joyce's 'Ulysses'*, introduction by Des Hickey (Dublin: Lilliput Press, 2004).
[158]Committee on Finance. – Vote 42 – Posts and Telegraphs (Resumed). https://www.oireachtas.ie/en/debates/debate/dail/1966-10-27/4/.
[159]'Hollywood Shuts Book on "Ulysses"; Fox Permits Option on Work by James Joyce to Lapse', *NYT*, 7 February 1964, 38.
[160]*CE*, 7 August 1962, 6.
[161]Mark Chalon Smith, 'Strickly Speaking About "Ulysses"', *Los Angeles Times*, 1 July 1993. https://www.latimes.com/archives/la-xpm-1993-07-01-ca-8941-story.html.

Every step of Strick's film's journey was followed with interest in the Irish papers. It had a low budget of $450,000 and the actors 'worked for minimum wage'. In the end, however, it 'paid for itself at least three times over'. Strick modestly noted in 1993 that its 'popularity may have been due as much to the wild publicity "Ulysses" generated as it was to the movie's merits'. He continued:

'We opened in London, and the film was promptly attacked as dirty, as nasty. Ironically, the publicity (helped keep it) playing in London for a year. Right there, we got back the money it cost to make.' The movie also met with cries for censorship in America, where it was given an X rating (primarily for the adult themes and language; there is little nudity) and showed up mostly in art houses.

The *Irish Times* republished a *New York Times* article describing the marketing strategy for the United States. The film would be released for 'simultaneous three-day runs [...] in 135 theatres' and 'each would show it four times'. The executive producer, Walter Reade Jr, said, 'The purpose was to call the public's attention to the "adult nature" of the picture and to give what he terms "the blue-noses" as little time as possible to hamper the film's release.'[162] It worked. The *Irish Press* noted that the film had made £357,000, 'the amount spent in making it on location in Dublin – after its first session of three-day runs in selected U.S. cities.' The successful 'out-manoeuvring of the American censors, official and unofficial' was praised and seen 'as a brilliant piece of organisational work by the distributors. Indoctrinated scouts have visited these cities in advance of the showing and have lectured pressmen, broadcasters, civic leaders and even churchmen on the classic qualities of Joyce's *Ulysses*'.[163] Cork's *Evening Echo* was among the papers to note the very positive responses in the United States, such as Archer Winsten's in the *New York Post*: 'Its artistic quality is such that shock soon dissolves in astonishment and admiration. This is no pandering to low tastes, no feast for smut-seekers.'[164]

Despite this, Strick's *Ulysses* received mixed reviews in Ireland and was officially banned in 1968. Ciaran Carty in *The Sunday Independent* described it as 'a sincere if rather tedious homage to Joyce – very much a filmed book. It is totally innocuous visually. The dialogue, admittedly outspoken, is taken directly from the novel, which has never been banned in Ireland'.[165] Seamus Kelly in the *Irish Times* praised Strick for capturing 'the flavour of Joyce' and thought it 'a marvellously comic film'. He singled

---

[162]'Special Plans for Release of *Ulysses*', *IT*, 1 September 1966, 6.
[163]'US Success for Film of *Ulysses*' *IP*, 20 March 1967, 5.
[164]'*Ulysses* delights U.S. Film Critics', *Evening Echo*, 15 March 1967, 12.
[165]'*Ulysses* Banned Here', *SI*, 4 February 1968, 1.

out Wolfgang Suchitzky's black and white camera work as 'pure poetry' and
Milo O'Shea's Bloom as 'the best straight performance I have seen from this
actor, and very much better than Zero Mostel's interpretation of the same
character'. T. P. McKenna won credit for his portrayal of Buck Mulligan
but Maurice Roeves (who got the part of Stephen on Laurence Olivier's
recommendation) failed to convey the character's 'intrinsic arrogance' while
Joe Lynch was 'a marvellously strutting rutting bull of a Blazes Boylan'.[166]

In the *Evening Herald*, Gerald O'Reilly denounced it as 'sex-riddled!',
'neither entertaining nor artistic' and 'the greatest shocker of a film ever to
have been seen by even the most ultra-liberal of filmgoers'.[167] Horrified by
what he called 'embarrassingly offensive [...] pornographic filth', O'Reilly
particularly objected to the opening scene, which he called 'the appalling
blasphemous sneer at one of the most profound mysteries of the Catholic
Faith' and declared it 'inexcusable, and totally unacceptable to any Christian.
[...] Never, in a lifetime of film-going and theatregoing have I witnessed such
unrelenting behaviour or heard such language in a cinema or theatre'. This
review provoked a string of indignant responses, which would not have
been so forthcoming even a decade earlier, in defence of Joyce and Strick.
One reader, who pushed back strongly, claimed:

> It may be safely assumed that anyone who finds a work by Joyce or Strick
> corrupting must also be corrupt. For either *Ulysses* the film or *Ulysses* the
> novel to be pornographic they must be designed solely to stimulate the
> sexual appetites. Can one say that they do [...] or that *Ulysses* the novel is
> concerned with sex as, say, some of the books, which [...] circulate freely
> at Smithfield?[168]

Another letter writer, signing himself 'Stephen Dedalus', described *Ulysses*
as being 'in a class of its own' and 'fifty or more years ahead of its time [...]
so penetrating and alive that even today it cannot be fully appreciated. To
hear *Ulysses* being called trash is just showing the backward, paralytic, if
not catatonic state of mind of most Irish readers'.[169] Not everyone agreed.
A certain 'N. D.' wrote to praise Mr. O'Reilly and claimed 'the vast majority
are with him. They don't want "Ulysses," or any other sexual sewage of
that kind. They want a good, clean, healthy Christian world where moral
values are respected, and where men are proud that they are not unspirited
animals'.[170]

Belfast City Council was of similar mind with Councillor Mrs. Eileen
Paisley (wife of the Reverend Ian) proving that puritan attitudes were not

---

[166]Seamus Kelly, '*Ulysses* Film Has the Right Flavour', *IT*, 3 May 1967, 6.
[167]Gerald O'Reilly, 'Pornographic and Blasphemous', *EH*, 12 August 1967, 6.
[168]'*Ulysses* Accused of Injustice to Joyce and Strick', *EH*, 23 August 1967, 6.
[169]Stephen Dedalus, 'Dribbling Nonsense about Joyce', *EH*, 29 August 1967, 6.
[170]N. D. 'Lunatic Fringe Wrecking Our Society', *EH*, 1 September 1967, 10.

the sole preserve of strict Irish Catholics. She declared: 'We don't want dirt from Dublin brought to Belfast'[171] and claimed that the film 'will encourage young people to practice immorality. [...] It will help fill the isolation wards of our hospitals with venereal disease which is the direct result of immorality. And it will help to encourage drinking and vile language'.[172] Republican Labour Councillor, P. Kennedy, disagreed, noting that *Ulysses* 'was one of the masterpieces of English literature'. He proposed that the film be shown only to viewers who were over twenty-one. This proposal 'was lost on a voice vote'.[173] Similarly, in London, Lady Dartmouth, the Greater London Council representative for Richmond, described Joyce's book as 'the most disgusting book she had ever read' and said the film was 'degrading and filthy'. She suggested that the British Board of Film Censors 'create a double X category which could mean that his film could be seen by people over 21'. In the end, it was given an X-cert (suitable for sixteen and older). The Irish papers noted with a certain fascination the fate of the film around the world and expressed bemusement at the decision in New Zealand to show it to 'segregated audiences of persons aged 18 and over'.[174]

The Bodley Head issued a special edition of *Ulysses* to tie in with the film. Unusually, it had two dust jackets: the outer featured stills of Molly Bloom *in flagrante* with Blazes Boylan and Leopold Bloom; the inner featured the more classical and iconic Homeric bow. It was a clever marketing ploy. A *Sunday Independent* article noted a rise in sales of the novel as a result of publicity around the film 'which got panned in Cannes and banned in most places' (including Ireland) to the extent that it 'has become a best seller again at 45 years of age'. According to the article, British sales were approaching 1,000 copies per day, while 'Irish booksellers report rapid clearance of stocks that have graced their shelves for many moons'.[175]

RTÉ planned to broadcast the film in 1979, however, following a protest from the League of Decency; it cancelled this screening. One writer objected to the cancellation: 'If the lesbian cavorting of "Executive Suite" and the lipstick be-decked bosoms of "Pennies from Heaven" plus the crass vulgarity of "Are you Being Served?" and the mindless violence of other programmes have met the approval of the League, why pick on *Ulysses*?'[176] Mary Whitehouse might well have best answered that question. She had objected back in 1973 when it was aired on the BBC. She was reported as having 'slipped away from a dinner [...] to watch the BBC2 film in her room at King's College where she was attending the Royal Television Society's convention'. In her view, it 'set new limits in obscenity. It was verbally

[171]'Belfast Won't See Film of *Ulysses*', *EH*, 2 September 1967, 3.
[172]'*Ulysses* Not to be Shown in Belfast', *Belfast Telegraph*, 1 September 1967, 1
[173]'Belfast Won't See Film of *Ulysses*', *EH*, 2 September 1967, 3.
[174]'*Ulysses* Sets Them Apart', *EH*, 19 April 1967, 6.
[175]*SI*, 14 May 1967, 16. The film was eventually 'unbanned' in 2000.
[176]Leo Mahon, 'Why Pick on *Ulysses*', *II*, 16 June 1979, 9.

far-and-away the most obscene thing ever seen on television'.[177] The film was also the subject of much controversy at the Cannes Film Festival where organizers covered the French subtitles on the film with a grease pencil and, after a row, Strick withdrew it. The cinema ban was not lifted in Ireland until 2000.

In 1977, Strick struck again with a film version of *A Portrait*, which he shot in Dublin with an entirely Irish cast and crew (with the exception of John Gielgud as the preacher) that included Bosco Hogan, T. P. McKenna, Rosaleen Linehan and Maureen Potter. The world première was held simultaneously in Toronto, London and at the Curzon cinema on Dublin's Middle Abbey Street. A TV adaptation, featuring Donal McCann as Stephen Dedalus, had already been broadcast by the BBC in 1972.

If the 1960s had shown a notable change in attitudes to Joyce in Ireland, the 1970s, a decade dominated by the international oil crisis, unemployment, industrial strikes and relentless strife in Northern Ireland, brought 'All Kinds of Everything' to quote the title of Dana's winning entry in the 1970 Eurovision Song contest. There was no dramatic advance in perceptions of Joyce or of *Ulysses* although gradually and inexorably they moved towards the mainstream. Irish contributions to Joyce studies continued to come, for the most part, from outside the ranks of academia. Prominent among them was Stan Gebler Davies' biography, *James Joyce: A Portrait of the Artist* (1975). Davies, in the words of John Calder, 'belonged to a breed that one no longer encounters, a rake-hell, rumbustious, very Irish, journalist of great charm, who loved to shock'.[178] In reality, his heavily publicized work was disappointing for reasons clearly set out by Suzette Henke:

> Davies is anxious to convince us that James Joyce was merely a hard-drinking, skirt-chasing Irishman. [...He] dwells with salacious fascination on all the most titillating details of remote biographical relevance. he conjectures about Joyce's adolescent sexual interests, his visits to the Dublin red light district, his payments to prostitutes, his fears about (and possible contraction of) venereal disease, his elopement with and triumphant defloration of Nora Barnacle.[179]

The late 1970s saw the emergence of Trinity's David Norris as an important popularizer of Joyce's works. He performed in an early show initially in company with Ronnie Drew of the *Dubliners*, who owed their name to Joyce's collection. Luke Kelly had been reading *Dubliners* when they were looking for a catchier band name than 'The Ronnie Drew Ballad

[177]'*Ulysses* Obscenity', *Evening Echo*, 8 September 1973, 1.
[178]John Calder, 'Obituary: Stan Gebler Davies', *The Independent*, 23 June 1994. https://www.independent.co.uk/news/people/obituary-stan-gebler-davies-1424755.html.
[179]Suzette Henke, *The Virginia Quarterly Review*, vol. 53, no. 4 (Autumn 1977): 772–6, 776.

Group' as they were originally called. Their interest in Joyce's works was genuine and there was nothing accidental in Drew's appearing along with Norris in the first enunciation of his well-known Joyce show, 'Do You Hear What I Am Seeing?' Initially they performed it together as a two hander at Players in Trinity and subsequently Norris developed it into a highly popular one-man show, which he performed to a great variety of enthusiastic audiences in Ireland and abroad. His energy and infectious zeal for Joyce's works were perfectly channelled in what was an entertaining initiation into the writer's world.

A small group of seasoned readers, meanwhile, was consolidated in 1973 with the founding of the James Joyce Institute of Ireland which offered a meeting place – Newman House – for academic and non-academic Joyceans to gather. Notable among the group were Gerard O'Flaherty (appreciated by generations of academics at home and abroad for his generous support of their scholarship), John Garvin, Eileen McCarvill and J. C. C. Mays (both UCD lecturers), Niall Montgomery, Seamus Kelly, Donal Foley and Vivien Igoe. Although the composition of the group has changed over the years, it still meets today, no longer at Newman House but across the river at the James Joyce Centre in North Great George's Street.

In 1979, with the headline, 'Computer is producing the "authentic" *Ulysses*', the *Evening Herald* announced what would become one of the biggest international Joyce stories of the 1980s. The article described how Hans Walter Gabler of the University of Munich had begun 'the Herculean task' of producing a corrected *Ulysses* text. Dr Gabler and his team were described as feeding various versions of *Ulysses* into a computer and 'working from comparisons' with the aim of producing 'the *Ulysses* James Joyce would put his name to if he were alive today'.[180]

In the same year, both the National Library and the Trinity College Dublin library turned down the chance to buy the Harriet Shaw Weaver collection which had been offered to them by the National Book League in Britain. The collection, which included twenty autographed first editions and original etchings by the French artist, Matisse, for an American edition of *Ulysses*, was sold to the University of Tulsa for £40,000.[181] The *Evening Herald* spoke for many when it wrote in 1979:

> In Dublin we will find it difficult to take James Joyce to the bosom of our soul. Cold, alien and remote, he reveals none of those traits which we associate with the Irish quality. Once again, however, Joyce's faults were exacerbated by scholarship: his near-canonisation by academics has separated him from the human level by an almost unbridgeable distance. [...] There are some who hold – and we feel inclined to agree with them –

[180]*EH*, 1 March 1979, 7.
[181]'Row Brews over Sale of Joyce Collection', *II*, 25 July 1977, 3.

that *The Portrait* was the last novel written by Joyce. *Ulysses* is close to being a literary exercise while *Finnegan's Wake* [sic] is almost the typical word salad, the verbigeration of a schizophrenic.[182]

Things, however, were about to change. Joyce's centenary – 1982 – was on the horizon and would be a fitting occasion to finally embrace the author and *Ulysses* with a little more warmth and conviction.

---

[182]'Read Joyce and be Wary!' *EH*, 26 August 1974, 9.

CHAPTER EIGHT

Coming of age in the 1980s

The 1980s in Ireland were a time of economic pain and political uncertainty as the country lurched from one short-term government to another, with Fianna Fáil's Charlie Haughey and Fine Gael's Garret Fitzgerald alternating in power. Both struggled to manage a recession that saw emigration return to the alarming levels of the 1950s. In Northern Ireland, not a week passed without violence and death while the hunger strikes dominated the early part of the decade. There were also occasional bright spots: the arrival of MTV, Stephen Roche's Tour de France, Johnny Logan's Eurovision wins and the rapid rise of a band called U2. The year 1982 was the year of 'the big snow', but also, to quote leading Irish Joyce scholar, Terence Killeen, the one in which 'official Ireland finally made its peace with James Joyce'.[1] He was not exaggerating. Joyce's centenary proved to be the turning point in his reception in Ireland, although no one would have bet on this happening at the outset when things looked less than promising.

Bloomsday 1981 had been a damp squib with just 130 visitors turning up at the Joyce Tower on 16 June, seventy of whom 'were schoolgirls from the Navan Road who came to see the ballet in Dun Laoghaire, found it closed and came on here instead'.[2] Given the economic and political instability, there was little interest in and even less public money available for Joyce celebrations. At a meeting of Dublin City Council, crocodile tears flowed as councillors from all sides of the political spectrum 'expressed regret that they cannot pay adequate tribute to the 100th anniversary of the birth of James Joyce, due to severe financial stringency. [...] the coffers are bare'. Some, such as Mr Ned Brennan, leader of the Fianna Fáil group, saw the lack of money as a blessing and warned that the city should not go overboard in celebrating

---

[1]Terence Killeen, 'Forty Years on, Joyce Is Given an Official "Wake" at Last', *IP*, 15 June 1982, 3.
[2]*IT*, 17 June 1981, 9.

the writer: 'The average man in the street,' he declared approvingly, 'had never heard of Joyce.' In an aptly entitled article, 'No Public Pence for the City's Prophet', Sean Kilfeather reported that Gus Martin's proposal for a statue on St Stephen's Green, which would be the first significant public memorial to Joyce in the country, had met with opposition. Dublin City Council felt it 'should be funded by the alumni of UCD in view of Joyce's association with the college'. Tony Gregory and the chairperson, Mary Freehill, regretted that so little was being done when 'cities like Trieste and other European centres would organise bigger tributes'.[3] A proposal, made in 1982 by poet James Liddy, to rename Beresford Place as Nora Barnacle Place, was also turned down by the Council.

Pressure to divvy up and celebrate Joyce in Dublin was increased by news that he was being commemorated abroad in London and Lancaster, in Egypt, France, Greece, Italy (Rome and Trieste), in the Lebanon, the Netherlands, Portugal, Switzerland and in various cities in the United States. Trieste would be unveiling a bust to Joyce and the city's Mayor, Manlio Cecovini, declared from Brussels: 'James Joyce is entitled to be considered an eminent local writer, notwithstanding the fact that he was not born here.'[4] But in Dublin, on the eve of the centenary, the City Council was still arguing about what to do. Tomás MacGiolla (Workers Party) expressed his surprise and disappointment: 'His birthday is tomorrow, but we are not doing anything until June 16th which is not his birthday, just Bloomsday. [...] We will only be doing that because we will have a lot of Americans around at that time.' Fine Gael Councillor, Gay Mitchell, said he was 'flabbergasted' and called the failure to mark 2 February 'a slur on our city'.[5]

This was exactly the kind of news that the capital had hoped to avoid. *The Washington Post* alluded to a series of 'controversies' over Joyce's 'allegedly pornographic writing' and wondered if 'the financially troubled city (Dublin) has the money to honour the author properly'.[6] The *New York Times* side-stepped any controversy, stressing instead the 'joyful exuberance' of the celebrations and noting 'how totally the official view of Joyce had now changed that the Government's own television network (RTE) tonight broadcast an adoring two-hour portrait of him, and that the Foreign Ministry is spending $30,000 to send posters, films and lecturers from Ireland to various parts of the world where the centenary is being celebrated'.[7] The involvement of the department of Foreign Affairs was a sign that official Ireland was stepping up attempts to attract tourism from abroad through the Joyce name (this had started as early as the fifties) even if it continued to be frugal when it came to investing in Joyce heritage at home.

---

[3]Frank Kilfeather, 'No Public Pence for City's Prophet', *IT*, 26 January 1982, 1.
[4]William Dillon, 'Italians to Honour Joyce', *II*, 26 March 1981, 26.
[5]Frank Kilfeather,' Dublin to Honour Centenary', *IT*, 2 February 1982, 5.
[6]Mark Hosenball, 'US Reaction to James Joyce Centenary Events', *IT*, 4 February 1982, 9.
[7]Ibid.

Despite the last-minute nature of preparations and the lack of funds, the centenary was celebrated successfully in Ireland. The national newspapers were full of it, many of them printing multiple page supplements on 2 February. Most reporting was constructive but the arrival of foreign visitors did provoke some hostile reaction: 'No man in the history of modern literature has attracted so many literary locusts as James Joyce', claimed the *Irish Press*. 'They still swarm across the Atlantic searching for crumbs in the rubble of the past that will help ferment another thesis.'[8] Joyce was the subject of several editorials, couched mostly in 'whether we like it or not' qualified praise. The *Irish Independent* noted that he would be 'celebrated this year not as a great Irishman but as one of the world's great writers deserving of a place at the very top of the literary tree'. Joyce 'would not be surprised that, among his fellow-Irishmen, there are not a few who take a decidedly jaundiced view of him, his life and his work':

> Yet, whether we like it or not, we have a genius on our hands, a man who wrought works which have been hailed by a world-wide reading public as masterpieces. He brought a new style to writing. [...] it can be admitted here that, taken in isolation there are 'objectionable' chapters in his works. [...] Joyce's ability to recognise the diversity of human nature brought him into collision with people and courts – but that is in the past. It should now be time to honour one of our great men.

The Irish Times was warmer: 'When Joyce came to publish his books, the censorious Ireland of the 1920s and 30s looked away disapprovingly, insofar as it paid any attention at all. However amends are now being made, as is right. Joyce by his writings paid great honour to the city of his birth, and the compliment should be returned.' Having noted that 'Joyce is receiving more attention this week in his native land than in all the decades since the publication of Dubliners in 1914', the *Irish Press* focused on the belatedness of this recognition, wondering if 'the attention which Joyce is receiving is of quite the best kind', and detected 'a faint tinge of surprise [...] as if we had unearthed the annals of some long-sleeping giant. [...] Joyce's work, it seems, has been woken from the sleep of the academies and given back into the hands of the man in the street, whoever he may be'. After scholars had established that Joyce produced 'a work of great, enduring and, above all, serious art [...] now the tide has reversed. Suddenly we are assured that Joyce is fun; that he was writing about ordinary things, for ordinary people; that one does not need a university degree to read his work'. The editorialist insists, however, that Joyce's work 'is difficult, demanding, and at times obscure' and to 'pretend otherwise is to attempt a deception, which will benefit neither the reader, nor Joyce's reputation'.[9]

---

[8] Liam Robinson, 'Out in Search of Mr. Joyce', *IP*, 2 February 1982, 9.
[9] 'Honouring Joyce', *IP*, 2 February 1982, 8.

Raising funds for the centenary was like getting blood from a stone. Having taken stock that 'Irish companies were not "very generous or spontaneous"', the Centenary Committee looked further afield and sought funds from an American company to pay for the statue to commemorate Joyce on Stephen's Green. Within forty-eight hours, American Express obliged.[10] While Ulick O'Connor described the decision to erect the monument as a 'great recognition of Joyce and a confirmation that Dublin does honour its great writers',[11] Joyce's increasingly recalcitrant grandson, Stephen, disagreed and declined to attend the unveiling. He let it be known that 'had the State donated the bust he would have been delighted to attend'.[12] The *Irish Press* commented: 'It did not go unnoticed that American Express had made the bust possible, and that Joyce could have done with a card in his lifetime.'[13]

The statue of Joyce, by Marjorie Fitzgibbon, carried the words from *A Portrait* – 'Crossing Stephen's, that is, my green' – and was unveiled by President Hillery on Bloomsday. Later in the year, a second bronze bust of Joyce, by Joe McCaul, was donated to University College Dublin by Galway's Royal Tara China which, in Augustine Martin's words, had 'redeemed the nation's honour'.[14] It was unveiled in October 1982 by NUI Chancellor Ken Whitaker, who called Joyce 'UCD's most renowned student'.[15] Martin and Peter Costello (who had recently published *Leopold Bloom: A Biography*, a work described as 'one that will make the more pious academics recoil with horror'[16]), organized an exhibition entitled 'Portraits of a Student' at Newman house which enjoyed an extended run. A special centenary number of UCD's *Third Degree* with articles by, among others, Brian Cosgrove, Christopher Murray, Gus Martin, Aidan Higgins also marked the Centenary. Editor Patrick Gallagher pulled off a coup in also managing to include Umberto Eco among the contributors with 'The aesthetics of Chaosmos', which foreshadowed his book *The Middle Ages of James Joyce: The Aesthetics of Chaosmos* published by Harvard in 1989.[17] UCD's prestigious literary journal, the *Irish University Review*, published a special Joyce issue featuring a host of leading contemporary writers reacting to their great predecessor. Val Mulkerns found Joyce less awesome than comforting while John Montague celebrated Joyce as 'central to European consciousness'. Brian Moore found in Joyce 'the exemplar of what the writer

[10]'US Firm Has to Fund Joyce Bust for Green', *IP*, 6 April 1982, 7.
[11]'U.S. Firm Funds Joyce Bust', *IP*, 18 March 1982, 8.
[12]Paddy Butler, 'Joyce Casts a Wry Eye at the Profiteers', *IP*, 17 June 1982, 1.
[13]Liam Robinson, 'Dublin Has a Rare ould Time on Special Bloomsday', *IP*, 17 June 1982, 3.
[14]*II*, 19 October 1982, 3.
[15]'Bronze of Joyce Unveiled', *IT*, 19 October 1982, 7.
[16]Peter Costello, *Leopold Bloom: A Biography* (Dublin: Gill and Macmillan, 1981). See Ronan Farren, 'At Last, the Real Story of Leopold Bloom?', *EH*, 5 November 1981, 8.
[17]Patrick Gallagher, *The Third Degree, Special Joyce Centenary Number* (Dublin: UCD, 1983). I am grateful to Aidan Collins for drawing this to my attention.

should be'. Francis Stuart, in 'A Minority Report', faulted *Ulysses* for its evasion of 'mysterious elements' but praised it as 'the funniest book I have read'. In her review, Patricia Hutchins was none too impressed and suggested that the contributors were happy to be associated with Joyce but few were genuinely interested in his work. Ita Daly's 'Joycelessness' encapsulated this. She 'finds she is much more interested in exploring herself as an Irishwoman in what has become a global village. In fact most of these writers are obeying Yeats' command not to dismount at the graveyard "Horseman, pass by!"'[18]

This was certainly not true of Brian Moore's contribution. He recalled discovering, as an eighteen-year-old in 1939, 'hidden behind some innocent titles' in a friend's house, 'the two-volume Odyssey Press edition of *Ulysses*, published in Hamburg, Paris, Bologna, and bearing the warning: Not To Be Introduced Into the British Empire Or the U.S.A'. His friend told him it was a dirty book bought by his brother in Paris:

> I settled in to read it openly in search of the 'hot bits.' It was, of course, a dirty book, more explicit about sexual matters than any other I had read until then. But it was, for me, stimulating in an altogether different way. On Sunday night, when it was time to leave, I hid both volumes in my suitcase. It was the first and only time that I have committed theft and today, forty years later, I still have both volumes, much worn, carefully preserved, the only books I have carried with me throughout my life.[19]

Moore made no secret of the fact that Joyce became the model to follow:

> From those first readings, *Ulysses* changed, if not my life, then my ideas about becoming a writer. It both inspired and intimidated me. [...] For in my twenties, before I began to write myself, Joyce was already, for me, the exemplar of what a writer should be: an exile, a rebel, a man willing to endure poverty, discouragement, the hardships of illness, and the misunderstandings of critics, a man who would sacrifice his life to the practice of writing.[20]

A few years later, Terence Killeen would take stock of Joyce's influence on Irish writing and conclude that the early Joyce was most influential in setting 'the pattern for the Irish short story'. One of the finest of the many short stories to pay homage to Joyce while making fun of the academic Joyce industry is William Trevor's 'Two More Gallants'. It imagines a University literature scholar, Professor Flacks, being gulled by two of his

---

[18]Patricia Hutchins, 'The Last of Summer's Bloom', *IP*, 12 August 1982, 6.
[19]Brian Moore, 'Old Father, Old Artificer', *Irish University Review*, vol. 12, no. 1 (1982): 13–16, 13.
[20]Ibid., 14.

students into believing that they have discovered the original servant girl
on whom Joyce based his story 'Two Gallants'. It turns out to be a hoax
pulled by two modern-day 'gallants', called Heffernan and Fitzpatrick, who
owe much to Joyce's original pair. The 'effect of *A Portrait* on subsequent
Irish fiction has been almost incalculable', according to Killeen, who noted
the 'formidably real' influence of Joyce on figures such as Brian Moore,
John McGahern and John Banville.[21] The 'later Joyce', on the other hand,
'mattered only to a hardy few' and the influence of *Ulysses* and *Finnegans
Wake* was still 'largely evaded' although exceptions were to be found, such
as Flann O'Brien, Beckett and Edna O'Brien, whose *Night* was 'obviously
indebted, both its situation and in its style, to Molly Bloom's monologue'.
Killeen concluded: 'Joyce is still very much a live presence in Irish writing.
Like it or not, his shadow has not grown any less.' In other words, Irish and
perhaps in particular Dublin novelists were still labouring under an anxiety
of influence. This was certainly the view of novelist and Film Director,
Ferdia Mac Anna, who claimed colourfully that Joyce or better the Joyce
myth 'intimidated the bejazus out of Dublin writers of the 60s, 70s and 80s'
and 'was inhibiting Dublin's artistic and literary development':

> It made writers feel that anything that could or should have been written
> about Dublin had already been penned by the man himself. In effect, the
> great man – the colossus of Irish writing, the writer of 'dirty bukes', the
> jejune jesuit – had hijacked the city and imprisoned it in his writings, out
> of the reach of ordinary people and other writers.[22]

With few exceptions, such as James Plunkett and later figures such as
Dermot Bolger and Michael O'Loughlin, it would take many more years
for many Irish novelists to fully come to terms with Joyce but their poet
colleagues had already begun to grapple far more creatively with and to be
inspired by his example.

One among them was the Irish language poet, Seán Ó Ríordáin, who,
in Derval Tubridy's words, 'found in Joyce a way out of the Irish Ireland
that threatened to stifle the emerging poet. [...] The struggle between the
modern Irish writer and the Gaelic language that Joyce circumvented rather
than resolved became the central struggle for Ó Ríordáin'. Rather than
go the route of Gaelic purism that his early teacher, Daniel Corkery, had
advised, Ó Ríordáin looked – through Joyce – to modernism and would
play with and expand the Irish language and the Irish poetic tradition
in part by following Joyce's example with English. His copies of Joyce's

[21]Terence Killeen, 'The Old Artificer Still Presents a Challenge to Our Young Writers', *EP Souvenir*, 1989, 16.
[22]Ferdia Mac Anna, 'The Dublin Renaissance: An Essay on Modern Dublin and Dublin Writers', *The Irish Review*, no. 10, Dublin/Europe/Dublin (Spring 1991): 14–30, 18.

works and his 1966 paperback edition of Ellmann's biography are quite heavily annotated and show that his statement that 'the worst mistake Daniel Corkery ever made was to say that James Joyce's work wouldn't last' was based on his own personal experience of reading Joyce.[23] As Ó Ríordáin battled between the pulls of Irish and English, he was particularly interested in Joyce's struggle as an Irish writer working within the confines of the English language. Sometimes he notes a key phrase that addresses his own linguistic predicament, such as 'You are an Irishman and you must write in your own tradition [...] what is in your blood', which Joyce did through English and Ó Ríordáin would predominantly do through Irish. Occasionally, he translates relevant phrases by Joyce such as 'Je suis au bout de l'anglais' directly into Irish: 'Táim ag deire an Bhéarla'. Towards the end of his career, he wrote 'Joyce', a substantial 'laoi ardmholta/ praise-poem'[24] in which he describes Joyce as being 'as much part of myself /as the alphabet and gospels/his distinct geometry /euclidising my brain'. In a sense he has become Joyce and now is 'tripping in his wake' in both senses of the word 'tripping', both stumbling and getting high in his long shadow of his legacy.[25] Ó Ríordáin would be criticized for writing in an Irish that was not pure or traditional enough and might perhaps have agreed with Thomas Kinsella's words when he wrote (after Joyce), 'We are all what we are, and that/Is mongrel pure. What nation's not?'[26]

James Simmons, in his sardonic poem 'The Catholic Church's Revenge on James Joyce' (1983), addressed a very different series of concerns, taking issue with Joyce for constructing a work of such complexity that people would 'cower/coming near his creation and sidle in, astounded,/and wait for official experts to show them how to read it'. Simmons, in Fintan O'Toole's words, 'accused the great novelist as having reproduced the very thing he had rebelled against by creating, in opposition to the church's authoritarian majesty, "a towering Gothic prose cathedral"'.[27] Derek Mahon is differently playful in addressing Joyce directly in his 'Joycentenary Ode' (commissioned by the BBC), which imitates the language of the *Wake* and directly addresses 'Jems... In the Flutherin Symatery':

---

[23]Seán Ó Ríordáin, *Mise* (Dublin: UCD 1987), 19.

[24]Frank Sewell, 'Seán Ó. Ríordáin: Joycery-Corkery-Sorcery', *Irish Review*, no. 23 (Winter 1998): 42–61, 47. For a broader discussion, see Sewell's very insightful, 'James Joyce's Influence on Writers in Irish' in Geert Lernout and Wim Van Mierlo, eds., *The Reception of Joyce in Europe*, Volume 1: Germany, Northern and East Central Europe (London: Thoemmes Continuum, 2994n 469–81.

[25]The full poem is quoted in both Irish and English in Frank Sewell, 'Seán Ó. Ríordáin: Joycery-Corkery-Sorcery', 47.

[26]Thomas Kinsella, *Thomas Kinsella: Collected Poems 1956–1994* (Oxford: Oxford University Press, 1996), 142.

[27]James Simmons, 'The Catholic Church's Revenge on James Joyce', *IT*, 25 June 1983, Weekend, 4. Fintan O'Toole, 'Putting God on the Stage is a Bold Act of Commission', *IT*, 12 July 2008.

> What pome of mine might
> Healp aliviate
> Youretournal night?
> What news of the warld
> You loft bihand
> Widdamuse you now?

What, he wondered, would Joyce make of the new Americanised Ireland?

> The bairdboard
> Bombardment screen
> And gineral californucation
> Have revolationized
> Ourland beyand raggednition.[28]

The year 1984 was the year in which Seamus Heaney published his great collection, *Station Island*. It is no accident that in the title poem the final ghost encountered by Heaney is not Yeats but Joyce, a paternal figure like Virgil for Dante, who, bearing his ashplant, urges Heaney to pursue his own individual path towards art. Joyce's exhortation is liberating rather than prescriptive as he tells the poet 'it's time to swim/out on your own':

> What you must do must be done on your own
> so get back in harness. The main thing is to write
> for the joy of it. [...] And don't be so earnest,
> let others wear the sackcloth and the ashes.'

If Irish poets were gathering strength and inspiration in Joyce's slipstream, the Irish Jesuits were finally acknowledging their most famous Irish product. Although some work was done in this direction by Brendan Duddy SJ in lectures given at summer schools in the 1960s and 1970s (he focused mainly on Joyce's Thomism), the publication of Fr Bruce Bradley's carefully researched *James Joyce's Schooldays*, took the acknowledgement to a whole new level. It came complete with an introduction by Richard Ellmann whose *imprimatur* was often sought but rarely given in this period, Ellmann, inevitably feted as the doyen of Joyceans, was somewhat uncomfortable with the growing army of Joyce scholars and admirers and was quoted as complaining that 'the bandwagon was getting a little crowded'.[29] However, he saw the symbolic importance of Bradley's book, which was launched as part of Belvedere's 150-year celebrations.

Many of the city's major national cultural institutions played their part in the centenary. The National Library mounted an exhibition entitled

---

[28]Derek Mahon, *The Hunt by Night* (Oxford: Oxford University Press, 1982), 145–8.
[29]John Doyle, 'Never let on you're related to that fella James Joyce', *II*, 16 June 1988, 7.

'Those Young Men', which framed Joyce and his contemporaries not as pre-Independence revolutionary spirits, but as post-Parnellites. Over at City Hall, the international exhibition 'James Joyce and the Dublin of his Time' opened (it had previously been shown in Beirut), while the Douglas Hyde Gallery showed 'The *Ulysses* Project' featuring works inspired by Joyce by Irish artists such as Brian Bourke, Barrie Cooke, Phelim Egan, Patrick Hickey and Charles Tyrrell. RTÉ Radio One broadcast Gerald Victory's Joyce-inspired 'Six Epiphanies of the Author' from the National Concert Hall.

The station also broadcast an acclaimed thirty-hour Bloomsday reading of *Ulysses*. Dublin-based English *Finnegans Wake* expert (and biology lecturer) Roland McHugh was textual advisor to the ambitious project, which was 'a fullscale version with different voices for all the characters in the book, sound effects, music'.[30] McHugh saw this as a last chance to record 1904 Dublin phraseology with any kind of authenticity. His first task was to quietly fix many misprints and errors in the text of *Ulysses* (the Gabler edition was not yet available) by consulting the hugely valuable copies of the *James Joyce Archive* (edited by a team led by Michael Groden), at the National Library, which contain facsimiles of Joyce's manuscripts. The ensemble reading, directed by William Styles and produced by Micheál Ó hAodha, was a triumph. In Tom O'Dea's words, 'the service rendered Joyce by RTÉ – both radio and television – over the course of that day and a bit was superb. For hour after hour, we were smoked with Joyce, as a flitch of bacon is smoked, until he had penetrated every pore of us and cured us'.[31] Veteran Joycean, Niall Montgomery, was one of the very few to demur. At the announcement of the event, he said that although Joyce 'was literate and wrote for a literate audience, the idea of reading Joyce's work to a vast illiterate audience' was 'supererogatory'.[32] His comments were either evidence of the limits of the approach to appreciating Joyce that his generation had adopted and of their insistence on Joyce's personality and Irishness over the power and broad appeal of his actual words or, ever the provocateur, he was drawing attention to the general public's disinterest in Joyce's works. Whichever way it was, RTÉ's broadcast was an apt response to Beckett's belief that Joyce's writing 'is not so much to be read – or rather it is not only to be read. It is to be looked at and listened to'.[33] Montgomery's attitude was a throwback to a time that was fading when *Ulysses* was, in Barry McCrea's description, 'the preserve, not of the ordinary élite, the cultivated upper-middle classes (as

---

[30]Roland McHugh, 'The 30-hour *Ulysses*', *IT*, 16 June 1982, 10.
[31]Tom O'Dea, 'Joyce, Soccer, Tennis and Joyce', *IP*, 19 June 1982, 8. In 2005, an alternative full version of *Ulysses* was recorded by Jim Norton and Marcella Riordan for Naxos Audiobooks who produced twenty-two CD box set.
[32]*IT*, 15 December 1981, 6.
[33]Samuel Beckett, 'Dante… Bruno, Vico… Joyce' in Ruby Cohn ed., *Disjecta: Miscellaneous Writing and a Dramatic Fragment* (London: John Calder, 1983), 19–33, 27.

Proust in France or Goethe in Germany) but of a small, marginal, bohemian segment of the population'.[34] Montgomery, and Anthony Cronin after him, would, at times, seem to mourn the passing of the 1950s when to read and admit to reading *Ulysses* was still something of a rebel act.

RTÉ also broadcast Anthony Burgess's musical version of the novel entitled 'The Blooms of Dublin', despite an initial refusal by a number of the RTÉ singers to participate on the grounds of the text's indelicacy, and despite the opposition of Councillor Ned Brennan, and a call to the chairman of the RTÉ authority from STOP (Society to Outlaw Pornography) appealing for it to be cancelled. The appeal was sent on behalf of a considerable group of influential organizations including the Irish Countrywomen's Association, the Knights of Saint Columbanus, the Irish Federation of Womens' Clubs, the Joint Committee of Women's Societies and Social Workers, the Council of Social Concern and the Congress of Catholic Secondary School Parent Associations.[35] *Exiles* was also broadcast on both radio and television in addition to a series of twelve Thomas Davis lectures on Joyce (given by a strong academic cast including Richard Ellmann, Augustine Martin, Maurice Craig, James Plunkett and Seamus Deane). Eavan Boland was the one female contributor and focused on Joyce as a young writer who 'pioneered an artistic stance that released him from the meshes and toils of that most insidious European ideology, romanticism'.[36] In November, Seán Ó Mordha's memorable RTÉ 'Is There One Who Understands Me?' documentary won an Emmy New York (and was the first Irish documentary ever to do so). Narrated by T. P. McKenna and scripted by Colbert Kearney with music by Seoirse Bodley, it was justly hailed as 'a feast of facts, music and commentary [...] a fitting tribute to his genius'.[37]

Dublin City Council decorated the streets with flags and bunting on 16 June in a similar manner to what was usually done for St Patrick's Day or an All-Ireland final. There was also a more formal aspect to the celebration evident in the printing of a commemorative Joyce postage stamp and the unveiling of a plaque at Leopold Bloom's fictional birthplace, 52 Upper Clanbrassil Street. Hugh Kenner did the honours. For this event, the Lord Mayor in a horse-drawn open carriage led a procession through the city centre by as part of what the *Irish Independent* called 'a Bloomsday extravaganza that brought the city back to the splendours of its Edwardian past, for a day'.[38] Locals were said to have 'watched with incredulity and

[34]Barry McCrea, 'Privatising *Ulysses*: Joyce before, during and after the "Celtic Tiger"' in R. Brandon Kershner and Tekla Mesnóber, *Joycean Unions Post-Millennial Essays from East to West, European Joyce Studies*, Volume: 22, 81–95, (Amsterdam: Rodopi, 2013), 84.
[35]Letter to the Editor', *EP*, January 29 1982, 23.
[36]'Eavan Boland on James Joyce'. https://www.listennotes.com/it/podcasts/davis-now-lectures/eavan-boland-on-james-joyce-_n0XhLANfJO/.
[37]Brendan Glacken, 'Precedence for Mr Joyce', *IT*, 9 February 1982, 8.
[38]*II*, 17 June 1982, 9.

amusement' at the unveiling of a plaque to a fictional character.[39] Among the distinguished guests present were novelists Thomas Flanagan, Dennis Potter and Anthony Burgess, who also gave a riveting symposium lecture to a packed audience at the Mansion House on Joyce and Hopkins' use of language. He was a fixture at all Joyce celebrations over the coming years, so much so that Frank Delaney would describe him as 'a subsidiary company in the Joyce industry'.[40]

Politicians also got in on the Joyce act. Ireland's European Commissioner, Richard Burke, held a Brussels reception to celebrate Bloomsday and said that Joyce's *Ulysses* celebrated 'the unity of the European imagination by recreating at one extremity of Europe [...] a heroic myth which originated more than 3,000 years before at the other extremity of today's European Community'. A resolution of the European parliament, inspired by the SDLP's John Hume, was signed by sixteen Socialist colleagues of various nationalities. It declared 'this day Blooomsday 1982, a day of special commemoration of James Joyce'.[41]

There was an embarrassment of Joycean riches in the Dublin theatres in 1982. Siobhan McKenna appeared in *All Joyce* at the Abbey. She had already performed her acclaimed *Here Are Ladies* at the Gate in 1975 and introduced female figures from works by Synge, Yeats, Stephens, Shaw, O'Casey and Lennox Robinson but it was Molly Bloom and Anna Livia Plurabelle who stole the show. Her new show was all Joyce. A lukewarm Mary Moloney in the *Evening Press* called it a 'fairly decent introduction' that 'never comes to terms fully with the writer's life and times. The bulk of last night's audience was provided by coachloads of American tourists'.[42] In the *Irish Times*, the often grudging David Nowlan described McKenna's as 'the best Molly Bloom characterisation in the world' and suggested that a rival performance by Fionnula Flanagan 'suffered by comparison because she seemed more concentrated on the sex'. He noted that Patricia Leventon was also performing as Molly at Bloom's hotel and felt the presence of Poldy asleep beside her 'upside down' added pathos to her words.[43] Gerry Stembridge's *Betrayals*, a drama set on the night of Joyce's departure from Ireland, directed by Eilis Mullan, won plaudits for the Dublin Youth Theatre while an old stager, Eamon Morrissey, returned once more with his evergreen 'Joycemen', which won singular praise from Nowlan:

> Morrissey's format was deceptively simple: he picked some of the characters from *Ulysses* and portrayed them as cameo, set them around a few set pieces of dialogue of which the scene in Barney Kiernan's pub

[39]Terence Killeen, 'Forty Years on', *IP*, 15 June 1982, 3.
[40]Frank Delaney, 'Joyce and Sex', *II*, 10 June 1989, 8.
[41]Brian Donaghy, 'Ulysses Myth Unites Gourmets', *IT*, 17 June 1982, 7.
[42]Mary Moloney, 'Siobhan Hasn't Got Jim's Joys', *EP*, 10 June 1982, 4.
[43]David Nowlan, 'The Spoken Joyce', *IT*, 25 June 1982, 12.

was the undoubted comic pinnacle with the lone actor playing, with meticulous precision, about seven characters and one mongrel dog.[44]

In David Norris's view,

> the most memorable event of that year was the re-enactment by Horizon Theatre Productions of the 'Wandering Rocks' episode of *Ulysses* [...] This was really the first time that a large scale costume re-enactment of one of the episodes of the book took place and the citizens of Dublin, all of whom wittingly or unwittingly played the role of extras, responded enthusiastically to the rich gallery of colourful and eccentric characters dressed in period costume.[45]

Ironically, Horizon's show was organized by John Farrell and Bill Wertz from the basement of No 35 (later the Joyce Centre) where Horizon had been effectively squatting for several years. It was but the first of many such large-scale, colourful street entertainments that would characterize the Bloomsday celebrations over the following decades.

The year 1982 also saw Dublin hosting its biggest international symposium, which attracted almost 700 participants. Morris Beja recalled that the public events included 'the first welcome at a Symposium by a head of state, Dr. Patrick Hillery, the President of Ireland'. The Taoiseach, Charles Haughey, hosted a reception at Dublin Castle but perhaps more importantly provided public funding for the event (this was a first). David Norris described asking Anthony Cronin, the Taoiseach's cultural advisor, for money for the Symposium: 'He asked me to hang on a minute. When he returned he said, "The man [Haughey] says we can have ten grand. You do what you want with it, but he says you can then fuck off because you are not getting anything more."'[46] Among the illustrious guests at the Taoiseach's reception was 'Carroll O'Connor, who before Archie Bunker had played Blazes Boylan in the original production of *Ulysses in Nighttown*', his director, Burgess Meredith, was also present, 'as were Simon and Garfunkel, Tom Stoppard, Anthony Burgess, and E. L. Doctorow. Later in the week, Jorge Luis Borges made an unannounced appearance at the Bloomsday banquet'.[47] The morning after, a bemused *Irish Press* journalist noted that there 'were more foreign photographers in Dublin than near the Falklands' (the war had ended there on 14 June): 'Last night there were carousels in pubs and banquets in hotels. Today will be Doomsday. While Bloom sleeps there will be boozer's gloom and brewer's droop.'[48] The same paper reported

---

[44]Ibid.
[45]David Norris, *II*, 16 June 1995, 9.
[46]David Norris, *A Kick against The Pricks*, 188.
[47]Morris Beja, 'A Symposium All His Own', *JSA* 12, 134.
[48]Liam Robinson, 'Dublin Has a Rare ould time on Special Bloomsday', *IP*, 17 June 1982, 3.

that trade in Joyce books had been brisk at Fred Hanna's, mainly thanks to German, Dutch, Italian and Japanese visitors but that there had been little interest among Irish customers.

Commemorations were held outside Dublin in places with Joyce connections. The Triskell Arts Centre in Cork hosted an exhibition called 'Joyce's Ireland', which, true to the local spirit, focused almost entirely on the Joyce family's presence in nineteenth-century Cork. Mullingar also claimed its Joyce connection, thanks to local activist Leo Daly (author of *James Joyce and the Mullingar Connection*[49]), who was the main mover behind the placing of a Joyce waxwork at the Greville Arms Hotel in 1982. This wax Joyce Statue had previously held the place of honour as part of Westmeath Community Development Ltd's trade mission to the Paris Agricultural Show. This would be the closest Joyce would ever come to being the 'bullockbefriending bard' he mentions in *Ulysses*.[50] An exhibition on Joyce's Trieste was held in Letterkenny and celebrations were also held in Galway where Padraic O'Laoi's biography, *Nora Barnacle Joyce*, was published and well received (in part for correcting some errors in Ellmann and reiterated in Gebler Davies 1975 biography).[51] Five years later, again in Galway, Mary and Sheila Gallagher bought and restored the Barnacle home on Bowling Green, which had been derelict for over ten years. They subsequently ran it as a private museum displaying documentary evidence about the Barnacle family. In the words of Sheila Gallagher, 'the Barnacle house is of interest in that, apart from the installation of the small Liffey range sometime in the late forties, the house virtually remains the same as it was when Joyce and Nora came there'.[52] The careful efforts to preserve the Barnacle house contrasted with the failure to preserve much of Joyce's heritage in the capital.

One work which had a major impact among readers in Ireland and abroad in the 1980s was Frank Delaney's *James Joyce's Odyssey: A Guide to the Dublin of Ulysses* (1981).[53] In some ways, Delaney was the ideal guide for the intimidated future reader of *Ulysses* (he had failed his Leaving Cert and did not have a university degree but went on to become a leading literary journalist on radio and television in the UK and later in the United States). Delaney liked to tell of how he found his first copy of the novel in a brown paper bag left on a Dublin bus and had to overcome his own reservations before reading it. Full of what Terence Killeen describes as 'infectious enthusiasm',[54] Delaney's 'plain man's guide' was aimed at a popular rather than an academic audience: 'Reading *Ulysses* is one of the

[49]Leo Daly, *James Joyce and the Mullingar connection* (Dublin: Dolmen Press, 1975).

[50]*Westmeath Examiner*, 28 February 1998, 20.

[51]Padraic O Laoi, *Nora Barnacle Joyce* (Galway: Galway, Kennys Bookshops and Art Galleries Ltd., 1982).

[52]Sheila Gallagher, 'Letter to *JJQ*', vol. 26, no. 4 (Summer 1989): 635–7, 637.

[53]Frank Delaney, *James Joyce's Odyssey* (London: Hodder and Stoughton, 1981).

[54]"Frank Delaney Author, Broadcaster and Champion of James Joyce's Ulysses', *IT*, 25 February 2017, 12.

pleasures of life. It is a vast, entertaining, funny, absorbing, exciting, complex, immensely enjoyable novel [...] a book to be [...] relished, savoured, a work of intelligence and delight.'[55] In 2010, he launched a hugely popular weekly *Ulysses* podcast and would record over 400 instalments over the following years right up to his death in 2017 getting about one-third of the way through Joyce's book. At the time of this death, his eloquent, informed, lively, musical and dramatic short commentaries had been downloaded over 2.5 million times (mostly in the United States), making him, arguably, the most successful Joyce popularizer of them all.

Perhaps not surprisingly, some felt that the Joyce that was being celebrated in the early 1980s was a diluted version of the real thing. In an article in the *Irish Press*, Seamus Deane looked at Joyce's legacy and expressed his perplexity at the concentration 'particularly in the USA' on 'the punster, the wordsmith, the proliferation of useful but limited studies of his allusions, hints, parallels and so forth'. This focus on language had, in his view, 'completely obscured the radical nature of his enterprise and so entirely converted it to a literary phenomenon'. Reacting to a growing tendency to read the political in literary texts – among many others, Edward Said's highly influential *Orientalism* had appeared in 1978 and was soon followed by Fredric Jameson's *The Political Unconscious* (1981) with the famous exhortation 'Always historicize!'[56] – Deane sought to reinstate Joyce's Irish politics and took issue with the widespread belief that Joyce 'did in fact surrender all pretence to any form of political commitment'. This mirrored a similar debate that was already raging in Yeats' studies in which Deane and others were attempting to delineate and assess Yeats' often uncomfortable political ideas with regard to Ireland and Europe. In Deane's view, 'Joyce certainly was sceptical about the narrowness of Irish nationalism, although he never lost sight of its justification; he lost interest in socialism'. Stating that 'nothing in Irish writing' since Joyce had 'come remotely near' to his ambition, Deane lamented that the country's writers laboured under 'a false sense of division between political commitment and art, for which Joyce has become an example, we have made the absence of politics from writing a sign of its integrity as art. This is a sad distortion'.[57] Deane would spend the next decades establishing an Irish literary canon through the Field Day Anthology, but also working on his project of re-historicizing and re-politicizing those same texts. His work and that of many others who followed in his critical footsteps on Joyce would be an important part of this.

The Centenary was also the occasion of the legal transfer of the house at 35 North Great George's Street from Dublin Corporation to the (Irish)

---

[55]Frank Delaney, *James Joyce's Odyssey*, 9.
[56]Fredric Jameson, *The Political Unconscious: Narrative as a Social Symbolic Act* (London: Methuen, 1981), 9.
[57]Seamus Deane, 'The Daunting Achievement', *IP*, 2 February 1982, 9.

James Joyce Foundation that would eventually refurbish it and convert it into what would become the James Joyce Centre. David Norris had come up with the idea of the Centre around the time of the 1977 Symposium in Dublin – and there, matters rested but nothing came of it until 1982. Bloomsday in the centenary year fell just weeks after the famous 'Gregory Deal'. One part of this arrangement saw Taoiseach Charles Haughey instruct Dublin Corporation (in which his brother was a very senior figure) to call a halt to the ongoing demolition of the north inner city. The deal became operative on 9 March and on 16 June while Lord Mayor Alexis Fitzgerald was promenading in the Lord Mayoral Carriage, playing the part of the Earl of Dudley, his deputy, the notoriously conservative Fine Gael Councillor, Alice Glenn, ceremonially handed over the key of No 35 North Great George's Street to David Norris. Although the key was handed over, there was no lease and Dublin City Council never imagined that Norris and his supporters would be able to refurbish the Centre. They fully expected to get the key back in due course and the strategy was to await its return. But as things turned out, a 'full restoring' lease was eventually effected, albeit nine years and much effort later and the building was eventually restored from near-dereliction. The newspaper reports of the Bloomsday 1982 ceremony record, for example, that local T. D. Tony Gregory was present (at what was one of the first material manifestations of his famous deal, even if not included in its express terms). The ceremony was interrupted by a protest involving various artists led by Kalichi James Donahue and associated with the Grapevine Arts Centre around the corner in North Frederick Street who disapproved of the city extending largesse to celebrate someone long dead while many contemporary artists struggled to make a living.

Number 35 had originally been the home of Valentine Browne, first Earl of Kenmare and a part of it was later used by Professor Denis J. Maginni, who ran a dance academy there in Joyce's time and is immortalized in *Ulysses*. The building had been allowed to deteriorate and faced demolition. Ken Monaghan, who had long called for more attention to be paid to Joyce's connections to the north inner city (rather than or in addition to Sandycove where he only spent a couple of nights), campaigned, with David Norris, to raise funds for its restoration over the decade that followed. It was gradually refurbished from the top down, starting with a new roof in 1983. The first administrator was Des Gunning.

Despite a shaky start, the 1982 Centenary had delivered for Joyce and *Ulysses* and there was a noticeable leap in Irish interest in and acceptance of the author. In 1988, the *Irish Times* journalist, Fergus Brogan, looked back on the centenary year as a crucial turning point:

> Watching the annual Joycean ritual one would be forgiven for assuming that it was the Feast Day of some popular saint and not the day set aside for Ireland's most irreverent writer. [...] 1982, the year that he was forgiven for being a dirty-minded school boy, the anti-Christ who

took the... out of the literary establishment and mocked at all we hold sacred.[58]

The secular saint was even given the tribute of a ballad entitled 'Finnegan, are ya reely dead?' penned by Shay Healy (author, among other things, of Johnny Logan's 1980 Eurovision winner 'What's Another Year?') and performed by the popular folk singer, Danny Doyle. It carried echoes mostly of *Ulysses* and concluded: 'Ah, Dublin, how your son has served you! All across the world, his words are read./Ah sure he was the quare one, fol the diddle... ; Finnegan, are you really dead?' It would later become a staple in some of the pubs that would spring up in Temple Bar.

Even Joyce's grandson, the increasingly volatile Stephen Joyce, seemed moderately and momentarily happy and announced (from Paris) during the symposium: 'Wherever Nonno and Nonna are, I know they will be smiling, even grinning broadly with malice and pleasure at the festivities and especially the lectures and theories expounded by the learned Joyceans.' But he did not let the occasion carry him away entirely and took a cut at the commercial side of the celebrations: 'They might have been less amused by the at times grotesque Madison Avenue type over-commercialization of the event; but who knows.'[59] Undoubtedly, the commercialization of Joyce and Bloomsday reached unprecedented levels in the 1980s but many companies who sought to be associated with the author also made important contributions to the costs of the celebrations. A good example was Guinness Ireland, which commissioned twelve paintings by Gerald Davis and accompanying texts by Terence Brown for its centenary exhibition entitled 'Wine of the Country', echoing the 'Cyclops' episode of *Ulysses*. It was held at the Guinness Visitor Centre and aimed at recapturing the character of Dublin pub life in the Joyce years. The star attraction was the recreated Victorian pub. Dublin actor Dermot Lynskey performed Joyce readings inside the 'pub'. The advertisement, under the banner 'James's Choice' (echoing both James Joyce and James's Gate, site of the Guinness brewery), notes: 'When it came to writing slogans Mr. Joyce was no slouch either. He suggested replacing "Guinness Is Good For You" with "Guinness – The Free, The Flow, The Frothy Freshener"!' The slogan is from *Finnegans Wake* where HCE boasts of his excellence as a brewer of stout: 'I brewed for my alpine plurabelle, wigwarming wench, (speakeasy!) my granvilled brandold Dublin lindub, the free, the froh, the frothy freshener' (*FW* 553.25). Porter and Dublin (*Dubh Linn*) become synonymous is the word 'lindub' meaning 'stout' and indeed desolation (*lionn dubh*). Decades earlier, the Colums claimed that Joyce 'was actually disappointed that Guinness did not use it instead of the commonplace "Guinness is good for you"'.[60]

[58]Fergus Brogan, 'Joycean ritual', *IT*, 17 June 1988, 12.
[59]Niall Kiely, 'Joyce's Centenary Celebrated', *IT*, 15 June 1982, 5.
[60]Mary and Padraic Colum, *Our Friend James Joyce*, 156.

Guinness was far from alone in attempting to capitalize on its Joyce connection. Noted Dublin butchers F. X. Buckley regularly ran an advertisement that quoted two mentions in *Ulysses* while Mackey's seeds cited 'Ithaca' and descriptions of Bloom's garden proposals 'Flowerville'. Others had even less of a connection, such as the Molly Bloom boutique, which opened in Galway in 1981. Other companies that would publish Joyce-inspired advertising included Barry's Tea, Bewleys, Mulligans, Davy Byrne's The Bailey, Switzers, the EBS (multiple yes'es), while Clery's proudly claimed that 'Gerty Mac Dowell, as readers of Joyce's *Ulysses* will know, hunted all one Tuesday afternoon for a hat to match that eggblue chenille trimming. At last she found just what she wanted at Clery's summer sales'.[61]

The year 1986 brought controversy around the commercialization of Joyce, which sat so uncomfortably beside the continuing failure to secure the Joyce Tower in Sandycove through public funds. Stephen Joyce cancelled a bequest to the Tower that was to have included a portrait of Joyce by Augustus John, the manuscript of 'Ecce Puer', signed and dated on Stephen's birthday in 1932, two letters to Joyce from his father, a ring owned by Joyce and a necklace given by Joyce to Nora, so as to give voice to his concern over the financial security and future of the museum: 'If the museum has to sell Bloomsday soap and ties to finance itself what guarantee can there be of its continuation?'[62] Joyce was annoyed at the sale through Sotheby's of a Joyce death mask (one of just three originals) for £16,500 to the Irish firm, Guinness Peat Aviation. He believed it belonged to the James Joyce Tower and that Michael Scott's family had no right to put it up for sale. Dublin Corporation attempted to intervene to buy the mask, which had been, for more than two decades, a key exhibit in the Tower, but this was opposed by Stephen, who did not believe that there should be any sale at all.[63] Fritz Senn intervened in the *Irish Times* pointing out that selling 'something as personal and intimate as a death mask' was 'at the very least, in poor taste'. He also underlined that the mask had been a gift from Mrs Carola Giedion-Welcker to the Tower and that she had visited and been pleased to see it there during the fourth symposium in 1973.[64] On the same day, Michael Scott announced that he had agreed to rescind the sale and would give the mask to the Government even if he did not think the Joyce Tower was a suitable place for it to be preserved.[65] A month later it was agreed that Dublin Eastern Tourism Organisation (DETO), the owners of the Tower, would be allowed to continue to exhibit the mask.

---

[61]*EP* Bloomsday Supplement, 15 June 1989, 48.
[62]John Armstrong, 'Joyce's Grandson Cancels Bequest to Dublin Museum', *IT*, 18 November 1986, 10.
[63]'Corpo's Death Mask Move Opposed', *II*, 10 September 1985, 9.
[64]Fritz Senn, 'Joyce Death Mask', *IT*, 17 September 1985, 9.
[65]Elgy Gillespie, 'Scott Not to Sell Joyce Death Mask', *IT*, 17 September 1985, 6.

Despite his role in supporting the 1982 symposium and other Joyce initiatives, Anthony Cronin was caustic about the Joyce fervour in Dublin, which he saw as little more than an attempt to exploit the writer's name for business or tourism ends. In an *Irish Times* article, he focused on Swan Blooms hotel, which, after an initial £1.5 million investment, opened on Anglesea Street in the late Spring of 1980. Much like the *Ulysses* restaurant on Parliament Street and Molly Bloom's flower shop on Dawson Street, which opened soon afterwards, Blooms hoped to exploit a non-existent Joyce association to stimulate custom. At the outset Blooms 'relied heavily on the posthumous fame of James Joyce' in the hope of attracting a wealthy clientele: 'There were dining areas named after the saintly Leopold and his wife, Molly. There were table mats providing an inaccurate and ungrammatical synopsis of the book in which they appeared. The décor was a sort of demented post-modernist Edwardian.' To Cronin's satisfaction, Blooms eventually got rid of most of the Joyce connections and hung on only to the name: 'There was a disco bar [...] but no aspidistras, no chintz, no Buck Mulligan bar or Anna Livia room.' With the changes introduced, the 'whole thing was about as Edwardian as a nuclear reactor.' Cronin complimented the management on 'their realism'.[66] His article, however, went on to compare how Dublin was using Joyce to lure tourists with a description of how visitors to Crete were brought to visit a former leper colony so they can go home feeling they've got a bit of culture:

> The vast majority of the tourists who come here have never heard of James Joyce. But they are passive, have already been regimented and are anxious to learn whatever it is that somebody thinks they should learn. Since they must be bussed somewhere, they are bussed to the so-called Joyce tower.

Gradually, the visitors became convinced 'that they came here because of Joyce' and the Irish went along with this 'since most of us do not know or care very much about James Joyce either, and have no clear idea why he is important'. The Irish adopted the line of least resistance that 'the object of a reasonable being' should be to 'humour' and 'gull' the tourists: 'Yes, all in all, the management of Bloom's hotel is to be congratulated.'[67]

Complain though he might, Cronin was fighting against a growing tide which brought ever larger-scale Joyce celebrations in the 1980s. One of the standout events was the release of John Huston's acclaimed version of *The Dead*, featuring Donal McCann and Angelica Huston, which was a big international success. Huston, who had become an Irish citizen in 1964 having lived in the country for twelve years, had supported the Joyce

---

[66]Anthony Cronin, 'Joyce and the Leper Colony', *IT*, 17 June 1986, 10.
[67]Ibid.

cause for decades and had unsuccessfully tried to make a film of *Stephen D.* The filming of 'The Dead' between Dublin and Los Angeles was widely reported on in the Irish media and on its release shortly after Huston's death, it was hailed as his triumphant swansong, a brilliant and faithful treatment of Joyce's original, and a splendid example of ensemble acting. It premiered at the 1987 Dublin Film Festival with Angelica Huston in attendance. 'No other America film-maker has ended a comparably long career on such a note of triumph', enthused the *New York Times* while the *Wall Street Journal* called it 'a remarkable adaptation of a great piece of literature'.[68] Other notable Joyce films in this period included *James Joyce's Women* with Fionnula Flanagan (1982) and Michael Voysey's adaptation of *A Painful Case* (1987), starring Sian Phillips and Mick Lally. This was one of a group of film adaptations of Irish short stories made in co-production with Britain's Channel 4, produced by John Lynch, packaged under the title 'Love Stories of Ireland' and shown both on RTÉ and on the Film on Four slot on Channel 4.

The publication of the long-awaited new critical and synoptic edition of *Ulysses,* produced by the team led by Hans Walter Gabler, was far more controversial. It attracted quite a bit of attention in 1984 with headlines such as 'Joyce and the 5,000 bloomers'.[69] Initially, Gabler's attempt to reconstruct an 'original' text closer to what Joyce intended was welcomed in Ireland (and by influential scholars around the world). Journalists warmed to the idea of 'a new book' being painstakingly created over a seven-year period. Richard Ellmann's enthusiastic endorsement also helped its initial reception. Gordon Paterson called it 'an absolutely stunning achievement',[70] but David Norris was among the dissenters, dismissing it as 'nothing but a gardening job'.[71] Later, at a conference on the subject in Monte Carlo, he pointed to mistakes in Gabler's text (e.g. turning 'naggin' into 'noggin', 'goner' into 'doner') in a paper which he called the 'Clinic for Textually Transmitted Diseases'. By Norris' own admission, this 'went down like a lead balloon with the scholars, but in the end I was proved right by greater minds than my own'.[72] This is an overreach on Norris's part. The reality is that neither he nor the vast majority of reviewers were adequately equipped to evaluate Gabler's text for the innovative scholarly enterprise it was. And that included the American critic, John Kidd, who published a very harsh attack on the Gabler text in *The New York Review of Books*, pointing to what he saw as flaws in Gabler's methodology, and highlighting 400 instances in which Joyce's style had been lost to what he considered 'inauthentic' changes. Kidd claimed Gabler had inserted as many new errors as he had taken out and that the

---

[68]Quoted in Sean Cronin, '"The Dead" Has as Living Monument', *IT,* 18 December 1987, 8.
[69]Gordon Paterson, 'Joyce and the 5,000 Bloomers', *II,* 9 June 1984, 1.
[70]Ibid.
[71]Quoted in 'Joyce Re-written', Letter to the Editor, *II,* 13 June 1984, 8.
[72]David Norris, *A Kick against The Pricks,* 169.

edition was brought out to ensure a new and lucrative copyright that would run for a further seventy-five years. Ireland's involvement in this 'war of wits and words' was marginal and for the general reader, as Richard Birchall concluded, 'Kidd's painstaking scholarship will be of as little importance as a rusty boot on Dollymount strand'.[73] Kidd's scholarship, as it turned out, was less than painstaking, but his interventions had the effect of turning opinion against Gabler's edition. In 1991, Penguin withdrew 'The Corrected Text' from its title. With much fanfare, Kidd, by then *in situ* as director of a new James Joyce Research Centre at Boston University, promised a new edition as part of what was to be a seven-volume edition of Joyce's works. To date, this new edition has not appeared. The Centre has long since closed.

By now, Davd Norris was the uncontested Irish popularizer of Joyce. Although he occupied an academic position in Trinity College Dublin, he was not, by his own cheerful admission, particularly academic and he liked nothing more than taking public pot shots at his more scholarly Joyce colleagues, both at home and abroad. In his biography, he would write:

> One of the great problems Joyce presents to the reader is the grim and deadly earnestness of the Joycean critics. They reminded me of a convention of lunatic clockmakers, surrounded by cogs, wheels and springs yet scarcely one of them able to tell you the time. A special jargon grew up around Joyce, and the experimental nature of his later novels meant he became a sort of Rorschach blot on which critics could project their own lunacies. This all helped to distort the essential meaning. They were taken in by the appearance of the text and had little understanding of the way Joyce's mind worked.[74]

He made an exception for three 'great critics' while misspelling two of their names as he did so: 'Ellman, Hugh Kenner and Harry Levine.'[75] Although a rather extreme example, Norris was far from being alone among Irish academics who, while embedded in what was sometimes the solipsistic world of academic Joyce studies, also felt the need to regularly express their distance from it. They often did so while failing to acknowledge that their own more generalist approaches would have been far less securely moored had they not been able to draw on the less flashy (often American) academic legwork of others. One such broadstroke Joycean was Declan Kiberd who, in 1984, wrote a polemical piece denouncing overly specialized approaches to Joyce studies: 'Specialisation', he declared, 'is the modern form of self-love'. Kiberd expressed the belief that scholarship had 'become big business; and to succeed in business you specialise in a single line or a single text. [...]

---

[73]Richard Birchall, 'Kidd Sparks off Joycean War of Wits', *SI*, 31 July 1986, 16.
[74]David Norris, *A Kick against The Pricks*, 168.
[75]Ibid.

In the process, critical ideas are dying a slow death, as is the notion of the lay, non-specialist intellectual'.[76]

The 1988 Dublin Millennium, which also saw the city assume the role of European Cultural Capital, was the occasion of yet another round of Joyce celebrations. It was in this year that University College Dublin launched what was to become its annual James Joyce Summer School, founded and directed by Augustine Martin (with Terence Dolan), at Newman House. Speaking at the launch, Martin drew attention to the enduring ambivalence in the College towards its most famous graduate: 'There was no particular aversion to Joyce – he was on the UCD course when I was an undergraduate in the late Fifties.'[77] Over the decades that followed, the school would provide a vital opportunity for both scholars and enthusiasts – the majority of whom came from abroad – to gather in an evocative Joyce setting to discuss his works in a way that was more accessible than the bi-annual symposia. The Trieste Joyce School, founded in 1997, though entirely independent, was an offspring of this event and fulfils a similar role.

As part of the Millennium, RTÉ radio broadcast the opera-drama 'Bloomenleid', with soprano Joan Merrigan in the role of Molly. This production won the prestigious Nordring European Radio Competition. Joyce was also given a place of honour in a literary parade of plaques established beside St Patrick's Cathedral in St Patrick's Park featuring Dublin's most illustrious writers (unfortunately, he was cited as the author of 'Finnigans Wake' [sic] which took away some of the lustre). For the now blossoming Bloomsday, 1988 was just another year in which Joyce enthusiasts from home and abroad, many decked out in straw-boaters and striped blazers, and brandishing parasols, took part in a vast variety of events, ranging from Bloomsday breakfasts, Joyce plaque unveilings, Joyce lookalike competitions, vintage car or messenger bike rallies, Bloomsday pub of the year competitions, walking tours, Bloomsday Balls, garden parties, re-enactments and dramatizations of sections of Ulysses, celebrity readings (mostly by diplomats, politicians and writers), best-dressed character from Ulysses competitions, and even Joyce-inspired road races and fun runs.[78]

In the words of the Irish Independent, 'hovering over the whole, commercialised free-for-all was Big Brother – or should that be Big Uncle. Uncle Arthur. Guinness was called "the wine of the country" in Ulysses, so Guinness have poured big sponsorship bucks into Bloomsday'.[79] Popular local participation grew over these years although how many people were actually encouraged to read Joyce's works remains an open question. The scepticism of many was voiced in the Irish Independent, which

---

[76]Declan Kiberd, 'Scholarship Dogged by the Specialist', IT, 28 June 1988, 8.
[77]'Joyce Summer School Launched', IT, 29 June 1988, 9
[78]'Joycean Actress Declines to Run in Race', II, 17 June 1985, 5.
[79]Miriam Lord, 'Blooming hell', II, 17 June 1995, 5.

declared: 'Some people say that Bloomsday is culture dressed up as crack. We say it's crack dressed up as culture.'[80] The 'crack' side of things tended to be underlined in newspaper headlines, such as 'Plastered literati on trail of Bloom',[81] but the commercial spinoff was not to be sniffed at and 16 June in Dublin was normally marked by the positive news that 'Business is Blooming'.[82] Many Joyceans – those who actually had read the books – found it off-putting and over the top. Bruce Arnold dismissed it as 'just a load of old Dublin coddle' and declared that 'Bloomsday has gone to pieces; since the centenary year it has gone steadily downhill. Joyce has become an excuse for publicity, an excuse to sell food, an excuse for excess'.[83] A letter to the *Irish Times* made a similar claim, complaining of 'folkloric merrymaking worthy of Disneyland' and suggesting 'converting Joyce's anniversary to a festival in honour of Buck Mulligan. Is his not the philosophy being celebrated as that of Joyce?'[84]

Although Bloomsday expanded, the formula fed to the public through the newspapers never changed. David Norris was inevitably centre stage grinning broadly while breathless journalists fussed about for copy, not knowing whether to cheer or sneer. No Bloomsday coverage was complete without interviews with random passers-by, the vast majority of whom proudly professed to never having read *Ulysses* or admitted to having abandoned it after a few pages. A random American would usually also be found (or invented) who would declare it 'a splendid book' that merited being read times over. The conclusion was often: 'Everybody knows that the only person in Dublin who has read it is David Norris.'[85] He regularly pointed out that Joyce was good for the image of Dublin and Ireland, as a unique cultural icon capable of raising interest abroad. From his standpoint, the promotion of Joyce was a vital element in the cultural promotion of the country. In these years, Norris was also busily leveraging serious financial support for the James Joyce Centre of which he was founder and co-director. In 1989, he described how he had been 'asked to take top American industrialists around the Custom House Docks with a view to investing and I found the first thing they wanted to see was Joyce's Dublin. That suggests that Joyce is economically as well as morally important in Ireland'. With characteristic understatement, he concluded: 'I would say that Bloomsday is to Dublin what Christmas is to Bethlehem.'[86] Six years later, describing Bloomsday, he declared:

---

[80]Ibid.
[81]*II*, 17 June 1993, 7.
[82]*II*, 16 June 1994, 8.
[83]Quoted in the *II*, 17 June 1991, 3.
[84]Letter from R. Watson, 'Post-mortem on Bloomsday', *IT*, 25 June 1994, 19.
[85]Maura O'Kiely, 'So, Who Actually Reads Joyce?', *EP*, 15 June 1989, 37.
[86]*II*, 10 June 1989, 8.

An atmosphere of mardi gras prevails, walking tours set out in the footsteps of the master and whole city is bathed in turn-of-the-century nostalgia. Cultural tourism is now big in Ireland and nothing so disinfects the reputation of even so iconoclastic a writer as Joyce more rapidly than the tinkle of coins and the crinkle of notes in the civic till. As Joyce himself wrote of Parnell in his short story, 'Ivy Day in the Committee Room', 'we all respect him, not that he is dead and gone'.[87]

In 1991, then Tánaiste, John Wilson, a former classics teacher, spoke warmly in favour of Joyce and in the hope that he would soon actually be read by more readers in Ireland: 'He is increasingly significant and contrary to what some high-minded persons might maintain, *Ulysses* is a very spiritual uplifting book.' He added that he would like to see the ordinary, non-specialist reader adopt Joyce's works 'the way every Italian regards opera'.[88]

Some complained that Joyce was getting far too much attention at the expense of other writers. At the opening of the All-Ireland Fleadh Cheoil in Sligo, Labhras O Murchú, the director of Comhaltas Ceoltóirí Éireann, hit out at what he called the 'James Joyce lobby', which was 'enjoying a "monopoly" of media attention to the exclusion of other Irish literary figures'. He encouraged a return to Charles Kickham, who was

> an antidote to the sentiments and philosophy of Joyce. It would be an exercise in equality, balance and literary maturity if each year, when *Ulysses* is being hyped and analysed by the national media, if *Knocknagow* were to be presented in all its nobility and humanity as an alternative viewpoint. This is not a matter of urban versus rural, or conservative as opposed to liberal; it is merely a suggestion that a major portion of the population who might be labeled traditionalist would not be ostracized.[89]

How times had changed. Joyce was now part of Ireland's 'official culture' of its accepted cultural mainstream having replaced more traditional Irish literary figures who had for so long been revered. He was by now so uncontroversial that the President, Patrick Hillery, during his official visit to the Vatican in April 1989, could present the library of St Isidore's Franciscan College in Rome with 'a three-volume facsimile edition of James Joyce's *Ulysses*'.[90]

The sustained level of activity around Joyce and *Ulysses* suggests that O'Murchu was not entirely wrong. Joyce, who had been for so long marginalized because his works and his lifestyle were seen to undermine

---

[87]David Norris, 'Joyce's Dublin Is a City Frozen in Time', *IT*, 2 August 1995, 34.

[88]Eileen Battersby, 'Cream of the Joyce World Mark Anniversary', *IT*, 14 January 1991, 2.

[89]Lorna Siggins, 'Comhaltas Director Criticises Joyce "monopoly" of Attention', *IT*, 24 August 1991, 5.

[90]Joe Carroll, 'President Visits Oldest Irish College in Rome', *IT*, 22 April 1989, 6.

the very identity of the new Irish nation, to destabilize the very premises –
Catholic, Nationalist, Gaelic – on which it was built, was now being offered
the best seat in the national front room. His name was proving a useful
catch all symbol of the new, modern and urban 'European' Ireland that
was replacing the more traditional version of the country. In a mere decade
or so, a carnival of previously suppressed literary voices, from outside the
conventional Pale and led by Joyce, began to become the frame of reference
of the new Ireland, which had, all of a sudden, caught on to his usefulness.

Theatrical works inspired by or simply about Joyce and *Ulysses* continued
to appear. Beckett actor, Barry McGovern, performed a Joyce show to
great acclaim while Paul O'Hanrahan won Edinburgh Festival Fringe First
awards for his one-man productions from *Ulysses* and *Finnegans Wake*.
O'Hanrahan was a founding member of the Balloonatics Theatre Company
in 1984 and they have been putting on adaptations of Joyce's works (among
others) ever since becoming a popular Bloomsday fixture. Ulick O'Connor
also scripted the entertaining and accessible *Joyicity*, which was memorably
performed, firstly in 1989, at the Peacock, by Vincent O'Neill (Caroline
Fitzgerald directed) and later on tour in the United States where the *New
York Times* declared: 'No prerequisite reading or homework is necessary.
"Joyicity" can be a primer for anyone daunted by Joyce's reputation as an
Olympian writer of incomprehensible gobbledygook, yet at the same time
delight and entertain genuine Joyceans.'[91]

Another important element in what we might call the sacralization of
Joyce in Dublin was the proliferation of Joyce plaques and statues sometimes
in spots where buildings associated with Joyce or his characters had long
since been bulldozed. The year 1983 saw the placing of An Gallán Gréine
do James Joyce [The Sun Pillar for James Joyce] on Sandymount Strand.
Over four metres high, it resembles a single open-quotation mark, which is
perhaps unintentionally ironic given Joyce's distaste for 'perverted commas',
which he famously did not use. The sundial has equation designs on its sides
that were inspired by Dr Ian Elliott of Dunsink Observatory. Just a mile or
two further south, a monument raised by Dun Laoghaire Corporation to
mark the centenary. It also carries a brief quotation from *Ulysses*: 'He gazed
southward over the bay, empty save for the smokeplume of the mailboat
vague on the bright skyline and a sail tacking by the Muglins.' In 1985, it
was the turn of Lombard Street West where a plaque was unveiled in honour
of the fact that Leopold Bloom had lived there. Dublin Corporation also
planted a tree on the street 'to commemorate the spot where Joyce placed
Bloom's home, now demolished'.[92] The year 1988 saw the installation of

[91]Wilborn Hampton, 'Getting to the Heart of Joyce with His Own Words', *New York Times*,
11 September 1992. http://query.nytimes.com/gst/fullpage.html?res=9E0CE4D6173CF932A2
575AC0A964958260&sec=&spon=&pagewanted=all.
[92]Elgy Gillespie, 'Dublin to Revive Joyce Legend', *IT*, 15 June 1985, 21.

fourteen pavement plaques marking the path of Leopold Bloom as a kind of secular *via crucis*.

The placing of statues is an important communal act intended to celebrate and commemorate those who have made a special contribution to the greater community. Joyce, being Joyce, had long since contested this idea and claimed that a statue is a memento which 'honours the dead by flattering the living, and has the further supreme advantage of finality, since, to tell the truth, it is the most efficient and courteous way yet discovered of ensuring a lasting oblivion of the deceased' (*OCPW*, 127). Among the many proposals put forward in the 1980s was one to put Bloom on top of a restored version of what had been Nelson's pillar but now, presumably, would become Bloom's pillar. In 1987, Declan Kiberd pertinently objected to this 'modish proposal' and suggested that Bloom 'would be mortally embarrassed by the publicity'. As to Joyce, 'such a self-iconoclast would not wish to be embalmed or mummified in a statue'. Joyce was all too well aware that 'people are commemorated on statues only when they have lost their power to threaten and disturb'.[93] This may have been precisely why the Dublin City Business Association or better the North Earl Street Business Association commissioned a Joyce statue by Marjorie Fitzgibbon, which was eventually placed on North Earl Street in 1990. In her sculpture, Joyce is seen walking or rather better posing with a cane in his hand and his hat tilted at 'the Kildare angle' in this piece which is often called, with an uneasy Dublin mixture of begrudging pride and scorn, the *Prick with the Stick*. It was originally hoped 'that the statue, standing seven feet tall on a granite plinth, would be erected on the traffic island at the apex of D'Olier street and Westmoreland Street'.[94] The Business Association stated that the Joyce statue was part of their policy of depoliticizing Dublin street art. As the association's website put it, they worked to sponsor and install 'street art in public places – notably the statues of James Joyce, the ladies with the shopping bags, the girl swinging from a lamppost and Molly Malone. All of these statues were a significant departure away from revolutionary, political and religious images to reflect a more people-friendly, peaceful democracy'.[95] Perhaps by keeping in mind Joyce's brief role as a city trader – running the Volta Cinema in Mary Street in 1909 – they were thus able to align him with Molly Malone, herself a famous city street hawker.

Not all Dubliners were thrilled. Ken Monaghan recalled standing in front of the statue during one of his Joyce walking tours when a Dublin man pushed his way into the audience to try to see who the statue was of. He eventually backed away disgruntledly before telling his friend, 'James fucking Joyce, if you don't mind.' It seems he had thought it was a statue

---

[93]Declan Kiberd, 'Not One of the Pillars of State', *IT*, 12 May 1987, 5.
[94]Frank McDonald, 'A Bronze Joyce May Stand by His Anna Livia', *IT*, 5 December 1987, 1.
[95]Dublin City Centre Business Association, http://www.dcba.ie/index.cfm/loc/2-1-2.htm.

of Jack Charlton, who led the Irish soccer team to the finals of Euro 88. Yet the monumentalizing of Joyce continued apace. The year 1988 saw the release of plans for the £200,000 Smurfit millennium fountain on O'Connell Street close to where Nelson's pillar had stood. One of those to object was John Kelly of Fine Gael, a 'frequent scourge of Dublin Corporation'. He likened the design to 'the late and unlamented Tomb of the Unknown Gurrier on O'Connell Bridge', more formally known as An Tóstal 'Bowl of Light', which had been erected in 1953 (a large concrete box with tubular steel bars supporting a plastic flame). The 90-foot-long Smurfit monument, designed by Éamonn O'Doherty and Sean Mulcahy, was eventually placed at the heart of O'Connell Street.[96] The controversial piece of street art features Anna Livia sitting in the gushing waters of the river Liffey. It immediately entered Dublin folklore with various nicknames, such as the *floozy in the Jacuzzi*, the *Hoor in the Sewer*, *Bidet Mulligan* and *Viagra Falls*. More than a monument to Joyce, many saw it as leading Irish entrepreneur Michael Smurfit's monument to himself. He commissioned and paid for it giving it as a gift to the city on condition that it carry a dedication to his own father. The monument was eventually removed to make space for the Millennium spire, which was unveiled in 2003. After a decade in a council storage depot in Raheny, a refurbished version of the Anna Livia was relocated to the far less prominent Croppies Memorial Park near Heuston Station in 2011.[97]

There is a thin line between genuine commemoration and mere tourist packaging. Many visitors do indeed come to Dublin out of genuine interest in Joyce following in the footsteps of one of the earliest pilgrims, his friend Frank Budgen, who visited in the 1930s with the express intention of visiting the places most associated with the author. But from the 1980s on, a visitor would struggle to distinguish between locations with authentic Joyce connections and those just trying to cash in on his name. Commerce and tourism rather than a concern with raising citizens' knowledge and awareness of Joyce's writings were clearly the drivers behind many of Dublin's statues of the writer.

Robert Nicholson, author of the much appreciated *The Ulysses Guide: Tours through Joyce's Dublin* (Methuen, 1988), captured the sense of Joycean overkill when he wrote: 'Bars and restaurants are named after Joyce and his characters, and enterprising merchants are busy hawking Joycean wares. Books, brochures, posters and even tea towels are adorned with misrepresentations of the unfortunate novilist [*sic*], looking variously sick, seedy, senile, simian and constipated.'[98]

---

[96]'The Case for the Smurfit Fountain', *IT*, 24 February 1988, 12.

[97]Allison Bray, 'Dubliners Re-Joyce at Return of the Floozie', *II*, 25 February 2011. https://www.independent.ie/irish-news/dubliners-rejoyce-at-return-of-the-floozie-26708030.html.

[98]Robert Nicholson, 'Patron Saint of Irish Tourism', *EP* Supplement, 15 June 1989, 51.

CHAPTER NINE

Joyce in Celtic Tiger Ireland

Nobody in Ireland saw the 1990s coming. It was to be a time of profound change in the country, much of which would be positive. The decade opened with the transformational election of Mary Robinson as the first female president and closed with the historic signing of the Good Friday Agreement in 1998. In between, after emigration had peaked in 1989, in a matter of just a few years Ireland went from being a net exporter of its people to an unfamiliar new status as a society suddenly capable of absorbing a conspicuous number of immigrants.

The unexpected success of Jack Charlton's Irish soccer team at the World Cup in Italy (they were eventually knocked out by Holland in the quarter finals) kept the country transfixed and was a harbinger of a decade of success and economic growth that would exceed all expectations. Between 1991, when Dublin enjoyed the honour of being European Capital of Culture, and the 2000 Millennium, the city grew and renovated as never before. One of the major motors of this expansion was its rapid development as a financial services centre. Alongside this, the city gradually became a tourist destination in a country that had, up to that time, almost exclusively sold itself as a rural and coastal idyll. The city's cultural heritage received a substantial financial boost from local sources and European structural funds. The results were most visible in Temple Bar, which had risked demolition but was saved and developed after the government established a not-for-profit company in 1991, called Temple Bar Properties, to oversee the regeneration of the area as Dublin's cultural quarter.

Culture often found itself conscripted to add a touch of respectability to capital ventures. This happened in 1987 when Taoiseach Charles J. Haughey announced plans for what would become the International Financial Services Centre in the docklands. He lost the rhetorical run of himself (and risked giving off a whiff of anti-Semitic prejudice) when citing the Jewish Leopold Bloom as the guiding light for the arriving venture capitalists: 'Yea, on the word of a bloom, ye shall ere long enter into the Golden city which is to be the new Bloomusalem in the Nova Hibernia of the future'.[1] This brave new Ireland would be built on the basis of a preferential corporation tax rate and a network of double taxation agreements for companies locating in the Custom House Docks and could not have been further in its philosophy from Bloom's prudent notions of economy or from Joyce's rather more extravagant ones. However, such a small detail proved no obstacle to Joyce being dragged into an unexpected marriage of convenience between literature and international investment.

The post-nationalist, anti-Catholic, pro-European (but more crucially pro-capital) Ireland of the 1990s – proudly the world's most global economy – found the perfect symbol in Joyce, who had earlier rejected so many of the pieties that the country was now finally beginning to question and demolish. It was almost as if Robert Hand's words in *Exiles* provided the convenient motto for the country, which was suddenly a dynamic player within the European Union: 'If Ireland is to become a new Ireland she must first become European.'[2] It was precisely the older liberal internationalist, cosmopolitan view of Joyce, rather than the updated nationalist version that was being constructed in the 1990s by postcolonial critics, that made Joyce so useful to an Ireland in search of 'authentic' images that might be said to embody the city and the nation. Thus, Joyce could be paraded as the creator of the quintessential Dublin in *Ulysses* while his chosen exile from and still relevant criticism of the country was airbrushed out of the picture. Ireland of the 1990s was a country anxious to connect and economically engage with its diaspora, the descendants of exiles and emigrants, who, like Joyce, had fled the country in decades past. The question was not so much what the country could do for them but what they could now do for their country.

Ireland was also constantly in search of images to bolster its European credentials (in this regard Joyce was a card to play along with the learned monks who carried their faith and erudition to Europe in the dark ages, and with the Wild Geese). As early as 1973, Fine Gael Education Minister, Richard Burke, played up Joyce's claims to be 'a European artist', who 'submitted eagerly to European influences [...] unlike most English writers of his time'.[3] In the light of Europe but also of Ireland's acknowledgement of and reconnecting with its diaspora – as personified by Joyce – the key intervention came from President Mary Robinson in her celebrated address to a joint sitting of the Dáil and Seanad.

When James Joyce went to Europe, he set out on a historic paradox of exile and recall. He reclaimed his birthplace by leaving it. He went away

---

[1]Quoted in David Nally, 'Desmond: Head on the Block', *ST*, 3 May 1992, C5.
[2]James Joyce, *Poems and Exiles*, 158.
[3]'Minister on Joyce the European', *IT*, 24 May 1973, 12.

with the purpose, so he wrote later, of creating 'the uncreated conscience of my race'. We stand at a distance from that time; but we can still be struck by that phrase. I had in mind all our exiles, all our emigrants – past and present – when I put the light in the window at Áras an Uachtaráin. I was not prepared for the power and meaning which a modest emblem would have. But we have reason to know in Ireland how powerful symbols are; that they carry the force of what they symbolise. Joyce's words remind us – that light reminds us – that the community of Irish interest and talent and memory extends far beyond our boundaries, far beyond Europe's boundaries.[4]

Just as Joyce was becoming a useful pinup for the newly affluent country, postcolonial critics were working hard to prove above all else that it had a 'third-world history', reading his works as the definitive act of resistance to its colonial inheritance. At the same time, *Ulysses* was becoming the *ur*-text for Dublin as a vibrant but compact capital even as the city seemed set on relentlessly destroying all traces of the city Joyce had rendered immortal. For all its newfound wealth, Ireland was still a country struggling to distance itself from its past, from the spectre of repressive Catholicism and an unpredictable republicanism. Who better to represent this than Joyce who had forthrightly challenged these ideologies in his fiction. Ireland in the 1990s was a country that was also preoccupied with being less Catholic, more modern and less threatening to that part of the island's population belonging to the Protestant and Unionist majority in the North. Joyce's ascent, in this regard, came at the expense of Yeats, who, although Anglo-Irish, was associated with Irish Nationalism in a way that Joyce was not. Indeed, the rise of the exiled Joyce over a Yeats who stayed in Ireland to labour against the conservative Catholic tide was, in its convenient politics, as simplistic as the return to favour of Michael Collins in the 1990s at the expense of Eamon de Valera.

Posthumous validations of Joyce were the means for various interest groups in 'post-Nationalist' Ireland to legitimize themselves through refraction. But to have Joyce as the vehicle for all these aims was to expect him to be all things to all men and to expect *Ulysses*, the book that mattered most, to be the same. Thus *Ulysses* 'suddenly became almost Ireland's emblematic national text, a chief cultural icon of Dublin, a symbol, like the Book of Kells, of Irishness itself',[5] even if most people would have struggled to explain what either Joyce's novel or the new 'Irishness' actually meant.

Joyce studies and indeed Irish studies forged ahead, largely detached from the new corporate culture in the country. Both however were occasionally beneficiaries of that world. In 1991, Baileys became the sponsor of the UCD James Joyce Summer School. It also funded a number of high-profile UCD lectures organized by Augustine Martin and featuring international names,

---

[4]Full text here: http://www.irlgov.ie/oireachtas/Addresses/08Jul1992.htm.
[5]Barry McCrea, 'Privatising *Ulysses*', 85.

such as Marilyn French, Anthony Burgess, Umberto Eco, William Kennedy, Melvyn Bragg, Thomas Kenneally, Mario Vargas Llosa, all of whom came in Joyce's name. By now, official Ireland was less averse to endorsing Joyce, at home or abroad, and *Ulysses* came to be looked on 'as a special kind of Irish luxury, like top-quality golf courses, organic smoked salmon [...] or oysters with Guinness',[6] although no one was actually expected to read it. Rather it was part of the package to entice visitors to the country.

In 1991, the fiftieth anniversary of Joyce's death, both the Irish Ambassador to Switzerland and the Lord Mayor of Dublin travelled to Zurich to take part in a commemoration. This was in marked contrast to the Trieste symposium in 1971, which had invited the mayors of Zurich, Paris and Dublin to attend. The only no-show was the mayor of Dublin. In 1991, Bruce Arnold, an English journalist who had been, for decades, a key component of the Irish literary establishment, published his book, *The Scandal of Ulysses*.[7] It was also broadcast as a TV documentary. Arnold covered the so-called Joyce wars of the 1980s, with its many rows about copyright, corrections and cash, all of which would otherwise have passed the Irish Joyce world by had it not been for his work. Arnold outlined the entire publishing history of *Ulysses* before describing how its copyright was due to expire in 1992. He claimed that this impending deadline had played a part in the Joyce Estate's decision to support Hans Walter Gabler's synoptic edition with its many controversial textual changes, which had appeared to a blaze of publicity in 1984. It had Richard Ellmann's imprimatur while Anthony Burgess called it 'a grand literary event' although he later retracted this endorsement, partly because of John Kidd's shrill objections. It was not simply a question of Gabler supposedly adding as many errors as he removed. Kidd claimed that the entire enterprise was based on dodgy editorial strategies. Gabler, an immensely conscientious scholar, turned out to be his own worst enemy. In defending his work, he came across as dogmatic when diplomacy was required and alienated some of his earlier supporters. Some reviewers followed Kidd and commented on the financial motivation behind the Joyce Estate's endorsement. While most believed that Gabler's motives were pure, his edition guaranteed the publishers and the Estate a newly copyrighted *Ulysses*.

Some mainstream Irish academic Joyceans were, in the meanwhile, engaged in fighting an altogether different war all of their own. In a 1990 interview with Kathryn Holmquist in the *Irish Times*, Augustine Martin announced that the 'real war' was 'between a small solidarity of "old-fashioned" Irish critics' (himself, David Norris, Terence Brown and Sean J. White) and an 'international brigade of French, Germans and Americans armed with the

---

[6]Ibid., 88.

[7]Bruce Arnold, *The Scandal of Ulysses: The Sensational Life of a Twentieth-century Masterpiece* (London: Sinclair Stevenson, 1991). A new, substantially revised edition appeared in 2004.

abstract, deconstructionist theories of Derrida and LaCan [*sic*], which are not the names of cars but of critics'. In Holmquist's words, 'Professors Martin and Norris argue that the sensual enjoyment of Joyce's text is the point of reading the book, rather than the intellectual one-upmanship which has at least 500 of the scholars in Monte Carlo all believing they have found the secret to *Ulysses* or *Finnegans Wake*'. This view was shared by Ferdia Mac Anna, who complained that the 'deluge of academic analysing, critical debate and Freudian theorising over Joyce's multi-faceted vision of city life in *Ulysses* and the mini-industry of critical works which sprang up around it, put Dublin into a literary black hole run by deconstructionists and professors for the benefit of serious students of High Art who would one day themselves go on to become deconstructionists'.[8] Robert Nicholson, then of the Dublin Writers Museum, chimed in: 'Joyce was given a bad name by the sort of critic who was able to find symbolism under every stone, making *Ulysses* seem an obscure and inaccessible work that could only be appreciated by American professors or with the help of books written by them.' Martin used the article to push the belief that an 'international James Joyce industry of hard-nosed careerist academics has burgeoned, turning Joyce scholarship into an exclusive academic club and employment agency'. The international symposium was little more than 'a massive hiring fair where the Joyceans show their wares [...] a horrendous thought. A concentration of 700 Joyceans all blathering away'. Martin mischievously concluded his comments by adding 'I'm a Yeatsian by the way'.

There is little doubt that the writings of some members of this menacing massed army of Joyce scholars added a layer of complexity to his works and even the vituperated Jacques Derrida told a Joyce symposium in Frankfurt in 1984 that 'nothing intimidates me more than a community of experts in Joycean matters'.[9] This, however, does not adequately explain why Irish Joyce critics felt so threatened by their international counterparts or did not engage more wholeheartedly in pushing back against their theories and, at times, their plainly misguided readings. Although the Irish critics wished to claw Joyce back from foreign clutches, sniping newspaper reviews written for a non-academic weekend readership was never going to be an effective means of achieving this. Yet, having chosen to remain detached from Joyce and more so from the Joyce industry for decades, now, increasingly, Irish literary critics wanted a slice of the action at a time when political and corporate Ireland was already well ahead of them in claiming the author. The Taoiseach's cultural advisor, Anthony Cronin, believed that Joyce criticism was still in the hands of foreign critics because Irish academics had simply not put in the hard work needed to make a proper claim for him: 'We

---

[8] Ferdia Mac Anna, 'The Dublin Renaissance', 18.
[9] Jacques Derrida, 'ULYSSES GRAMOPHONE: Hear Say Yes in Joyce' in *Acts of Literature*, ed., Derek Attridge (New York: Routledge, 1992), 279.

Irish are too lazy to write criticism ourselves. Real criticism is hard work.'[10]
Eileen Battersby agreed:

> The Irish intelligentsia amuses itself by sneering at the earnest and often
> not very inspired American academics who approach the text with the
> meticulousness of a research scientist. But the joke backfires on Joyce's
> countrymen. A major international Irish Joycean scholar is yet to emerge.
> [...] Perhaps the UCD-masterminded Joyce Summer School, now in its
> fourth year, will discover an Irish Joycean with a textual rather than an
> anecdotal agenda.[11]

To be fair, there was some movement in the Irish academic undergrowth
and the Joyce School was just one manifestation of this. Much of the effort
was spurred by the belief that Joyce was under academic siege and needed
to be liberated. Bruce Arnold gave credence to this line of thinking when he
claimed that in the 1980s 'Joyce was a prisoner. He was possessed by the
legions of academics, most of them American'. But he also rightly pointed
out that Joyce 'was more tightly-controlled, in terms of the publication
of his writings through copyright, by the James Joyce Estate, which was
authoritarian in its general approach'.[12] Now the tide was turning. A
widespread 'greening' of James Joyce was about to begin in earnest. Irish
critics were finally doing some of the hard work necessary to allow them to
find their voice, although they would be fighting against a sceptical critical
mass. Some, like the once influential American-based Italian academic,
Franco Moretti, sounding like a latter day Ezra Pound, felt such an enterprise
was a waste of energy:

> If Joyce were an Irish writer, comprehensible and containable without
> any loose threads within Irish culture, he would no longer be Joyce; if
> the city of *Ulysses* were the real Dublin of the turn of the century, it
> would not be the literary image *par excellence* of the modern metropolis.
> Cultural phenomena cannot be explained in the light of their genesis
> (what ever has emerged from the studies that interpreted Joyce on the
> basis of Ireland?).[13]

Although Moretti was quite wrong, the results of this Irish endeavour
would be mixed and did not always gain much traction outside of the
country's academic environment. One decidedly positive development was
the involvement of two 'independent' Irish scholars, Vincent Deane and

[10]Kathryn Holmquist, 'Will Anyone Remember This Date?' *IT*, 16 June 1990, 23.
[11]Eileen Battersby, 'Where Are all the Irish Joycean Scholars?' *IT*, 2 February 1991, 26.
[12]'Joyce Back Home Again', *II*, 13 June 1992, 11.
[13]Franco Moretti, *Signs Taken for Wonders* (London: Verso, 1983), 189–90.

Danis Rose, in a prestigious international project to publish the *Finnegans Wake* notebooks as part of the editorial team that included Geert Lernout of the University of Antwerp and Daniel Ferrer of the Institut des textes et manuscrits modernes (École Normale Supérieure-CNRS) in Paris. Closer to home, Peter Costello produced the first credible biography of the young Joyce by a fellow Irishman, entitled *James Joyce: The Years of Growth*. It offered an important reconstruction and contextualization of Joyce's Irish years, while drawing on many sources unseen by Ellmann. David Pierce, an English academic born of Irish parents, produced a handsome illustrated volume, *James Joyce's Ireland*, which fleshed out important elements of Joyce's Irish backgrounds and influences, examining Joyce's identification of the key role of class in preventing change in Ireland and pointing to the impact of his Catholic education in his depiction of sexuality and gender.[14]

Augustine Martin's 1990 volume *The Artist and the Labyrinth*[15] reflected his desire to foster Irish Joyce scholarship and to make Joyce less distant from the so-called 'ordinary reader'. It received mostly positive reviews but his UCD colleague, Seamus Deane, was more hostile. His *Sunday Tribune* review might be read as a short sequel to what some of their fellow academics referred to as the 'Deane-Martin' show, or better the ongoing struggle between UCD's Professor of Anglo-Irish literature and its Professor of Modern English and American literature. It showed that even if Irish critics were finally getting down to work on Joyce they were not doing so in unison. Without making the least pretence to having read what he calls the volume's 'gallimaufry of delights' (apart from the first page of the introduction which he quotes), Deane lets rip at the resistance to any adequate consideration of the political in Joyce's writings. He sarcastically quotes Martin who expressed the desire, in his introduction, 'to redress a little' what he saw as the tendency of post-structuralist criticism to remove Joyce 'from the world of the ordinary reader'. Deane responds:

> I would have thought that Joyce had done that very effectively himself. Anyway, no-one in this collection seems to know or care much about poststructuralism, even though most of the contributors unwittingly share the poststructuralist conviction that literature needs the detergent effect of regular washing and commentary to keep it free of any social or political germs and viruses. That moving wallpaper, known as 'back ground', is all we need to know; otherwise we might not see the thing itself, the wonderful, labyrinthine text, coiled like solid smoke on a coffee table that is surrounded by experts and mobbed by the media.

---

[14]Peter Costello, *James Joyce: The Years of Growth 1882–1915* (Cork: Roberts Rinehart, 1992). David Pierce, James Joyce's Ireland (New Haven: Yale University Press, 1992).
[15]Augustine Martin, *James Joyce: The Artist and the Labyrinth* (London: Ryan Publishing, 1990).

Any attempt to rethink the relation between text and background is even yet liable to be regarded as resentment, Denis Donoghue's current word for the condition of mind experienced by those who disagree with his exquisitely phrased naivete.[16]

Deane reads the volume as evidence 'that the Free State had at least learned to absorb Joyce', who is 'not a modernist [...] a semiotician [...] a Franco-Amercan possession'. Joyce, in the choral view expressed in Martin's collection, is 'above all, ordinary, ours, a cultural prodigal come home at last to a smiling welcome, his exile as domestic as unemployment, his anxious texts best known here, within the tribe, unshackled from those absurd exogamous relationships that made them appear so disturbed and disturbing'. Deane mocks the provincialism in the supposed repatriation of Joyce the volume presumes to effect: 'Joyce the European has come home to the Free State he never saw, his Babylonian captivity over. It is a touching moment.' Deane's two-pronged criticism is aimed at Irish scholarship that suffers, in his view, from failing to come to terms with what is happening in the worlds of critical theory elsewhere and from thinking that it can go it alone. Secondly, he identifies a failure among Irish critics to deal with the political implications of the texts they scrutinize, a tendency to read Joyce's politics in terms of Parnell (if at all) and less in terms of the politics of the generation of which he was part. This reflects a greater political failure of the country itself to face up to the political legacy of 1916 and its aftermath. Deane closes by accusing the Free State of refusing to take adequate note of the Northern question as enshrined in the 1922 Treaty: 'By 1992 we shall have absorbed 1922 – the year of *Ulysses*, though wasn't the political background interesting in that year too?'

The Irish political content of Joyce's works was foregrounded in a series of new editions that were edited, with mixed results, by leading Irish critics under Deane's general editorship (although ironically, they were published in England by Penguin). Writing of the project in 1991, Deane declared: 'It is time to reinvent him as an Irish author and rescue him from the implacably authoritarian nostalgias of early twentieth-century America'.[17] The *Irish Independent* initially supported 'this reclaiming of Joyce by Irish writers and scholars, and his publication, post-copyright, by Irish publishers', hailing it as 'an enormously welcome change in the Joyce industry, and a power-shift in the Joyce empire'.[18] Terence Killeen described the editions 'as an Irish recuperation of Joyce, a rescuing from the alleged annexation and depredations of (mostly) U.S. critics'.[19] Bruce Arnold, however, soon

---

[16]Seamus Deane, 'Joyce "the European" Comes Home', *ST*, 10 February 1991, Books, 3.
[17]Seamus Deane, 'Editing Joyce in 1991', Special Supplement to the *II*, 12 January 1991.
[18]Bruce Arnold, 'Joyce Back Home Again', *II*, 13 June 1992, 11.
[19]Terence Killeen, 'Irish (Men) Recuperate Joyce', *JJLS*, vol. 7 (Fall 1993): 16.

dismissed what he described as an attempt to present 'Joyce as a social commentator on Ireland's oppression by the British'.[20] His was a somewhat snippy reading of a more complex effort which contributed effectively to introducing a more Irish Joyce, delineating an Irish aesthetic, and teasing out Joyce's complex engagement with both nationalist and imperialist politics.

Arnold might equally have taken issue with the somewhat loose editorial practices that lay behind these new editions. Apart from the introductions, which highlighted the 'Irishness' and the political nature of Joyce's texts, there was very little that was new. *A Portrait*, edited by Deane, is the 1964 Chester Anderson revised edition with some silent error correction while Declan Kiberd's *Ulysses* is essentially a reprint of the 1960 Bodley Head edition. Equally there is nothing new, apart from the introduction, which declares the text 'boring', 'tedious' and 'unreadable', in Deane's edition of *Finnegans Wake*. It was a rehash of the original 1939 edition and disregarded any subsequent corrections suggested by Joyce himself or by later critics. Commenting on the four volumes, Killeen pointed out that only the J. C. C. Mays' *Poems and Exiles* volume could 'properly speaking' be considered an edition insofar as 'it establishes and justifies a text on the basis of study of manuscripts and other sources. All the others merely adopt an already existing text and reproduce it'.[21]

Declan Kiberd's introduction to *Ulysses* was part of the concerted project of teasing out the political elements in Irish writing through the adoption of a postcolonial approach. He popularized these readings in his newspaper columns, giving shorthand versions of ideas worked out more carefully in his books. In one, he argued: 'If *Ulysses* can never be fully celebrated or understood by some Europeans, that may simply reflect the fact that Ireland, by history and fate, has as much in common with the experience of the "Third World" as with the "First."' Kiberd saw *Ulysses* in parallel with *One Hundred Years of Solitude* and *Midnight's Children* 'which take the epic form and concern themselves, as epics do, with "the birth of a nation"'.[22]

The popularity of these readings in the 1990s was at odds with the country's new image of itself as an economic powerhouse and occasionally look, in retrospect, a little like the Tiger was licking old wounds and preferring to see the relevance of Joyce to its difficult past and the achievement of statehood rather than to its changing contemporary reality. That said, what Denis Donoghue ruefully called 'the political turn', by which he meant readings that attempt to judge the politics of a text and in his view 'defeat the literature in advance', was far from unjustified.[23] Joyce was profoundly concerned with the matter of Ireland and with the realities of its changing

---

[20]Bruce Arnold *JJQ*, vol. 29, no. 3 (Spring 1992): 695–8, 698.
[21]Terence Killeen, 'Irish (Men) Recuperate Joyce', 16.
[22]Declan Kiberd, 'Weeding out the Blooming Critics', *IP*, 11 October 1994, 17.
[23]Denis Donoghue, 'The Political Turn in Criticism', *Salmagundi*, vol. 81 (Winter 1989): 104–22, 112.

politics and now, finally, it was no longer possible to accept what M. Keith
Booker called 'the virtual unanimity of Joyce critics for decades that Joyce
was an aestheticist writer with no interest in politics or history whatsoever'.[24]
For the next two decades the principal interest of Irish Joyce critics (and
many of their international counterparts) would lie in exploring his role in
inventing Ireland (to borrow the title of Kiberd's ground-breaking work) or
in parsing his response to its ongoing development.

The politics of Joyce's works would cease to be seen as mere wallpaper and
the longstanding image of him as an apolitical European, an internationalist,
a high-modernist canonical figure would be interrogated and undermined.
Joyce himself was partially responsible for being cast within the frame of
what Emer Nolan called 'benign multiculturalism',[25] having authorized
Herbert Gorman to proclaim grandly that he 'did not meddle in politics
in any way. He was above the conflict as were all the wise impassioned
minds of the time and his entire devotion and travail were concentrated
on the development and perfection of his art'.[26] Various of Joyce's friends
also argued in favour of reading his texts in an ahistorical manner; among
them, Ezra Pound disputed the need for local knowledge of Dublin in order
to read *Ulysses* while confuting the importance of Molly's Irishness and
claiming: 'she exists presumably in Patagonia as she exists in Jersey City or
Camden'.[27] Ellmann prolonged and developed an internationalist reading of
Joyce in his monumental biography that became the last word on so many
Joyce subjects for so long.

In the late 1970s, Colin McCabe was among the first to draw attention
to how criticism had elided the political potential of Joyce's works, at times
even trivializing it.[28] He was particularly referring to Richard Ellmann
who, as early as 1977 in *The Consciousness of Joyce*, had begun revising
his previous readings and now claimed: 'Joyce's politics and aesthetics were
one. For him the act of writing was also, and indissolubly, an act of liberating.
His book examines the servitude of his countrymen to their masters Church
and State, and offers an ampler vision.'[29] Dominic Manganiello expanded
and added substance to this claim in a thesis supervised by Ellmann and
later published as *Joyce's Politics* (1980). Now in the 1990s, Marxist
and postcolonial approaches led by figures, such as Fredric Jameson and
Seamus Deane, took it a stage further with Deane's pithy, ground-breaking

---

[24]M. Keith Booker, *Ulysses, Capitalism and Colonialism: Reading Joyce after the Cold War* (Westport, CT: Greenwood Press, 2000), 108.

[25]Emer Nolan, *James Joyce and Nationalism* (London: Routledge, 1995), 3.

[26]Herbert Gorman, *James Joyce* (New York: Farrar & Rinehart, 1939), 257.

[27]Ezra Pound, 'Paris Letter', *Dial*, May 1922, 626–8.

[28]Colin MacCabe, *James Joyce and the Revolution of the Word* (London: Macmillan, 1978), 141.

[29]Richard Ellmann, *The Consciousness of Joyce* (New York: Oxford University Press, 1977), 90.

essay, 'Joyce the Irishman',[30] an important focal point which opened up a critical territory that would be explored by many at a time in which, in Enda Duffy's words, 'the Troubles seem to be exhausting themselves and another settlement of the "Irish question" again seems possible'.[31] Emer Nolan added considerable ballast to the Irish contribution with her 1995 *James Joyce and Nationalism*, the first full-length book on Joyce by an Irish academic who was actually working in an English department in the country (Maynooth).

Nolan took Franco Moretti to task for underestimating the importance of Joyce's Irishness in his *Signs Taken for Wonders*, which she criticized for its claim that *Ulysses* 'belongs fully to a critical turning point of international bourgeois culture'. Another target was Terry Eagleton, who, in his pre-Irish nationalist phase, wrote of how Joyce's *Ulysses* deploys 'the full battery of cosmopolitan modernist techniques' in order to recreate Dublin 'while suggesting with its every breath just how easily it could have done the same for Bradford or the Bronx'.[32] When dealing with *Ulysses*, Nolan heads straight for 'Cyclops', the episode in which Irish critics have tended to feel most at home, and challenges what she calls the inadequate 'post-structuralist opposition between Bloom and the Citizen as one between multivocal dialogism and a monolingual monocular bigot'.[33] She launches what Duffy described as 'a lively defense of the Citizen's gossip and invective, which she sees as a radical attack on the official newspaper discourse of the episode's interpolations and of the windy declaimers of "Aeolus"'. Turning more conventional readings upside-down, Nolan insists that the 'citizen's lowly satire exists [...] in a mimetic relation to Joyce's satire in the novel as a whole; both attempt to invert the (British) opposition between British citizen and Irish barbarian. The interpolations, not the Citizen, are the comic butt of this episode, and Bloom's pacifism is merely the masochistic "pacifism of the oppressed"'.[34] Nolan contests the common view that Joyce detested violence and draws attention to what she sees as his persistent ambivalence with regard to terrorist violence, reading 'Circe' 'as an ironic representation of the Easter 1916 Rebellion' so as to counter the charge that the Rising is the novel's 'most noteworthy historical elision.'[35] Given that *Ulysses* is set in 1904 to talk about the Rising as a deliberate omission was something of a stretch.

Ulysses, in Nolan's view, is all about depicting 'strategies of resistance to imperialist domination' and not merely involved in proving, at the level

---

[30]Seamus Deane, 'Joyce the Irishman', in Derek Attridge, ed., *The Cambridge Companion to James Joyce* (Cambridge: Cambridge University Press, 1990), 31–54.
[31]Enda Duffy, Review, *JJQ*, vol. 35, no. 2/3, *ReOrienting Joyce* (Winter–Spring 1998): 492–8.
[32]Emer Nolan, *James Joyce and Nationalism*, 9.
[33]Ibid., 96.
[34]Duffy, 495.
[35]Nolan, *James Joyce and Nationalism*, 121.

of form, evidence of 'demystification and subversion'.[36] This was, to adopt Seamus Deane's terminology, an attempt to contest what she calls the 'recruitment of the writer as a "soft" Irish nationalist by Richard Ellmann' and others, and to move beyond what Deane would see as a 'Free State' Joyce and an attempt to portray him or to conscript him as a more committed Republican writer.[37] Although Nolan's book sought to show how the traditions of nationalism and modernism complemented each other, Terence Killeen, noting the centrality of teleology to nationalism, complained: 'This book is not just about nationalism; it is itself part of nationalism, a contribution to the discourse and self-definition of that ideology.' Joyce had been dragged full circle back into the kind of everyday Irish politics he had left the country to avoid.

While Nolan's work represents one of the most significant indigenous readings of Joyce, hers was but one of a bevy of studies that teased out the historical, political and ideological content of his texts. For a decade at least, reading Joyce's Irishness in a postcolonial key was the only game in town. Vincent Cheng's *Joyce, Race, and Empire*, along with works by Trevor Williams, and latterly, Andrew Gibson,[38] among many others, contributed to a long process that slowly refined what was initially too often a very broad stroke approach and only gradually became more attuned to Joyce's passion for political nuance and detail. The publication, after a delay, of *James Joyce Occasional, Critical, and Political Writing*, edited by Kevin Barry, usefully made available the texts that were being selectively mined and in some cases given excessive importance by these critics.[39] In his long introduction, Barry underlined the ambiguity present in many of Joyce's so-called 'political writings' and undermined the belief that a coherent overall political stance could be evinced.

This remained a minority view and at times in the 1990s and beyond it felt like Joyce was being enlisted to a nationalist cause by critics straining to establish links and affinities, for example, between Joyce and Pearse, between Joyce and IRA bombs, between *Ulysses*'s successful shattering of novelistic form and the violence of 1916. At the extreme end of the spectrum, it seemed that *Ulysses* could only be judged in terms of its ability

---

[36]Ibid., 120

[37]Terence Killeen, 'Claiming Joyce for the Nationalists', *IT*, 14 January 1995, 36.

[38]Vincent J. Cheng, *Joyce, Race, and Empire* (Los Angeles: University of Southern California, 1995); Enda Duffy, *The Subaltern Ulysses* (Minneapolis: University of Minnesota Press, 1994); Declan Kiberd, *Inventing Ireland: The Literature of the Modern Nation* (Cambridge: Harvard University Press, 1995); Trevor L. Williams, *Reading Joyce Politically* (Gainesville: University of Florida Press, 1997); Andrew Gibson, *Joyce's Revenge* (Oxford: Oxford University Press, 2002); *The Strong Spirit: History, Politics, and Aesthetics in the Writings of James Joyce 1898–1915* (Oxford: Oxford University Press, 2013).

[39]Kevin Barry, *James Joyce Occasional, Critical, and Political Writing* (Oxford: Oxford University Press, 2001).

to contribute to the Irish cause. In *The Subaltern Ulysses* (1994), US-based Irish academic Enda Duffy read it as *the* postcolonial text, *par excellence, the* 'text of Ireland's independence [...] the starred text of an Irish national literature', 'a terrorist act', whose chief aim was to strike out against British imperialism.[40] This reading provincialized Joyce's work by ensnaring him in those very nets he spent his entire creative life untying. What was forgotten by many was that as an exile, Joyce tried to change Ireland from abroad, not by committing straightforward literary acts of terrorism, but rather by creating complex, multi-layered fictions that can be profitably read with only minor recourse to their Irish content (as was successfully done for decades). At the same time, a work like *Ulysses* responds to Ireland partly by attempting to invent a different Ireland of the future in fiction, one that is superimposed on the original and which is more tolerant, more open to diversity, more cosmopolitan, more transnational. My own contributions in *James Joyce: A Passionate Exile* (1999) and *The Years of Bloom: James Joyce in Trieste 1904–1920* (2000) were partly an attempt to give voice to a more nuanced and rooted European or Triestine Joyce, as a counterweight to what seemed at the time to be a cyclopean and not adequately balanced focus on Ireland. Perhaps only a Joycean from Dublin could have got away with asserting that *Ulysses* could not have been imagined in Ireland (or only in Ireland) and claiming the underlying contribution of Trieste to the principal characters of Leopold and Molly Bloom. In any case, a more composite historicized view of Joyce writing against empire and colonial oppression but also against narrow nationalism – be it Irish or English – eventually came to be generally accepted. In 2000, Marjorie Howes and Derek Attridge provided a middle-way in their proposal that Joyce be read as a semi-colonial figure, arguing

> that the full measure of Joyce's achievement cannot be understood without relating it to the Irish struggle for independence – regarded not merely as a storehouse of images, characters, and narrative possibilities, but as a bitter, complex, and protracted struggle, with a history still alive in Irish political memory, a constantly changing course during Joyce's lifetime.[41]

In a word, Joyce criticism had finally made it to where a handful of prescient Irish commentators in the 1920s had intuited it should go.

The year 1992 was an important year for Joyce's legacy in Ireland. Paul Léon's bequest of a trunk full of Joyce correspondence to the National Library, which had arrived in 1947, was finally opened. Léon had heroically

---

[40]Enda Duffy, *The Subaltern Ulysses* (Minneapolis: University of Minnesota Press, 1994), 1–2.
[41]Derek Attridge and Marjorie Howes, eds., *Semicolonial Joyce* (Cambridge: Cambridge University Press, 2000), 16.

returned to occupied Paris in 1940 to rescue and entrust these materials to Count O'Kelly. His son Alex recalled:

'I remember my father going to Joyce's flat, with my mother and uncle, in spite of the curfew. He put Joyce's papers into 19 brown manila envelopes and brought them to the Irish Embassy, with the proviso that they should not be opened for 50 years to protect people still living', says Leon. 'A number of Joyce's things were being put up for auction, because he had not paid rent for some time, and my father, mother and uncle went to the auction and bought back as much as they could. My father felt this was a duty and you would do it for a friend.'[42]

Later, he was captured and killed by the Nazis. In the lead-in to the opening of the hoard there was widespread interest and speculation in the Irish newspapers as to the exact contents of the 'secret Joyce papers'. Librarian Catherine Fahy explained that there were 'about 3,000 papers in all including 200 letters from Joyce'.[43] The materials were formally unveiled for the public at the National Library by Taoiseach, Albert Reynolds, in the presence of Stephen Joyce and Léon's son, Alexis. The one major downside was that at the express request of Stephen, some of the papers were not made public and were put back under wraps until 2050. It was also alleged that items were removed and destroyed by him so as to protect the privacy of his grandparents.

The year 1992 also saw the return of the international Joyce brigade to Dublin for what was a rather different welcome from a more confident and active local Joyce community. The recently elected Mary Robinson opened the Joyce symposium (Dublin's sixth), which was organized by what was now, in many ways, a new 'old guard' of David Norris, Gus Martin and Seán J. White (with Murray Beja representing the International James Joyce Foundation). President Robinson used the occasion to point to the changing perception of Joyce:

Joyce's work outraged conventional wisdom of his time and was widely banned. Here in Ireland Joyce fared no better, and we were, perhaps, more suspicious of his motives than most. To have moved from that position to the situation today, where Bloomsday is fast becoming our second great national day, is a testament not only to Joyce's genius and artistic integrity but also to our growing maturity and confidence as a nation. We are no longer afraid to see ourselves in the mirror that the artist holds

[42]'In memory of true friendship' IT, 29 October 1998. https://www.irishtimes.com/culture/in-memory-of-true-friendship-1.208492.
[43]'Joyce Letters Opened 50 Years on', CE, 6 April 1992, 5.

up to us and now appreciate artists like Joyce who were prepared to challenge the orthodox and to shatter complacency.[44]

Her words were all the more relevant precisely because Joyce was rapidly becoming part of what passed for orthodox in the country. By now, his journey towards respectability and even secular sainthood was gathering pace and soon both the Joyce and *Ulysses* brands would be relentlessly turned into commodities in the capitalist 'miracle' that was Dublin in the second half of the 1990s and the early years of the new Millennium. In 1993, his gaunt face was rounded out to adorn the green Irish 10-pound note designed by the Dublin artist, Robert Ballagh. One of a generation of Irish artists who openly admitted to having been inspired by Joyce, Ballagh noted: 'If Joyce has been a major influence on contemporary Irish art, it has been more for his ideas than for any specific references to art. Thus Brian King finds inspiration in the cyclical and circular nature of *Ulysses* and *Finnegans Wake*. Louis Le Brocquy's famous head series derives much from their multi-layered view of things.' What appealed to Ballagh in Joyce was the 'meticulous attention to detail', which he saw as a legacy of the Book of Kells. Joyce was 'a liberating influence [...] Particularly when you're young and trying to break free of myths and shibboleths, it's enormously encouraging and reassuring to find all that you're going through already in a book. I still go back to Joyce a lot, rather like a Fundamentalist returns to the Bible to confirm his faith – or prejudices'.[45]

Liberation, however, was the last thing on the mind of the Central Bank when it placed Joyce on the tenner alongside Catherine McAuley, founder of the Sisters of Mercy, on the fiver, Daniel O'Connell on the 20-pound note and Douglas Hyde on the 50. Charles Stuart Parnell took the place of highest honour on the 100-pound note. These choices suggested that the Central Bank and the State were hedging their bets. While the placing of Joyce on the country's currency – its most diffuse image of itself – could be read as the ultimate validation of the artist, it came at the cost of being claimed to validate contemporary Ireland. Stephen Joyce for one and for once was most impressed and claimed, at the launch, to have 'discussed these events' with his grandparents at their graveside, before commenting: 'How times have changed. [...] This is the man who was vilified, who was maligned, who was banned, who was condemned, and who struggled to get his books out – and now he is legal tender.' Having his grandfather on an Irish banknote was 'the ultimate recognition'.[46] In some ways it was in the

---

[44]'Welcome Address by the President of Ireland, Mary Robinson, on the Occasion of the Opening of the Thirteenth International James Joyce Symposium, 15 June 1992', in Morris Beja and David Norris, eds., *Joyce in the Hibernian Metropolis* (Columbus: Ohio State University Press, 1996), xviii.

[45]Ciaran Carty, 'Had no time for the art he influenced', *SI*, 28 March 1982, 13.

[46]Paul O'Kane, 'Joyce Is Indeed a Noted Author', *IT*, 18 September 1993, 5.

new world of Celtic Tiger Ireland, a place and a mindset that valued its own economic boom over all else.[47]

Further dubious honour awaited Joyce in 1996 when the *Irish Times* reported a reawakening of the sporadic debate over what to put in the long-since destroyed Nelson's Pillar. Of particular interest was the centre-right Progressive Democrats' proposal.

> 'Berlin has the Brandenburg Gate', they say in their appropriately titled 'What Next?, a new vision for Dublin' document presented yesterday, 'Paris has the Arc de Triomphe, Rome has the Colosseum, Dublin has nothing.' But fear not [...] they have the answer: a competition to design a suitable replacement for Nelson's Pillar. The objective would be to create a new focal point for Dublin, celebrating the millennium (not that one, the next one), 'celebrating Dublin's growing civic self confidence and celebrating its recent rediscovery as a great European city'.

The PDs proposed to place Joyce on a rebuilt pillar. This was a legitimate suggestion although the motivations given were rather less so: 'The PDs favour Joyce as their "ideal candidate" because he is "the quintessential Dubliner, whose works celebrate Dublin as no other city has ever been celebrated in modern literature". He is also "non political, non military, non sectarian, and non divisive", they say.'[48] Whatever about the non-military and the non-sectarian, both of which could be argued for, the empty rhetoric of this formula is not just Joyce-lite, it is Joyce emptied of everything his works expressed and beaten into shape as a legitimizing godfather to the newly cosmopolitan Celtic Tiger Ireland where the attraction of foreign capital seemed the main priority. In a stroke, it seemed that all former objections to Joyce could be cast aside. As David Norris later put it, 'nothing so disinfects a reputation as the clink of money in the till'.[49] This was part and parcel with what John Daly called 'a Joycean love affair':

> where any savage observations of his native soil have been swept conveniently under the carpet in a stew of adoration whose aroma threatens to make scholars of us all. [...] Today in Dublin it will seem that this unique and frankly, weird literary hero was the love-child of Michael Collins and Jack Charlton, such is the hoopla surrounding his memory.[50]

[47]Two decades later, Joyce's *Ulysses* was misquoted on a new commemorative €10 coin issued in 2013. The Central Bank, amid much embarrassment, had to apologize while collectors rushed out to purchase the coin.

[48]Patsy McGarry, 'Pillar of Irish Society Being Sought for Top Post', *IT*, Friday, 29 March 1996. http://www.ireland.com/newspaper/ireland/1996/0329/96032900005.html.

[49]Eimear Flanagan, 'James Joyce: Exhuming Bones and Resurrecting House of *The Dead*', BBC *News*, 19 November 2019. https://www.bbc.com/news/world-europe-50390837.

[50]John Daly, 'Portrait of the Artist as the Coolest Cat in Tiger Town', *Examiner*, 16 June 1998, 11.

Stephen Joyce voiced his displeasure from Paris in an article in the *Sunday Tribune*:

> During his lifetime he was ignored, condemned, vilfied in his native land. The tide began to turn in the 1950s. Today, in Ireland, the about-face is complete. The attitude vis-à-vis him has, more than not, become patronising. From a virtual pariah Joyce has not only become over-exploited and grossly over-commercialised but has been made into something pervasive and overbearing, a kind of obsession which already has begun to stifle Irish letters.[51]

The commercially driven love affair (or marriage of convenience) saw the Joyce and *Ulysses* brands spread to the walls of several dozen Dublin hostelries, most of which had only the most spurious connections with the writer or his work, and even to the sides of beer glasses, beer mats and the tops of thimbles. Some institutions, such as his alma mater, University College Dublin, had more legitimate claims in renaming its Arts Faculty library as the James Joyce Library, although 'Finnegan's Break' in the Arts Block, which itself had been renamed as the John Henry Newman building, was more opportunistic. As mentioned earlier, a Dublin street was belatedly named after Joyce in 2000. It was the former Corporation Street (and before that Mabbot Street which features so prominently in the 'Circe' episode of *Ulysses*), located in the heart of the new city rising behind the Financial Services Centre but it was a rather modest choice and a singular downgrade from what had been proposed back in 1982, when Dublin City Council had debated the possibility of renaming Eccles Street as 'Bloom Boulevard'.[52] The year 2003 brought a more impressive acknowledgement when the new bridge designed by Santiago Calatrava was named the 'James Joyce Bridge'. It led, very appropriately, from Ellis Quay on the north of the river to Usher's Island, site of the house in which 'The Dead' was set. In 2000 this property was bought by Dublin barrister, Brendan Kilty, who spent the following years working tirelessly to restore it with his own funds so that it could function as a Joyce museum.

With less justification, Blooms hotel in touristy Temple Bar, haven of English bachelor parties, continued to trade off a cynical, false narrative that *Ulysses* was essentially 'a marathon pub crawl' during which 'the two boys' [Bloom and Stephen] travel across the city:

> Every year a bunch of Joycean enthusiasts re-enact this epic pub crawl. It's dressed up as literary event, don't let that fool you, its [sic] drink broken up by a bit of walking. The event is known as Bloomsday. [...] The Catholic Church would have beatified Leopold Bloom if he really

---

[51]Stephen J Joyce, 'Don't Let Joyceans Scare You off', *ST*, 13 January 1991, 22.
[52]Tony O'Brien, 'Dublin to Get a "Joyce Street"', *II*, 16 March 1982, 7.

existed, and wasn't Jewish. We decided to name the liveliest and loveliest hotel in Temple Bar after the great literary character – Blooms Hotel.[53]

Elsewhere in Dublin, those wishing to listen to their radios could, from 1992 on, tune into 'Dublin's number 1 Special Interest Radio station 103.2 Dublin City Anna Livia FM',[54] while those flying out of Celtic Tiger Ireland could fork out €25 to relax in the 'Anna Livia Departure Lounge' at Dublin airport. Alternatively, from 2001 on, travellers could take the Irish Ferries €100 million ship, *Ulysses*, and 'discover a little bit of Leopold Bloom's Dublin' in 'Nora Barnacle's Food Emporium', at the 'Volta Picture Theatre', in 'Silly Milly's Fun House' or the 'Cyclops Family Entertainment' or finally along 'the Sandycove Promenade Deck'. It almost seemed like there were more 'authentic' Joyce experiences available on board then there were on the streets of Dublin.

Dermot Bolger expressed exasperation in an outspoken talk at the 1992 James Joyce Summer School pointing out that 'the city that I and others write of did not exist in his day' and venting his frustration at being constantly asked if he lived as a writer in the shadow of Joyce:

I do not share a city with Joyce. The heart has been knocked out of his city and the new bits frequently named after him by developers who are happy to invoke his name without having ever read a word of his work. [...] For the modern Dublin politician Joyce is the equivalent of the cupla fuchla [*sic*].

Describing Bloomsday as a day allowing some 'people to dress up in silly clothes, frightening the dogs in the street', he concluded: 'I admire the work, but I despise the circus.'[55] He recalled reading *Ulysses* at fourteen and returned regularly to it. In 1995 he published his stage adaptation *A Dublin Bloom*[56] which was given a public reading in the United States but for various reasons, mostly to do with copyright, did not enjoy a full production in Europe until 2012 (by Tron Theatre in Glasgow). It would finally make a successful visit to the main stage of the Abbey in 2017.

Like Bolger, there were few Irish writers who did not have something to say about Joyce and very few saw him in the terms proposed by Desmond O'Grady when he wrote in a verse letter to Derek Mahon: 'Joyce and Beckett are *cul de sac*/from which the only out's turn back'.[57] By now, for many, Joyce had displaced Yeats as the dominant figure in the Irish literary

[53]http://www.blooms.ie/joyce.htm.
[54]www.dublincityannaliviafm.com.
[55]*IT*, 23 July 1992, 5.
[56]Dermot Bolger, *A Dublin Bloom: An Original Free Adaptation of James Joyce's Ulysses* (Dublin: New Island and London: Nick Hern, 1995).
[57]Desmond O'Grady, *My Fields This Springtime* (Belfast: Lapwing Publications, 1993), 10.

pantheon as writers sought out their own place while occasionally tipping their hats. As early as 1985, Dillon Johnston could publish his *Irish Poetry after Joyce* without it seeming a misnomer. Poets from Heaney to Longley to Muldoon to Ní Chuilleanáin employed versions of Joyce's method of mixing the mythical and the quotidian although few reached as comprehensively into the classics as he had done. What Joyce opened up for them most of all was the unlimited possibility offered by language. Initially this was the English language, as Heaney attested in 'Station Island' XII where he listens to Joyce's advice: 'Who cares,'/He jeered, 'any more? The English language/ belongs to us.'[58] To follow Joyce was not just a political choice of English but a choice to revel in language itself. In the words of Paul Muldoon, 'Joyce is marvellous, extraordinary; he has been an influence even on poets in Ireland as well as novelists in terms of his allowing for all the possibilities of language'.[59] Few if any, more than Muldoon, revelled so playfully in the freedom to be found in his slipstream.

John Montague, by this time a senior Irish poet, expressed the centrality of Joyce in very different terms, sculpting a reverential image of Joyce as a wise elder in his poem, 'James Joyce':

> It could be my
> Father or yours;
> any worn, life-
> tempered man if
> the caption lacked
> the detail – bright
> as heresiarch or fallen
> angel – of his name.[60]

For Montague, Joyce was 'the major influence on contemporary Irish writing, including that light industry, modern Irish poetry'. Thomas Kinsella, among many others, was 'steeped in Joyce' and enabled by his writing: 'The persona of the young civil servant in *Nightwalker* halts under the Martello Tower to invoke: "The father of authors" with his "milky spectacles" to give him the strength to contemplate the career of Charles J. Haughey.' Dillon Johnson noted Joyce's central role in leading poets on the path from a predominantly pastoral to a new urban aesthetic: 'Poems such as Clarke's "Ancient Lights," "Inscription for a Headstone," and "Emancipation," Kavanagh's "If Ever You Go to Dublin Town" and his canal-bank sonnets, and Kinsella's "Baggot Street Deserta" had established before 1960 a new urban landscape that owed its foundation to Joyce, whom Kinsella confesses was "definitely

[58]Seamus Heaney, *Station Island* (London: Faber & Faber, 1985), 93.
[59]Paul Muldoon, 'Interview', *Contemporary Authors*, 129, 311.
[60]John Montague, 'James Joyce', *New Collected Poems* (Oldcastle: Gallery Press, 2012).

his [early] hero."'[61] Montague also attributed Joyce's central influence to his being 'the greatest Catholic writer since Dante. All too Catholic, all too Irish: the reasons for his great influence are obvious, since most of us share that same background.' But he also noted that non-Catholic writers, such as Derek Mahon, had been inspired by Joyce as a model of 'audacity' and 'integrity'. Montague concluded his article by claiming that the challenge was to see through the Joyce circus and rediscover the power of his words, a power that was systematically ignored by those most keen to exploit his value to the country: 'The case of Joyce has a satisfying ring of ironic justice, for in my lifetime I have seen him turned from a public embarrassment to a national asset. No writer could fail to be moved by such a subtle vengeance.'[62]

Not all writers and especially not all novelists, however, felt comfortable in Joyce's wake. Neil Jordan admitted:

> I did my best to avoid this literary Tower of Pisa collapsing on me. I located my stories in landscapes which Joyce had not described, such as the little seaside towns north of Dublin. I tried to address themes which were different from his. Every Irish writer has to devise his or her own stratagems to avoid the crippling influence of Joyce. My ultimate stratagem was to start writing films.[63]

Maeve Binchy, like most women writers, was far less traumatized. She told the *Irish Times*: 'I was never afraid of *Ulysses*. I thought it a great rollicking story of my own home town.'[64] On being asked if Joyce overshadowed Irish women writers, she replied:

> No indeed, not for writers like Kate O'Brien or Mary Lavin. Women would have seen a totally different Ireland from what he saw, divided not only by time and circumstance, but by outlook. Women would not have been formed in the hell-fire tradition. The sermons we heard never regarded us as great sinners in ourselves, more as being likely to let sin happen to us through men. Our own sexuality wasn't brought much into play, since it wasn't really assumed to exist.[65]

Similarly, the poet, Paula Meehan, felt little burden of influence when giving voice to her very different Dublin. This was recognized by Brendan Kennelly

---

[61]Dillon Johnston, *Irish Poetry after Joyce* (Notre Dame, IN: University of Notre Dame Press and Mountrath, Ireland: The Dolmen Press, 1985), 32–3.
[62]John Montague, 'The Father of All Authors', *IP*, 11 October 1994, 19.
[63]Ferdia Mac Anna, 'The Dublin Renaissance', 19.
[64]'Name the Greatest Irish Novels', *IT*, 27 September 2003. https://www.irishtimes.com/news/name-the-greatest-irish-novels-1.379196.
[65]Maol Muire Tynan, 'Facing difficult Joyces, Binchy affirms women's writes', *IT*, 4 August 1990, 2.

in his poem 'It takes trees in summer', which was written for Meehan. Reversing the usual dynamic whereby the contemporary writer would seek out Joyce, here it is Joyce who 'would love to meet her':

> not only because she could take him
> to avenues parks squares lanes
> he bypassed, didn't bother with,
> but also she could tell him how
> to listen to his ancestors,
> question the dead
> about love and loss,
> unknown edges of a known world [...].[66]

Despite his ubiquity, despite the appropriation and commodification of Joyce by both public and private sectors, and despite his growing influence on those working in the Irish creative sector, Joyce's works continued to feature only sporadically and marginally in mainstream Irish school curricula. In 1996, a new Leaving Certificate English curriculum again found no place for Joyce. Prominent Fine Gael MEP, Mary Banotti, wrote to the *Irish Times* to say that she thought it

> quite amazing, if not outrageous, that the new literature curriculum for the Leaving Certificate does not include any of the works of James Joyce. Students from all over the world, many of them younger than Leaving Certificate students, are already enthusiastically studying Joyce's texts. Those who chose the texts should be called to account for having excluded our most distinguished and most famous Irish and European writer.[67]

The *Irish Times* published a reply from Leaving Cert student, Jonathan Dockrell, who said that excluding Joyce from the literature curriculum was akin to leaving de Valera out of the Irish history curriculum.[68] Another reader, Peter C. Jackson, disagreed and stated that Joyce was 'not up to standard', not 'in the same league as Charles Dickens or Jane Austen', and concluded: 'If any work of James Joyce is included, it should be stated his work is not in the same league as the traditional classics. The most important task is to maintain standards.'[69] He need not have worried. Apart from the occasional appearance of *A Portrait*, Joyce was kept off the syllabus. Somewhat bizarrely in 2016, Frank McGuinness's adaptation of 'The Dead' (rather

---

[66]Brendan Kennelly, 'It takes trees in summer', *An Sionnach: A Journal of Literature, Culture, and the Arts*, vol. 5, no. 1 & 2 (Spring & Fall 2009): 25.
[67]Mary Banotti, 'An amazing omission', *IT*, 19 March 1996, 11.
[68]Letter to *IT*, 16 April 1996, 36.
[69]Peter C. Jackson, 'Joyce Not up to Standard', *IT*, 30 April 1996, 34.

than Joyce's original short story) was made part of the Leaving Certificate curriculum. This may well have been due to an unwillingness on the part of the Joyce estate to yield copyright. When Niall MacMonagle was editing his anthology for fifteen-year-olds, *TEXT A Transition Year English Reader*, he assembled, in the short stories section, a broad miscellany including Tobias Wolff, Hemingway, Alice Munro, Jhumpa Lahiri, and Irish authors including Roddy Doyle, Anne Enright, Joseph O'Connor, Claire Keegan, John McGahern, but Stephen Joyce refused permission for Joyce's 'Clay' on the grounds that Ireland had treated his grandfather so badly. Money was not an issue.[70] Today, *Kingdom 2*, the principal English textbook for Junior Cert English, includes 'Eveline' and the Clongowes excerpt from *A Portrait*. *Dubliners* and *A Portrait* are also among a large selection of texts that can be studied during 'transition year' (a gap year before the final cycle into the leaving certificate). The Joyce Tower, the Joyce Centre and, more recently, the new MoLI museum offer workshops on these texts for students. There is still no trace of *Ulysses*.

Meanwhile, the pace of new Irish Joyce publications noticeably increased in the 1990s. Having produced (with Bernard McGinley) a very fine annotated and illustrated edition of *Dubliners*,[71] John Wyse Jackson teamed up with Peter Costello and published *John Stanislaus Joyce. The Voluminous Life and Genius of James Joyce's Father*.[72] This copiously detailed account of the life, trials and times of Joyce's father and of the Joyce family ancestry furnished a rich tapestry of Irish backgrounds and sources. In the same year, David Norris and Carl Flint published their *Joyce for Beginners*, which offers a light-hearted introduction to the writer while Viviene Igoe's *Joyce's Dublin Houses* was greeted as 'a fascinating portrait of the early years, charting his family's descent from gentility to poverty and the impact this had'.[73]

The year 1997 brought a legal battle between the James Joyce Estate and another Irish Joyce scholar, Danis Rose, over his 'Readers' edition' of *Ulysses*, which claimed to have corrected Joyce's text. Published by Lilliput Press, this limited edition was to have a run of 1,000 copies, 100 of which were leather-bound contained a signed foreword by John Banville and costing the rather immodest sum of £400 each. The remaining 900 were priced at £75. A trade edition was to be published in London by Picador.[74] Rose made over 10,000 grammatical, punctuation and spelling amendments

---

[70]Niall MacMonagle, *TEXT A Transition Year English Reader* (Dublin: The Celtic Press, 2009).

[71]*James Joyce's 'Dubliners': An Illustrated Edition with Annotations*, eds., John Wyse Jackson and Bernard McGinley (New York: St Martin's Press, 1993).

[72]John Wyse Jackson and Peter Costello, *John Stanislaus Joyce: The Voluminous Life and Genius of James Joyce's Father* (London: Fourth Estate, 1997).

[73]Vivien Igoe, *James Joyce's Dublin Houses* (London: Mandarin, 1990). John Mulqueen, 'Finding the Fun in Jimmy Joyce', *CE*, 14 June 1997, 83.

[74]James Joyce, *Ulysses: A Reader's Edition*, ed. Danis Rose (Dublin: The Lilliput Press, 1997 and London: Picador, 1998).

to the text so as, in his words, to restore the 'undisturbed flow of the text'. He sought, in Sam Slote's words,

> to redress what he calls 'textual faults', which he defines as something that 'can be suspected when one realizes that there is 'something wrong' with a particular sentence in the isotext, not simply when a word is misspelled but more subtly where the sentence is saying something that it should not, where the logic of the narrative is inexplicably broken.[75]

In the *Times Literary Supplement*, Rose described his edition as an attempt to bypass the 'coterie of academics' designed to appeal to a 'general public'.[76] He took major liberties with what some considered his dumbing down of Joyce's novel and Lawrence Rainey, among others, accused him of engaging in an act of 'editorial despotism' by overruling Joyce at every turn. Rose had long been a member of the same scholarly Joyce community he now attacked: 'Rose decrees, by *fiat*, the reign of an editorial theory which violates every principle and procedure of critical editing, replacing it with nothing more than "making sense" as construed, tautologically, by Danis Rose.' An appalled Stephen Joyce protested in the *Irish Times*: 'To have had the audacity, the effrontery to put the name James Joyce on this outrageous misrepresentation of *Ulysses*, my grandfather's unique masterpiece, often referred to as the novel of the century, is demeaning to his creative, imaginative genius. [...] The integrity, the essence of James Joyce's innovative writing has been obliterated.'[77] This 'ill-fated Reader's Edition' [...] which was denounced by the estate as 'the equivalent of drawing a moustache on the Mona Lisa' was suppressed 'after a long and bitter court case in London'[78] that was won by the Estate. It was only a partial victory because the judge did not award damages to the Estate and while the Estate won the copyright claim, they lost the passing off claim (which was an attempt to try and make bad editing illegal). This allowed Rose to release an emended version of his edition in 2004 which deleted various short passages that were under copyright.[79] That Marcel Duchamp had in fact drawn such a moustache on the Mona Lisa in his famous modernist work of art, L. H. O. O. Q, was presumably lost of Stephen.

The decade closed with Edna O'Brien's biography, *James Joyce A Life*, which managed to get his dates of birth and death wrong among a myriad of errors that overshadowed what was a heartfelt, and sometimes lyrical

---

[75]Sam Slote, *Ulysses in the Plural: The Variable Editions of Joyce's Novel* (Dublin: The National Library of Ireland Joyce Studies, 2004), 36.

[76]Danis Rose, *TLS*, 11 July 1997, 17.

[77]Don Lavery, '"New *Ulysses*" Angers Joyce', *SI*, 29 June 1997, 2.

[78]Frank McNally, 'Revised "Ulysses" Set to Anger James Joyce Estate', *IT*, 12 June 2004, 1.

[79]James Joyce, *Ulysses*, ed. Danis Rose (Cornwall: Houyhnhnm Press, 2004). I am grateful to Sam Slote for his input on this point.

tribute to the writer. O'Brien took little stock of scholarship post-Ellmann or indeed of any scholarship at all in her impressionistic version of the author's life. It was well received outside the Joyce community with the *Meath Chronicle* describing it as a 'succinct little gem [...] written in the stream-of-consciousness guise of the Old Artificer himself'. O'Brien is praised for providing 'the true substance' of Joyce's life in prose 'as limpid as boulders glimpsed through a clear-running stream– but overshot with her own familiarly urbane rhetoric'.[80] O'Brien's hymn to Joyce was also an act of self-identification as his female counterpart in breaking the boundaries of fiction, but also as a female respondent who had a whole other world to paint, even if she could borrow techniques and words from Joyce without any of the agonizing that seemed to afflict the earlier generation of predominantly male Irish novelists. Her first novel, *The Country Girls*, carried many Joycean reverberations as can be seen in this exchange between Caithleen and Baba:

> 'Will you for Chrissake, stop asking fellas if they've read James Joyce's *Dubliners*? They're not interested. They're out for a night. Eat and drink all you can and leave James Joyce to blow his own trumpet.'
> 'He's dead.'
> 'Well, for God's sake, then, what are you worrying about?'
> 'I'm not worrying. I just like him.'[81]

None of this was particularly surprising given O'Brien's own words about Joyce's dazzling effect on her:

> The first book I ever bought-I've still got it – was called *Introducing James Joyce*, by T. S. Eliot. It contained a short story, a piece from *Portrait of the Artist*, some other pieces, and an introduction by Eliot. I read a scene from *Portrait* which is the Christmas dinner when everything begins pleasantly: a fire, largesse, the blue flame of light on the dark plum pudding, the revelry before the flare-up ensues between people who were for Parnell and those who were against him. Parnell had been dead for a long time, but the Irish, being Irish, persist with history. Reading that book made me realize that I wanted literature for the rest of my life.[82]

---

[80]*Meath Chronicle*, 11 September 1999, 67.
[81]Edna O'Brien (1960), *The Country Girls Trilogy* (London: Penguin, 1988), 150. For a discussion of the Joyce–O'Brien connection see Ellen McWilliams, 'James Joyce and the Lives of Edna O'Brien' in Paige Reynolds, ed., *Modernist Afterlives in Irish Literature and Culture* (London: Anthem Press, 2016), 49–60.
[82]David Heycock, 'Edna O'Brien Talks to David Heycock about Her New Novel, *A Pagan Place*' in Alice Hughes Kersnoswki, ed., *Conversations with Edna O'Brien* (Jackson: University of Mississippi, 2014), 8–13, 10.

As the 1990s drew to a close Irish newspapers were more concerned with the present than with the lingering shadow of history and sought to put a figure on Joyce's value to the economy. It was reported that the Bloomsday celebrations were 'just the most visible part of a multi-million pound industry':

> After Guinness and perhaps U2, James Joyce is our most famous export. He put Dublin on the world map. [...] Admittedly of the 4.7 million people who came here last year, only a small proportion came for Joyce alone. And although Bórd Fáilte cannot say what fraction of the $440.7 million generated from visitors last year can be attributed to Joyce, they insist that his presence is central to their marketing strategies. Literary Ireland is one of the range of tourism attractions that we identified in the late '80s. And we have since aggressively targeted that niche market.[83]

The price to be paid for this was that Joyce was at times reduced to being 'an Irish Mickey Mouse of sorts, his squinty visage sagely purveying from every second pub wall across the capital's trendier stretches– James Joyce is today more feted as a badge of Irish artistic triumph than actually enjoyed by the average book lover, no matter how the Nation's scholars coo and simper over his oozing prose and chaos-theory grammar'.[84] Anthony Cronin also expressed his dismay at 'the semi-official aspects' of Bloomsday and pointed out that

> in 1954 it was a subversive gesture [...] but now it's an establishment thing which I don't think fits easily on Joyce. [...] It's just got to be too jolly in the wrong way. Most of Joyce's people were outcasts or failures [...] and that is not reflected in the general jolly atmosphere that dominates the day. It's like all the jagged edges have been removed from the thing and it's been turned into something safe for tourists.[85]

Elsewhere Cronin called the 'Bloomsday cavortings [...] an insult to the depth and complexity, the greatness and compassion of our country's greatest book'.[86] All such complaints were batted away by David Norris:

> It makes me sick to hear those shrivelled-up begrudgers who think that it's not proper to make a party of it all; they call it a circus. Well, I want to tell them that people have a ball at circuses. Why should ordinary people

---

[83]Mary Carr, 'Why Next Monday's Bloomsday Celebrations Are Just the Most Visible Part of a Multi-million Pound Industry', *EH*, 13 June 1997, 20.
[84]Edward Power, 'Purists Furious over Cleaned-up Version of Joyce's Finest Work', *IE*, 26 June 1997, 30.
[85]Mary Carr, 'Dublin Is Blooming', *EH*, 16 June 1998, 22.
[86]Ibid.

234   CONSUMING JOYCE

be excluded? The elite have obfuscated Joyce in an appalling manner and tried to keep the ordinary people out. Joyce wanted desperately to communicate. I think he would have heartily approved. People who criticise the party are wizened old farts.[87]

For Norris, one of the positive spinoffs of what was by now the week-long Bloomsday Festival was that the James Joyce Centre on his beloved North Great Georges Street became the focal point for all activities and was now a tourist attraction in itself: 'Without Joyce's international reputation many of the wonderful buildings and, in particular, the Joyce Centre in North Great Georges Street, would long ago have been demolished. This fact alone justifies Bloomsday.'[88] With Joyce's grandniece, Helen Monaghan, in the role of administrator in the late 1990s, the European Union and various other private and public sources (especially Guinness Ireland) invested over 1 million pounds in the refurbishment of the centre. In 1995, the Eccles Street door was transferred there from the Bailey pub and became a prime exhibit. In 1998, the centre organized a worldwide internet reading of excerpts from *Ulysses* involving the new President, Mary McAleese, the Taoiseach Bertie Ahern, and many other luminaries including Frank McCourt in New York, Kader Asmal in Capetown, Australian actress Beverley Dunn at Molly Bloom's Hotel, in Melbourne. Fifteen cities around the world were involved in this event which was broadcast live from the Jameson Distillery in Smithfield. The text chosen for the reading was based on a version of *Ulysses* that had been prepared between 1992 and 1995, the period in which Joyce's works were out of copyright. The James Joyce Estate, however, was not impressed and took a case against the newspaper which was settled out of court 'on very far-reaching terms involving not only the payment of costs and damages to the Estate but also agreement to a permanent injunction, which would prevent any future webcast'.[89] David Norris expressed anger and dismay in the Seanad: 'Immediately, the James Joyce estate took action against us. There were no reasonable or cultural grounds for such action – it was a case of pure, unmitigated spite against which we should be protected.'[90] He was far from wrong.

What Stephen Joyce failed to see was that Bloomsday, for all its excesses, successfully drew people into Joyce's vortex and helped foster the reading of *Ulysses* and his other works. This spirit was captured well in the words of Irish novelist, Joseph O'Connor, who remembered as a young boy asking

[87]John Daly, 'Portrait of the Artist as the Coolest Cat in Tiger Town', *CE*, 16 June 1998, 11.
[88]'It's Bloomin' Great!', *EH*, 12 June 1999, 8.
[89]Marie McGonagle, Sharon McLaughlin and Tarlach McGonagle, *Media Law in Ireland* (The Netherlands: Wolters Kluwer, 2018), n.p.g. (electronic edition).
[90]David Norris Copyright and Related Rights Bill, 1999: Second Stage. Copyright and Related Rights Bill, 1999: Committee Stage (Resumed). https://www.oireachtas.ie/en/debates/debate/seanad/1999-06-29/8/.

his grandmother what the stories of *Dubliners* were about and she replied 'ordinary people like ourselves'. He then recalled overhearing 'an old man on a number 8 bus in Sandycove. [...] The old man said that James Joyce was nothing but a dirty little tinker who had never done an honest day's work, and who had "run Ireland down for money"'. Turning to Bloomsday, he noted that some people

> say it's phoney, but I don't think so. In other countries, they commemorate battles and victories and death. But we in Ireland, for all our faults, celebrate the work of the dirty little tinker who ran us down for money and made our small insignificant city glorious everywhere, and turned the lives of ordinary people just like ourselves into the most spellbindingly beautiful prose ever written in the language. What a wonderful idea that is. Yes.[91]

Lest there should be any doubt, Irish public policymakers had a more cynical view of Joyce's worth but so too did the Joyce Estate. Many Joyce scholars, many actors and performers had waited in the hope that all Joyce copyright would expire on the fiftieth anniversary of Joyce's death and so it did. The year 1992 promised to be a new dawn but the seeming freedom only lasted for a few short years before the new EU Copyright Term Directive revived copyright over these works in 1995, as the rules extended the lifetime of copyright to seventy years after the author's death. In 1999, the Irish government passed the Copyright and Related Rights Bill, in order to bring Ireland's laws in this regard into line with the European directive. As a result, Joyce's works would remain under the control of the Joyce Estate in the European Union until 2012 even if in other jurisdictions they remained in the public domain, because copyright had expired. The Estate was particularly aggressive in policing his revived copyrights. Stephen Joyce, as the self-appointed 'keeper of the flame', 'relied upon threats of legal action to discourage the production of derivative works based upon the canonical texts of the novelist. The Estate also jealously guarded the reputation of the author by vetoing the use of his work in various scholarly productions'.[92] In other words, the Estate actively paralysed the efforts of the very people working to build and popularize Joyce's reputation. The Estate's prohibitive actions stymied scholarly projects, such as new editions of Joyce's letters to replace the three volumes produced by Gilbert and Ellmann, which, to this day, remain patchy and incomplete and were subject to silent cutting. The Cork University Press *Irish Writing in the Twentieth Century: A Reader*, edited in 2001 by David Pierce, was left with a gaping hole as

[91]Joseph O'Connor, 'Ordinary People Like Ourselves', *ST*, 20 June 1993, A13.
[92]Matthew Rimmer, 'Bloomsday: Copyright Estates and Cultural Festivals', *Script-ed*, vol. 2, no. 3 (September 2005): 383–428, 383.

pages 323–346 had to be removed from the 1,350-page volume. Pierce had wanted to publish 'The Dead' and six short extracts from *Ulysses* but the Estate had sought an exorbitant fee of £7,000 sterling – half the budget for the entire project. Similarly, when RTÉ asked to broadcast excerpts from *A Portrait*, Stephen, after some haggling, finally agreed on a fee: 'The demand was £50 sterling a minute, and with the broadcasts running to a total of 70 minutes, this meant a total of £3,500 – far bigger than the payments sought by other literary estates.' To put the icing on the cake, he then demanded that the fee 'be delivered to him by courier at a certain time on a certain date in a Dublin hotel'.[93] Similarly, Barry McGovern was asked to pay royalties of £27,000 sterling for a special *Ulysses* on Bloomsday 2000 (he had paid the Beckett estate £20 for a similar event a year earlier).

Despite overwhelming evidence to the contrary, Stephen Joyce seemed convinced Joyceans were getting rich through their scholarship or performances and he seemed to get a kick from drawing those engaging with his grandfather's work into interminable negotiations, often demanding excessively high fees for permission to use relatively short quotes. He motivated his vigilance as follows:

> Joyce should be given back to the reader, the general public. [...] Nonno has never ever been allowed to belong to the reader; having been barred, even usurped, by Joyceans and critics who have fashioned him into the unscalable mountain which is the figure of their own tortured twisted minds. When the parasites, scavengers, muckrakers are stripped away it will become self-evident that James Joyce does not need them; nor do you. But they need him![94]

But the reality was that his actions were actually one of the major hurdles to Joyce being made more accessible to Irish readers as RTÉ literary critic and radio producer, Seamus Hosey, commented: 'Joyce's work informs Irish culture and society in a similar way to the Book of Kells. Stephen Joyce's behaviour is blackly comic, but it is very serious; Irish people have a moral and cultural right to access the ideas in a range of ways.'[95]

Stephen was particularly stubborn about allowing derivative creative works, such as musical adaptations, dramatic performances and films, to make any use of Joyce's words. In 2000, he refused permission to a young Irish composer, David Fennessy, to quote just eighteen words from *Finnegans Wake* and regularly blocked broadcasters from quoting even small extracts. Those straying into the realm of biography risked becoming the targets of particular vigilance and indeed reprobation. Stephen rarely held back in

[93]Ronan Farren, 'Why Joyce Is Out of the Big Picture', *SI*, 18 February 2001, 57.
[94]Stephen J Joyce, 'Don't Let Joyceans Scare You off', *ST*, 13 January 1991, 22.
[95]Medb Ruane, 'The War of Words over Joyce's Literary Legacy', *IT*, 10 June 2000, 9.

applying copyright law and as a result alienated many of those in the Joyce community who had sympathy with his desire to protect his family from excessive probing.

The 1990s drew to a close with *Ulysses* being named as the finest English language novel of the twentieth century by the Modern Library. However, despite 'the hoopla surrounding the annual Bloomsday shenanigans' and all the efforts to popularize it, *Ulysses* remained conspicuous for its absence from the Eason's Top 100 selling novels in Ireland over the previous fifty years. For the record, Maeve Binchy's *The Glass Lake* topped the list, closely followed by John Murphy's *Little Irish Cookbook*.[96]

[96]Colin Lacey, 'A Nation of Sweethearts', *The Examiner*, 7 August 1998, 14.

CHAPTER TEN

Millennial Joyce

The first two decades of the third millennium were a roller coaster for Ireland. Initially it seemed that the only way was up as the increasingly globalized Republic worked to consolidate the hard-earned peace in the North and enjoyed a period of unprecedented economic expansion. Multinational companies flocked to the country to take advantage of its English-speaking population, friendly tax regime, well-qualified workforce and ready access to the European market. The population grew rapidly for the first time since the mid-nineteenth century as the country attracted tens of thousands of migrant workers and many Irish returned home from the diaspora. A robust Fianna Fáil-Progressive Democrat coalition was in power, led by the hugely popular Bertie Ahern. Tánaiste, Mary Harney, the leader of the Progressive Democrats, caught the bullish spirit of the time when she declared in 2000: 'Our economic success owes more to American liberalism than to European leftism [...] geographically we are closer to Berlin than Boston. Spiritually, we are probably a lot closer to Boston than Berlin.'[1] The expanding economy, however, was not as secure as many wanted to believe and it was managed wastefully. The drive for continued growth became increasingly dependent on the construction sector and on spiralling property prices where a more balanced or enlightened approach might have sought the gradual achievement of a fairer or more just society.

At a time when Ireland was at the height of its economic boom (June 2004), the government held a contentious referendum on citizenship. Just five years earlier, a previous amendment had agreed to insert a clause into Article 2 of the constitution that guaranteed 'the entitlement and birth right

---

[1]Quoted in Diarmuid Ferriter, 'Twenty-First Century Ireland' in Richard Bourke and Ian McBride, eds., *The Princeton History of Modern Ireland* (Princeton: Princeton University Press, 2016), 169.

of every person born in the island of Ireland … to be part of the Irish Nation'. This had done little more than restate what had long been effectively the case in the country. Now the government sought to reverse this with another amendment restricting the right to citizenship solely to those with a parent who was an Irish citizen or who was entitled to be one. The motivation for this was thin anecdotal evidence of foreign women coming to Ireland to give birth so that their children could claim Irish citizenship. The referendum was rushed through and many voters had little understanding of the issue at hand. An open letter, written by a leading group of artists and intellectuals in support of a no vote, began by citing the section in *Ulysses* where 'Joyce has the Citizen pose the question of his famous Jewish hero. "What is your nation, if I may ask?" Mr Bloom has no hesitation in replying: "Ireland. I was born here. Ireland"'.[2] The signatories asserted that 'right to citizenship through birthplace is a beautiful concept', one that expresses 'the better part of ourselves'. Yet, what the government was proposing 'means that in future, a baby born in this country must depend on the exact circumstances of its parents before he or she can be deemed to be Irish. The beautiful idea will be gone forever'.[3] A no vote was the only way to safeguard this right. With the Catholic Church's authority now greatly diminished (it did, to be fair, argue for a no vote), the signatories enlisted Joyce in their attempt to occupy a moral void. The referendum passed in what was a bad day for Ireland of the welcomes, a bad day for a country that had for centuries watched so many of its sons and daughters emigrate and find shelter and a life elsewhere around the globe becoming, in the Citizen's words, 'our greater Ireland beyond the sea' (*U*12.1365).

More mistakes would be made when the economy faltered during the Great Recession and when the government intervened on 21 December 2008 to bail out the Irish banks. The populace looked on powerlessly as the once-unstoppable blaze of the Celtic Tiger dwindled into the bonfire of the nation's economic vanities. By the end of the decade, Ireland's illusion of economic sovereignty was in tatters and the State found itself relying on bailout funds. The long dominant Fianna Fáil suffered in the polls as never before and Fine Gael was swept to power in a coalition led by Enda Kenny. The process of rebuilding the economy began and continued under successive governments until the unprecedented new scenarios that were Brexit and Covid-19 came to dominate.

The other chastening collapse that came during these turbulent twenty years was in the authority and credibility of the Catholic Church as people absorbed the horrors of the Ferns Report (2005), and the Ryan and the Murphy reports (2009) on child abuse. It was clear that a repressive culture of secrecy and denial – hinted at in 'The Sisters' and troublingly present

[2]Robert Ballagh et al., Letter 'Referendum on Citizenship and Birth', *IT*, 4 June 2004, 21.
[3]Ibid.

between the lines of all of Joyce's works – and an avoidance of scandal at all costs had driven the Church's decisions for decades and undone much of its undoubtedly positive contribution to society in the fields, for example, of education and health. The dark, disgraceful realities of abuse turned people irrevocably against what had been the country's unquestioned and unquestionable dominant force. A majority of people now believed what Joyce and others had denounced a century earlier, that is, that clerical power had been grossly and recklessly abused.

In 2004, a special Joyce issue of the Jesuit periodical *Studies* paid homage to Joyce as the most famous product of Irish Jesuit education. The editor, Fr Fergus O'Donoghue SJ, made reference to the collapse of the official Church and claimed that Joyce would have been uneasy at 'our wholesale rejection of tradition' but 'delighted' at the disappearance of Dublin's slums. With a heavy dose of revisionism, he averred that it was 'natural for a Jesuit journal to join the centenary celebrations of Bloomsday' and correctly noted that *Studies* had been publishing articles about Joyce since 1956. More oddly, he described Joyce, perhaps the most atypical product to which the Irish Jesuits could lay claim, as 'a typical product of the Victorian Irish Catholic middle classes, who used commerce and education to advance themselves'.[4] He contended that 'one of Joyce's most Irish traits was his (incorrect) feeling that he was not appreciated in his own country. Such a feeling may even be an aspect of voluntary exile. [...] the critical comments of Oliver St. John Gogarty, Flann O'Brien and others were evidence of a healthy critical atmosphere which has since vanished'. To claim that Joyce was 'incorrect' in believing that he was not appreciated in Ireland was simply wrong and the idea that this was 'an aspect of voluntary exile' was tone deaf with regard to the diaspora. Joyce simply could not have been Joyce if he had stayed in Ireland. The freedom he found in an often painful exile was essential. Furthermore, it seems evident that Fr O'Donoghue never read the critical comments of either Gogarty or O'Brien because to lump them together in this way was an unintended slight on both. Regardless of their common scepticism about Joyceans, their views on Joyce could not have been more different.

The editorial's principal theme was the extraordinary changes in the world since Joyce's time: 'So much that seemed permanent has vanished: colonial empires, European world hegemony, monarchy as politically significant, and the churches as a central feature of European life.' He did not speculate on what Joyce might have felt about such change but did admit that in Joyce's era, the Catholic hierarchy spoke as if 'articulating the national mindset' while now that role had been taken by some commentators. Here he failed to acknowledge that the public once cowered in fear when the hierarchy or

---

[4]Fergus O'Donoghue, 'Editorial', *Studies: An Irish Quarterly Review*, vol. 93, no. 370 (Summer 2004): 119–20, 119.

the clergy spoke (on behalf of a people many of them believed incapable of speaking or thinking for themselves), whereas in more recent decades, the media has offered a variety of opinions, each of which can be contested or ignored with a shrug and without fear of consequences.

Studies was launched in Belvedere College where Fr O'Donoghue admitted that the Jesuits' view of Joyce had, in the past, been 'uncomfortable'. Fr Bruce Bradley expressed the belief that Joyce would be pleased at how cosmopolitan Ireland had become; however, 'he would not like some of the tawdriness and the way in which his name is exploited'.[5] It would have been hard to disagree. Some did, however, and felt that Joyce was the perfect symbol for the decadent new Ireland that had, in all its degraded modernity, become the Joycean image of itself. In a letter to the *Irish Times* entitled 'Bloomsday: the national feast?', Thomas P. Walsh responded to a suggestion that the country abandon Saint Patrick and adopt Leopold Bloom and James Joyce as national patrons:

> After all, such coarse characters have it to their credit that they make manifest a vulgar display of various bodily functions such as defecating, urinating, masturbating, vomiting, belching, picking one's nose and scratching itchy pimples in public.
>
> And isn't this just what we spontaneously do ourselves every Saturday night on the streets of Dublin? [...] Away then with St Patrick. What need have we of a patron who was prayerful and humble, and who devoted his life to the disinterested spiritual service of his fellow man? A dignified icon such as this is out of place and much too old-fashioned and passé for the New 'honky-tonk' Ireland we are busily building today.[6]

Later in the same year, influential *Irish Times* critic, Eileen Battersby, claimed that *Ulysses* was 'monolithically overrated' and that its reputation owed more to academic critics and 'the culture industry' in Ireland than to 'loyal readers'. Joyce's novel was mean-minded and intent on 'milking the cynicism' of 'the Irish experience'.[7] The so-called Joyce industry was not however to be deterred. The decade began with the arrival in Dublin of the famous Rosenbach manuscript of *Ulysses* that Joyce had reluctantly sold to John Quinn in 1919. It was exhibited, along with Joyce artefacts and photographs, at the Chester Beatty library. This was but a prelude to what was to come.

In an aptly entitled article in the *Irish Times*, 'Time for Ireland to say yes to *Ulysses*', Terence Killeen reported that the 'lost' typescript of the

---

[5]Ben Quinn, 'Jesuits Celebrate Joyce's Imagined Take on No-longer-pious City', *II*, 2 June 2004, 6.
[6]Thomas P. Walsh, 'Bloomsday, the National Feast?', *IT*, 27 June 2003, 19.
[7]Eileen Battersby, 'Joyce Reigns Supreme… but Are We Still Waiting for the Great Irish Novel?' *IT*, 18 October 2003, 39.

'Circe' episode, known as the Quinn draft, was up for sale at Christies, New York. He described it as 'a truly important manuscript, a genuine trace of Joyce's amazing creative energy in the writing of *Ulysses*' and 'as much a part of Ireland's heritage as the Rock of Cashel or the Cliffs of Moher'.[8] It was the broadly held view of Joyce scholars that nowhere could offer a more fitting home for the twenty-seven-page draft and the first significant Joyce manuscript to emerge in forty years than the National Library. With good reason, Killeen concluded his article provocatively with the question: 'So, how about it, Síle?' He was appealing directly to the then Fianna Fáil Minister for Arts, Heritage, Gaeltacht and the Islands, Síle de Valera, granddaughter of former President, Éamon de Valera – 'the devil era' of *Finnegans Wake* (FW 473.07). The Minister, who presumably had been listening to her advisors rather than picking up on echoes from the past and from her famous ancestor, sanctioned the acquisition at a cost of 1.4 million dollars. On 16 December 2001, using language more often adopted for the return of an Olympic Gold medal winner or a victorious Irish rugby team, the newspapers reported that the manuscript had 'made a triumphant arrival at Dublin airport'.[9] An *Irish Times* editorial celebrated the purchase, which went 'a long way to ending the anomalous situation whereby virtually no Joyce manuscripts were kept in this State'.[10] The Library put the manuscript on exhibit the following summer.

Perhaps high on the success of this acquisition, the National Library followed up in July 2001 with the purchase of what was thought to be an original Joyce death mask at Sotheby's for £55,000. No sooner was it purchased, however, than it was brought to the attention of the Library that the mask was, in fact, only a copy (once owned by John Huston) and the sale was hastily cancelled. An unexpected silver lining lay in the fact that the mask in the Joyce Tower in Sandycove, which had earlier been the subject of controversy, now acquired some belated lustre on being re-identified as one of just three in the world (the others being at the Zurich James Joyce Foundation and the Library of Congress in Washington).

Despite this setback, the Library was back in the buyers' corner just a year later when, in May 2002, it acquired a previously unknown archive of manuscript material that had been rescued by Paul Léon from Joyce's Paris flat (or bought by him during a sell-off of the contents by Joyce's landlord). The materials, which were passed down to Léon's son, Alexis, were acquired through the agency of Sotheby's after Léon indicated that he wanted the NLI to be granted first refusal on the collection. Alexis hoped the materials would find a home at the Library given that it already held the extensive

---

[8]Terence Killeen, 'Joyce Document due Home Today', *IT*, 9 December 2000, 11.
[9]'Joyce Odyssey over as *Ulysses* Episode Home for Good', *IT*, 16 December 2000, 1.
[10]'*Ulysses* in Dublin', *IT*, 16 December 2000, 19.

collection of the Joyce–Léon letters, donated by his father decades earlier. Thus, the NLI became, overnight, 'the world's foremost repository of Joyce manuscripts' after a top secret, eighteenth-month negotiation led by director Brendan O'Donoghue.[11] As many as 500 manuscript pages and 200 pages of proofs, along with typescripts and early notebooks, were included in the monumental package, which also contained the early 'Pola Notebook'. The cost worked out at €24,000 a sheet. Despite the massive price tag of €12.6 million, there was general approval of library's 'remarkable success'. On arrival back from London with the materials, Minister de Valera was met at Dublin airport by Taoiseach, Bertie Ahern, who described the collection as 'probably one of the most important cultural milestones for Ireland in living memory'.[12] The Government paid €5.4 million using monies from the recently established heritage fund and the remainder was donated by Allied Irish Banks, which obtained tax relief on the sum. Subsequently, there was some grumbling and speculation, mainly on the internet, about a lack of transparency around the purchase. The Irish political and current affairs magazine, *The Phoenix*, and the Joyce Estate, which resented having been kept out of the loop during the secret negotiations, questioned whether the Léons actually had legal title to the documents. It was established that although the library held the papers, copyright would remain with the Joyce Estate until 2012 (when European copyright on all his works would expire).

All of this formed the backdrop to an ever-greater use of Joyce as a cultural magnet to draw tourists to the capital, particularly for the *Ulysses* centenary, which was named 'Rejoyce Dublin 2004'. The annual Bloomsday bash became a sprawling five-month affair run by a thirteen-person committee, dominated by high-powered public servants from the Department of Arts, Sport and Tourism, from Dublin Tourism, the Abbey Theatre, the National Library, the Joyce Centre and representatives from the leading universities. One of its centrepieces was a Bloomsday 'breakfast' for several thousand people on O'Connell Street (inspired by the fact that Bloom witnesses the 'nextdoor girl' purchase 'a pound and a half of Denny's sausages' (*U*4.147–8) in Dlugacz's butcher's shop). Asked about this and about what was by now a relentlessly consumerist approach to Joyce in general and *Ulysses* in particular, an exasperated Roddy Doyle claimed: 'They'll be serving Joyce Happy Meals next.'[13] Irish papers reported that he 'elicited gasps from the New York literati when he took a swipe at James Joyce, saying *Ulysses* "could have done with a good editor"'.[14] Doyle's complaints seemed more

---

[11]Geraldine Collins, '"Silence, Exile and Cunning" in €12m Joyce Deal', *II*, 31 May 2002, 4.
[12]Fergus Black, 'Trove of Joyce Papers Flown Home as €12m Deal Clinched', *II*, 30 May 2002, 3.
[13]John Crowley, 'Dublin's Celebration for Joyce Overshadowed by *Ulysses* Copyright Row', *Daily Telegraph*, 14 June 2004.
[14]Nicola Anderson, 'James Joyce, Ha Ha Ha, Says Roddy', *II*, 11 February 2004, 3.

to do with 'the inevitable comparisons between Joyce and other Irish writers' and perhaps as the reluctant heir to Joyce's brilliant renditions of pub-dialogue, he took issue with how so many Irish writers were said to have 'lifted from Joyce' as if he had invented the Dublin accent or the language as it was spoken in the city.

At the same time as the sausage-eating extravaganza, the city was also host to the largest international James Joyce symposium ever, which was addressed by President Mary McAleese, Seamus Heaney, John Banville and many others. It also hosted an exhibition of Joyce-inspired art entitled 'High Faluttin Stuff' at the Irish Museum of Modern Art (IMMA), and a 'Joyce in Art: Visual Art Inspired by James Joyce' exhibition at the Royal Hibernian Academy gallery curated by Christa-Maria Lerm Hayes (with Patrick T. Murphy) and featuring works by Man Ray and Matisse as well as by Joyce himself. Lerm Hayes also published an impressive volume from the exhibition.[15] But this was really only the tip of the iceberg. Joyce was everywhere and the symbolic Bloomsday homage of the hardy few in 1954 had become the Joycefest of the many, as thousands of travellers thronged to Dublin to participate.

Most of the bill for this celebration of Joyce as the King of Irish Carnival, a title he would be amused to share with Saint Patrick, was footed by the Irish government, which contributed close to €2 million. From across the water the *Observer* argued that this 'represented a long overdue "official" recognition of Joyce's status as Ireland's greatest writer'.[16] There is, however, no such thing as a free lunch, even for Joyce, and the government invested in the hope of a significant economic payback, which clearly arrived, according to Laura Barnes, chief organizer of Bloomsday 2004, and later director of the James Joyce Centre:

'There's nothing scientific', says Barnes, 'because we don't have entry or exit polls of people coming into Dublin. After 2004, the centennial, Dublin Tourism reported a 10% boost in hotel bookings. Bloomsday 2004 had over 1,500 media internationally. And that in of itself created a ripple effect because even if people did not come to Dublin in 2004 Dublin became a desirable tourist destination'.[17]

Of most lasting importance was the splendid Joyce exhibition, 'James Joyce and *Ulysses*', organized by the National Library in its newly refurbished and enlarged exhibition facility on Kildare Street. Displaying some of the

[15]Christa Maria Lerm-Hayes, *Joyce in Art: Visual Art Inspired by James Joyce* (Dublin: Lilliput Press, 2004).

[16]John Naughton, 'Joyce and Copyright: A Nightmare from Which Publishers Are Now Trying to Awake', *Observer*, 25 June 2006, 10.

[17]Dermot McEvoy, 'Bloomsday Enters Dublin's Stream of Consciousness', *Publisher's Weekly*, 14 June 2007. http://www.publishersweekly.com/article/CA6451190.html.

library's newly acquired Joyce materials and exploiting what was then quite advanced digital technology, the exhibition ran from 2004 until May 2006 and attracted some 58,000 visitors from all over the world. This, the central event of the Centenary, almost did not happen, however, because of the opposition of the Joyce Estate. Stephen Joyce warned the Irish government

> that the 'James Joyce and *Ulysses*' exhibition staged by the National Library of Ireland could breach copyright by displaying manuscripts and draft notebooks. He also threatened to sue the Irish government for breach of copyright if there were any public readings or recitations as part of the festival. He issued similar warnings to other organisations planning to use Joyce's words as part of their celebrations, including the National Library, national broadcaster RTE and the James Joyce Centre in Dublin; and he rejected a proposal by the Abbey Theatre to stage Joyce's play *Exiles*.[18]

The government, having made such a significant investment, was not going to be cowed and rushed through emergency legislation to ensure that the exhibition could go ahead (although the *Exiles* production remained cancelled). In a rare show of political unity, the opposition parties criticized but were largely supportive of the government's legislation. The *Irish Independent* reported:

> Fine Gael's Arts spokesperson Jimmy Deenihan said a positive outcome of the controversy was that an anomaly had been brought to light in terms of the loophole in the Copyright Act which could have affected other exhibitions. He said that while Stephen Joyce might feel that his grandfather was being taken for granted, the writer was now very much part of Ireland's artistic heritage and tourist industry. He described Joyce as the country's greatest ambassador.[19]

Once again, Joyce was being defended in Ireland, not so much in terms of his artistic achievement, an unknown quantity to the vast majority of politicians, but in terms of his usefulness to the country's tourist industry. That said, politicians from all sides, partly marshalled by Senator David Norris, stood firm against the threat of the Joyce Estate and ensured that the 2004 Festival was not emptied of Joycean content and significance. By now, it was clear that when given an inch, the arbitrary and capricious Joyce Estate would attempt to take a mile. Conor McPherson's experience is just one of many possible examples. He was approached by Judy Friel, the

---

[18]John Naughton, 'Joyce and Copyright', 10.
[19]Ben Quinn, 'Politicians Move Swiftly to End Joyce Censorship', *II*, 28 May 2004, 3.

literary manager of the Abbey, to adapt two of Joyce's short stories for the Peacock into a pair of one act plays:

> A few weeks later, I was forwarded a letter from Stephen Joyce explaining that his grandfather had been rejected by the Irish people in general – and the Abbey Theatre in particular – so he felt it was inappropriate that we now sought to profit from his name. Although I had been born 56 years after that Abbey rejection, given the forcefulness of his letter the matter was promptly dropped.[20]

Another example came when Sean Walsh attempted to make a new feature film based on *Ulysses* and Stephen Joyce refused him permission to use any quotations from Joyce's text. So the film – designed to celebrate and render Joyce's novel more accessible – was made despite rather than with the support of the Estate. After a long and complicated gestation, it had its world premiere at the 2004 Taormina Film Festival and its Irish debut at the Galway Film Fleadh. Featuring Stephen Rea as Bloom, Angeline Ball as Molly (she won the Best Actress at the Irish Film & Television Awards for her portrayal), and Hugh O'Conor as Stephen Dedalus, it was well received by critics as a faithful rendering of the spirit of *Ulysses*.

The other major Joyce film of the period was Pat Murphy's *Nora*, a project that she had initiated many years earlier with producer, Tiernan MacBride (son of the aforementioned Sean), who sadly passed away before filming began. She was later joined by Gerry Stembridge as co-writer. As its title suggests, the film's principal focus was Nora Barnacle, who was magnificently played by Susan Lynch. Murphy, an acclaimed feminist filmmaker, made what was essentially a love story exploring the relationship between Nora and Joyce (played by Ewan McGregor, fresh from *Star Wars*). It offered an elegantly shot close-up of the couple's relationship and focused on how Nora influenced Joyce's writing, very much in the spirit of the book on which it was based, Brenda Maddox's *Nora* (1986). Maddox told of the resistance to her project from prominent Joyceans, such as Richard Ellmann, who wrote and told her how much he disliked 'book-length studies of people who are clearly not of great importance themselves' and suggested that Nora's 'meagre correspondence and literary output would make it "possible neither to give a full character portrayal, nor to evolve a feminist tract"'.[21] Maddox persisted, pasted his letter on the wall of her toilet and proved him wrong. The Dublin Film Festival hosted the Irish premiere of *Nora* with Susan Lynch in attendance and the arrival of supermodel, Kate Moss, gave the event a little necessary glamour that made up for the no-show of Ewan

---

[20]Conor McPherson, 'Joyce', *IT*, 2 February 2012, 42.
[21]Brenda Maddox Obituary, *Guardian*, 28 June 2019. https://www.theguardian.com/books/2019/jun/28/brenda-maddox-obituary.

McGregor ('the Scottish heart-throb'). The film won both critical praise and five Irish Film and Television Awards.

One final major Joyce acquisition took place in 2006 when the National Library bought some crucial early manuscript sheets of *Finnegans Wake* through Sotheby's for €1.17 million. Allied Irish Banks made the purchase for the State in return for tax relief. The remarkable collection consisted of six large sheets containing eleven pages of text, all written between April and August 1923, and comprising drafts of the 'Tristan and Isolde', 'Mamalujo' and 'St Kevin' sections of *Finnegans Wake*. No sooner had the news of this coup been made public than controversy broke out when it was alleged that the library had been offered the material by a rare book dealer in Paris, Jean-Claude Vrain, two years earlier, for just €400,000 but had passed it up. Vrain had acquired it through the heirs of another bookseller who, in turn, had bought them at the auction organized in 1945 by Joyce's former landlord. They were bought in the interim by Laura Barnes who, in the words of the *Irish Independent*, 'nipped in under the nose of the NLI, overrode its supposed exclusivity arrangement and secured the sheets in December 2004'. At the time, she was the owner of rare books specialist store, Araby Books, in New York and was about to become the director of the newly reopened (again) James Joyce Centre (which was bailed out to the tune of €125,000 shortly before she took over). It would receive a further €250,000 the following year after the intervention of Taoiseach, Bertie Ahern, in whose constituency it was located. Well known for her role in the Bloomsday 2004 celebrations and indeed for her notable business acumen (a rare quality in a Joycean), Barnes was quoted in the *Irish Independent* as saying that 'she did not have privileged information, and that her dealings were "kosher, beyond kosher"'.[22] In the *Irish Times*, Christine Madden reported:

> The director of the National Library of Ireland (NLI), Aongus Ó hAonghusa, believed it had 'got a good deal' when he discussed it with *The Irish Times* a few months ago. He explained that the purchase through Sotheby's meant that the library had warranties about the ownership and provenance of the manuscript. He also told the *London Times* in May that the library had a good relationship with Sotheby's through another recent purchase: 'They know what we want in terms of ownership and provenance. It provides a level of reassurance that a small Parisian book-dealer could never do.'[23]

Given the controversy that followed both the aborted purchase of the death mask and the contested ownership of the 2002 acquisitions, the National

---

[22]Peter Carty, 'Rare Joyce Papers Delay Cost 800k', *SI*, 21 May 2006, 25.
[23]Christine Madden, 'A Business Head on Joycean Shoulders', *IT*, 15 June 2006, 14.

Library's caution was understandable but very costly. The massive price increase and the entire affair became the object of a good deal of newspaper speculation, awkward parliamentary questions and a Department of Arts internal enquiry.

To spend a total of €16 million on Joyce manuscripts and materials in just a few years would have been unthinkable even a decade earlier, but now, in an Ireland flush with cash, it almost seemed like the natural thing to do. There were many reasons why this was so, many of them to do with boosting the country's cultural image abroad. But none of it would have been possible had it not been by the commitment of Joyce scholars and enthusiasts who had, in various different ways, and sometimes at cross-purposes with each other, made the case for his work and helped establish his global reputation. His arrival at the pinnacle of the Irish cultural firmament was the result of many lifetimes of work. It is hard to imagine an event on the scale of the Joyce Centenary were it not for the fundamental commitment of a host of pioneering international scholars. Without their dedication, which was often taken for granted and, indeed, derided in Dublin, and, if Joyce had been dependent on Irish scholarship, *Ulysses* might not have been hailed as the great novel that it is, and Joyce might not have achieved his central place in the Irish canon or indeed in the canon of world literature. Literary critics, therefore, played a crucial role in establishing his lasting reputation although they were rarely given much credit for doing so, more often than not being accused of rendering Joyce's texts more impenetrable than they needed to be.

At the same time, many Irish writers, artists, actors, and journalists had also flown the flag down through the decades, long before Irish university scholars and critics were willing to do so. Now, in the new millennium, Irish scholarly interest, which had lagged for so long, finally emerged in the English departments of the country's principal universities. Following the untimely death of Gus Martin in 1995, Anne Fogarty had taken over as director of the Joyce Summer School. At the time, she was more of a Joyce convert than a *prima facie* specialist but then again Martin had been the same. Ten years later, in 2006, Fogarty became UCD's first professor of James Joyce Studies and she would go on to serve with distinction as the first Irish President of the International James Joyce Foundation from 2008 to 2012 (she was also one of the principal organizers of the 2004 Dublin symposium).

The Joyce professorship was the brainchild of the then UCD President, Hugh Brady, a professor of medicine recently returned to Ireland after a long spell at Harvard and keen to build and brand the university following the American private model. His desire to boost Joyce Studies – in the hope of attracting a new wave of fee paying postgraduate students from abroad – was greeted with a mixture of bemusement and resentment by the members of English department and the Arts faculty, who were already up in arms because of the closure of several 'minor' departments, but it proved a shrewd move. Following Fogarty's appointment, Trinity College responded by hiring American textual scholar, Sam Slote, as its own resident Joyce specialist. These appointments, along with a further posting at UCD for Luca Crispi, who had served very successfully as the James Joyce and W. B. Yeats Research Scholar at the National Library of Ireland from 2003 to 2007 and as co-curator of the 'James Joyce and *Ulysses*' exhibition at the NLI, further reinforced the work that had been done over previous decades by many older colleagues working in the field of what was still called, for want of a better term, Anglo-Irish literature. Crispi and Slote worked together to publish the highly regarded 2007 volume, *How Joyce Wrote Finnegans Wake*.[24] Slote also published a hugely popular edition of *Ulysses* (containing 9,000 notes). His chosen version was the last (and best) of the Odyssey Press printings of *Ulysses*, published in 1939. He also produced a well-reviewed monograph entitled *Joyce's Nietzschean Ethics* published by Palgrave, and his massive annotations to *Ulysses* will be published by Oxford University Press in time for the Ulysses centenary.[25] In 2009, Fogarty launched what became an annual James Joyce Research Colloquium held each spring and the *Dublin James Joyce Journal*, which is co-published annually by the UCD James Joyce Research Centre and the National Library, and which she co-edits with Crispi. Favouring, but not limited to Irish scholarship, its contributions tend to focus on historical and archival investigations of Joyce, which make active use of the impressive Irish archival, documentary and manuscript resources, many of which were made available online by the National Library in April 2012 to counter a move by Danis Rose, who had published the material on his own initiative in very expensive editions. He was claiming to be the copyright holder of these manuscripts in the EU on the grounds that he had been the first person to publish them (even if he did not own them and arguably had no right to do so). He said that 'he temporarily holds these rights in trust for scholars, librarians and artists but added that he would "make over to the Irish State such rights in the Joyce text in the *Ulysses* documents that I have acquired"'. The director of the NLI, Fiona Ross, said that the library's primary function was 'lawfully to make available to the public the material in its care' and was now doing so.[26] Rose replied by asserting that the copyright was his (even if the actual manuscripts were not): 'The legal situation now is that the library is in continuing infringement of my copyright, but has itself acquired economic rights in the EU (excluding the UK) over all of the materials published by them *other than those included in my edition*.'[27]

---

[24]Luca Crispi and Sam Slote, eds., *How Joyce Wrote Finnegans Wake: A Chapter-by-chapter Genetic Guide* (Madison: University of Wisconsin Press, 2007).

[25]James Joyce, *Ulysses*, ed., Sam Slote (Alma, 2012). Several updated editions have appeared since then. See Sam Slote, Marc A. Mamigonian, John Turner, *Annotations to James Joyce's 'Ulysses'* (Oxford: Oxford University Press, 2021). Sam Slote, Joyce's Nietzschean Ethics (London: Palgrave, 2013).

[26]Terence Killeen, 'Joyce Collection Published Free on Web', *IT*, 12 April 2012.

[27]Danis Rose, *IT*, 17 April 2012.

As interest in Joyce flagged somewhat in the United States, long the engine of Joyce Studies, Irish critics, based both at home and abroad, as well as foreign critics based in the county, now resoundingly found their voices. The single most useful volume published in Ireland or anywhere in this period to orientate readers of Joyce's *Ulysses* was Terence Killeen's 2004 *Ulysses unbound*.[28] Killeen provides a crystal-clear introduction to Joyce's work but does not simplify; he draws on his intimate knowledge of Joyce's text, of Dublin and of generations of Joyce criticism to guide his readers. This work became a reference point not only for novices but also for Joyce veterans. A gem of a rather different hue was Niall Murphy's *A Bloomsday Postcard*.[29] Murphy, an antiquarian, spent some twenty-five years gathering postcards connected to the Dublin of *Ulysses*. The result is an engaging verbal and visual narrative account of the eighteen episodes of the novel, featuring 250 brilliantly chosen postcards from Murphy's Joyce-related postcard collection, which the National Library acquired a short time earlier. The book provides a useful entry point into *Ulysses* for new readers and a treasure trove of visuals of Edwardian Dublin. The Library also published *A Joycean Scrapbook*. Carefully compiled by Katherine McSharry, a principal researcher for the Library's 'James Joyce and *Ulysses*' exhibition, the rich cornucopia of images chosen from the exhibition is divided into two sections: 'Home' and 'Abroad'.

Frank Shovlin's book, *Journey Westward*, mixes history and close readings of *Dubliners* while examining Joyce's reworking of the Revival's myth of the West as a place of authenticity. He concentrates on three Irish subjects: the Irish whiskey industry, the memory of failed Jacobite intervention in Ireland, reading 'The Dead' as an elegy 'for the fallen of Aughrim and the last of Gaelic Ireland', and the Irish Literary Revival.[30] This last section, among much else, explores Joyce's 'imaginative absorption of stray material',[31] which is the subject of more prolonged focus in Luca Crispi's *Becoming the Blooms*, a work that made ample use of the National Library's Joyce collection. Crispi's book was an important contribution to the ongoing re-evaluation of how Joyce actually composed *Ulysses*. It focused on 'the construction of the central characters of *Ulysses*' studying 'the genesis and evolution of their life-stories across all the relevant episodes in all of the relevant surviving manuscripts and note repositories'.[32] The great strength of his work is the ease with which it sifts through Joyce's sometimes

---

[28]Terence Killeen, *Ulysses Unbound: A Reader's Companion to James Joyce's Ulysses* (Wicklow: Wordwell, 2004 and Florida: University Press of Florida, 2018).
[29]Niall Murphy, *A Bloomsday Postcard* (Dublin: Lilliput, 2004).
[30]Frank Shovlin, *Journey Westward: Joyce, Dubliners and the Literary Revival* (Liverpool: Liverpool University Press, 2012), 121.
[31]Ibid., 150.
[32]Luca Crispi, *Joyce's Creative Process and the Construction of Characters in Ulysses Becoming the Blooms* (Oxford: Oxford University Press, 2015), 3.

fragmentary, often borderline-illegible body of writing – his notes, drafts, fair copies, typescripts and proofs – that combine to form the Joyce corpus of manuscripts. By employing his geneticist's eye, Crispi provides the reader with a remarkably rich sense of Joyce's not always consistent or regular, process of textual assembly and accretion.

Cóilín Owens, a member of the older cohort of Irish Joyceans stationed in the United States, published two studies, each of which honed in on one short story from *Dubliners* as a means of focalizing a hugely detailed, historicized study of the contexts in which Joyce worked. 'A Painful Case' and 'After the Race' are both treated as microcosms of the methods and interests that would be developed in Joyce's later works.[33] Another study to appear, again by a veteran Irish academic, was Brian Cosgrove's *James Joyce's Negations*. Distancing himself from the postcolonial debate, he inserted himself into what he considered a bigger discussion about Joyce's place in the European tradition. Cosgrove's work explores what he calls the 'cul-de-sac into which ironic negation, and the related textual indeterminacy can lead' and examines Joyce's writings through a study of how their use of irony (as derived from Schlegel and Flaubert) and indeterminacy undermines any sentimental or political readings of his works.[34] Irony, in Joyce's hands, is said to represent detachment and the exercise of formal control. Indeterminacy is pushed to further extremes in *Ulysses*, and it is difficult if not impossible to assert a hierarchy of value from the proliferation of details and narrative perspectives. Thus the novel, far from being life affirming, as so many critics claim, gives voice to meaninglessness, even nihilism.

It would be hard to find a book further from this set of assertions than Declan Kiberd's *Ulysses and Us*. In this popular work, Kiberd, former professor of Anglo-Irish Literature at UCD, sees *Ulysses* as a hymn to normality and an epic of everyday life, a work redolent with meaning, much of it positive and life affirming. Kiberd combines much of the humanistic worldview that he inherited from his one-time doctoral supervisor at Oxford, Richard Ellmann, with a concern with the political resonance of Joyce's texts. *Ulysses*, he reminds the reader, was written in time of European war and Irish revolution, and Joyce, writing against a backdrop that risked wiping out ordinary life as it was known, sought to re-assert the importance of the quotidian. Kiberd argues that the 'openness of form and the multiple viewpoints in a book like *Ulysses* implicitly challenge the sort of zealotry which had led to the carnage'[35] of the First World War. Like many an Irish

---

[33]Cóilín Owens, *James Joyce's Painful Case* (Gainesville: University Press of Florida, 2008); Cóilín Owens, *Before Daybreak: 'After the Race' and the Origins of Joyce's Art* (Gainesville: University Press of Florida, 2013).

[34]Brian Cosgrove, *James Joyce's Negations Irony, Indeterminacy and Nihilism in Ulysses and Other Writings* (Dublin: University College Dublin Press, 2007), viii.

[35]Declan Kiberd, *Ulysses and Us: The Art of Everyday Life in Joyce's Masterpiece* (New York: Norton, 2009).

commentator before him, Kiberd, does not shy away from the irony that 'a book which set out to celebrate the common man and woman', has 'endured the sad fate of never being read by many of them'. His volume is a spirited and stylishly written attempt to wrest Joyce's novel from what he considers the obfuscation of 'specialist elites' and to make it accessible to the 'common reader'[36]. He does so by downplaying the fact that *Ulysses* is difficult and that this very difficulty is an integral part of its art. At times, while seeking to reinstate the Dublin setting, the study reads like a hymn to the city in the rare old times and a lament for a lost civic harmony.

Luke Gibbons, like Kiberd, reinstates Joyce's cultural and political heritage in *Joyce's Ghosts, Ireland, Modernism, and Memory*.[37] This book is exemplary in its engagement with other critics and theorists but also with the nuts and bolts of Joyce's own texts. As Katherine O'Callaghan comments:

> The importance of James Joyce's Irish cultural heritage and its extraordinary influence on all of his texts were notably absent from much of the first strand of critical response to his work. Gibbons rightly places this book as a part of a corrective to the absence and explains, 'Dublin and Irish culture did not just provide local color or background to innovations in form that Joyce acquired elsewhere (from European modernism, or the international avant-garde): they were constitutive of his most advanced stylistic achievements' (28). Dublin and Irish culture instead offered Joyce a textual fabric capable of articulating porous temporal and spatial paradigms. For Gibbons, 'the boundaries between inside and outside, past and present, come apart in Joyce's Dublin' (186), a concept explored in relation to what is generally articulated as the 'stream of consciousness' technique.[38]

Gibbons claims that much of the genius of Joyce's writing derives, not so much from the often vaunted 'stream of consciousness', but from the author's use of 'the more elusive narrative device of free indirect discourse',[39] from the rendering of 'inner speech', which is 'not only a psychological phenomenon but also a cultural process, embodying the background knowledge, physical contexts, and somatic responses through which we negotiate the external environment as well as inner life'.[40]

Voices on Joyce, almost exclusively written by Irish academics and edited by UCD's Anne Fogarty and Fran O'Rourke (who is also known for his performance of songs associated with Joyce's work, accompanied on Joyce's own guitar by John Feeley, the internationally renowned Irish classical

---

[36]Ibid., 10, 17.
[37]Luke Gibbons, *Joyce's Ghosts, Ireland, Modernism, and Memory* (Chicago and London: The University of Chicago Press, 2015).
[38]Katherine O'Callaghan, Review, *JJQ*, vol. 54, no. 3–4 (Spring–Summer 2017): 441–6, 442.
[39]Luke Gibbons, *Joyce's Ghosts*, 183.
[40]Ibid., 3.

guitarist),[41] did much to fill out the Irish contexts alluded to by Kiberd and Gibbons. One of its limits is that it contains just two contributions by female critics, a sign, this, of the historical lack of women to the forefront of Irish Joyce studies: a valuable piece by Fogarty on Joyce's varying treatments of Parnell, and a re-reading by Geraldine Meaney of 'The Lass of Aughrim', which, in her view, more than evoking the trauma of post-Famine Ireland, actually alludes to a 'history of the women who hid "their downfall" in the sea or were themselves hidden in mother and baby homes and Magdalene asylums'.[42] This lively compendium introduces many of the leading Irish Joyceans at work in 2014 and situates Joyce within the reach of Irish Studies more generally. Among the notable contributions is Cormac Ó Gráda's discussion of how Joyce's depiction of Bloom bears little or no resemblance to the realities of Jewish life in Dublin in 1904 (which does not mean, he is careful to point out, that it is not fictionally perfect, corresponding, as it does, to what he learnt about Jewish life from his time in Trieste).[43] Equally convincing contributions include Fran O'Rourke's 'Joyce and Aristotle', Terence Dolan on Joyce's use of Irish English and Adrian Hardiman's 'Suspecting, Proving, Knowing: Three Cases of Unnatural Death in Joyce's *Ulysses*'. Following Hardiman's own untimely death, his 'fascinating, painstaking book',[44] *Joyce in Court. James Joyce and the Law*, was published posthumously to acclaim in 2017. In the words of his friend and legal wingman, the historian and senior counsel, Frank Callanan, 'Hardiman's great theme is Joyce's embrace of juridical doubt as part of a larger questioning of conventionally received facts, which also marked his treatment of history'.[45] Hardiman enjoyed taking (often unfair) aim at Joyce scholars whom he claimed 'feel a professional need to obfuscate what Joyce has written'. The central thesis of his book, however, is useful. For Hardiman, Joyce's 'legal concerns are in part an oblique but persistent assertion of the need for philosophical and judicial doubt as a proper, moral and humane reaction to the inadequacy of evidence. Joyce's epistemological concern was centred on how the law resolved the uncertainties of a case'.[46]

An equally remarkable study, this time of Joyce's legal troubles in the United States, was penned in the same year by another (Irish-American)

---

[41]Anne Fogarty and Fran O'Rourke, eds., *Voices on Joyce* (Dublin: University College Dublin Press, 2015).

[42]Ibid., 293.

[43]A decade earlier, Ó Gráda had published his fascinating economic and demographic history of the Irish Jewish community in the late nineteenth and early twentieth centuries, *Jewish Ireland in the Age of Joyce: A Socioeconomic History* (Princeton: Princeton University Press, 2006).

[44]Colm Tóibín, 'Joyce in Court and The *Ulysses* Trials Review – The Law, Murder and Obscenity', *Guardian*, 6 July 2017. https://www.theguardian.com/books/2017/jul/06/joyce-court-ulysses-trials-law-murder-obscenity-adrian-hardiman-joseph-hassett-legal-cases.

[45]Frank Callanan, 'Reasonable Doubt', *DRB*, 1 September 2017. https://www.drb.ie/essays/reasonable-doubt.

[46]Adrian Hardiman, *Joyce in Court: James Joyce and the Law* (London: Head of Zeus, 2017).

UCD graduate, lawyer and literary critic, Joseph Hassett. *The Ulysses Trials: Beauty and Truth Meet the Law*[47] was hailed as

> groundbreaking, going against the general view – in Richard Ellmann's biography of Joyce, for example, or in other, more recent versions of the story – that Quinn, under the circumstances, did his best in a case that was unwinnable. Instead, Hassett establishes that Quinn disliked the novel's more sexually explicit passages, and was not willing to argue the case for its literary merit, one that might have succeeded in an appeals court. Hassett shows that Quinn was not merely incompetent but cynical and almost malevolent as he argued the case.[48]

Adding further ballast to the legal angle was Margaret Kelleher's *The Maamtrasna Murders*,[49] which, among much else, dedicated a fascinating chapter to Joyce's response to the trial and hanging of Myles Joyce. Again from the legal angle, 2015 saw the publication of Frank Callanan's long essay 'The Parnellism of James Joyce' in *Joyce Studies Annual*. He offers an important evaluation of how Joyce saw Parnell and asserts that the latter's 'taciturn elusiveness within his own myth' is 'a defining feature of Parnell's spectral presence in Joyce's writing'.[50] His eagerly awaited *James Joyce: A Political Life* will be published by Princeton University Press in 2023.

Another innovative, interdisciplinary work was Liam Lanigan's 2014 *James Joyce, Urban Planning and Irish Modernism: Dublins of the Future.* It reconnects Joyce to Dublin as an urban centre but challenges the common reading that underlines Joyce's exceptionality by showing how his work was part of a larger literary commitment to writing about urban modernity as seen in the works of George Moore, James Stephens and Seumas O'Sullivan.[51] What singles out Joyce's work is his ability to creatively suggest 'what the Irish city might become' rather than merely document what it was like in 1904. Focusing on 'Circe', he describes how Joyce reimagines the sprawling red-light district of Monto as a container 'for desires and fears that are suppressed elsewhere in the city'.[52]

The year 2016 saw the publication of *The Real People of Joyce's Ulysses: A Biographical Guide* by veteran Joycean, Vivien Igoe. Peter Costello described it as

---

[47]Joseph Hassett, *The Ulysses Trials: Beauty and Truth Meet the Law* (Dublin: Lilliput Press, 2017).

[48]Colm Tóibín, 'Joyce in Court and The Ulysses Trials Review – The Law, Murder and Obscenity', *Guardian*, 6 July 2017. https://www.theguardian.com/books/2017/jul/06/joyce-court-ulysses-trials-law-murder-obscenity-adrian-hardiman-joseph-hassett-legal-cases.

[49]Margaret Kelleher, *The Maamtrasna Murders: Language, Life and Death in Nineteenth-century Ireland* (Dublin: UCD Press, 2018).

[50]Frank Callanan, 'The Parnellism of James Joyce', *JSA* (2015): 73–97, 88.

[51]Liam Lanigan, *James Joyce, Urban Planning and Irish Modernism: Dublins of the Future* (London: Palgrave 2014).

[52]Ibid., 178.

an exhaustive biographical dictionary of real people, either as themselves, or as the inspiration or model for characters in the works of Joyce. [...] By creating such a database of carefully researched information, supported by portraits in many instances (in itself an heroic task), Vivien Igoe has created a resource of immense value to all students of Irish life and history.[53]

Costello used his review to acknowledge Igoe's long contribution to Joyce's reception in Ireland, remembering that she had been

one of a small group of people who, through their promotion of Joyce's life and work, could be said to have played a significant part in the modernisation of Ireland that took place between the early 1950s and the late 1960s. James Joyce became then a token of what made Irish culture interesting and important to the rest of the world.

Costello also sounded what was perhaps a necessary note of caution: 'We are getting to the stage where experts know more about some of the people in Joyce's Dublin than Joyce himself could possibly have known. Many of them he knew only second-or even third-hand, through his father's gossip and what was said in the papers.'[54]

The very necessary work of excavation that was carried out by generations of Irish Joyceans is perhaps coming to an end. Of course, there will be more excavation, more necessary local mapping and some unexpected discoveries, but if Irish Joyce studies are to have a future it will not be solely concerned with looking back into Irish contextual history. Rather it will involve an interdisciplinary delving into multiple other areas of interest in Joyce studies. Which is exactly what is already happening in works like Clare Hutton's *Serial Encounters*,[55] which examines how Joyce's *Ulysses* was first serialized and shows how its initial reception impacted Joyce's final version of the book. Catherine Flynn's *James Joyce and the Matter of Paris* does what French critics have failed to do in recent times, that is, it makes the case for the central influence of the French capital on Joyce from as early as his initial time there in 1902–3 but more importantly from 1920 onwards. In his review, Terence Killeen writes:

'Paris', for Flynn, is more than just a place. She does give an account of Joyce's actual stays in Paris, especially the first one, but that is not her

[53]Peter Costello, *Studies: An Irish Quarterly Review*, vol. 107, no. 425 (Spring 2018): 128–32, 129 and 131.
[54]Ibid.
[55]Clare Hutton, *Serial Encounters: Ulysses and the Little Review* (Oxford: Oxford University Press, 2019).

primary focus, and those who come to it expecting such a history will be disappointed.[56]

Another, less academic, book by another Irish writer, Conor Fennell's *A Little Circle of Kindred Minds: Joyce in Paris*, deals in a more straightforward but likeably lively biographical manner with Joyce and his circle in Paris and was warmly praised by Luca Crispi as 'a commendable introduction to the cultural scene' and one told with 'contagious passion'.[57] Returning to Flynn's book, Killeen continues:

> For her, Paris is an attitude, a symbol, a state of mind. It stands, in the first place, for the full force of modernity – the speed, the dislocation, the depersonalisation – among other things. It also stands, though, for artistic resistances to, along with co-dependency on, these processes and she wants to put Joyce at the centre of all these streams.

Flynn is one of an exciting younger generation of Irish Joyce critics that includes Ronan Crowley, and Katherine O'Callaghan, who, with Oona Frawley, edited an innovative volume of essays entitled *James Joyce and Cultural Memory*.[58]

In the last twenty years, Irish Joyceans have made themselves at home in the international field of Joyce Studies by doing the hard work needed to make a fundamental and lasting contribution. In their hands, Irish Joyce Studies have moved closer to centre stage and have started to play a key role in the international debate. Lots more is yet to come and *Ulysses* still has a lot to give. So too does Joyce, more generally, and *Finnegans Wake* in particular. There is still much we need to know about Joyce's compositional methods and even his publishing history. A major contribution to this has been made by two old hands, Danis Rose and John O'Hanlon. Diehard mavericks, they know Joyce inside out and their James Joyce Digital Archive is an extremely useful resource for scholars though it may represent more of a challenge for readers.[59] Launched in June 2018, the Archive is the culmination of four decades of research into Joyce's manuscripts for *Ulysses* and *Finnegans Wake* and provides a complex interactive account of their

[56]Terence Killeen, 'The Capital of Modernity', *Dublin Review of Books*, 1 April 2020. https://www.drb.ie/essays/the-capital-of-modernity.
[57]Conor Fennell, *A Little Circle of Kindred Minds: Joyce in Paris* (Dublin: Green Lamp Editions, 2011). Luca Crispi, 'Defining Dublin in the City of Light', *IT*, 16 June 2011.
[58]Oona Frawley and Katherine O'Callaghan, eds., *Memory Ireland Volume IV: James Joyce and Cultural Memory* (Syracuse: Syracuse Press, 2014). Frawley had earlier edited *A New and Complex Sensation: Dubliners in the 21st Century* (Dublin: Lilliput Press, 2004) and *New Dubliners: Stories to Celebrate James Joyce's Dubliners* (Dublin: New Island Books, 2005).
[59]http://jjda.ie/main/JJDA/JJDAhome.htm.

compositional histories. As a website, it has the added benefit of being able to absorb constant updating of new materials.

A proper, genuinely new Joyce biography remains to be written while Ellmann's sits in state, like a 1959 Rolls Royce, in the Joyce family carpark, splendid but untouchable, its inner and outer workings belonging to another age and not particularly fit for purpose for today's scholars or readers of Joyce. Gordon Bowker's workmanlike *James Joyce: A New Biography* failed to put a dent in the Ellmann edifice but perhaps a biography to challenge that will only come after Joyce's collected letters have been published in full. A team, including Bill Brockman, Kevin Dettmar, Robert Spoo and Ronan Crowley, is currently at work on a digital first volume, but it is proving to be a slow process and more than 1,500 letters remain unpublished. Crowley, who was a Marie Curie Fellow at the Centre for Manuscript Genetics at the University of Antwerp, was also responsible, along with Joshua Schäuble, for the publication in 2018 of *A Digital Critical and Synoptic Edition of Ulysses* (based on the Gabler text).[60]

The challenges of our own times and, one suspects, of future times continue to find unexpected resonance in Joyce's works. A ground-breaking book by the Trinity-trained American critic Alison Lacavita, *The Ecology of Finnegans Wake*, is a good example of this. Within the field of Irish Studies, it is pioneering in the way it blends genetic criticism and ecocriticism in reading Joyce's works, while at the same time furnishing a hefty quantity of historical and bibliographic information. UCD-trained Malcolm Sen, originally from India, author of the forthcoming *Unnatural Disasters: Irish Literature, Climate Change and Sovereignty* (Syracuse University Press), is also among those, trained in Ireland, who are leading Joyce Studies and Irish Studies more generally into crucially relevant new areas of investigation.

While Irish academic Joyceans appear to have found their voice, the popular points of contact with Joyce have had to continually adapt just to stay above water. The James Joyce Centre on North Great George's Street, which enjoyed almost a decade of stability under the management of Mark Traynor until 2017, is under increasing pressure today, in part because of a paucity of funding, in part because it has only a small collection of Joyce materials with which to attract a paying public. On the plus side, its sell-out 'Ulysses for All' reading groups, which gather each spring under the guidance of Caroline Elbay, attract new clusters of readers. Another staple activity is its lively selection of walking tours and schools workshops, which were continuing apace until the onset of Covid. Darina Gallagher, known for her excellent 'Songs from Joyce' show, which she devised and performs with Sinead Murphy, was appointed director in 2020.

The Tower in Sandycove has also had its difficulties. In 2012, for the first time in over thirty years, it was forced to close due to staffing issues at Fáilte

---

[60]http://ulysses.online/exist/apps/ulysses/index.html.

Ireland. The closure was brief thanks to local intervention. A Friends of the Joyce Tower Society was formed and brought together a group of over 150 volunteers who took over the running of the Tower, keeping it open 365 days a year right up until the onset of Covid. All signs are that when the pandemic has passed, the Tower too will resume its activities.

One of the most encouraging developments over the past decade or so has been the growth of Joyce reading groups taking on both *Ulysses* and *Finnegans Wake*. Sweny's Pharmacy, which has been run by volunteers marshalled indefatigably by P. J. Murphy since 2009, runs a variety of reading groups in several languages when it is not selling the famous lemon-scented soap or other Joycean knick-knacks, books or paraphernalia. This shop, which ceased trading as a chemist in 2010, still has the same Victorian fittings today as were in place on the day when Leopold Bloom visited in 1904. It depends entirely on volunteers and on donations and almost had to close in 2019 when the landlord doubled the rent. It was saved only when Bernard Walsh, managing director and co-founder of Carlow-based Walsh Whiskey, the maker of Writers' Tears and The Irishman whiskeys, made a substantial financial contribution. Since the closure of Joyce's House of 'The Dead', which for many years hosted a popular annual dinner on 6 January to celebrate Joyce's great story, Sweny's and the Joyce Centre have come together to organize a similar event, firstly at the Gresham and then in Wynn's. The centrepiece is the singing of 'The Lass of Aughrim' by renowned Irish tenor Noel O'Grady, who is also well known for his one-man show in which he renders songs relating to Joyce, a cappella. Another group called 'Joyceborough' was founded in 2012 and is led by Des Gunning (who earlier had served as the first curator of the James Joyce Centre). It organizes readings and performances, and is playing an important role in building a strong community of Joyce afficionados. Many of its events are held in Sweny's, although it started out as part of the 'Phizzfest', the Phibsborough Community & Arts Festival in 2012, which organized a production of Declan Gorman's successful one-man show, 'Dubliners Dilemma', to mark the centenary of Joyce's final departure from Dublin. Even during lockdown, the group has been extremely innovative and has held a series of high-quality online Joyce readings, performances and seminars, such as 'Virag in Hades', a rehearsed reading of an excerpt from 'Circe', with Barry McGovern, and the 'Heaventree of Stars', presented from Dunsink Observatory in association with the Dublin Institute for Advanced Studies.

Fitzgerald's in Sandycove is also home to weekly reading groups. This old Victorian pub has a long-standing interest in Joyce whose presence permeates the premises in pictures, paintings, posters and newspaper cuttings. Each episode of *Ulysses* is featured on the pub's stained glass windows. Currently up for sale, it is to be hoped that the new owners will maintain the Joycean flavour. *Ulysses* is also read regularly in adult education courses held in places such as Coláiste Chiaráin in Leixlip and in the People's College on Parnell Square.

One feature of Bloomsday over the past decade is that while it has gone global and is celebrated in multiple cities around the world, from Montreal to Mumbai, often with the support of Irish embassies and consulates, it has also gone nationwide. Local celebrations are regularly held in a range of towns and cities, from Belfast to Bruff (spearheaded by Donal Thurlow), Galway to Cork to Mullingar, and are driven not so much by a desire for tourism as by a genuine local or community interest. In Dublin, several local Bloomsdays are held in places like Blackrock, Sandycove and Glasthule, and a collective known as 'Bloomsday in the villages', supported by Dublin City Council, sees events taking place in locations such as Ranelagh, Sandymount and Terenure. Of course none of this guarantees that everyone will read *Ulysses* and online polls, which can for the most part be taken with a pinch of salt, are not entirely encouraging in this regard. The *Journal. ie* posted some interesting results on Bloomsday 2012. Asked 'Have you read *Ulysses*?' 39 per cent of respondents said 'no', 22.8 per cent 'I don't care', 17.5 per cent 'I started it, but I quit before the end', while 12.1 per cent said they had read all of it. A further 7.8 per cent admitted to having pretended to have read it.[61]

The destiny of what is arguably the most iconic setting in Irish literature, Joyce's house of 'The Dead', built in 1775, by now seems clear. Despite considerable personal investment (in terms of both time and money), Brendan Kilty was eventually forced to sell the property, simply because of a lack of funds. When neither the State nor Dublin Corporation showed any interest in purchasing the house, which retains the uniquely valuable interior and character so splendidly described in 'The Dead', it was bought by developers intent on converting it into a fifty-six-bed hostel. This plan was contested by an international group of writers, such as Salman Rushdie and Ian McEwan, Colm Tóibín, and Edna O'Brien, and by a large group of leading academics, by local conservation groups, and even by Angelica Huston, but An Bord Pleanála gave permission in the spring of 2021 to proceed. Aside from handwringing, local and national politicians do not have the will to intervene and save the house in its current architectural layout. This is a shameful and contradictory state of affairs, especially so in Dublin which has, since 2010, enjoyed the status of being one of a handful of UNESCO Cities of Literature. This precisely because, in the absence of great iconic monuments like the Eiffel Tower or the Colosseum, the country inevitably turns to its great writers to attract a share of global attention. At the same time, the Irish State continues to trade off the Joyce name internationally and in 2014 even had the gall to name a weaponized Irish Naval Service patrol ship after him (and another one after Beckett).

The continued lack of joined up thinking when it comes to the country's and the city's approach to Joyce, and indeed to its writers and to culture

---

[61] 'Poll: Have You Read *Ulysses*?' *theJournal.ie*, 16 June 2012. https://www.thejournal.ie/poll-have-you-read-ulysses-489561-Jun2012/.

in general, is hard to credit. While the house of 'The Dead' was being left to crumble, €10 million was raised for the wonderful MoLI – the Museum of Literature Ireland. This is a collaborative project between the National Library and University College Dublin, based in Newman House. Five million euros came from philanthropists Martin and Carmel Naughton, Fáilte Ireland contributed €2.5 million and the remainder was raised through the generosity of donors. MoLI opened in September 2019 and, under the guidance of its Director, Simon O'Connor, the founding curator of the nearby Little Museum of Dublin, it is expected that the museum will eventually employ between twenty-five and thirty people. Yet, it is hard to conceive of MoLI without Joyce. It was, in fact, originally intended to be called 'The *Ulysses* Centre' and Joyce is front and centre, the very backbone of the structure which contains, among other things, the first copy of *Ulysses*, donated by Harriet Shaw Weaver to the National Library, along with a hanging display of writers called 'Joyce's Century of Writers', and installations called 'A River Run of Language', and 'Dear, Dirty Dublin'. While it would be easy to dismiss this as just 'another Joycean enterprise to beguile the international tourists visiting the capital city',[62] or 'a cynical bid to merchandise Joyce all the more',[63] so much of what MoLI is about is the stimulation of current and future creativity. But given the weight placed on Joyce's shoulders here, it seems mean spirited in the extreme that the city cannot find a way to save what is probably the most emblematic setting in Irish literature, 15 Usher's Island, especially when so many other places that he immortalized from 7 Eccles Street to Barney Kiernan's pub to the Ormond Hotel have been disfigured beyond recognition or simply demolished. There is urgent need for a plan to secure the long-term viability and safeguarding of the city's Joyce infrastructure.

Increased familiarity with Joyce works today means that the dilemma once felt by the Irish writer working in his wake and caught, in John Banville's words, 'kneeling speechless' before 'a great looming Easter Island effigy of the Father', 'in filial admiration' but at the same time left 'gnawing his knuckles, not a son, but a survivor', is no longer felt so intensely.[64] Contemporary Irish writers over the past two decades have shown themselves increasingly at home with Joyce's works. This was partly because many of them would have studied him at University and have been able to look at him as an inspiration without sharing the feeling of being pre-empted that earlier generations experienced. Thus Patrick McCabe can combine appreciation with criticism, while at the same time understanding the weight of Joyce for earlier generations of writers:

---

[62]John Donohue, 'The MoLI – An OverJoyced Lady!' *Meath Chronicle*, 2 November 2019, 79.
[63]Mary Kenny, 'MoLI: Yes, Yes, or No?' *II*, 30 November 2019, 15.
[64]John Banville, 'Survivors of Joyce' in Augustine Martin, ed., *The Artist and The Labyrinth*, 73.

The Joyce I liked best was the humorous, humane and, arguably, less obtuse one. The dreary dogmas of Stephen often quite bored me, not to say irritated, as did exasperatingly elliptical maternity hospital quizzes. But anytime Bloom happened along I rallied, finding myself delighted more than anything by the sheer exactitude of the reported speech and the phenomenon of his language. Joyce's use of language is the area of greatest interest for me – that perfectly-tuned aural orchestra which perhaps frustrated Flann O Brien more than anyone, who when he went to it, was to find the treasure chest of working and middle class Dublin speech more or less empty, with nothing remaining but a little poignant printed card: JJ was here.[65]

Joseph O'Connor is more than willing to express reservations, to call Joyce pretentious, to claim that *Ulysses* is sometimes 'too experimental' and 'too long', while still concluding that 'Joyce is to literature what Bob Dylan and the Sex Pistols were to music: the be all and end all'.[66] Equally, Conor McPherson has no hesitation in calling Joyce as 'my literary north star' and marvelling at 'how the work seems to change and grow and speak to me anew at every age'.[67] In a 2014 article in *The Guardian*,[68] Eimear McBride could admit without hesitation:

Joyce really set my universe on its end. Reading *Ulysses* changed everything I thought about language, and everything I understood about what a book could do. I was on a train on the way to a boring temp job when I was about 25; I got on at Tottenham, north London, and opened the first page of *Ulysses*. When I got off at Liverpool Street in central London, I don't think it is an exaggeration to say the entire course of my life had changed.

She does not see him as a mythic frightening figure against whom to measure herself but appreciates that he 'provides a great lesson for writers who don't at first succeed'. Accused of letting Ireland down by writing about it the way he did, 'he stuck to his guns' and never shied away from his necessarily 'wideawake language'. Today's Irish writers revel in Joyce's achievement while avoiding the crippling hero-worship. And they can follow his way of sticking to his guns at a time when it is more crucial than ever that writers invent new ways to ask questions of society, of the institutions of society, and of the individual within society.

---

[65]Patrick McCabe, 'Metemdepsychoswandayinarkloan; James Joyce and Me', *Writings on Joyce UCD James Joyce 2012*. https://www.ucd.ie/ucdonjoyce/writings-on-joyce/articles/joyce-and-me-patrick-mccabe/index.html.
[66]Andrea Smyth, 'James Joyce: Literary Genius or in Need of a Good Editor?', *II*, 16 June 2016. https://www.independent.ie/entertainment/books/book-news/james-joyce-literary-genius-or-in-need-of-a-good-editor-34804929.html.
[67]Conor McPherson, 'My Joyce', *IT*, 2 February 2012, 42.
[68]Eimear McBride, 'My hero: Eimear McBride on James Joyce', *The Guardian*, 6 June 2014. https://www.theguardian.com/books/2014/jun/06/my-hero-eimear-mcbride-james-joyce.

Joyce's importance to Ireland's creative and arts communities has been underlined, in recent years, by President Michael D. Higgins, who has hosted an annual Bloomsday event at Áras an Uachtaráin to mark Joyce's unique achievement and to celebrate creativity in all its forms.

The so-called 'ordinary readers' too, can draw on *Ulysses* in multiple ways. Reading *Ulysses* can bring a heightened sense of our history, of our society, of our country and of the world and of our place in the world, past and present. It teaches us to take nothing for granted. *Ulysses* was written during the 1916 Rising and the Anglo-Irish War, during the First World War and the Spanish Flu, all of which threatened to sweep away so much that had been gained over the long nineteenth century both in Ireland and in Europe. In the face of disorientation, darkness and death, it was the only modernist text to maintain its vital sense of humour. It exhalted and exalts the value of everyday life, decency, civility, and justice, of basic human survival against the backdrop of a number of life-changing challenges. Thus, it is appropriate that in this most recent decade, Dublin will have hosted two Joyce symposia (in 2012 and 2022), both mostly based in Trinity College but also with events at UCD. They effectively bookend the Decade of Centenaries (1912–23) and assert the relevance of Joyce, once more, in the ongoing national debate. The 2022 event will particularly focus on *Ulysses* at 100.

In a recent dialogue with Jeet Thayilaipur and Paul Muldoon on the enduring value of *Ulysses*, Colm Tóibín states: 'If you are looking for a political message you won't get one.'[69] And in the narrow, party political sense, this is true. Yet, at the same time, Muldoon points out that 'the notion of home is a constant' (home in both a domestic and a national sense) and talks of Joyce's method of 'inclusion' while Tóibín sees the book as 'a blueprint against insularity [...] suggesting a sort of openness that Ireland might embrace as it becomes a State'. This reading is not too far from what the earlier Irish reviewers, unhappy in the Ireland that was forming, had to say 100 years ago. And it speaks to the value of Joyce and *Ulysses* for Ireland in our contemporary globalised world.

Today, in Ireland and elsewhere, we face many challenges on a par, at least, with those faced by Joyce's generation. *Ulysses* remains as relevant as ever in teaching us the limits of what we know, in acquiring a sense of perspective, and in pushing us to better read the world and to value what is important and what is not. It does not provide answers but it does help us ask the questions. *Ulysses* will continue to be mined and consumed from a extraordinary range of angles. It has long been a uniquely fertile terrain for feminists, Marxists, post-colonial critics, deconstructionists and so many others. So too it is and will be for the digital humanities, for the environmental, global and urban humanities (among many others), and all

---

[69]'Celebrating Bloomsday: Paul Muldoon and Colm Toibin in Conversation with Jeet Thayilaipur', Jaipur Literature Festival, 16 June 2020. Festival. https://www.youtube.com/watch?v=CCtQ0vprqc4.

of these areas or methods of investigation will reveal rich new unexpected sides to Joyce's work.

One hundred years after *Ulysses* was first published in book form, it is timely to ask if Ireland has consumed or exhausted its most famous modern book. To consume means 'to use up, eat, waste' but also to 'to destroy by use' and 'to engage the full attention and energy of'. Ireland has sought to dine out on Joyce and *Ulysses* or a caricature of Joyce but it has far from used him up or given him its full attention. The celebration and critical appreciation in Ireland of *Ulysses* and of Joyce has been both sporadic and, in another sense, constant and multifaceted.

Down through the century the country has looked the gift horse that is Joyce in the mouth as often as it has embraced the opportunities that his works and his achievement have offered. And yet, *Ulysses* now sits in state, (the very first printed copy does so quite literally on its pedestal in MoLI), like *Hamlet* or the *Divina Commedia*, both commercialized for local and foreign visitors to consume but also canonical object of reverence for literary scholars and readers. This status should not deter its being approached by readers, nor does it take anything away from its revolutionary literary qualities that are as powerful today as ever they were. Like all humans who are canonized, who become saints – religious, secular or literary – the extreme nature of their choices sometimes tends to be forgotten. So too, the radical nature of the life Joyce led in order to pursue his art and the extraordinary originality of that art are too often forgotten and need to be unlocked anew by each coming generation. What will continue to be most relevant is a sense of *Ulysses* as a work of literature, in Tóibín's words: 'What matters in the book is its literary content [...] the idea of the literary is what still makes the book sing to us.' It is, above all, this unique quality that makes *Ulysses* live on today. Far from being consumed, *Ulysses* is an enduringly rewarding work of literature and an extraordinarily rich compendium of life and language that will give at least as much to Ireland and the world in its second hundred years of life as it gave in its first.

SELECT BIBLIOGRAPHY

Journals and newspapers

Ariel
Belfast News Letter
Belfast Telegraph
Bell
Books Ireland
Capuchin Annual
Catholic Bulletin
Catholic World
Connacht Tribune
Criterion
Current History
Daily Telegraph
Dial
Dublin Magazine
Dublin Review
Economist
Envoy
Evening Echo
Evening Herald
Evening Press
Everyman
Furrow
Guardian (previously Manchester Guardian)
Hound and Horn
Independent
International Forum
Irish Book Lover
Irish Independent
Irish Monthly
Irish Press
Irish Times
James Joyce Yearbook
Kerryman
Kilkenny Magazine
Klaxon
Limerick Leader

Listener
L'Osservatore Romano
Meath Chronicle
New Republic
New Statesman
Nation
Nationalist & Leinster Times
Nirsa
Observer
Publisher's Weekly
Quarterly Review
Quest
Redemptorist Record
RTÉ Guide
Salmagundi
Separatist
Sinn Féin
Sligo Champion
Spectator
Studies: An Irish Quarterly Review
Sunday Independent
Sunday Tribune
Tatler and Bystander
Times Literary Supplement
Tuam Herald
Truth
Twentieth Century Studies
Waterford New and Star
Westmeath Examiner
Yale University Library Gazette

Manuscript collections

McFarlin Library, University of Tulsa
Beinecke Library, Yale
Harry Ransom Center, University of Texas (HRC)
National Library of Ireland (NLI)
Pontificio Collegio Irlandese, Rome
Trinity College Dublin
University College Cork
University College Dublin
ZJJF Jahnke Collection
Fitzgerald Papers, University College Dublin archives.

Published works

Aldous, Richard, ed. *Great Irish Speeches* (London: Quercus, 2009).

Allen, Nicholas. 'Free Statement: Censorship and the Irish Statesman' in *Last Before America – Irish and American Writing*, ed. Fran Brearton and Eamon Hughes (Belfast: Blackstaff Press, 2001), 84–98.

Allen, Nicholas. *Modernism, Ireland, and Civil War* (Cambridge: Cambridge University Press, 2009).

Anderson, Margaret. *The Little Review Anthology* (New York: Horizon Press, 1953).

Anderson, Margaret. *My Thirty Years' War* (New York: Horizon Press, 1969).

Andrews, C. S. *Man of No Property: An Autobiography*, Vol. 2 (Dublin: Mercier Press, 1982).

Mac Anna, Ferdia. 'The Dublin Renaissance: An Essay on Modern Dublin and Dublin Writers', *The Irish Review*, Vol. 10 (Spring 1991), 14–30.

Arnold, Bruce. *The Scandal of Ulysses: The Sensational Life of a Twentieth-century Masterpiece* (London: Sinclair Stevenson, 1991).

Attridge, Derek. *The Cambridge Companion to James Joyce* (Cambridge: Cambridge University Press, 1990).

Attridge, Derek and Marjorie Howes, eds. *Semicolonial Joyce* (Cambridge: Cambridge University Press, 2000).

Banta, Melissa and Oscar A. Silverman, eds. *James Joyce's Letters to Sylvia Beach 1921–1940* (Oxford: Plantin Books, 1987).

Beckett, Samuel. 'Dante… Bruno. Vico.. Joyce' in *Disjecta: Miscellaneous Writing and a Dramatic Fragment*, ed. Ruby Cohn (London: John Calder, 1983), 19–33.

Beckett, Samuel. *Disjecta: Miscellaneous Writing and a Dramatic Fragment*, ed. Ruby Cohn (London: John Calder, 1983).

Beckett, Samuel. *The Letters of Samuel Beckett Volume 1: 1929–40*, eds., Martha dow Fehsenfeld, Lois More Overbeck, (Cambridge: Cambridge University Press, 2009).

Behan, Brendan. 'Brendan Behan on Joyce'. A Lecture Delivered before the James Joyce Society at the Gotham Book Mart in New York City, 1962.

Beja, Morris. 'Synjoysium: An Informal History of the International James Joyce Symposia', *JJQ*, Vol. 22, No. 2 (Winter 1985), 113–29.

Beja, Morris and David Norris, eds. *Joyce in the Hibernian Metropolis* (Columbus: Ohio State University Press, 1996).

Birmingham, Kevin. *The Most Dangerous Book: The Battle for James Joyce's Ulysses* (London: Head of Zeus, 2014).

Bolger, Dermot. *A Dublin Bloom: An Original Free Adaptation of James Joyce's Ulysses* (Dublin: New Island/London: Nick Hern, 1995).

Booker, M. Keith. *Ulysses, Capitalism and Colonialism: Reading Joyce after the Cold War* (Westport, CT: Greenwood Press, 2000).

Bourke, Richard and Ian McBride, eds. *The Princeton History of Modern Ireland* (Princeton: Princeton University Press, 2016).

Bowen, Elizabeth. *Elizabeth Bowen's Selected Irish Writings*, ed. Eibhear Walshe (Cork: Cork University Press, 2011).

Boyd, Ernest. *Ireland's Literary Renaissance*. Rev. edn. (Dublin: Maunsel, 1923).

Boyd, Ernest. 'Order Established in the Literary Choas [*sic*] of James Joyce', *NYT*, 2 March 1924, BR7.

Boyd, Ernest. (Dublin Boyd) 'Modern Transitional Literature', *The New Statesman*, 16 August 1930, 593.

Boyd, Ernest. 'Joyce and the New Irish Writers', *Current History* (New York), 1 March, Vol. 39, No. 6 (1934), 699–704.

Bradley, Bruce, SJ. *James Joyce's Schooldays*, foreword by Richard Ellmann (Dublin: Gill and Macmillan, 1982).

Bradley, Bruce, SJ. 'James Joyce and the Jesuits: A sort of Homecoming', 30 November 1999. https://www.catholicireland.net/james-joyce-and-the-jesuits-a-sort-of-homecoming/

Bradshaw, David and Rachel Potter, eds. *Prudes on the Prowl Fiction & Obscenity in England, 1850 to the Present Day* (Oxford: Oxford University Press, 2013).

Briggs, Austin. 'The First International James Joyce Symposium: A Personal Account', *JSA*, Vol. 13 (Summer 2002), 5–31.

Brockman, William S. 'Learning to Be James Joyce's Contemporary? Richard Ellmann's Discovery and Transformation of Joyce's Letters and Manuscripts', *Journal of Modern Literature*, Vol. 22, No. 2 (Winter 1998/1999), Special Issue: Joyce and the Joyceans, 253–63.

Brooker, Joseph. *Joyce's Critics: Transitions in Reading and Culture* (Madison: University of Wisconsin Press, 2004).

Brooker, Joseph. 'A Balloon Filled with Verbal Gas: Blather and the Irish Ready-Made School', *Precursors and Aftermaths*, Vol. 2, No. 1 (2004), 74–98.

Brown, Stephen S.J. *Ireland in Fiction: A Guide to Irish Novels, Tales, Romances, and Folk Lore* (Dublin and London: Maunsel and Company, 1916).

Brown, Terence. *Ireland: A Social and Cultural History, 1922 to the Present* (Ithaca and London: Cornell University Press, 1985).

Brown, Terence. *Irish Times: 150 Years of Influence* (London: Bloomsbury, 2015).

Burke-Savage, Roland. 'Literature at the Irish Crossroads', 23 January 1936, Houghton Library: bMS Am 1691 (29).

Butler, Hubert. Manuscript 'James Joyce in Trieste', pp. 3–4. Crampton family papers, Bennettsbridge, Co. Kilkenny [papers in possession of the Crampton family]. Cited in Robert Benjamin Tobin, 'The Minority Voice: Hubert Butler, Southern Protestantism and Intellectual Dissent in Ireland, 1930–72', PhD Thesis, Merton College, Oxford, 2004.

Butler, Stephen G. *Irish Writers in the Irish American Press, 1882–1964* (Amherst and Boston: University of Massachusetts Press, 2018).

Byrne, J. F. *Silent Years: An Autobiography with Memoirs of James Joyce and Our Ireland* (New York, Farrar, Straus and Young, 1953).

Callan, Patrick. '"One and eightpence too much" – Suing James Joyce through the agency of the BBC, 1954 to 1955'. *Dublin James Joyce Journal* (forthcoming).

Callanan, Frank. 'The Parnellism of James Joyce', *JSA* (2015), 73–97.

Carey, James J. *Exploring English 2: An Anthology of Prose for Intermediate Certificate* (Dublin: Gill and Macmillan, 1967).

Carlson, Julia, ed. *Banned in Ireland* (London: Routledge, 1990).

Carpentier, Martha C., ed. *Joycean Legacies* (London: Palgrave, 2013).

Cheng, Vincent J. *Joyce, Race, and Empire* (Los Angeles: University of Southern California, 1995).

Colum, Mary M. 'The Confessions of James Joyce', *The Freeman*, Vol. 123 (19 July 1922), 450–2. Reprinted in *The Selected Works of Mary M. Colum*, ed. Denise A. Ayo (2013), http://marycolum.com/articles/confessions-ofjames-joyce/

Colum, Mary M. *Life and the Dream* (New York: Doubleday, 1947).

Colum, Mary M. and Padraic Colum. *Our Friend James Joyce* (Garden City, NY: Doubleday, 1958).

Conner, Marc C. 'James Joyce's Painful Case by Cóilín Owens (Review)', *JJQ*, Vol. 46, No. 1 (Fall 2008), 142–6.

Corkery, Daniel. *Synge and Anglo-Irish Literature - A Study* (Cork: Cork University Press, 1931).

Cosgrove, Brian. *James Joyce's Negations Irony, Indeterminacy and Nihilism in Ulysses and Other Writings* (Dublin: University College Dublin Press, 2007).

Costello, Peter. *Leopold Bloom: A Biography* (Dublin: Gill and Macmillan, 1981).

Costello, Peter. Review of *Joyce and the Joyceans* by Morton P. Levitt, *Studies: An Irish Quarterly Review*, Vol. 91, No. 363 (2002), 308–11.

Costello, Peter. 'James Joyce and the Remaking of Modern Ireland', *Studies*, Vol. 93, No. 370 (Summer 2004), 121–32.

Costello, Peter. 'Review of *The Real People of Joyce's Ulysses: A Biographical Guide*', *Studies: An Irish Quarterly Review*, Vol. 107, No. 425 (Spring 2018), 128–32.

Costello, Peter. *James Joyce. The Years of Growth, 1882–1915* (London: Roberts Rinehart, 1992).

Crispi, Luca and Sam Slote, eds. *How Joyce Wrote Finnegans Wake: A Chapter-by-Chapter Genetic Guide* (Madison: University of Wisconsin Press, 2007).

Crispi, Luca. *Joyce's Creative Process and the Construction of Characters in Ulysses Becoming the Blooms* (Oxford: Oxford University Press, 2015).

Cronin, Anthony. *A Question of Modernity: Essays on Writing with Special Reference to James Joyce and Samuel Beckett* (London: Secker & Warburg, 1966).

Cronin, Anthony. 'The Advent of Bloom' in *Joyce. A Collection of Critical Essays*, ed. William M. Chace (New York: Prentice-Hall, 1974), 84–101.

Cronin, Anthony. *No Laughing Matter. The Life and Times of Flann O'Brien* (London: Grafton Books, 1989).

Curran, C. P. 'Literature and Life. French Critics and Irish Literature', *Irish Statesman*, 15 September 1925.

Curran, C. P. *James Joyce Remembered* (London and New York: Oxford University Press, 1968).

Curtayne, Alice. *The Irish Story: A Survey of Irish History and Culture* (Dublin: Clonmore & Reynolds, 1962).

Curtis, Keiron. *P. S. O'Hegarty (1879–1955): Sinn Féin Fenian* (London: Anthem Press, 2009).

Daly, Leo. *James Joyce and the Mullingar Connection* (Dublin: Dolmen Press, 1975).

Dawson, Hugh J. 'Thomas MacGreevy and James Joyce', *JJQ*, 25 (Spring 1988), 305–21.

Deane, Seamus. *Heroic Styles: The Tradition of an Idea* [Field Day Pamphlets, No. 4] (Derry: Field Day, 1984).

Delaney, Frank. *James Joyce's Odyssey* (London: Hodder and Stoughton, 1981).

Deming, Robert. *James Joyce: The Critical Heritage*, 2 Vols (London: Routledge & K. Paul, 1970).

Dettmar, Kevin J. H. and Stephen Watt, eds. *Marketing Modernisms: Self-Promotion, Canonization, and Rereading* (Ann Arbor: University of Michigan Press, 1996).

Dettmar, Kevin J. H. and Stephen Watt. 'The Joyce That Beckett Built', *JJQ*, Vol. 35/36, Vol. 35, No. 4 – Vol. 36, No. 1 (Summer–Fall 1998), 605–19.

Devane, R. S. *Indecent Literature: Some Legal Remedies* (Dublin: Browne and Nolan, 1925).

Dillon, Brian. '"The Statue Affair": Diplomatic Notes on the Reinterment of James Joyce', *The Dublin Review*, No. 26 (Spring 2007), 64–77.

Duff, Charles (1932). *James Joyce and the Plain Reader* (New York: Haskell House, 1971).

Duffy, Enda. *The Subaltern Ulysses* (Minneapolis: University of Minnesota Press, 1994).

Eglinton, John. *Irish Literary Portraits* (London: Macmillan, 1935).

Eliot, T. S. et al. *The Complete Prose of T. S. Eliot: The Critical Edition: Tradition and Orthodoxy, 1934–1939* (Baltimore: Johns Hopkins University Press, 2017).

Eliot, T. S. et al. *The Letters of T. S. Eliot* Volume 8, 1936–1938, eds. Valerie and John Haffenden (London: Faber and Faber, 2019).

Ellmann, Richard. *The Consciousness of Joyce* (New York: Oxford University Press, 1977).

Ellmann, Richard. *James Joyce*. Rev. edn. (New York: Oxford University Press, 1982).

Fanning, Bryan. 'Hidden Ireland, Silent Irelands: Seán O'Faoláin and Frank O'Connor versus Daniel Corkery', *Studies – An Irish Quarterly Review*, Vol. 95, No. 379 (Autumn 2006), 251–9.

Fennell, Conor. *A Little Circle of Kindred Minds: Joyce in Paris* (Dublin: Green Lamp Editions, 2011).

Fitch, Noel Riley. *Sylvia Beach and the Lost Generation: A History of Literary Paris in the Twenties and Thirties* (New York: W. W. Norton & Company, 1985).

Flanagan, Frances. *Remembering the Revolution: Dissent, Culture and Nationalism in the Irish Free State* (Oxford: Oxford University Press, 2015).

Fogarty, Anne and Fran O'Rourke, eds. *Voices on Joyce* (Dublin: University College Dublin Press, 2015).

Forkner, Ben, ed. *A New Book of Dubliners: Short Stories of Modern Dublin* (London: Methuen, 1988).

Foster, R. F. *Vivid Faces: The Revolutionary Generation in Ireland, 1890–1923* (London: Penguin, 2015).

Foster, R. F. 'A Revolutionary Generation' in John Crowley, Donal O Drisceoil and Mike Murphy, eds. *Atlas of the Irish Revolution* (Cork: Cork University Press, 2017), 116–25.

Fox, Brian. '"land of breach and promise": James Joyce and America', Unpublished PhD Thesis, Royal Holloway, University of London, 2014.

Frawley, Oona. *A New and Complex Sensation: Dubliners in the 21st Century* (Dublin: Lilliput Press, 2004).

Frawley, Oona. *New Dubliners: Stories to Celebrate James Joyce's Dubliners* (Dublin: New Island Books, 2005).

Frawley, Oona and Katherine O'Callaghan, eds. *Memory Ireland Volume IV: James Joyce and Cultural Memory* (Syracuse: Syracuse Press, 2014).

Gallagher, Patrick, ed. *The Third Degree, Special Joyce Centenary Number* (Dublin: UCD, 1983).

Garvin, John. *James Joyce's Disunited Kingdom and the Irish Dimension* (Dublin: Gill and Macmillan, 1976).

Garvin, Tom. 'O'Hegarty, Patrick Sarsfield (P. S.)' in James McGuire and James Quinn, eds., *Dictionary of Irish Biography* (Cambridge: Cambridge University Press, 2014).

Gibbons, Luke. *Joyce's Ghosts, Ireland, Modernism, and Memory* (Chicago and London: The University of Chicago Press, 2015).

Gibson, Andrew. *Joyce's Revenge* (Oxford: Oxford University Press, 2002).

Gibson, Andrew. *The Strong Spirit: History, Politics, and Aesthetics in the Writings of James Joyce 1898–1915* (Oxford: Oxford University Press, 2013).

Girvin, Brian. 'Political Culture, Political Independence and Economic Success in Ireland', *Irish Political Studies*, Vol. 12, No. 1 (1997), 48–77.

Givens, Seon, ed. *James Joyce: Two decades of criticism* (New York: The Vanguard Press, 1963).

Gogarty, Oliver St. John. 'A Fellow Dubliner', 'The Veritable James Joyce According to Stuart Gilbert and Oliver St. John Gogarty', *International Forum*, Vol. 1, No. 1 (July 1931), 13–17.

Gogarty, Oliver St John. 'Roots in Resentment James Joyce's Revenge', *The Observer*, Vol. 7 (May 1939), 4.

Gogarty, Oliver St John and Mary Chenoweth Stratton, eds. *My Dear Gogarty: Being a Previously Unpublished Critical Essay Together with Selections Taken from the Correspondence of Oliver St. John Gogarty, Poet, Doctor, Statesman, & His Friends in the Irish Literary Renaissance: All Drawn from the Collection in the Ellen Clarke Bertrand Library* (Pennsylvania: Bucknell University & the Press of Appletree Alley, 1991).

Goldberg, S. L. *The Classical Temper: A Study of James Joyce's 'Ulysses'* (London: Chatto & Windus, 1961).

Gorman, Herbert. *James Joyce, His First Forty Years* (New York: Huebsch, 1924).

Gorman, Herbert. *James Joyce* (New York: Farrar & Rinehart, 1939).

Gray, John, ed. *Thomas Carnduff Life and Writings* (Belfast: Lagan Press, 1994).

Griffin, Gerald. *The Wild Geese; Pen Portraits of Famous Irish Exiles* (London: Jarrolds, 1938).

Gunn, Ian. 'Mr Burgess Goes to Eccles Street', *James Joyce Broadsheet*, No. 97 (1 February 2014).

Gunn, Ian. 'No 7 Eccles Street. The Demise of Ithaca', *James Joyce Online notes*. http://www.jjon.org/joyce-s-environs/no-7-eccles-street.

Hardiman, Adrian. *Joyce in Court: James Joyce and the Law* (London: Head of Zeus, 2017).

Harmon, Maurice, ed. *The Celtic Master: Being Contributions to the First James Joyce Symposium in Dublin* (Dublin: Dolmen Press, 1969).

Harmon, Maurice. 'The Rejection of Yeats: The Case of Clarke and O'Faolain', *Studies: An Irish Quarterly Review*, Vol. 82, No. 327 (Autumn 1993), 243–56.

Hassett, Joseph M. *The Ulysses Trials: Beauty and Truth Meet the Law* (Dublin: Lilliput Press, 1916).

Healey, George H. *The Complete Dublin Diary of Stanislaus Joyce* (Ithaca: Cornell University Press, 1962).

Heaney, Seamus. *Station Island* (London: Faber & Faber, 1985).

Heckard, Margaret. 'The Literary Reverberations of a Fake Interview with John Stanislaus Joyce', *JJQ*, Vol. 13, No. 4 (Summer 1976), 468–71.

Hickey, Des and Gus Smith, eds. *A Paler Shade of Green* (London: Leslie Frewin, 1972).

Hickey, Kieran. *Faithful Departed: The Dublin of James Joyce's 'Ulysses'*, introduction by Des Hickey (Dublin: Lilliput Press, 2004).

Hobson, Bulmer. *Saorstát Eireann Irish Free State official handbook* (Dublin: Talbot Press, 1932).

Hogan, Robert, ed. *The Experiments of Sean O'Casey* (London: St. Martin's Press, 1960).

Houston, Lloyd. '(Il)legal Deposits: Ulysses and the Copyright Libraries', *The Library*, 7th series, Vol. 18, No. 2 (June 2017), 131–51.

Hutchins, Patricia. *James Joyce's Dublin* (London: Grey Walls Press, 1950).

Hutchins, Patricia. 'Review of James Joyce's *Ulysses*' by Stuart Gilbert, *Irish Writing*, No. 18 (March 1952), 55–6.

Hutchins, Patricia. 'James Joyce's Correspondence', *Encounter*, Vol. 7 (August 1956), 49–54.

Hutchins, Patricia. *James Joyce's World* (London: Methuen, 1957).

Hutton, Clare. *Serial Encounters: Ulysses and the Little Review* (Oxford: Oxford University Press, 2019).

Hutton, Clare and Patrick Walsh, eds. *The Oxford History of the Irish Book Vol V The Irish Book in English, 1891–2000* (Oxford: Oxford University Press, 2011).

Igoe, Vivien. *James Joyce's Dublin Houses* (London: Mandarin, 1990).

Igoe, Vivien. *A Literary Guide to Dublin* (London: Methuen, 1994).

Igoe, Vivien. 'Early Joyceans in Dublin', *JSA*, Vol. 12 (Summer 2001), 81–99.

Igoe, Vivien. *The Real People of Joyce's Ulysses: A Biographical Guide* (Dublin: University College Dublin Press, 2016).

Imhof, Rudiger, ed. *Alive Alive O! Flann O'Brien's at Swim-two-birds* (Dublin: Wolfhound Press, 1985).

Jackson, John Wyse and Peter Costello. *John Stanislaus Joyce: The Voluminous Life and Genius of James Joyce's Father* (London: Fourth Estate, 1997).

Jameson, Fredric. *The Political Unconscious: Narrative as a Social Symbolic Act* (London: Methuen, 1981).

Jordan, John. *Crystal Clear: The Selected Prose of John Jordan*, ed. Hugh McFadden (Dublin: Lilliput Press, 2006).

Johnston, Dillon. *Irish Poetry after Joyce* (Notre Dame, IN: University of Notre Dame Press and Mountrath, Ireland: The Dolmen Press, 1985).

Joyce, James. *Poems and Exiles*, ed. J. C. C. Mays (London: Penguin, 1992).

Joyce, James. *'Dubliners': An Illustrated Edition with Annotations*, eds. John Wyse Jackson and Bernard McGinley (New York: St Martin's Press, 1993).

Joyce, James. *James Joyce Occasional, Critical, and Political Writing*, ed. Kevin Barry (Oxford: Oxford University Press, 2001).

Joyce, James. *Ulysses: A Reader's Edition*, ed. Danis Rose (Dublin: The Lilliput Press, 1997 and London: Picador, 1998).

Joyce, James. *Ulysses*, ed. Danis Rose (Cornwall: Houyhnhnm Press, 2004).

Joyce, James. *Ulysses*, ed. Sam Slote (London: Alma Books, 2012).

Joyce, Stanislaus. 'Joyce's Dublin', *The Partisan Review*, Vol. 19 (1952), 103–9.

Joyce, Stanislaus and Ellsworth Mason, eds. *The Early Joyce The Book Reviews, 1902–1903* (Colorado Springs: The Mamalujo Press, 1955).

Joyce, Stanislaus. *My Brother's Keeper,* ed. Richard Ellmann with a preface by T. S. Eliot (New York: Viking, 1958).

Kain, Richard. *Fabulous Voyager: James Joyce's Ulysses* (New York: The Viking Press, 1959).

Keating, Anthony. 'Censorship: The Cornerstone of Catholic Ireland', *Journal of Church and State*, Vol. 57, No. 2 (Spring 2015), 289–309.

Kelleher, Margaret. *The Maamtrasna Murders: Language, Life and Death in Nineteenth-century Ireland* (Dublin: UCD Press, 2018).

Kelly, Joseph. *Our Joyce: From Outcast to Icon* (Austin: University of Texas Press, 1998).

Kennedy, P. J., ed. *New Intermediate Certificate Poetry* (Dublin: M. H. Gill & Son, 1955).

Keogh, Dermot. *Ireland and the Vatican: The Politics and Diplomacy of Church–State Relations, 1922–1960* (Cork: Cork University Press, 1995).

Keown, Gerard. 'Sean Lester: Journalist, Revolutionary, Diplomat, Statesman', *Irish Studies in International Affairs*, Vol. 23 (2012), 143–54.

Kersnoswki and Hughes, Alice, ed. *Conversations with Edna O'Brien*, (Jackson: University of Mississippi, 2014).

Kiberd, Declan. 'Writers in Quarantine?' in *Crane Bag Book of Irish Studies* (Dublin: Blackwater Press, 1982), 341–53.

Kiberd, Declan. *Inventing Ireland: The Literature of the Modern Nation* (Cambridge: Harvard University Press, 1995).

Kiberd, Declan. *Ulysses and Us: The Art of Everyday Life in Joyce's Masterpiece* (New York: Norton, 2009).

Kiely, Benedict. *The Waves behind Us* (London: Methuen, 1999).

Killeen, Terence. 'Ireland Must Be Important… ', *JSA*, Vol. 14 (2003), 19–36.

Killeen, Terence. *Ulysses Unbound: A Reader's Companion to James Joyce's Ulysses* (Dublin: Wordwell, 2004).

Killeen, Terence. 'The Capital of Modernity', *Dublin Review of Books*, 1 April 2020. https://www.drb.ie/essays/the-capital-of-modernity

Laird, Heather, ed. *Daniel Corkery's Cultural Criticism: Selected Writings* (Cork: Cork University Press, 2012).

Lane, Dermot A. 'Vatican II: The Irish Experience', *The Furrow*, Vol. 55, No. 2 (February 2004), 67–81.

Lanigan, Liam. *James Joyce, Urban Planning and Irish Modernism: Dublins of the Future* (London: Palgrave, 2014).

Lanters, Jos. *Missed Understandings: A Study of Stage Adaptations of the Works of James Joyce* (Rodopi: Amsterdam, 1988).

Larbaud, Valery. 'The "Ulysses" of James Joyce', *The Criterion* Vol. 1, No. 1 (October 1922), 94–103.

Leonard, Hugh. *Stephen D* (London: Evans Brothers, 1964).

Lerm-Hayes, Christa Maria. *Joyce in Art: Visual Art Inspired by James Joyce* (Dublin: Lilliput Press, 2004).

Lernout, Geert. *The French Joyce* (Ann Arbor: University of Michigan Press, 1992).

Lernout, Geert and Wim Van Mierlo, eds. *The Reception of James Joyce in Europe* 2 Vols (London: Continuum, 2004).

Leventhal, A. J. 'The *Ulysses* of Mr. James Joyce', in *Klaxon* (Winter 1923–24), 14–20. http://www.ricorso.net/rx/library/criticism/major/Joyce_JA/Leventhal_AJ.htm

Liddy, James. 'Coming of Age: James Joyce and Ireland', *Kilkenny Magazine*, Vol. 5 (1961), 25–9.

MacCabe, Colin. *James Joyce and the Revolution of the Word* (London: Macmillan, 1978).

MacCarvill, Eileen. *Les Années de formation de James Joyce a Dublin* (Paris: Éditions Minard/Lettres Modernes, Archives des lettres modernes, n° 12, 1958).

MacCarvill, Eileen. *The Collection of Joyce Exam Papers and University Calendars*, Unpublished Manuscript, Zurich James Joyce Foundation.

MacDonagh, Donagh. 'The Reputation of James Joyce: From Notoriety to Fame', *University Review*, Vol. 3, No. 2 (Summer 1963), 12–20.

MacMonagle, Niall. *TEXT: A Transition Year English Reader* (Dublin: The Celtic Press, 2009).

MacManus, M. J. *So This is Dublin!* (Dublin: Talbot Press, 1927).

Mac Réamoinn, Seán. Bloomseve, a documentary presented on RTÉ Radio 1, 20 June 1969.

Mac Réamoinn, Seán. 'Bloom Sunday', a Documentary presented on RTÉ Radio 1, 20 June 1971.

Mahon, Derek, *The Hunt by Night* (Oxford: Oxford University Press, 1982).

Martin, Augustine. 'Inherited Dissent: The Dilemma of the Irish Writer', *Studies: An Irish Quarterly Review*, Vol. 54, No. 213 (Spring 1965), 1–20.

Martin, Augustine, ed. *James Joyce: The Artist and the Labyrinth* (London: Ryan Publishing, 1990).

Martin, Augustine. *Bearing Witness: Essays on Anglo-Irish Literature*, ed. Anthony Roche (Dublin: University College Dublin Press, 1996).

Martin, Peter. *Censorship in the Two Irelands 1922–1939* (Dublin: Irish Academic Press, 2006).

McCabe, Patrick. 'Metemdepsychoswandayinarkloan; James Joyce and Me', *Writings on Joyce UCD James Joyce 2012*. https://www.ucd.ie/ucdonjoyce/writings-on-joyce/articles/joyce-and-me-patrick-mccabe/index.html

McCleery, Alistair. 'The 1969 Edition of *Ulysses*: The Making of a Penguin Classic', *JJQ*, Vol. 46, No. 1 (Fall 2008), 55–73.

McCourt, John. *The Years of Bloom: Joyce in Trieste 1904–1920* (Dublin: Lilliput Press, 2000).

McCourt, John, ed. *James Joyce in Context* (Cambridge: Cambridge University Press, 2009).

McCourt, John, ed. *Roll Away the Reel World: James Joyce and Cinema* (Cork: Cork University Press, 2010).

McCrea, Barry. 'Privatising *Ulysses*: Joyce before, during and after the "Celtic Tiger"' in *Joycean Unions: Post-Millennial Essays from East to West (European Joyce Studies, Vol. 22)*, eds. R. Brandon Kershner and Tekla Mecsnóber, 2013 (Rodopi: Amsterdam, 2012), 81–95.

McGinley, Bernard. *Joyce's Lives. Uses and Abuses of the Biografiend* (London: University of North London Press, 1996).

McGonagle, Marie, Sharon McLaughlin and Tarlach McGonagle. *Media Law in Ireland* (The Netherlands: Wolters Kluwer, 2018), npg (electronic edition).

McHugh, H. A. C. SS. R., D. C. L. 'Dark Angel The Tragedy of James Joyce', *The Redemptorist Record*, July–August 1953, 98–100.

McHugh, Roland. *Annotations to Finnegans Wake* (London: Routledge & Kegan Paul, 1980).

McNelly, Willis E. 'Twenty Years in Search of a Footnote', *JJQ*, Vol. 9, No. 4 (Summer 1972), 452–60.

McWilliams, Ellen. 'James Joyce and the Lives of Edna O'Brien' in *Modernist Afterlives in Irish Literature and Culture*, ed. Paige Reynolds (London: Anthem Press, 2016), 49–60.

Meaney, Geraldine. 'Rosamond Jacob and the Hidden Histories of Irish Writing', *New Hibernia Review/Iris Éireannach Nua*, Vol. 15, No. 4 (Geimhreadh/Winter 2011), 70–4.

Monaghan, Ken. 'Dublin in the Time of Joyce', *JSA*, Vol. 12 (2001), 65–73.

Montague, John. *New Collected Poems* (Oldcastle: Gallery Press, 2012).

Montgomery, Niall. 'Joyeux Quicum Ulysse', *Envoy,* Vol. 5 (1951), 31–43; 'The Pervigilium Phoenicis', *New Mexico Quarterly*, Vol. XXIII (1953): 437–72.

Moretti, Franco. *Signs Taken for Wonders* (London: Verso, 1983).

Moore, Brian. 'Old Father, Old Artificer', *Irish University Review*, Vol. 12, No. 1 (1982), 13–16.

Mullin, Katherine. *James Joyce, Sexuality and Social Purity* (Cambridge: Cambridge University Press, 2003).

Murphy, Niall. *A Bloomsday Postcard* (Dublin: Lilliput, 2004).

Murphy, William M. *Prodigal Father. The Life of John Butler Yeats (1839–1922)* (Ithaca and London: Cornell University Press, 1978).

Murray, Peter. 'Belting the Irish State with US Croziers. Theatre, Tourism, UN Policy and Church–State Relations, 1957–58', *Nirsa*, No. 54 (December 2009).

Nash, John, ed. *Joyce's Audiences*, *European Joyce Studies* 14 (Amsterdam: Rodopi, 2002).

Nash, John. 'In the Heart of the Hibernian Metropolis"? Joyce's Reception in Ireland, 1900–1940' in *A Companion to James Joyce,* ed. Richard Brown (London: Blackwell, 2008), 108–22.

Nicholson, Robert. '"Signatures of All Things I am Here to Read": The James Joyce Museum at Sandycove', *JJQ*, Vol. 38, No. 3/4, Joyce and Trieste (Spring–Summer 2001), 293–8.

Nicholson, Robert (1988). *The Ulysses Guide: Tours Through Joyce's Dublin* (Dublin: New Island, 2019).

Ní Dhuibhne, Éilís. 'Joyce's Shadow' (2012). https://www.ucd.ie/ucdonjoyce/writings-on-joyce/articles/joyces-shadow-eilis-ni-dhuibhne/index.html

Nolan, Emer. *James Joyce and Nationalism* (London: Routledge, 1995).

Norris, David. *A Kick against The Pricks: The Autobiography* (Dublin: Transworld Ireland, 2012).

O'Brien, Edna (1960). *The Country Girls Trilogy* (London: Penguin, 1988).

O'Brien, Edna (1999). *James Joyce* (London: Penguin, 2019).

O'Brien, Kate. 'The Art of Writing', Lecture delivered to Graduates' Association, 2nd May, 1963, *Irish University Review*, Vol. 48, No. 1 (2018), 145–53.

O'Callaghan, Katherine. 'Joyce's Ghosts: Ireland, Modernism, and Memory by Luke Gibbons (review),' *JJQ*, Vol. 54, No. 3–4 (Spring–Summer 2017), 441–6.

O'Casey, Sean. *The Letters of Sean O'Casey 1910–1941*, ed. David Krause, Vol. 1 (New York: Macmillan, 1975).

O'Casey, Sean. *The Letters of Sean O'Casey*, ed. David Krause, Vol. III (Washington, DC: The Catholic University of America Press, 1989).

O'Casey, Sean. *The Letters of Sean O'Casey*, ed. David Krause, Vol. IV (Washington, DC: The Catholic University of America Press, 1992).

O'Connor, Frank. 'James Joyce: A Post-Mortem', *The Bell*, Vol. 5, No. 5 (February 1943), 363–75.

O'Duffy, Eimar. *The Wasted Island* (New York: Dodd, Mead, 1920).

O Faoláin, Seán. 'The Cruelty and Beauty of Words', *Virginia Quarterly*, Vol. IV (April 1928), 208–25.

O Faoláin, Seán. 'Style and the Limitations of Speech', *Criterion*, Vol. VIII (1928), 67–87.

O Faoláin, Seán. 'Ah, Wisha! The Irish Novel', *The Virginia Quarterly Review*, Vol. 17, No. 2 (Spring 1941), 265–74.

O Faoláin, Seán. 'Fifty Years of Irish Writing', *Studies*, Vol. 51, No. 201 (Spring 1962), 93–105.

Ó Gráda, Cormac. *Jewish Ireland in the Age of Joyce: A Socioeconomic History* (Princeton: Princeton University Press, 2006).

O'Grady, Desmond. *My Fields This Springtime* (Belfast: Lapwing Publications, 1993).

O'Hegarty, P. S. 'Mr. Joyce's *Ulysses*,' *The Separatist*, Vol. 2 (September 1922), 4.

O'Hegarty, P. S. *The Victory of Sinn Fein* (Dublin: Talbot Press, 1924).

O'Laoi, Padraic. *Nora Barnacle Joyce* (Galway: Kennys Bookshops and Art Galleries Ltd., 1982).

O'Malley, Ernie. *On Another Man's Wound* (Dublin: Sign of the Three Candles, 1936).

O'Neill, Christine. 'Niall Montgomery: An Early Irish Champion of Joyce', *Dublin James Joyce Journal*, No. 1 (2008), 1–16.

O'Neill, Christine. *Niall Montgomery Dublinman: Selected Writings* (Dublin: Ashfield Press, 2015).

Owens, Cóilín. *James Joyce's Painful Case* (Gainesville: University Press of Florida, 2008).

Owens, Cóilín. *Before Daybreak: 'After the Race' and the Origins of Joyce's Art* (Gainesville: University Press of Florida, 2013).

Pierce, David. *James Joyce's Ireland* (New Haven: Yale University Press, 1992).

Potts, Willard. 'Joyce's Notes on the Gorman Biography', *ICarbS*, Vol. IV, No. 2 (Spring–Summer 1981), 83–100.

Pound, Ezra. 'The Non-existence of Ireland', *The New Age*, Vol. XVI, No. 17 (25 February 1915), 452.

Pound, Ezra. *Literary Essays of Ezra Pound*, ed. T. S. Eliot (Norfolk, CT: New Directions, 1954).

Pound, Ezra. *Pound/Joyce: The Letters of Ezra Pound to James Joyce, with Pound's Essays on* Joyce. Edited and with Commentary by Forrest Read (New York: New Directions, 1970).

Power, Arthur. *Conversations with James Joyce* (London: Millington Publishers, 1974).

Quinn, Antoinette. *Patrick Kavanagh: A Biography* (Dublin: Gill and Macmillan, 2001).

Quinn, Edward. *James Joyce's Dublin* (London: Secker & Warburg, 1974).

Reid, B. L. *The Man from New York: John Quinn and His Friends* (New York: Oxford University Press, 1965).

Reynolds, Paige, ed. *Modernist Afterlives in Irish Literature and Culture* (London: Anthem Press, 2016).

Rimmer, Matthew. 'Bloomsday: Copyright Estates and Cultural Festivals', *Scripted*, Vol. 2, No. 3 (2005), 383–428.

Rodgers, W. R. 'Portrait of James Joyce' (transcript), Broadcast on BBC Third Programme, 13 February 1950.

Rodgers, W. R. *Irish Literary Portraits* (London: BBC, 1972).

Ryan, Desmond. *Michael Collins* (Dublin: Anvil Press, 1932).

Ryan, Desmond. *Remembering Sion: A Chronicle of Storm and Quiet* (Dublin: Arthur Barker, 1934).

Ryan, Desmond. 'Still Remembering Sion', *University Review*, Vol. 5, No. 2 (Summer 1968), 245–52.

Ryan, John, ed. *A Bash in the Tunnel* (Brighton: Clifton Books, 1970).

Ryan, Phyllis. *The Company I Kept* (Dublin: Town House, 1996).

Ryan, W. P. *The Pope's Green Island* (Boston: Small, Maynard, 1912).

Savage, Robert J. *A Loss of Innocence? Television and Irish Society 1960–72* (Manchester: Manchester University Press, 2010).

Scary, John. 'James Joyce and John McCormack', *Revue belge de philologie et d'histoire*, tome 52, fasc. 3 (1974), 523–36.

Senn, Fritz. *Joycean Murmoirs: Fritz Senn on James Joyce*, ed. Christine O'Neill (Dublin: Lilliput Press, 2007).

Sewell, Frank. 'Seán Ó. Ríordáin: Joycery-Corkery-Sorcery', *The Irish Review*, No. 23 (Winter 1998), 42–61.

Shannon, Gerard. 'The Sinn Féin Rebellion? Arthur Griffith's Easter Week 1916', *The Irish Story* (5 April 2015), http://www.theirishstory.com/2015/04/05/the-sinn-fein-rebellion-arthur-griffiths-easter-week-1916/#.V76z1Y9OLcs.

Sheehy, Eugene. *May it Please the Court* (Dublin: C. J. Fallon, 1951).

Shovlin, Frank. *Journey Westward: Joyce, Dubliners and the Literary Revival* (Liverpool: Liverpool University Press, 2012).

Sigler, Amanda. 'Joyce's Ellmann,' *JSA*, Vol. 21 (2010), 3–70.

Slocum, John J. and Herbert Cahoon. 'A Note on Joyce Biography', *The Yale University Library Gazette*, Vol. 28, No. 1 (July 1953), 44–50.

Slocum, John J. and Herbert Cahoon. *A Bibliography of James Joyce, 1882–1941* (London: Rupert Hart-Davis, 1957).

Slote, Sam. *Ulysses in the Plural: The Variable Editions of Joyce's Novel* (Dublin: The National Library of Ireland Joyce Studies, 2004).

Slote, Sam. *Joyce's Nietzschean Ethics* (London: Palgrave, 2013).

Stanford, W. B. 'Ulyssean Qualities in Joyce's Leopold Bloom', *Comparative Literature*, Vol. 5, No. 2 (Spring 1953), 125–36.

Stewart, Bruce. 'Another Bash in the Tunnel: James Joyce and the Envoy', *Studies: An Irish Quarterly Review*, Vol. 93, No. 370, (Summer 2004), 133–145.

Strong, L. A. *The Sacred River: An Approach To James Joyce* (London: Methuen & Company, 1949).

Téry, Simone. *L'Île des bardes. Notes sur la littérature irlandaise contemporaine. Yeats, Synge, Joyce, Stephens* (Paris: Flammarion, 1925).

Tóibín, Colm. *Mad, Bad, Dangerous to Know: The Fathers of Wilde, Yeats and Joyce* (New York: Viking, 2018).

Ulin, Julieann Veronica. 'Philatelic Ulysses', *JSA* (2018), 51–85.

Ussher, Arland. *Three Great Irishmen, Shaw, Yeats, Joyce* (New York: The Devin-Adair Company, 1953).

Veale, Vivien. 'The Martello Tower', *JJQ*, Vol. 3, No. 4 (Summer 1966), 276–7.

Wells, 'H. G. James Joyce', *Nation*, Vol. xx (24 February 1917), 710, 712.

Whyte, J. H. *Church and State in Modern Ireland, 1923–79* (Dublin: Gill and Macmillan, 1980).

Williams, Trevor L. *Reading Joyce Politically* (Gainesville: University of Florida Press, 1997).

Yeats, W. B. *The Collected Letters of W. B. Yeats*, gen. ed. John Kelly (Oxford: Oxford University Press [InteLex Electronic Edition], 2002).

Yeats, W. B. and Thomas Kinsella. *Davis, Mangan, Ferguson? Tradition and the Irish Writer* (Dublin: Dolmen Press, 1970).

INDEX